INSIDE TEXAS

Texas Christian University Press / Fort Worth

INSIDE TEXAS

Culture, Identity, and Houses, 1878–1920

by Cynthia A. Brandimarte

Cynthia A. Brandimarte

15/50

Copyright © 1991 Cynthia A. Brandimarte

Library of Congress Cataloging-in-Publication Data

Brandimarte, Cynthia A.
Inside Texas : culture, houses, and identity, 1878–1920 / by Cynthia A. Brandimarte.
p. cm.
Includes bibliographical references and index.
ISBN 0-87565-092-9.
1. Interior decoration—Texas—History—19th century. 2. Interior decoration—Texas—History—20th century. 3. Interior decoration—Texas—Human factors. I. Title.
NK2003.5.B7 1991 91-10249
747.2164—dc20 CIP

Publication of *Inside Texas* was in part made possible by a generous grant from the Summerlee Foundation.

Cover photograph: The parlor of the Gregor Carmichael McGregor home in Waco, 1896. For a discussion of the image, see figure 10.1. (Courtesy William M. and Frances P. Harris)

Back cover photograph: Entry hall of the Henrietta Chamberlain King house, Corpus Christi, ca. 1893. For a discussion of the image, see figure 13.10. (Courtesy Architectural Drawings Collection, Architecture and Planning Library, General Libraries, University of Texas at Austin)

Title page photograph: Detail of the parlor of the Albert G. Boyce house, Channing, ca. 1890. For the complete image, see figure 11.8.

Design and production: Whitehead & Whitehead

To Mark

CONTENTS

Preface

Inside Texas is about people and houses, using domestic material culture, documented in photographic images, to study Texans from 1878 to 1920. How did they set about fashioning homes for themselves and their families? What image or images did they wish to project in their homes? What messages did they want to communicate? What objects were privileged as revealed by their frequency and placement within rooms? Was the state's cultural identity revealed in its houses? If so, how? By examining a specific region as a case study, *Inside Texas* provides a pilot for future studies.

The book began to take shape in 1982 with a search for historic interior photographs in institutional collections and private holdings. The response to letters, questionnaires and news releases set a pattern for nearly 15,000 miles of research travel, crisscrossing the state.

My survey of photographs revealed that, like many Americans in the late nineteenth and early twentieth centuries, Texans eagerly embraced the technology offered by the camera to document social, religious, commercial, and domestic life. Photographs of parades, picnics, and social groups reinforced the sense of community. Photographs of churches and religious activities testified to spiritual strength. Photographs of businesses advertised specific stores and documented the commercial vitality of a given locale. And photographs of a house documented a homeowner's status, the ability to muster the resources both to build a house and to have a record of it made.

But interior views of Texas buildings are discouragingly rare. For every 500 or so portrait photographs and 300 exterior views, I found only one interior view. At the turn of the century the technology of the camera made it difficult to shoot in low-light spaces; further, it was expensive to hire a professional photographer, presuming you could find one, or to own a camera. Even the earliest Kodak camera in 1888 cost $25 and $10 more to reload the film.[1]

When many middle-class wage earners received only $2.50 a day, a camera represented a considerable investment.[2]

Still, many Texans of the period took interior photographs when they completed, furnished, or redecorated their houses. They took pictures to commemorate holidays, weddings, anniversaries, and other family celebrations. Occasionally the photograph was taken as a portrait of a family member, and interiors were frequently "caught" in the composition, merely attractive backdrops. Some of these images were taken by traveling photographers who, without a studio, approximated a formal portrait in the house interior. Some views exist because architects or interior decorators wanted a portfolio record of their expertise to show prospective clients. Other interior views survive for insurance purposes. Still others appear to have no narrative function and may have been taken as private records of intimate spaces.

After nine years of research, I located more than 600 interior views of Texas houses. Of these, nearly 300 are published here — the largest published collection of pre-1920 interior photographs of Texas homes to date. Photographs included were initially selected by the condition of the original — if it was of publishable quality, a photo met the first criterion. Next, I chose images that provided a good geographical and socioeconomic range. Finally, I selected photographs that presented useful information about people and their furnishings.

Any reading and interpretation of interior photographs must be cautious. The wealthy were more likely to photograph their homes, and they tend to be overrepresented in samples. Public rooms — parlors, dining rooms, and sitting rooms — were photographed more frequently than private or service areas — bedrooms, bathrooms, servants' rooms, and back-stair halls. And photographers rarely provided more than a partial view of a room, focusing on a bay window, a piano, or a fireplace, forcing us to make judgments about the appearance of the rest of the room. Moreover, interior views were often unlabeled, the provenance lost, and the images themselves faded and foxed.

Photographs alone cannot convey the visual harmonies and cacophonies of the late nineteenth and early twentieth centuries. These black-and-white images neutralize that colorful landscape: exteriors were painted in yellows, reds, and browns, and interiors shone with deep carmine, gilt, and sky blue. Black-and-white film in the nineteenth century was not panchromatic, so shades seen may not accurately represent the shades of the actual colors; for example, blue registers as very light and red as black.[3]

We must also be wary of the truthfulness of the photographs. At mid nineteenth century, photographs were deemed preferable to paintings because people believed photographs precisely duplicated the natural world. In effect, a photograph could not lie, although a painting might. Some mid-century critics were convinced that photography might make landscape painting obsolete.[4] But interior photographs could be and *were* posed, staged as easily as a painting.

Despite these limitations, the photographs reveal much. Their liabilities — such as narrow focus — may not help us recreate a historic interior precisely, but they become assets by making the photos valuable documents of American culture. The repetition of certain elements or focal points in these pictures is an index to features considered important by turn-of-the-century Americans: bay windows and pianos, for example. The often photographed hearth and mantel served as the synecdoche of the home. In many cases the placement of objects in these spaces indicates a conscious composition. Such manipulation is another index of the way householders wished to present themselves: these are photographs of people — and their homes — as they wanted to see themselves and be seen by others, "stories that people tell themselves about themselves."[5]

★ ★ ★ ★

I hope *Inside Texas* will have many audiences — historic preservationists, architects, historians, historic archaeologists, and anyone interested in historic house recreation. Many have given assistance: architects have noted interior finishes, interior architectural details, and lighting fixtures; preservationists and historic house planners have paid special regard to furnishings; historic archaeologists have concentrated on ceramics and other accessories; and cultural historians have read the photographs for information concerning the values and behavior of the people who decorated and lived in the rooms.

In my search for interior views, I visited many private and public collections around the state. People who learned about my research from newspapers and friends invited me into their homes from Panhandle to Alice, from Palestine to El Paso, and many cities and towns between. Staffs from the following public collections also welcomed me, and I am grateful: Abilene Historical Photograph Collection, Richardson Research Center, Hardin Simmons University, Abilene; African-American Cultural Heritage Center, Dallas; Amon Carter Museum, Fort Worth; Architectural Drawings Collection, Architecture and Planning Library, the General Libraries at The University of Texas, Austin; Austin History Center, Austin; Big Spring Museum, Big Spring; Brazoria County Historical Museum, Angleton; Carson County Square House Museum, Panhandle; City-County Pioneer Museum, Sweetwater; Colorado City Museum, Colorado City; Corpus Christi Public Library, Corpus Christi; Courthouse-on-the-Square Museum, Denton; Dallas County Heritage Society, Dallas; Dallas Historical Society, Dallas; Deaf Smith County Historical Museum, Hereford; Eugene C. Barker Texas History Center, Austin; Fayette Heritage Museum and Archives, La Grange; Fort Bend County Museum, Richmond; Fort Concho National Historic Landmark, San Angelo; Fort Davis National Historic Park, Fort Davis; Annie Riggs Museum, Fort Stockton; Galveston Historical Foundation, Galveston; George Washington Carver Museum, Austin; Gregg County Historical Museum, Longview; Harris County Heritage Society, Houston; Harrison County Historical Museum, Marshall; Harry Ransom Humanities Research Center, Austin; Houston Metropolitan Research Center, Houston; Huntsville Public Library, Huntsville; Institute of Texan Cultures, San Antonio; Kell House, Wichita Falls; The Library, Daughters of the Republic of Texas at the Alamo, San Antonio; Magoffin Home State Historical Park, El Paso; McFaddin-Ward Historic House Museum, Beaumont; Midland County Museum, Midland; Morton Museum of Cooke County, Gainesville; Museum of American Architecture and Decorative Arts, Houston; Museum of the Big Bend, Alpine; Museum of the Llano Estacado, Plainview; Nelda C. and H. J. Lutcher Stark Foundation, Orange; Overland Trail Museum, Fort Davis; Panhandle-Plains Historical Museum, Canyon; Permian Historical Society, University of Texas of the Permian Basin, Odessa; Rosenberg Library, Galveston; Sam Bell Maxey House State Historical Park, Paris; San Antonio Conservation Society, San Antonio; San Jacinto Museum of History, La Porte; Sherman Historical Museum, Sherman; Smith County Historical Society and the Goodman Museum, Tyler; Southwest Collection at the El Paso Public Library, El Paso; Southwest Collection at Texas Tech University, Lubbock; Texas Collection at Baylor University, Waco; Texas and Dallas History Collection at the Dallas Public Library, Dallas; Texas State Library and Archives, Austin; Wallisville Heritage Park, Wallisville; West of the Pecos Museum, Pecos; Wichita Falls Museum and Art Center, Wichita Falls; Winedale Historical Center, Winedale; and Witte Museum, San Antonio.

Many other groups and institutions participated by mail and by telephone: Brownsville Historical Association and the Stillman House, Brownsville; Crockett County Museum, Ozona; Crosby County Pioneer Memorial, Crosbyton; Fire Hall Museum, Crowell; Fort Sam Houston Museum, San Antonio; Heritage House Museum, Orange; Hidalgo County Historical Museum, Edinburg; John E. Conner Museum, Kingsville; Karnes City Library and Karnes County Historical Society, Karnes City; King Ranch Archives, Kingsville; McAllen International Museum, McAllen; Martin County Historical Museum, Stanton; Pan American University Library, McAllen; Ralph W. Steen Library, Special Collections, Stephen F. Austin University, Nacogdoches; Texas Forestry Museum, Lufkin; Wharton County Historical Museum, Wharton; and White Deer Land Museum, Pampa.

I am also grateful that most of the 254 county historical commissions kindly responded to my three inquiries.

Many individuals assisted my effort. I thank Arlinda Abbott, Blake Alexander, Fran Alger, Marge Alkek, the late Reba Alsup, Kenneth Ames, Elton and Lorene Archer, B. W. Aston, the staff of Austin Prints for Publication, Eve Bartlett, Holly C. Batson, Jim Baum, Cynthia Beeman, Gail Beil, Mrs. Paul Brooks Belding, Melleta R. Bell, Wayne Bell, Eunice Benckenstein, Suzanne G. Benefield, Margaret C. Berry, Callie Bevill, Jim Bigger, Mabel Birdsong, the late John Black, Mrs. John Black, Jan Blodgett, Preston Bolton, Mrs. Ford M. Boulware, George Donald Bowie, Hal Box, Gloria Britain, Lennie Brown, Willard E. Brown, III, Ed and Alice Buffington, Pat Butler, Betty Buttolph, Joan Cabaniss, Jean Carefoot, Mrs. Marvin F. Carruth, Fannie Simpson Carter, Kathy Carter, Beverly G. Case, Elizabeth Cauthan, Mr. and Mrs. Edward Cave, Mrs. Walter Caven, Ruby Cawthron, Betty Chapman, Bruce Cheeseman, Geniece Childress, Wade Choate, Robert Clark, Mrs. Earl Cliburn, Bert Clifton, Elaine Coffman, Richard and Susan Collins, Roger Conger, Thelma Conitz, John W. Cordray, Rodger J. Cramer, Cindy Crane, Cox Crider, Dan Crouch, Danelda Crouse, Hugh and Craig Cunningham, Wayne Daniel, Virginia Wood Davis, Edward R. Dedeke, Lynn Denton, the late Florence Fletcher Dessart, the late Frederick W. Digby-Roberts, Mrs. Frederick W. Digby-Roberts, Robin Doughty, Elinor Draeger, Richard Eisenhour, Virginia Eisenhour, Betty O. Ellis, Mrs. Jack Elms, H. Leslie Evans, Katie Falkenberg, Margaret Felty, Linda Ferris, Mrs. Eugene Fish, Tom A. Fort, Jessica Foy, Kristine Fredricksson, Bettie B. Gafford, George R. Gause, Elzira Ann Gibson, Lois M. Gililland, William Goetzmann, the late E. O. Goldbeck, Larry Goode, Don Graham, Bill Green, Casey Edward Greene, Beth Griggs, Justine Digby-Roberts Grisham, Jonnie Gunnels, Vivian and Mary Hackney, Ken Hafertepe, Mr. and Mrs. Wilson E. Hail, Jr., Dessie M. Hanbury, Bebe Harman, William M. and Frances P. Harris, Martha Hartzog, Barbara Harvey, Lois Harvey, Susan Hasker, Priscilla Hauger, Bill Hauk, Henry J. Hauschild, Margaret Hays, Esther Hearne, Mrs. Robert S. Heath, Cecelia Conitz Heinrich, Janet Hewlett, Norman and Loretta Hodde, Keva Hoffman, Virginia Holden, June S. Holly, Kathryn Hornby, Barney Hubbs, Elena Ivy, Mr. and Mrs. Mermod C. Jaccard, Jr., Carol Jackson, Patricia Chadwell Jackson, Lori Jacobson, Gloria Jaster, Glenn J. Jessee, A. Lloyd Jones, Josephine Simmang Jones, Mrs. Roland T. Jones, Margaret Kelley, Jane Kenamore, Jeanette Jackson King, Diana Kirby, Pat Kirkeminde, Bobbie Jean Klepper, Judy Rowe Koehl, Nezell K. Korges, Kevin Ladd, Leila S. LaGrone, Lisa Lambert, Nancy Land, Larry Landis, Kathryn Lang, Lee

Averill Lawrence, Mike Leslie, Johnnye Jean Weinert Lovett, Sharmyn Lumsden, May Ellen MacNamara, Jody McCall, Mr. and Mrs. William O. McCurdy, Dr. W. O. McCurdy, III, Eloise McDonald, James Patrick McGuire, Anne McIntyre, Clyde McKee, Dorothy McKee, Margaret Stoner McLean, Sherrie McLeroy, the late Mr. Oliver B. McReynolds, Mrs. Oliver B. McReynolds, Mr. and Mrs. Robert D. Maddox, Jane Manaster, John M. Manguso, Nelda Marcum, Jo Lynne Marlin, Helen Faltin Martin, Niny A. Massey, Peter Maxson, Albert Mayer, Polly Mays, Jeff Meikle, John Middleton, Barbara Bates Mills, Michael Moore, Zane Morgan, Peggy Moser, David Murrah, Ellen Murry, Dick Mycue, Lois E. Myers, Helen Cates Neary, the late Robert A. Nesbitt, Janet Neugebauer, Rosa Lee Neumann, Linda Cheves Nicklas, Nina L. Nixon, Jack Oswald, Glen Patton, Clark Pearce, Richard Pearce-Moses, Henri Elizabeth Pepper, Beverly Singletary Perdue, Ken Perry, Juanita Phillips, Jimmie Picquet, Genora B. Prewit, P. J. Pronger, III, Marie Reasonover, Elizabeth Redmond, Martha S. Reed, Myrtle Rice, Patricia Rice, Beatrice Richards, Carol Riggs, Carol Roark, Mrs. J. B. Roberts, Mary C. Roberts, Mrs. Gordon Robertson, Kathryn E. Rogers, Tom Rogers, Shirley Ruckman, Helen Rugeley, Marie Russell, Mary Sarber, Mrs. W. H. Savage, Robert L. Schaadt, Patricia Scott, June Secrist, Mary Kay Shannon, Pat Sharpe, Marvin T. Shickles, Robert W. Shook, Ada Simond, Blake Smith, Mr. and Mrs. Cullen Smith, Gary Smith, Ray Smith, Otha Spencer, Catherine Villaret Spinks, Charles D. Spurlin, Nelda C. Stark, Cecilia Steinfeldt, Nancy Steves, Joe A. Stout, Mrs. Bailey Summers, Margaret P. Surratt, Mrs. Fred Thompson, Mrs. William A. Thompson, Jean Bowie Thorpe, William Turner, Dannehl Twomey, Bebe Beasley Ulrich, Martha Utterback, Ronald E. Wade, Pauline Watkins, Katherine Watson, Kathryn Watson, Maria Watson, Terry Wayland, Bobby Weaver, John M. Weaver, Nellie Lee Weincek, Mary M. Welder, Verna Anne Wheeler, Mrs. C. D. Whitaker, Harold and Elizabeth Williams, Kemper S. Williams, Mary L. Williams, Douglas Barton Willingham, the late Michael Wilson, Gail Caskey Winkler, Jeanette Winters, Mr. and Mrs. Drew Wommack, and Rosa Lee Wylie.

I am also grateful to those organizations that helped to fund parts of the research: National Endowment for the Humanities, American Association for State and Local History, Texas Architectural Foundation, and Hugh M. Cunningham Foundation.

Inevitably some people stand out as particularly helpful. With longstanding support, a particular kindness, and assistance at a critical time or with a nagging problem, these people made the research less overwhelming: John Anderson, Alison Beck, Lynn Bell, Art Black, Ellen Brown, James H. Conrad, Ralph Elder, Susan Harwell, Brenda Jordan, Kent Keeth, Claire Kuehn, Bill Richter, Peggy Riddle, and Lila Stillson.

Those working with the photographic record of the entire state can have no better ally and friend than Tom Shelton of the Institute of Texan Cultures. I am glad he was both for me.

My friends and colleagues — Gena Dagel, Melissa Hield, Jane Archer Feinstein, Nancy Neff, and Margaret Caffrey — gave me something *almost* as important as pre-1920 interior photographs of Texas houses. Their encouragement sustained me during this work.

Catherine E. Hutchins edited the manuscript with insight and clarity that I did not have. It was a pleasure working with Kate and the manuscript so benefitted from her hand that I would undertake another project only with her help. I will stop just short of urging all others to do the same.

After working with Robert Mugerauer, I know that comments like "I could not have written this book without the help of . . ." can be understatements. Bob was generous with both his time and his ideas. I hope that I have the opportunity to work with him on other projects and that many students and colleagues will experience the enthusiasm that he brings to the study of "home."

I am grateful to my family, especially my parents, Betty and Al Brandimarte, who, although they have never known exactly what I do, taught me early that it was all right.

This book is dedicated to my husband, Mark Emmert, happily a person who does not keep score.

1

"All That Stuff"

AN INTRODUCTION

IN 1984 author-screenwriter Horton Foote called me to advise him on a set design for the movie *1918*, a semiautobiographical film shot in Waxahachie about the 1918 influenza epidemic. Foote explained that many scenes would recreate his family's home. He said he had some of the original furniture, which he described as "white." I suspected he meant an enameled bedstead, and a colonial revival dresser and matching dressing table. Foote explained that the film company's art department — a Texas crew who embraced Hollywood's vision of their state — rejected the white furniture in favor of Victorian furnishings. Since he had no family photographs, Foote requested interior photographs I had collected that would approximate a Waxahachie interior in 1918. He believed my photographs and my research on house interiors would bolster his position against the art department so that he could use the very furniture that had been in the house.

The art department did not want the real thing — the sort of furniture widely available in Texas stores in the 1910 – 1920 decade. They overlooked the important details of the movie characters' lives — that they were young and newly married and had the need of all newlyweds to furnish their home. Instead, they wanted to perpetuate the Hollywood stereotype of Texans as somehow singular and anachronistic, unaware of fashion and styles. Their syllogism went something like this: "If Texans have bad taste — and they do — and if so-called Victorian taste equals bad taste — and it does — then Texans in 1918 decorated their houses in that manner." According to the movie's set designers, Texans were also behind the times, and although Victorian decoration was disappearing by 1918, newly married young Texans (and older ones) would be avid consumers of it. My search for early interior views gave me the opportunity to test the notion that Texas houses — like most things Texan — are unique and

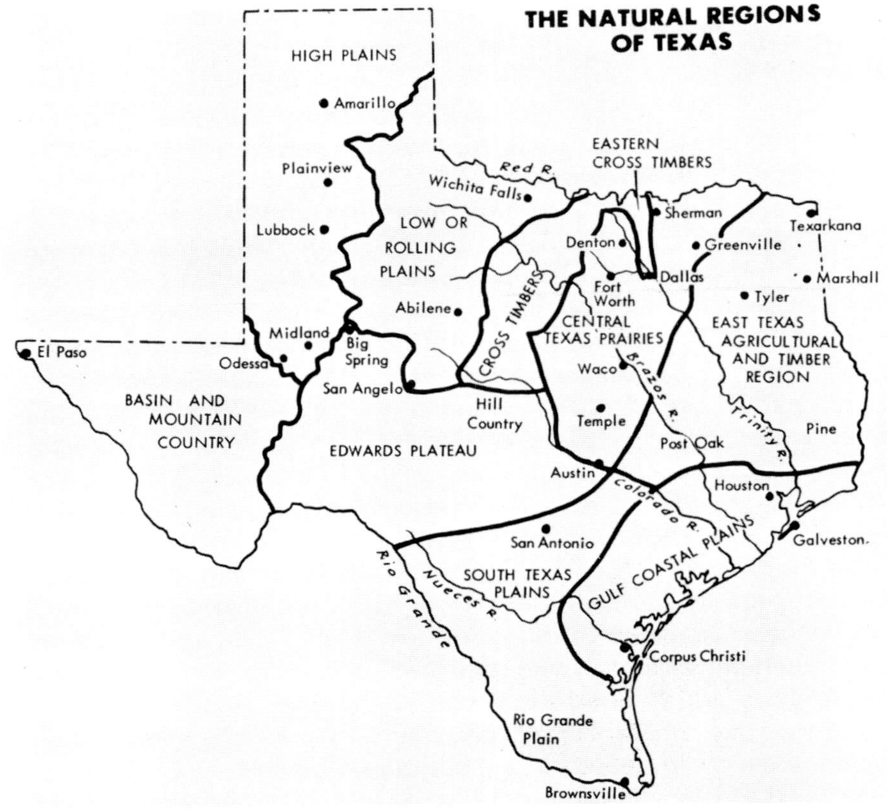

1.1. The natural regions of Texas (From Rupert N. Richardson, Ernest Wallace, and Adrian Anderson, *Texas: The Lone Star State*, 5th ed., Englewood Cliffs, N.J.: Prentice Hall, 1988, p.3. Based upon Stanley A. Arbingast, Lorrin G. Kennamer, and Michael E. Bonnie *Atlas of Texas*, Austin: Bureau of Business Research, University of Texas at Austin, 1967).

different and to debunk "the Hollywood art department fallacy."

Interior photographs contain much practical information not only for set designers but also for historic preservationists. Many people charged with historic house recreation either despair if their specific structure has no surviving photographic documentation or seize the first high-style East Coast interior photograph they can find and attempt to graft details upon a vernacular building in Texas. This is often understandable. But the published interior views always seem to be either too high-style or too low-style, too early or too late, too far west or too far east to have much to do with one's project. It is especially critical now to locate regional images as scholars increasingly recognize that people's creation of domestic environments depends in large part on factors relating to geography: climate, availability of goods, and ethnicity.

In nineteenth-century Texas, all three factors had an impact on household furnishings. Texas then as now had typically long and hot summers, and mild winters with occasional fierce blue northers. In West Texas, annual rainfall was sometimes less than ten inches, while in the eastern part of the state winds from the Gulf of Mexico brought frequent and heavy rains.

Soil and climate created conditions in which oak, hickory, and pine flourished in East Texas; oaks and mesquite grew intermittently in the central part of the state; and in West Texas, the land supported only grasses and shrubs, oaks, junipers, or cedars, and mesquite. In East Texas there was plentiful lumber; in southern and western areas, it was scarce (fig. 1.1).

At mid nineteenth century, transportation routes were starting to make available all kinds of goods, including household furnishings. Several ports connected settlers with markets in other parts of the country. Galveston was the most active; Matagorda, Indianola (destroyed by a storm in 1875, rebuilt, and again destroyed in 1886), and Port Lavaca were also busy ports. Prior to the 1880s, upon arrival in Galveston or other port cities, goods could be shipped — with considerable difficulty — over land routes or by riverboat to inland towns. Most of the major rivers — the Red, Sabine, Trinity, Brazos, Colorado, Nueces, and Rio Grande — were, at least in part, navigable and generally remained important transportation networks until the railroads eclipsed them in the 1880s.[1]

By the late nineteenth century, land routes were extending water transportation networks beyond New Orleans and the Texas Gulf Coast, and railroads were rushing into the state with goods from Chicago, St. Louis, Kansas City, Louisville, and other cities. Before the Civil War, there were fewer than 500 miles of intrastate tracks, and not before the early 1870s was the state linked with points outside its boundaries. But by the 1880s, incentives given to railroad companies helped to increase the number of miles to approximately 3,000 (fig. 1.2). And at the close of the decade, the number had almost tripled again.[2] Railroads were providing relatively swift, inexpensive, and dependable transportation in Texas.

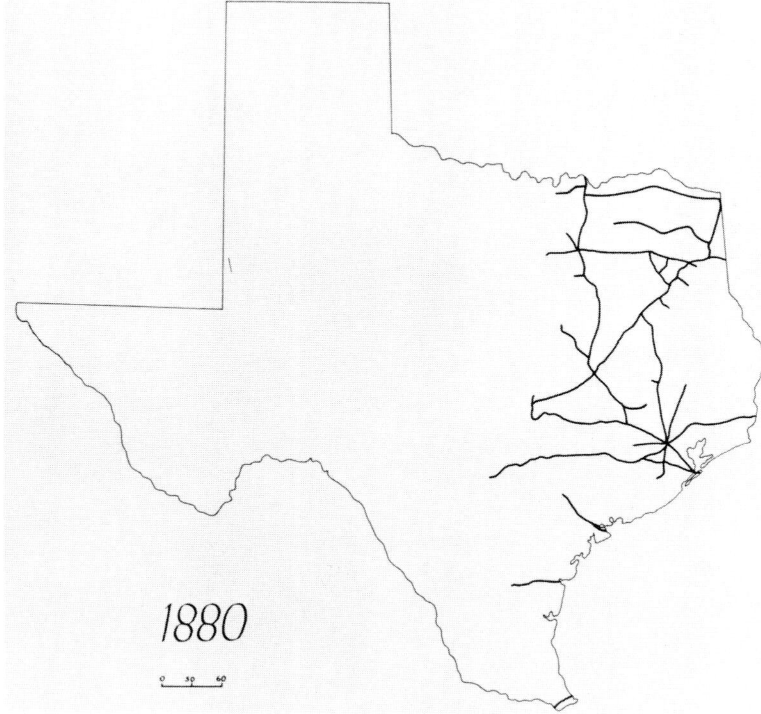

1.2. Railroad map, 1880 (From Charles P. Zlatkovich, *Texas Railroads, A Record of Construction and Abandonment* [Austin: Bureau of Business Research, University of Texas at Austin, and Texas State Historical Association, 1981], p. 109).

In 1880, 1.5 million people lived within the boundaries of Texas. Most people settled in the eastern half of the state. According to the 1880 federal census, 1,402,085 Texans lived in an area that the report broadly defined as "Southwest Central"; 154,821 clustered along the Gulf Coast; and only 34,843 lived in the vast "Western plains."[3] Large numbers of Anglos, Tejanos (or Spanish-speaking Texans), Germans, and blacks, and fewer Scandinavian, Polish, and other western European immigrants constituted the population.

The Lower South — Alabama, Georgia, Mississippi, and Louisiana — provided settlers to the eastern fifth of the state; northern sections — from the Central Texas prairies to the High Plains — were settled by many who

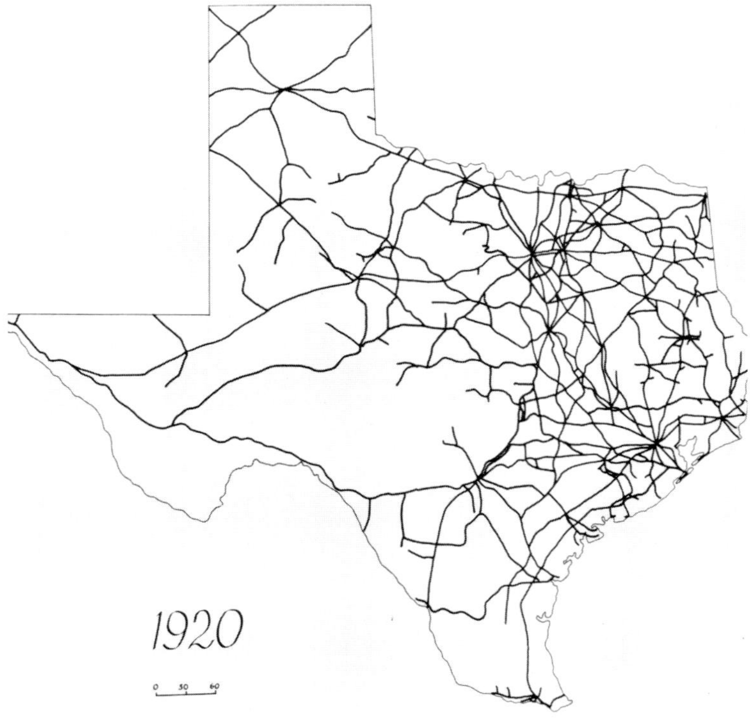

1.3. Railroad map, 1920 (From Charles P. Zlatkovich, *Texas Railroads: A Record of Construction and Abandonment* [Austin: Bureau of Business Research, University of Texas at Austin, and Texas State Historical Association, 1981], p. 113).

had left the Upper South — Virginia, Kentucky, Tennessee, and the Carolinas. Europeans, especially Germans and Czechs, converged in the east-central area of the state, joined by settlers from both the Lower and the Upper South. Germans settled the Hill Country near the center of the state. Tejanos occupied the area along the Rio Grande from western to southern Texas.[4]

In 1880 Texas had five major cities — Austin, Dallas, Galveston, Houston, and San Antonio — but most Texans lived in rural areas, earning a living in agriculture. A large number of people also worked as domestic servants, laborers, storekeepers and merchants, traders and dealers, railroad workers, and carpenters.[5]

By the early decades of the twentieth century, much had changed. In 1900 the population was more than 3 million; by 1920, more than 4 million. Many more Texans were living in the major cities: Dallas, Fort Worth, Houston, and San Antonio each had a population exceeding 50,000. In 1880 Texas had been less than 10 percent urban; forty years later it was more than 30 percent urban.[6] Occupational distribution was also shifting. While many working Texans were still engaged in agriculture in 1920, others sought and found employment in the lumber and mineral industries.[7]

Along with the increase in population and changes in the economic base came improved transportation systems. By 1920 the railroads had laid 16,000 miles of track throughout the state and spurred the development of inland cities (fig. 1.3).[8] On the coast, the natural ports, inadequate even in the days of light sailing craft and small steamers, were being improved. By the early twentieth century, the ports of Freeport, Port Aransas, and Houston had been upgraded, and by the 1920s the state was moving toward a deep-water port system.[9]

These statistics do not always conform to people's perceptions of Texas, however. For many people, Texas was exemplified then — and is now — by the dry, arid region of West Texas rather than the dense forests of East Texas, or conceived of as the extremes of desert and Dallas. Still others see only cowboys and ranchers, instead of farmers, sawmill operators, merchants, and railroad workers; and many think only of the large Tejano population, rather than the numerous Polish, Danish, and Germanic enclaves.

Decorative arts enthusiasts are just as prone to generalize. For some, both inside and outside the state, Texas furniture is too often equated with the masterful pieces of German cabinetmakers, rather than with the mantel clocks and rocking chairs from Sears, Roebuck.[10] Some people consider briefly the anomaly of Galveston's exuberant late-nineteenth-century structures and then observe that many nineteenth-century Texans lived in dugouts or log cabins before moving into ranch houses filled with horn furniture. These stereotypes are somehow more appealing than truthful — Texans lived in rooms resembling New Jersey parlors and Indiana kitchens.

Between 1878 and 1920, many changes affected the appearance of home interiors. Growing cities meant urban Texans were closer to large stores and outlets offering all types of consumer goods; new money from cattle and oil meant the power to purchase fashionable household furnishings; increasing population and greater wealth meant urban markets for design professionals; and vastly improved coastal and inland transportation networks blurred state and regional barriers.

Photographs taken between 1878 and 1920 show that *far from being insular, most Texans were well linked to mass markets and stayed reasonably current with decorating ideas and styles.* By the 1870s, and probably earlier, like other Americans, they were part of an emerging consumer culture. By the last decades of the nineteenth century, Texans could buy a respectable array of fashionable goods that were beginning to be offered in general stores, furniture stores, china and jewelry stores, and department stores. Mail-order catalogues like those of Sears, Roebuck encouraged further variety of household goods in Texas homes and made possible a democracy of place.

Choices for the Texas consumer had expanded greatly from the 1820s when Stephen F. Austin advised his family to abandon their furniture and piano in preparation for travel to Texas: "let our motto therefore be *economy* and *plain* living."[11] By the 1890s Texans were fashioning their home interiors in a manner far from plain, their ideas generated and supported both by experts who wrote columns and articles for various magazines that offered current fashion to women in the hinterlands and by local advisors, like paperhangers and furniture retailers. Texas consumers were confidently shopping in a varied marketplace and selecting diverse styles ranging from renaissance revival to Louis XVI.

Professional decorators were establishing offices and dispensing advice in urban centers. Some very prosperous Texans even went outside the state to enlist professional decorators. Within the state, a cadre of tastemakers began offering expertise through furniture or department stores in larger cities. There were also special decorating firms such as Doyle Decorating Studio in San Antonio, and individual craftsmen, such as Walther Tauscher of Dallas, who advertised their skills.[12]

In part to meet the growing sophistication and prosperity of some residents, increasing numbers of architects were also making their expertise available to the new Texas market. In 1860 Texas had only eight architects. Twenty-six years later, the Texas State Association of Architects was formed. By 1920 Texas boasted 495 architects.[13]

In Texas as elsewhere, a variety of styles of architecture and furnishings was embraced by householders during the period 1878 – 1920.[14] The styles overlap and lack a clear beginning and end. In exterior architecture, the Italian villa or Italianate, second empire, romanesque revival, stick, shingle, Queen Anne, Eastlake, and chateau styles allowed expression of the late-nineteenth-century aesthetic. At the turn of the century, architects also worked in the vocabularies of beaux arts classicism, Jacobean revival, and Georgian revival. And by the early twentieth century, the prairie style of midwestern architect Frank Lloyd Wright and the mission revival and bungalow styles met a ready reception.

Interior furnishings had similar changes and a weltering variety.[15] Few rooms and even fewer houses were fitted with furniture in a single style. Most turn-of-the-century Americans lived with an eclectic assemblage of furnishings — as we do today. Many styles lingered well after new ones appeared and still found a ready market. Some styles were updated by the attachment of elements from the new style. Conversely, some new styles were modified to make them more affordable to various socioeconomic levels. At the same time, the definition of stylishness was ever changing at the upper income level. Finally, there was neither a clear end of one style nor a clear beginning of another, nor was stylistic purity ever more than a chimera.

By 1850 householders in Texas could select furniture in the Grecian, Gothic, Elizabethan, and rococo-revival styles. But relatively few examples of these midcentury styles are found in Texas houses photographed between 1878 and 1920. Furnishings in these styles generally predate the period, and they are most visible in the households of older couples in established cities. Too, these midcentury styles were primarily manufactured outside the state during the era that transportation networks in Texas, and Anglo populations were limited. Accordingly these styles arrived in the state in relatively small numbers. There were fewer examples of them originally in Texas, and therefore fewer survive to appear in rooms photographed later.[16]

Late-nineteenth-century furniture styles found in abundance in Texas homes photographed between 1878 and 1920 include the renaissance and French-revival styles, as well as Eastlake. Neo-Grec and modern Gothic (also known as art furniture or Eastlake furniture) captured part of the late-nineteenth-century furnishings market. Americans' tastes in household decoration also turned to exotic peoples and cultures — Oriental, Egyptian, and Moorish.

By the end of the nineteenth century and early decades of the twentieth, few Americans could afford to follow the advice of Edith Wharton and Ogden Codman, Jr., in *The Decoration of Houses* (1897) to acquire expensive furniture based on French designs from Louis XIV through Louis XVI. More popular were other options available by then: arts and crafts-inspired mission, art nouveau, and colonial revival furniture.

These various furniture styles mirrored cultural changes taking place in the United States. In 1878, Victorianism — defined as an Anglo-American, transatlantic, bourgeois culture of industrializing Western civilization — was the dominant culture, one that placed value on rational order, competition, and modernization and one that was decidedly future oriented, didactic, serious, and concerned about religious tradition.[17] While we can generalize that Victorians tended to be middle-class, Anglo-American, and Protestant, certainly not all were. For our purposes, however, we can observe that many late-nineteenth-century Americans lived in or aspired to live in homes that were rich in detail and elaboration and characterized by "visual complexity and intricacy."[18] By 1920, many Americans lived in bungalows that looked far simpler.

★ ★ ★ ★

Intrigued but exasperated viewers of photographs in this study have often asked, "Why did Victorians have all that stuff?" Many are convinced that those who decorated their homes during these years dedicated themselves to a conscious assault on tasteful sensibilities of the generations following them (fig. 1.4). Indeed, it is fair to ask in a nonjudgemental tone, "Why did householders use such volumes of decorative accessories?"

Art historians observe that the late-nineteenth-century aesthetic system both in this country and abroad turned on the axis of "picturesqueness" and its concomitant qualities: variety, movement, irregularity, intricacy, and roughness.[19] Variety, for example, was achieved by multiple shapes and silhouettes. Roofs sprouted chimneys, towers, and gables; inside, rooms were divided in round, rectangular, and octagonal shapes and filled with a variety of exotic items. Movement was a consciously achieved effect of advancing and receding; in rooms, it was expressed in color and placement of objects. An attempt to avoid monotony and achieve visual surprise, irregularity was often conveyed by asymmetry, while juxtapositions of the natural and the artificial enhanced intricacy — cut flowers were placed among paper, embroidered, stenciled, or enameled flowers in many parlors. Allied with intricacy was contrast between original form and materials and social function, such as the use of cattle horns for furniture components. Finally, roughness appeared in objects conveying rusticity — rustic chairs, plant stands, picture frames, and easels — and in objects that signified "wild" or "savage," such as those using Native American motifs.

Architectural historian Carroll L. V. Meeks has suggested that during the late nineteenth century "the basis of taste was shifting from reason to sensibility," from a taste for classical buildings to romantic, picturesque structures.[20] A building's "picturesqueness" became the pri-

ROOM No. 10.

ARTICLE		ADDED		VALUE		DESCRIPTION
				DOLLS.	CTS.	
Carpets						
Rugs						
Mats						
Chairs						
Tables						
Lounges						
Sofas						
Piano						
Piano Stool						
Paintings						
Pictures						
Music Stands						
What Nots						
Etagers						
Chiffoniers						
Window Curtains						
Window Shades						
Portiers						
Bric-a-brac*						
Book Cases						
Bureaus						
Mirrors						
Bedsteads						
Toilet Sets						
Wash Stands						
Towel Racks						
Book Shelves						
Clocks						
Stoves						
Kitchen Utensils*						
Trunks						
China Ware & Dishes*						
Gas Fixtures						
Chandeliers						
Oil Lamps						
Wardrobes						
Musical Instruments						
Books*						
Mattresses						
Bedding*						
Silver Ware*						
Clothing*						
Bath Tubs						
Furnaces						
Hat Racks						
Umbrella Stand						
Matting						
Oil Cloths						
Tubs						
Coal						
Wood						
Sewing Machines						
Safe						
Refrigerator						
Fancy Brackets						
Writing Desks						

*As per Inventory.

1.4. Page from Herbert and Company, *Household Furniture Inventory Book*, Galveston Insurance Company, 1891 (Barker Texas History Center, Austin).

mary component in assessing its architectural beauty. But science, too, was shaping the way Americans lived.

There was great popular interest in science during the second half of the nineteenth century, especially after the 1859 publication of Charles Darwin's *On the Origin of Species.* For most Americans, "science" meant knowledge — specific, definite, and rational. Its opposite was mystery. Enthralled by science's seeming order, Americans applied a sort of "scientific method" to diverse and unlikely areas of their lives.[21]

Along with the "sciencing" of American life came an emphasis on rational functions. Plan-book writers insisted that each room in the house had a specific function.[22] Functional specificity meant that homeowners greeted visitors in the entry hall, entertained in the parlor, gathered in the sitting room, read in the library, and slept in the bedroom.

As certain spaces connoted certain activities, specific areas of the house connoted "actors" with an implied, sometimes stated, hierarchy. Servants remained in the service areas of the house — back-stair halls and third-level sleeping quarters. Space was either "public" or "private." The parlor, the most public room of the house, was different in function and decoration from the bedrooms or service areas. There were also gender distinctions for some rooms in the house. Sitting rooms and parlors were feminine; dining rooms, entry halls, and libraries were masculine.

Practicing correctly the elaborate rituals enacted in the parlor or dining room distinguished those who did from those who did not. In a society characterized by an influx of immigrants and a generally transient population, rules that governed social interaction were valued by the middle and upper classes. There was, for example, a sudden plethora of specialized eating utensils, dining services, and dishes — nearly a form for every food. One's ability to master these and other objects and to possess the knowledge and skills to act appropriately, whether in a dining room or a parlor, could determine one's progress up the social ladder.

The "scientific" prescription for progress and its taxonomic vision of the world clashed with the picturesqueness characteristic of the period; these two opposing forces joined other elements in American culture that directly influenced home interiors: the genteel tradition, cosmopolitanism, and domesticity.

Believing they had reached the pinnacle of civilization, Victorian Americans took it as their right to select and sample the best of the past. According to historian Howard Mumford Jones, the genteel tradition was "an operative fusion of idealism and the instinct for craftsmanship, which dominated high culture from 1865 to 1915 and which infiltrated the culture of the middle class."[23] In this idealism and appreciation of craft, Americans revived an old enthusiasm for the acknowledged great works of painting, sculpture, architecture, literature, classical music, and other aspects of European culture. Their homes became "memory palaces" where objects of refinement reminded householders of the world's cultural prizes.

Allied with this renewed appreciation for the best of civilization was cosmopolitanism, an interest in exotic cultures. In some cases this interest motivated travel, but in others it simply meant reading travel literature and foreign fiction, attending an international exposition, or making a trip to a museum or "foreign" restaurant.[24] These enthusiasms translated into exotic objects for the home that would recall foreign lands really or imaginatively visited, communicating a spirit of travel and suggesting the life of a cosmopolite.

Along with looking backward to the past and outward to the world was an unprecedented focus on and fascination with the home. Domesticity implied a devotion to that special sphere where women were to create a soothing environment distinct and separate from the materialistic world. The home was to be a place of spiritual renewal in which family members would want to gather and from which they would never wish to stray. While artistic pursuits were not allowed to take precedence over the orderly running of the household, they were valued because they contributed to the creation of a "suitable" environment.[25] Amateur art publications of the period agreed that "refined ornamentation in every room in the house" would "have a wonderful effect in developing character and preserving harmony."[26] The logic was clear: the more "tasteful" objects created by the woman, the more likely she and her family would be of high moral character, and their home life would be happy and harmonious. Her mandate was to fashion an environment that was spiritually and materially rich.

In part, this art activity was bolstered by the aesthetic and the arts and crafts movements, both of which evolved from design reform movements in Great Britain. Proponents of aestheticism encouraged the manufacture and consumption of artistically embellished domestic goods, including furniture, textiles, wallpapers, and ceramics, to enrich the home. They exalted art and urged wedding it to industry. Advocates of the arts and crafts movement sought to bring beauty into daily life, believing that artistic reform would induce social reform. They focused on handcrafted objects, emphasizing the creativity and autonomy of the individual worker and the quality of handwork over that done by machine.

Both the aesthetic and the arts and crafts movements supported women's art activity. But the arts and crafts movement also advocated simpler interiors, ultimately undermining the overornamentation and extravagance of many late-nineteenth-century home interiors.

By the turn of the century some householders in Texas and elsewhere were choosing different architectural and decorative models. Following the lead of Frank Lloyd Wright, architects and builders began constructing houses in the prairie style. For their interiors, designers and householders turned to the mission style, which called for furniture of heavy, square shapes and simple, angular construction.

In the minds of arts and crafts reformers, honesty, usefulness, and simplicity were necessary correctives to "picturesqueness." So-called honest construction was the opposite of the heavily upholstered and tufted furniture popular during the late nineteenth century. Exposed joinery was its own decoration. Honest objects were both beautiful and useful; étagères filled with trifles lacked utility.

Informality and restraint became the goals in home decoration. Pale tones and gilt were banished in favor of greens, browns, and shades of gold. Silk and damask were replaced by serviceable chintzes, burlaps, and grasscloths.

Variety and diversity, suggesting man's mastery of natural materials, gave way to a concern for unity, based in part on a romantic notion of the harmony of man with nature. In prairie-style dwellings and bungalows, indigenous materials provided construction elements, while the siting of a house reflected an awareness of the natural landscape. Structure and interior were united. Frank Lloyd Wright's built-in furniture expressed his belief that furnishings are "of the building itself, never fixtures on it."[27] Oak ceiling beams, paneling, floors, and furniture linked rooms, finishes, and furnishings.

Inside these new middle-class houses, function-specific rooms and elaborate house plans were replaced by unified spaces. Open floor plans featured spaces that blended into one another. Hallways flowed into living rooms (not parlors) and extended into dining rooms. Living rooms also served as libraries.

Decoration became a vehicle for unity. In prairie-style

houses, motifs were repeated throughout many rooms, linking spaces. Design strategies used in one space were applied to others — two or more rooms were furnished with mission furniture, and walls of several rooms were painted or covered with plain paper and topped by a frieze.

Openness and decorative unity blurred the hierarchical distinctions between public and private spaces, except in a few architect-designed homes of the very wealthy. In most middle-class homes, flowing, open areas expressed a new democratic ideal, muffling earlier demands for public and private spaces. Class, status, and ritual lost importance during the height of the arts and crafts movement, although some gender-distinctive elements remained.

The parlor — that feminine domain — was banished from new open house plans. Solid, sturdy, rectilinear mission oak furniture replaced the curvilinear shapes and excessive embellishment of the late nineteenth century in all rooms of the house, but especially in the library, traditionally a masculine space.[28]

In spite of the dramatic changes in room interiors, the design rhetoric of the second half of the nineteenth century resounded in the early twentieth. Comfortable houses encouraged families to stay at home; family members would not be tempted to leave the home and fall prey to immoral influences. Well-designed and well-decorated houses still made moral people.

Not everyone followed the arts and crafts movement precisely. Some turned to the colonial revival style which had received impetus at the International Centennial Exhibition in Philadelphia in 1876 and endured for many decades. The rage for old furniture afflicted middle-class and wealthy householders alike. While a few hunted for antiques, most turned to furniture companies, which by the end of the century were manufacturing colonial furnishings, some true to the prototypes, most not. Colonial revival furnishings were often combined with arts and crafts elements, but the blending was not contradictory. Colonial revival, folk, and Native American motifs were appropriate in an arts and crafts domestic setting because they were suitably simple, regional, and American.[29]

At the same time, other householders implemented the decorating advice of Elsie de Wolfe. On the heels of high-style critics Wharton and Codman, de Wolfe lambasted dark, cluttered interiors and helped transform middle-class houses across the country. Furniture was lighter colored and delicately proportioned, chintz and other colorful fabrics were used, and there was less clutter on tabletops and walls. A new simplicity reigned. "All that stuff," threatening an assault on the aesthetics of future generations, was passing from vogue.[30]

★ ★ ★ ★

Others have gathered interior images of late-nineteenth- and early-twentieth-century American houses. Such studies usually focus on styles of furnishings set forth in chronological order. *Inside Texas* offers a new model for viewing interior photographs thematically. The book also blends material culture with personal histories to present *room biographies.* Eight identities — occupation, family, ethnicity, social group, region, refinement, class, and style — provide the organization for this study. Arranged according to progressively widening spheres and concerns, the chapters address how some people reveal themselves as ranchers, Germans, lawyers, collegians, Texans, artists, and Southerners, for example. The categories are not exclusive; frequently, they overlap. Three concluding chapters discuss images that demonstrate personal identities interacting with the shaping forces of advice literature and designers — architects, builders, and interior decorators — as these new professionals standardized the previously highly personalized spaces of domestic interiors in Texas. Some houses show strong occupational and ethnic identities; others suggest that the homeowners relinquished personal identification and thus effected a standardization in house decoration implemented by the new design professionals. This does not happen suddenly or uniformly, but happen it does. And *Inside Texas* puzzles out the complex relationship among people, culture, identity, and houses.

2.1. Sitting room, Jim Ned Ranch, near Coleman, ca. 1888 (Courtesy Mrs. Ford M. Boulware).

2

Ranchers and Lawyers, Photographers and Artists

OCCUPATION

TEXANS were carpenters, clerks, domestics, farmers, lawyers, merchants, musicians, railroad workers, ranchers, and teachers. But no matter what their occupations, they often chose to signify their work in household decoration. Ranchers and lawyers, for example, outfitted their domestic environments with tools of their trade not only as a matter of practicality but also as an expression of who they were. Of course objects associated with some occupations were easier than others to incorporate into home decoration and to recognize as work related. Photographers who displayed a tasteful group of pictures in a public room could readily announce their profession; musicians and music teachers could display instruments to proclaim theirs. But merchants who dealt with both local and nonlocal markets might have to choose carefully a selection of goods showing the reach of their activities to communicate occupation.

Many families subtly conveyed the occupation of the head of the household in their decorations, but some women chose to decorate the parlor in a fashion that demonstrated their belief that the care and decoration of the home was a woman's business. Thus, some of the occupations announced by interior decoration were avocations, amateur pursuits, or hobbies, like the paintings of Vallie Fletcher, seen later in this chapter. But professional or not, many Texans identified with their activities or occupations enough to want to incorporate items representing them into the interior of their homes.

Three views document the Jim Ned Ranch, north of Coleman in Coleman County, circa 1888 (figs. 2.1, 2.2, 2.3). Ranch owners William and Frank Anson, standing and sitting respectively at the right in figure 2.1 were the sons of the Second Earl of Lichfield and, like many Englishmen, came to the Central Plains of Texas to pioneer in the state's cattle industry. Billy Anson lived in different areas of the state for three years before deciding that Cole-

2.2. Sitting room, Jim Ned Ranch, ca. 1888 (Courtesy Mrs. Ford M. Boulware).

man County, with its abundance of surface water and the best grazing country south of the Indian Territory, was the right location for his enterprise. His landholdings included a 20,000-acre grazing tract on which he bred cattle, including Herefords, and raised trotting horses, "high-class horseflesh."[1]

The men incorporated images of their work in their house decoration, favoring nineteenth-century genre scenes featuring horses: one hangs prominently over the fireplace, while another faces the camera on the table. Among the animate indicators of their profession are three valued sheep dogs who clearly received preferential treatment in the home. Jack stares at the photographer from his place in the arms of friend Johnny Eaton, who is reading the *Denton Mercury*; Punch naps in Frank's lap, and a puppy lies on the hearth rug near where Billy stands.

At the other end of the room (fig. 2.2), between the corner shelf and the window, a photograph of the patriarch Viscount Anson presides over the sitting room. According to family history, these English emigrants viewed their modest four-room dwelling with amusement; the home they left in England had twenty-five bedrooms. These photographs may have been taken to assure relatives in England that life in Texas was civilized and endurable.[2]

2.3. Frank's bedroom, Jim Ned Ranch, ca. 1888 (Courtesy Mrs. Ford M. Boulware).

There is nothing aristocratic about the four rattan and wicker rockers, several side chairs, center and side tables, two bookcases, piano, desk, overhead kerosene lamp, two kerosene table lamps, and two desk candles.

House decoration does not appear paramount in these ranchers' minds, as indicated by the wall shown just above the Viscount Anson portrait; someone miscalculated the length needed to border the low walls with a wallpaper frieze. Nevertheless, the Ansons have created an air of congenial domesticity in this all-male household. They have conformed to certain conventions in their arrangement of photographs of friends and family, primarily those of women, on various display surfaces — the mantel, draped bookcase, and side table. Presuming that the brothers purchased and draped their own curtains, they implemented what may have been a convention in England in the 1880s, anticipating by several years Edith Wharton and Ogden Codman's 1897 suggestion in *The Decoration of Houses* to hang the curtains high on the wall to conceal poor interior finishes. Wharton and Codman condescendingly explained that "in the modern American house, where the trim is usually bad, and where there is often a dreary waste of wall-paper between the window and the ceiling, it is better to hang the curtains close under

2.4. Office, New Headquarters, LS Ranch, Four miles south of Tascosa, 1897 – 1898 (Panhandle-Plains Historical Museum, Canyon).

the cornice."[3] Or perhaps the curtains were store bought, and rather than hem them, the occupants raised the rods. In any case, the Ansons suspended dark ball-fringe portières and horizontally banded curtains from rods and rings mounted in the middle of the wallpaper frieze, a foot and a half above the tops of the doors and windows. Other textiles cover most horizontal surfaces, including the bookcase behind Eaton that stores and displays valued possessions.

In a photograph taken in his bedroom, Frank presents an image of concentration (fig. 2.3). This space uses the same decorating strategies as the sitting room. The curtains, scarves, and table cover are similar to those in the parlor. A symmetrical mantel arrangement features cabinet cards of his sisters, friends, and mother, while family patriarchs and landscapes hang on the wall. Horses are the subject of the large mantel print.

Ranching was also the occupation of Charles Whitman, part owner of the LS Ranch. He built the New Headquarters at the base of a hill four miles south of Tascosa, a thirty-minute ride to the Fort Worth & Denver City Railroad depot and the LS warehouse. The headquarters included a long, low, one-room-deep frame house with a wide porch and an attached bunkhouse. During 1897 and 1898, this was home for Charles; his wife, Pauline; and their two sons. They had moved to the Panhandle from a fashionable home on Capitol Hill in Denver to take charge of ranch operations.[4]

Charles used one room of the house as his office (fig. 2.4). The activities implied by the desk, strewn with papers and ledgers and supporting a typewriter, distinguish this from many office-libraries photographed in Texas houses (see figs. 2.11, 10.6, 10.22).[5] Its Eastlake-inspired chairs, probably Denver purchases, can be pulled up to the meeting table positioned under the overhead kerosene lamp. Draped with a colorful print curtain, the corner cupboard serves both as a shelf for mounted butterflies, bottled medicine, and harnesses and a support for the Union Metallic Cartridge Company's promotional calendar. The pictures over the desk are symmetrically arranged on the board wall. The floors are covered with carpet or linoleum. Surmounting the painted raised panel door are steer horns, a common element in ranch decoration.

The bedroom combines features of household life and

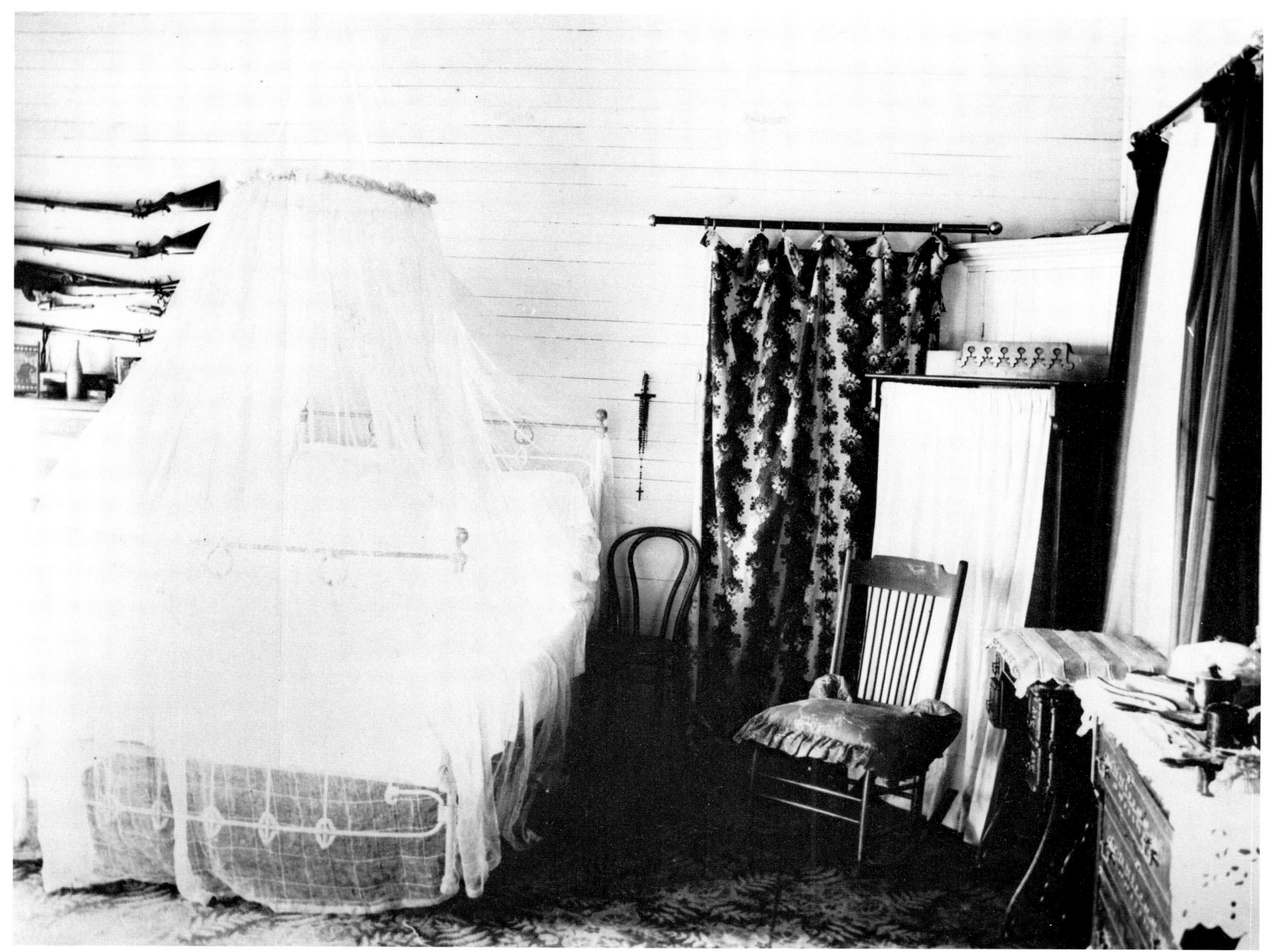

2.5. Bedroom, New Headquarters, LS Ranch, 1897 – 1898 (Panhandle-Plains Historical Museum, Canyon).

2.6. Bedroom, New Headquarters, LS Ranch, 1897 – 1898 (Pandhandle-Plains Historical Museum, Canyon).

occupation (figs. 2.5, 2.6). The white enameled iron bedstead dominates the 1897 – 1898 photograph. According to one facetious account, "The netting draped over the bed was mosquito protection. Larger pests were eliminated by the high-powered guns on the wall."[6] But guns and other weapons were popular late-nineteenth-century wall decorations, even in the homes of people who were not ranchers. Although ornamentally displayed here, in descending order of size, the rifles attest to some ranch duties. They also mark Charles' side of the bed, while a sewing machine, a child's folding bed, and a rosary decorate Pauline's.

Since multiple functions were carried on at New Headquarters, the Whitmans consciously attempted to achieve privacy in some areas of the complex. In their bedroom adjoining the parlor, they built a partition jutting out to-

2.7. Nursery, New Headquarters, LS Ranch, 1897 – 1898 (Panhandle-Plains Historical Museum, Canyon).

ward the foot of the bed to block from public view the daily rituals of washing and dressing; corner cabinets provide concealed storage. In their private space can be seen two crucifixes and a rosary, symbols of personal religious beliefs, as well as the fashionable bentwood and colonial revival chairs and foliate-pattern carpet.

A corner of the nursery (fig. 2.7) shows a built-in closet, decoratively constructed of beaded-wood panels painted in a light color, diagonally arranged and set within a frame painted a darker color. Such furniture reduced the need for large case pieces, always cumbersome and difficult to transport, especially to areas like the LS Ranch, which was some distance from the railroad. The furniture arrangement, possibly adjusted for the photograph, makes the closet almost inaccessible since a crib blocks the door. At the foot of the crib stands a draped changing table that

2.8. Kitchen, New Headquarters, LS Ranch, 1897 – 1898 (Panhandle-Plains Historical Museum, Canyon).

has had its legs shortened. A worn lightweight reed side chair stands nearby in front of the folding bed. The bed was probably considered to be in the Eastlake style with its incised decoration and scalloped crest. The condition of the furniture indicates that the best furniture was not used in the nursery.

A rare photograph of a kitchen (fig. 2.8) shows the space that served both the Whitman family and their ranch hands.[7] Blank, painted walls and bare, unfinished floors provide the setting for a service area furnished with a work table and chair, cooking utensils, pots and pans, and a shelf full of coffeepots (giving credence to the stereotype of the coffee-drinking cowboy). Serviceable cotton fabric covers the shelves, while the window, hung with a roller blind, is bare of textiles.

The focal point of the photograph as well as the kitchen is the Home Comfort No. 130 stove manufactured by the Wrought Iron Range Company of St. Louis. Its circular medallion features a scythe cutting shafts of wheat encircled by the firm's motto, "Economy. Strength. Durability. Good Cooking. Good Eating."

Unlike the other rooms of the house, with their painted horizontal wallboards, the Whitman parlor (figs. 2.9, 2.10) features wallpaper with a scrollwork pattern, a matching frieze, and ceiling paper. This treatment marks it as the most embellished and important room. Competing with the wallpaper design are framed prints and photographs, blind hung on the walls. Popular elsewhere, seascapes like the one shown here were especially prevalent decorative elements in houses on the landlocked plains of the Texas Panhandle. The couple's deceased first-born son, Colden, is commemorated in the large portrait. Floor coverings and textiles further refine the room. Animal-skin rugs are positioned at the piano, near the couch, and by the draped table. A chair cushion fashioned from fleur-de-lis-pattern fabric softens the wood seat and spindled back of the Windsor-style rocker. A small ceremonial fringed carpet marks the draped, simply constructed bookcase. In a room with no fireplace, the Whitmans have made mantels out of the tops of the bookcase, draped tables, desk, and piano. In this adorned space, signs of the owner's ranching activities are more subtle: LS cattle prize

2.9. Parlor, New Headquarters, LS Ranch, 1897 – 1898 (Panhandle-Plains Historical Museum, Canyon).

2.10. Parlor, New Headquarters, LS Ranch, 1897 – 1898 (Panhandle-Plains Historical Museum, Canyon).

ribbons are displayed on the striped curtain panels on the window adjacent to the front door.

At the turn of the century, Texas had a growing population of businessmen and lawyers in communities throughout the state. Library views document the houses of lawyers Samuel Bell Maxey of Paris in northeastern Texas and Alfred Brown Peticolas of Victoria in South Texas.

Maxey's library (fig. 2.11) expresses his identification with several occupations — soldier, lawyer, and statesman — pursued before he died in 1895. Kentucky-born Maxey graduated from the United States Military Academy at West Point, distinguished himself in the Mexican War, studied law under his father whose firm he then joined, and lost a bid for a seat in the Kentucky House of Representatives. In 1857 he moved to Lamar County where he was elected to the Texas Senate in 1861 but declined to serve, opting instead to join the Confederate army. In 1868, he and his wife of fifteen years, the former Marilda Cass Denton, built an Italianate house in Paris, the county seat. During the 1870s and 1880s, Maxey served Texas as a United States senator.[8]

This photograph of the library was taken soon after Maxey died. His portrait rests on the mantel along with a sword, the traditional symbol of a fallen soldier. A second sword, probably draped in red, lies atop the bookcases, which display Maxey's law books. The horn chair, a memento of his statesmanship, was a gift from rancher Richard King for his work on behalf of Texas. The chair was important enough to warrant special attention from the recipients. In 1881 Marilda asked her daughter Dora to

> go over to our house and get the tape measure you will find it in the Upper drawer of your father's writing desk and take the measure of my horn chair. — around and across the bottom — both ways across the bottom — then around the horns. You understand I want the measure around the horns in order to get the narrow trimming. You will see that is around them. . . . I want to get some crimson velvet to upholster it with, I am also going to get me a handsome velvet chair, and a stand for my engravings — and a few other things before I return.[9]

The Maxeys had both a sense of style and a sense of their duty to patronize local manufacturers in Paris. They bought furniture from Willet Babcock, a prosperous Paris

2.11. Library, Sam Bell Maxey house, Southwest corner of South Church and Washington streets (812 South Church Street), Paris, ca. 1895 (Texas State Archives, Austin).

2.12. Sitting room/library into dining room, Alfred Brown Peticolas house, Corner of Goodwin and Bridge streets (207 North Bridge Street), Victoria, 1906 (Courtesy Mrs. Marvin F. Carruth).

manufacturer and retailer. The renaissance revival bookcase and desk may have been purchased from one of several furniture companies active in the city during the late nineteenth century, such as the Rodgers-Wade Furniture Company, which continues its Paris business and is the oldest furniture manufacturing company in the state.[10] Among the indications of the Maxeys' sense of style are the stenciled border, oriental rugs on wooden floors, and art pottery vases filled with flowers cut from the family's extensive gardens. The fixture piped for gas and wired for electricity marks the Maxey house as being in an urban area. Like other libraries, Maxey's has a dictionary stand.

Lawyer A. B. Peticolas, a native of Virginia, settled in Victoria in South Texas in 1859. He practiced law and between 1881 and 1889 may have served as editor of the *Victoria Advocate*, a weekly newspaper. A multifaceted man, Peticolas wrote a memoir of his experiences as a soldier during the Civil War and composed the *Index Digest of Civil and Criminal Law of Texas*.[11] He sketched Victoria scenes and Texas landscapes, including waterways where he fished, and illustrated his Civil War diary. He was, in addition, an amateur cabinetmaker.[12] Some of Peticolas' enthusiasms are evident in the interiors of his home.

By summer 1906, if not before, the sitting room (fig. 2.12), with its paneled wainscoting below a dark border and fill, functioned as a library. The top of the bookcase, complete with law books, and the mantel are dotted with shells and ceramics on doilies. As was common elsewhere, a paper screen mounted on a small stand indicates summer as does the matting that stretches wall to wall in the upstairs and downstairs rooms.[13] Among Peticolas' artworks are a large portrait of his mother and a painting of Mission Concepción in San Antonio, possibly executed by Hermann Lungkwitz, a German-born artist who painted several San Antonio missions and other Texas scenes. The landscape to the right of the door may have been painted by Peticolas.

By the window with curtains trailing on the floor, a mission table supports a fern and what appears to be a writing box. His grandniece recalled that Peticolas made a small "chess table" that may be this one.[14] The only seating piece visible in the photo, a renaissance revival side chair with a leather-upholstered seat, is a dining chair from an earlier set that had been purchased with the renaissance revival sideboard in the adjacent room. The glimpse into the dining room provides a view of the newer Jacobean revival extension dining table and side chair. The large trophy on the wall attests to a successful fishing trip.

In the Maxey and the Peticolas houses, the two lawyers revealed their occupations and avocations in the libraries. But in a Houston residence circa 1920, the occupants, both musicians, expressed their profession throughout the first-floor rooms. The photographer has given a guided, room-by-room tour of the public spaces of this fashionable Houston Heights home: entry hall, living room, library, and dining room. The house was then about fifteen years old, having been built approximately a decade after Clement Edward Oliver had moved from Illinois to Houston in 1896 and established his music business. By 1913 the Oliver Music House was doing "a volume of $100,000 a year and . . . [had] a reputation more than Statewide."[15] His wife shared his enthusiasm for music and belonged to both the Mandolin Club and the Houston Heights Music Club.[16]

The entry hall wallpaper dates to about 1905 and may be the original paper (fig. 2.13). To the left are a mirror and a settee rather than the monumental hallstands common in some late-nineteenth-century houses; to the right, a boldly patterned carpet ascends the stairs. The photograph of the entry hall from just inside the living room

2.13. Entry hall into living room, Clement Edward Oliver house, 1739 Heights Boulevard, Houston, 1918 – 1920 (Harris County Heritage Society, Houston).

highlights the impressive planes and angles and the art glass, as it documents the immediacy with which visitors were confronted by the music making activity of the Oliver household (fig. 2.14). Violin cases rest in one corner, while a music cabinet framed by the windows is topped with a musician's bust.

A columned passage introduced the Olivers' guests and students to the living room, which reflects a newly fashionable sparseness (fig. 2.13). As in other houses, this "best" room features a more ornate mantel (fig. 2.15 *right*) and the newest furniture, here upholstered with a tapestry fabric. An American version of an oriental rug covers the central part of the wooden floor. The prominent arrangement of grand piano, music stand, and floor lamp is distinctive. Oliver emphasized the importance of the piano by leaving it in the living room, a space it dominates. The instrument signifies not only business but also display. The music stand suggests accompanists. Pre-Raphaelite scenes like the one hanging above the piano were popular after the turn of the century. The other print, a pastoral landscape, mimics the background into which it blends. Diagonally across the room from the piano, a colonial revival desk indicates that the Olivers' living room is a place of work.

The arch-framed alcove is defined by the semicircular window seat and three windows covered with sheer curtain panels, double hemmed and shirred on a rod, and window shades, pulled down at various levels to admit sufficient natural light for the photograph (fig. 2.16). Artfully posed, a footstool stands on a small rug, and a violin in its opened case rests on the padded seat.

Similar four-globe electric fixtures light the living room and the library: in the living room the fixture powers a floor lamp to illuminate the sheet music and keyboard; in the library, it powers a table lamp (see fig. 2.15). The library features a continuation of the living room wallpaper. Matching mission rockers with well-worn leather upholstery and colonial revival turnings are positioned to take advantage of the ceiling and window light. No musical instruments appear in the library, although the music stand adjacent to the stacked bookcase and small library table is piled high. A colonial revival mantel, simpler than

2.14. Living room into entry hall, Clement Edward Oliver house, 1918 – 1920 (Harris County Heritage Society, Houston).

2.15. Living room into library, Clement Edward Oliver house, 1918 – 1920 (Harris County Heritage Society, Houston).

2.16. Alcove off living room, Clement Edward Oliver house, 1918 – 1920 (Harris County Heritage Society, Houston).

the mantel in the living room, frames the library fireplace (fig. 2.17). The room accommodates the toys of children instead of the business of the adults. Tree-lined landscapes are blind hung against landscape wallpaper.[17] The bookcase and the mission desk display family photographs; the slim mantel is dominated by a figured clock.

The view of the dining room reveals an extension table, solid wallpaper, window shades behind sill- and floor-length sheer curtains, and access to a screened porch.[18] Above the server between the door and the window hangs a print of a young child playing a musical instrument. Every room echoes the musical theme.

The Olivers' dining room is furnished with restraint, exemplifying the shift from ornamentation to efficiency typical of the years just before 1920. In a measured show, the server displays a silver tray, and a single stand supports a chafing dish and coffeepot; the dining table features only a silver or pewter footed fruit bowl. The electric fixture, with an art glass shade beaded with fringe, is suspended by a chain wire.

Across the state in rural Fort Davis, Nick Mersfelder, like the Olivers, identified himself as a musician. His instruments and objects representing a variety of interests are apparent in photographs he took circa 1920. Born on Christmas Day 1858 in Bavaria, Mersfelder immigrated to Texas in the early 1870s, joined the Texas Rangers, and served as a guard for the international boundary engineers and mapmakers who surveyed the United States – Mexican border in Big Bend and West Texas. Mersfelder left the Rangers in 1880 and settled in Fort Davis, about 200 miles southeast of El Paso.[19] He became a barber, photographer, and justice of the peace, as well as a musician. Figure 2.18 shows Mersfelder in his photography and music studio; beyond the doorway in this multifunctional house is his barber shop and municipal office.

Mersfelder furnished his private space to accommodate his diverse interests. A corner office has a desk, lamp, and coat rack. To the right of the wardrobe in this view clusters a music stand and his orchestra of instruments. In the center of the room, where inexpensive side chairs, a table, and a rocking chair complete the assemblage, Mersfelder functions as his own photographer, his left hand control-

2.17. Library into dining room, Clement Edward Oliver house, ca. 1918 – 1920 (Harris County Heritage Society, Houston).

ling the device that trips the shutter as he sits in his Morris chair.

Many of the room's decorative items hang high on the wall or at the windows, out of the way as if decoration must not interfere with room functions. Commercial prints, family photographs, and possibly Mersfelder's own photographic work, along with a patriotic print of President William H. McKinley, form a frieze along the walls. Mersfelder has arranged these items carefully, aligning the bottom of each frame with the top of the door, tipping them out at the top and securing them with china pins at the bottom, a method of hanging wall accessories first popular at mid century.

The unpainted pine floor, only partially covered with a threadbare rug through which appears the pattern of shrinking wooden planks, tempts one to dismiss the room as lacking in decorative finishes. Yet the painted walls and ceiling have been embellished with stenciled decoration, and the wooden trim at the windows and doorways is painted to complement the color of the walls. Even a shaped valance hangs at one window.

At the other end of the room, a bedstead and dresser define the sleeping area (fig. 2.19). A corner pile of Mexican blankets balances the room diagonally. In the opposite corner, a trunk serves as both table and window seat, while the wide sill functions as a magazine rack. Mersfelder used this well-lighted window corner as his photography studio.[20] At night, he could light his reading areas with the overhead kerosene lamp, the table lamps, or the sconce near the desk. Mersfelder furnished his home pragmatically, shunning propriety and ceremony in favor of serviceability. Living with his Irish setter, this renaissance man of the Texas Big Bend had the luxury of using space in a manner that personally suited him.

About the same time but across the state in East Texas, artist Valentine "Vallie" Fletcher was transforming her studio at her family's Park Farm on the Neches River near Beaumont into a room-size cozy corner (fig. 2.20). Like Mersfelder, Fletcher decorated this room to suit her needs and her work. Her artistry dominates the darkened space. The table at the right holds her sketch pad, brushes, and other art supplies. The Elizabethan revival table, covered

2.18. Multipurpose room, Nick Mersfelder house, Fort Davis, ca. 1920 (Photography Collection, Harry Ransom Humanities Research Center, University of Texas at Austin).

2.19. Multipurpose room, Nick Mersfelder house, ca 1920 (Photography Collection, Harry Ransom Humanities Research Center, University of Texas at Austin).

2.20. Art studio, "Aunt Vallie's Studio at [Fletcher family's] Park Farm added to old house, built in early 1900s," near Beaumont, ca. 1900 (Courtesy Florence Fletcher Dessart).

2.21. Reception room, Joseph M. Maurer photography studio, 418 Tremont Avenue, Galveston, ca. 1903 (Rosenberg Library, Galveston).

with a hooked rug, supports a chafing dish, a tankard, and more art supplies.

The room also displays her art. One of her sketches is pinned to the wall netting.[21] The matching desk and chair decorated with trails of ivy may be examples of her wood-carving efforts. Even the arrangement on the tray in the corner looks like an artistic grouping, possibly the subject of a still life.

Fletcher's furnishings show a predilection for aestheticism and eclecticism: the rustic chair, German pipe rack, Japanese parasol and lanterns, stuffed peacock, netting supported by oars lining two walls, and a couch covered with unmatched pillows. The dark walls, relieved by the light, unfinished pine floor, provide a backdrop for the multiple patterns of the room's textiles. Fletcher has indulged her idiosyncrasies, creating an individualistic retreat and work space. This flamboyant stylishness could be its own goal, but in this room she blends eclecticism with her persona as "artiste."

Figures 2.21 and 2.22 show a Galveston studio of another sort. In 1903 photographer Joseph M. Maurer bought a thirty-six-year-old studio located in a space that had always been used as a photography studio. Justus Zahn, who earlier occupied the studio, had taught Maurer. After interning in St. Louis and Cincinnati and working as a traveling photographer, Maurer returned to Galveston and opened shop in the old Zahn studio. Thirty-five years later, Maurer had twice been elected president of the Texas Photographers' Association, had been the subject of a feature article in the *Galveston Daily News*, and was still proudly in business.[22]

Maurer's strong identification with his profession, demonstrated in his decoration of his studio, may account for his taking up residence in the building. Vague records indicate he lived there at least from 1903 to 1904 and possibly afterward.[23] The hammock and sleeping area, or cozy corner, curtained with one of two pairs of store-bought portières, are evidence that Maurer could have used this part of the studio for both working and sleeping.

2.22. Reception room, Joseph M. Maurer photography studio, ca. 1903 (Rosenberg Library, Galveston).

As a parlor projects good taste, moral character, and position in society, so does Maurer's studio/parlor, a refined commercial setting, display his professional expertise. Serving as seats for clients and as portrait props, picturesque wicker photographers' chairs furnish the reception spaces. As in many private residences, potted palms and ferns are also plentiful, some wrapped in florist's paper. A fashionable paper and frieze cover the walls; matting stretches wall to wall, while mats mark the seating areas and protect the matting from wear. Pillows in the chairs, the hammock, and corner lounge suggest comfort. Simply shaded bulbs are suspended from electric wires that crisscross the papered reception-room ceiling. An electric bulb hangs from the skylight, a common feature of photography studios.

Maurer's photographs line the walls, hang on an interior door, and sit on an armchair that functions more as an easel than a seating piece. Many of the photographic subjects are women, Maurer's favorites. After serving as a military photographer in Cuba for three years during the Spanish-American War and photographing funerals of yellow-fever victims, Maurer was invited by Colonel Theodore Baldwin to accompany his regiment to the Philippines. The Galveston native declined, declaring that while he had enjoyed photographing soldiers, horses, and cannons, he wanted to go where he could photograph beautiful women. He defined his own work and, thus, defined himself. Maurer gained fame as a photographer for bathing girl revues and beauty pageants.[24] At this time many other photographers, writers, and artists shared an interest in depicting American women; Maurer's preoccupation may well have had a cultural basis. Although she does not appear in any of the photographs hanging in the studio, his mother made her mark on his studio. Florist and "dealer in goldfish," Karolina Maurer kept him supplied with potted plants and goldfish in a bowl.[25]

In Central Texas in 1911 – 1912 another photographer, Fred "Gildy" Gildersleeve, took a series of interior and exterior views of the new bungalow he shared with his wife, Florence (figs. 2.23 through 2.27). His mother and sister Ellen, a medical doctor, lived next door. The dining room's only wall accessory, one of Gildersleeve's landscape panoramas, hangs above the corner fireplace (fig. 2.23). The room's furnishings consist of a pedestal table, a set of colonial revival dining chairs with leather-upholstered seats, and a china cabinet. The outstanding feature of the room is the conventionalized arts and crafts wallpaper, which extends approximately two-thirds the height of the room and is topped with a fashionable frieze of boldly pendent grapes. Fine woodwork forms the door head and jambs, paneled interior door, cupboard, and swinging door to the kitchen. The floor is oak, as is the mantel. Above the dining table, a three-globe electric fixture is operated by pull switches.

Without the bold rug and wallpaper border patterns, the room would seem bare; only the mass of china and glass in the cupboard relieves the bareness; the molding on the wall is too thin to function as a plate rail. Hand-painted ceramics — an earthenware jug with overglaze flowers and a china pitcher — are given prominence in the room's decorations. In the Christmas view of the dining room (fig. 2.24), the same pitcher is being used at the table, while a hand-painted lemonade pitcher is displayed prominently on top of the china cabinet.

For the holiday dinner, paper bells hang from foil streamers above the table. Documenting this occasion, Gildersleeve photographed the family group including himself opposite his wife, his sister and mother facing the camera, and two unidentified women. Gildersleeve, who knew the importance of sitting still during the long shutter opening, apparently has moved after activating the camera, blurring the image. The room differs slightly from the other dining room view — the rug has been reoriented lengthwise to match the run of the wooden boards. Gildersleeve has adjusted the window shade to illuminate his interior photograph better.

In the living room (fig. 2.25), only the stylishly up-to-date wallpaper border and the floor covering provide

2.23. Dining room, Fred A. Gildersleeve house, 2219 Ethel, Waco, ca. 1912 (Texas Collection, Baylor University, Waco).

2.24. Dining room, Fred A. Gildersleeve house, 2219 Ethel, Waco, ca. 1912 (Texas Collection, Baylor University, Waco).

color and pattern. The room is an amalgam of masculine and feminine imagery: the carved wall plaque of a stag hangs over the conventionalized wallpaper border, while a print of a kissing couple (a frequent image in Texas houses between 1905 and 1915) decorates the adjacent wall. The room serves multiple functions: it holds a parlor piano and the stacked bookcases, leather couch, and leather-seat rocking chairs often found in a library. The shelves of the bookcase display various matched sets of books; on top are albums such as those Gildersleeve filled with photographs. One of his landscape views hangs above.

The couple's bedroom (fig. 2.26) is also designed for multiple uses. A dining chair (on which is seated a photogenic cat) functions as an office chair at the desk; the living room rocker or its twin sits between the windows. The wall and floor treatments in this room are similar to those in other areas with slight variations. Below the plain ceiling and frieze, a border trims the top of the wallpaper, which is striped rather than solid as in other rooms. The rug is similar to those in the other spaces except here it lies atop matting instead of the exposed wooden floor.

The bedroom displays more wall-hung mementos than the public rooms. Those above the desk form a zigzag pattern; across the room, the paper border peeks through crossed tennis rackets. Small homemade wall decorations, including a heart-shape pincushion, and portrait photographs, the last probably Gildersleeve's work, fill out the room.

In what is probably the couple's spare bedroom (fig. 2.27) a folding bed and dresser stand diagonally across two corners.[26] The cat curled along the lines of the center medallion is very much a part of the room's decoration, evidence of the free rein domesticated animals enjoyed in some early-twentieth-century houses.

The solid wallpaper below the picture molding is topped with a border of rose festoons. An inexpensive straw and cane chest (a form that remained popular into the 1920s) functions as a window seat. The windows are covered by shades beneath sheer panels suspended from thin enameled curtain rods, the deep fold possibly a way to shorten store-bought curtains without cutting them off.

2.25. Living room into dining room, Fred A. Gildersleeve house, ca. 1912 (Texas Collection, Baylor University, Waco).

2.26. Bedroom, Fred A. Gildersleeve house, ca. 1912 (Texas Collection, Baylor University, Waco).

The sewing machine indicates that Florence used the room, while the absence of a protective cloth suggests she sewed regularly. The side chair on the right of the machine is from the dining room. The colonial revival rocking chair is used for relaxing, reading, or hand sewing. But even in this space that functions as Florence's sewing room and a guest bedroom, her husband's portrait photographs appear, joined by commercial greeting cards and prints at the dresser.

Of the images in this survey, few show evidence of a woman's occupation. Two images taken in a Catholic convent, however, express these women's identification with their vocation. In figure 2.28 a nun sits in what appears to be a domestic space. Her habit suggests that this interior was either Galveston's Ursuline Academy located at the south side of Avenue N between 25th and 27th streets or St. Mary's Cathedral School at the northwestern corner of Winnie and 20th.[27] In many respects the wall treatment and furnishing patterns are typical of turn-of-the-century houses. As in residential domestic settings of the period, the framed picture rests on an easel, the framed portrait is hung tipped out on the wall, ceramic ewers rest on a prominent display surface, and bordered portières cover the doorway. The stylized leaf- and floral-pattern wallpaper in this room was also found in many houses at this time, but the wide border pinned to the bottom of the wall was less common. Religious iconography sets this room apart, announcing the profession of its occupant.

Religious objects define, even overwhelm, the space. Paired on the handsome desk, probably made locally, tabletop icons reinforce the symmetry of the desk. Two dolls dressed in nuns habits flank a statue of the Sacred Heart, and a large shadow box bridges the desk's storage compartments. The box is flanked by two glass shades, popular tabletop decorations at mid century. In an earlier domestic setting, shades would have protected and displayed arrangements of shells, feathers, or leaves fashioned by women. Here, they shelter statues of Saint Francis of Assisi and Saint Mary. Below the shadow box a crucifix stands between two identical handmade frames enclosing cabinet cards and a pair of popular ceramic ewers with gilt handles. The nun herself is balanced in the photographic composition by the framed picture of the Sacred Heart on the easel. Like her costume, the icons define the subject's occupation and convey the belief system underlying it.

2.27. Bedroom, Fred A. Gildersleeve house, ca. 1912 (Texas Collection, Baylor University, Waco).

2.28. Parlor, Unidentified convent, Galveston, ca. 1895 (Rosenberg Library, Galveston).

Lay persons also displayed icons in private rooms of their homes, making personal references to their religious beliefs. Crucifixes, rosaries, or other symbols of religious belief were typically displayed in bedrooms rather than in sitting rooms or parlors (see fig. 2.5). Madonnas were popular subjects for wall-hung prints during the second half of the nineteenth century, appearing in public areas of the home, entry halls and parlors, but the image related less to Mary and the Christ child than to the sanctity of the homeplace, idealized womanhood, and the importance of paintings by masters like Raphael.

In the convent's multipurpose room (fig. 2.29), at least two of the wall-hung items express the occupants' identification with their religious mission and their belief system: a print of the Sacred Heart hangs above the sideboard near a print of two ascending figures. Both religious images and the unidentified certificate hang tipped out from the ceiling molding, secured by ceramic pins. A corner whatnot holds statuary, a framed portrait, and shells.

Light paint covers the horizontal wallboards; below the chair rail, a dado has been painted in a medium color. The slipcovers with dark piping protecting the renaissance re-

2.29. Multipurpose room, Unidentified convent, Galveston, ca. 1895 (Rosenberg Library, Galveston).

vival chairs indicate that it is summer and suggest that the space serves as a sitting room. Some of the slipcovers have been fashioned to protect the deep carving of the chair aprons beneath the cloth. Matting, which has been either stitched together at the seams or tacked or stapled directly to the floor, covers the floor wall to wall, while runners of ingrain carpeting or linoleum protect walkways.

The final image of occupational identity in this chapter is the sitting room of a shingle-style bungalow near Paris in Northeast Texas where Sheb Williams displays his ethnographic collections (fig. 2.30). Williams incorporated these objects into room decoration much as many other Americans purchased and used items of Native American design to create arts and crafts-inspired interiors. But he was one of the few actually to collect the objects by traveling to specific locales. In Williams' house, style and biography were united.

First a drummer, or traveling salesman, Williams was appointed United States marshal in 1894 by President Grover Cleveland, having jurisdiction over a portion of the Indian Territory. Later he began another career as explorer and developer of Alaskan mineral fields, shipping

steamboats "knocked down" overland to northern British Columbia and then on to the Yukon Territory. In 1908 he returned to his "splendid estate . . . improved with modern buildings and its beautiful country home, in sanitary arrangement, electrical equipment . . . the equal of almost any city residence in the southwest."[28]

His interiors express the arts and crafts movement: built-in furniture (a bench at the right); dining room sideboard, table, and chairs featuring hallmarks of the style; and a rug, possibly of Mexican origin, at the dining room doorway. Williams collected objects related to the Plains Indians: a rawhide parfleche hangs over the doorway, flanked by a bow and a quiver. Just out of view, a brick fireplace dominates the space, and tankards line the mantel. The floor and window treatments supply pattern and color to the backdrop of solid-color walls.

★ ★ ★ ★

Expressing identity with decorative elements that incorporated occupationally significant objects ranged from the practical display of books, to a stylish array of photographs, to a self-conscious display of artistry and implements. These interior views reveal that such displays were used less to relate to other members of the occupational group than as a statement of individual identity. Although some occupations were related to family and ethnicity, occupation was a basic and personal feature of one's identity, differing from identification with the broader family or ethnic group.

2.30 (facing page). Sitting room into dining room, Sheb Williams house, Paris, 1899 (Texas State Archives, Austin).

3.1. Bedroom, Sallie Wade house, Benjamin, ca. 1895 (Heritage Museum of Big Spring).

3

Ties That Bind

FAMILY

AMONG the household elements most expressive of an identification with family were crayon portraits, cabinet cards, cartes de visite, and snapshots of immediate family and relatives. Such images adorned middle- and lower-middle-class houses throughout the state. Texans, along with others, used the images to keep their past within their present reach.

Like other late Victorian Americans, Texans also sought to embrace and record their present. They showed enthusiasm both for their new situations and for the camera's new technology — some people even featuring photographic images of themselves as they posed for still another picture and incorporating many types of photographs into their domestic settings. Interior views reveal that crayon portraits were especially popular; their size and framed format made them desirable household accessories. Crayon portraits were life-size enlargements made from smaller formats, usually the carte de visite or cabinet card. A photographic process produced a faint image usually in a dark gray color on matte-surfaced paper that served as the underlying sketch hand finished with pastels or charcoal.[1] Contributing to the crayon portrait's popularity from the 1860s through the turn of the century was its low price and accessibility. In 1895, Sears, Roebuck advertised that if buyers mailed in a photograph, $1.98 could transform it into an 18-by-22-inch crayon portrait; for an additional $1.97, the buyer could purchase a beautiful frame.[2]

Cabinet cards, cartes de visite, and snapshots were smaller than the crayon portrait, but they were easily adapted to house decoration. Cabinet-card mounts measured 4½ by 6½ inches, and those of the carte de visite, 2½ by 4¼ inches. Although special sizes of photograph albums were created to fit these portrait photographs, many people chose instead to adorn their mantels and tabletops with the images. Small snapshots were glued to

3.2. Parlor, Unidentified house (possibly the George A. Miller house), Longview, 1897 (Courtesy Mrs. Paul Brooks Belding).

various-sized mounts as freestanding accessories or had holes pierced in their mounts to be strung together with ribbons as wall-hung photographic "ladders."

A single interior view of a bedroom shows how a house can exemplify family identification by means of a variety of photographic formats (fig. 3.1). While no members of the Wade family are seen in this photograph, the room is crowded with wall-to-wall Wades.

Widow Sallie Wade lived on a ranch outside Benjamin in Knox County with her son and daughter-in-law, Isaac and Etta, who operated the ranch. Figure 3.1 shows Sallie's bedroom circa 1895. Isaac Wade was "a prominent West Texas cattle man." He and Etta ranched in Oklahoma and in Howard, Knox, and Haskell counties in Texas more than fifty years before his death in 1934. One brief sketch written during the Great Depression noted that "Mr. and Mrs. Wade worked together on the range battling the elements as well as market fluctuations," a reference made at a time when such family solidarity would have been noted.[3] We can infer that the family had close ties by looking at their home's interior some four decades before the published comment.

Identically framed crayon portraits of Isaac and Etta Wade hang in the corner above the bed. Each displays the cabinet card upon which the enlargements were modeled. Crayon portraits are predominant in the bedroom, defining the space as one in which family identification is expressed. They line the painted, horizontally boarded walls like a frieze; they rest on cardboard trunks; and they serve as washstand splashboards. Such placements of typically wall-hung accessories could reflect limited space or an effort to include all the family in a single view — essentially a group family portrait.

At least three photograph albums rest on the dresser, probably arranged for the photograph. One album of cabinet cards and a pair of carte de visite albums flank the "mantel" clock, the dresser top functioning as a kind of mantel in the absence of a fireplace, giving a focal point to the room. This is a family interested in documenting itself and using the documentation to decorate their home.

The inferred small space of the Wade house may have reinforced familial interaction. Pairs of furniture forms — two beds, two rocking chairs, and two dressers — suggest use of this one room by many family members, including a child whose doll hangs on the wall. There is virtually no clear wall space around the room's perimeter, and although the crayon portraits may have been moved into the camera's view, it is unlikely that all the furniture was positioned into view as a show of wealth. There is so little wall space that the Wades have ignored the two windows covered with roller blinds, placing a bed and a dresser in front of one and concealing one corner of the other window with a framed print. Likewise, much of the floor space is occupied, the wall-to-wall rag carpet nearly obscured by the furniture in the crowded room.

Crayon portraits were also an integral element of home decoration in the public space of an East Texas house of the same period (fig. 3.2). Unlike the Wade bedroom, the Longview parlor is peopled. Outnumbered, even dwarfed, by his wife and children, the head of the household sits with his family in this home in 1897. Other women join the group by proxy in the two framed portraits by the windows. The family poses beside the grand piano, which is adorned with ceramic vases and small portrait photographs. The bookcase is topped by more photographs and a spray of dried grasses. Reinforcing family relationships is a print of a mother and daughter.

In this photograph, clothing textiles blend with decorative textiles. Indeed, it is difficult to see where the table scarf ends and the standing girl's dress begins. Younger children sit on pillows on animal-skin rugs atop a wall-to-wall carpet. Both case pieces are draped; chairs are ti-

3.3. Parlor, James Franklin Newman house, 701 James Street, Sweetwater, ca. 1890 (City-County Pioneer Museum, Sweetwater).

died and cushioned. As dress mediated between body and world, the home, especially the parlor, was the buffer between the family and the world. Home, the place of comfort, functioned to soften the effects of the outside world. Decorative textiles — upholstery, rugs, scarves, lambrequins, and tidies — rounded the edges and corners — literally and figuratively — and came to be synonymous with the comfortable home.

Two interior views of Sweetwater homes circa 1890 (figs. 3.3, 3.4) also illustrate the manner in which crayon portraits of family members were incorporated into house decoration. Born in Montgomery County, Arkansas, in 1849, James Franklin Newman was a child when his family moved to Navarro County, Texas. As a young man, "[h]e worked as a cowboy and beginning with 1867 he was on the trail a great many years, driving cattle from numerous Texas points to New Orleans, Louisiana, and later to Memphis, Tennessee."[4] He married Josephine Rushing of Navarro County in 1873, and they moved to the Nolan-Fisher counties region where they raised cattle, horses, and mules; cultivated cotton and grain; operated a cotton-seed oil mill; and eventually owned a bank, known as J. O. F. Newman and Sons. His family also owned "large quantities of real estate," including a private race course and a "fine home and ranch headquarters near Sweetwater."[5]

3.4. Parlor, Andrew Jackson Long house, Sweetwater, ca. 1890 (Courtesy Douglas Barton Willingham).

Circa 1890 the Newmans were photographed with three of their children in that fine home (fig. 3.3). The photographer probably composed this portrait some time just before or early in James Newman's tenure as sheriff of Nolan County between 1890 and 1896. Dressed in their finest clothes, they sit among framed photographs of themselves and absent family members. As if to emphasize the portraits hung at one level, Josephine has positioned embellished scarves in a slightly asymmetrical fashion on the picture frames.

Nonfamily elements are sparse. Little furniture is visible. A side chair, part of a parlor suite, partially balances the family composition. Behind the family, the top shelf of a corner whatnot displays a vase and pampas grass; the parents and youngest son sit on a settee or sofa draped with a Mexican blanket. A kerosene lamp hangs overhead. The windows are covered with medium-color, fringed roller blinds topped with ready-made lace curtains hung on wooden rings and poles.

Another Sweetwater family, the Andrew Jackson Longs, posed in their parlor about the same time (fig. 3.4). The family sits in a portrait gallery of relatives. The sitters include the maid (name unknown), Mabel Long, her great-grandmother Mary Cave Boren, Laurence and Andrew Long (standing), Andrew's wife, Queen, and their daughter Ailene. Deceased son, Emmitt, posthumously joins the group from his place on the easel, his portrait draped with banners rather than scarves.[6] Family photos top his portrait, fill the album sitting on the piano, and decorate the mantel.

The Longs' parlor resembles the Newmans'. In addition to a taste for draped crayon portraits, both share a preference for dried grasses, an aesthetic effect common in many American homes; the flowers dangling from the Longs' parlor lamp recall the bunch marking the chair back in the Newman parlor. This pair of photographs suggests a shared set of decorating ideas and preferences among these West Texans during the late nineteenth century, despite evident differences in wealth. The interior view of the Long house shows more prosperity than the Newman house, which lacks wallpaper, piano, and fireplace; however, these disparities may reflect a difference in the allocation of family funds, influenced by the presence or absence of daughters, and the strength of a wife's desire to decorate her home. The Long parlor reveals a stylishness made available by money or embraced by choice. The "extra" features of the Long parlor led to additional expenditures of time or money: a fireplace and a piano require more textiles. An embroidered and fringed mantel lambrequin hangs above the painted screen, and a dark scarf covers the piano top. The amount of drapery is extraordinary. The floral-pattern portière, suspended from a pole that exceeds the door width, has been hung low to allow opening of the transom.

In figures 3.1 through 3.4, crayon portrait enlargements are tabletop and wall-hung accessories. But in figures 3.5 through 3.8, snapshots, cabinet cards, and other photographic formats replace the larger images. Photographs of the Russell house document the annual summer pilgrimage of Josephine Flow Russell's five daughters, two sons, and grandchildren to her North Texas home. Russell was born and educated in Missouri and, after moving to Texas, taught in the first school established at Emmerson Chapel near Pilot Point. After five years, she devoted her "time and energies to her home and children."[7]

One of her sons was an amateur photographer who supplied Russell with a steady crop of new images (fig. 3.5). These photographs reveal the strong family bonds in the Russell home. By 1900, the time the photographs were taken, Russell lived alone. Photography provided room decorations and allowed Russell to have her family with her, at least visually, all year.

Russell chose to use the cabinet cards imaginatively. They decorate the door and window jambs and cluster around a wall shelf draped with a dark ball-fringe lambrequin. The shelf is a family altar of sorts, supporting a stereoscope, a device for viewing photographic images.

Secondary to the display of family, other details of the room include wallpaper patterned with conventional flowers and scrollwork, wall-to-wall carpet with a pattern of flowers and scrolls, lace curtains, a bamboo corner shelf, and pillows.

Two interior views indicate that the Russell sitting room also displayed a strong family identification (figs. 3.6, 3.7). Since one of her sons owned a department store, presumably Russell could have selected other accessories, but family photographs cover the walls and the tabletops. They march down the joint between door jamb and wall, buffering the edge. They hang accordion-style, suspended by ribbons strung through holes pierced in the mounts, a common arrangement for photographs in Texas interiors. And cabinet cards arranged horizontally on a scallop-edged fabric backing provide a family gallery. The framed floral still life, executed by daughter-in-law Agnes Norris Holford Russell, refers less to refinement than to a family achievement.[8]

In the Russell series, the photographer presents the antics of children in various rooms of the house.[9] Peeking

3.5. Parlor, Josephine Flow Russell house, Southwest corner of Grove and Hill streets (400 South Hill Street), Pilot Point, Summer 1900 (Courtesy Elaine Coffman).

3.6. Sitting room, Josephine Flow Russell house, Summer 1900 (Courtesy Elaine Coffman).

out from behind the portières, the children echo the ethos of visual surprise in the turn-of-the-century homes (fig. 3.6). Surprise in furnishings was expressed by variety. Thus it was acceptable for a combination case embellished with embroidered doilies to sit diagonally across the corner and for one Russell to peer from a homemade frame while others look out from simple mounts. Possibly Russell segregated the photographs according to room (in contrast, other Texans segregated types of images on various walls; see fig. 5.12): portrait photographs of the men adorn the parlor, while snapshots of the women and children decorate the less formal sitting room.

In figure 3.7 Genevieve Goff, Russell's grandchild, dances amid a background of late-nineteenth-century furnishings, including an inexpensive, plush-covered box lounge and a colonial revival rocking chair. The light, sprig-pattern wallpaper contrasts with the dark, unbordered wall-to-wall carpeting in a scrollwork design and with the dark festoon-pattern portières. Although this view offers additional details about the room's furnishings, these details appear secondary to the family photos.

The Russell entry hall continues the theme of identification with family in imagery and in function (fig. 3.8). The chair rail serves as a decorative ledge supporting still more family photographs. A geometric-pattern wallpaper with a quatrefoil design enclosed in circles, resembling clockworks, is illuminated by a kerosene lamp. Other details include two small rugs that break the spread of the scrollwork-pattern wall-to-wall carpet; a carpet of a different design ascends the steps. Small rugs, or mats, forestall signs of wear and mark the transitions into other rooms.

The photograph demonstrates Russell's attitude about the function of her hall. Scholars have argued that during the second half of the nineteenth century, the entry hall was an imposing space meant to impress guests or inhibit

3.7. Sitting room, Josephine Flow Russell house, Summer 1900 (Courtesy Elaine Coffman).

tradespeople.[10] But in 1900 in this home the area is more convivial, appropriate even for children's activity. The change in function is reinforced by the placement of the hallstand, which, rather than a sentinel to the door, is positioned at the back of the room, holding straw hats, a bonnet, a cap, a jacket, and an umbrella.

In the Avant household in the town of Dilley, southeast of San Antonio, family identification is emphasized as much as in the Russell household. Robert Fletcher Avant

3.8. Entry hall, Josephine Flow Russell house, Summer 1900 (Courtesy Elaine Coffman). The entry hall provides a backdrop where two of the children begin a game of crokinole and a third amuses himself by taking shells from the basket to his left and arranging them on a pillow, while looking longingly at the board game.

was born in Gonzales County in 1865, his father and grandparents having moved to Texas from De Kalb County, Tennessee, about 1852. Preferring the climate of South Texas, the young Avant moved to Dilley. He married Florence Annie James, whose father, a baker, had brought his family from Gloucester, England, in 1857 to settle in San Antonio. In 1899, the Avants designed their home, which was constructed by builder J. J. Yowell. The couple lived in the house until their deaths in 1951.[11]

Besides being postmaster and deputy sheriff, Robert Avant owned a general merchandise store and semiannually traveled by train to St. Louis to buy stock. Local and regional residents rushed to Avant's store when his new goods arrived, preferring to patronize him rather than travel the eighty miles to San Antonio.[12]

The 1908 photograph of the Avants shows strong family identification (fig. 3.9). Hanging above two small circular photographs of Mr. and Mrs. James, Florence's parents, on the unusual vertical board walls is a large oval portrait of the two Avant daughters, Lucille and Gladys. In this view, three of the four children pose while playing caroms; brother Russell rides the hobby horse in the corner. More family photographs sit on top of the folding bed, the large case piece behind Avant. The function of the room reinforces familial ties: the hobby horse, doll, game board, No. 2 Brownie camera, stereoscope, and magazines signal informal and shared family activities.

Judging from the poses, the home is a place of comfort and relaxation for Avant and the children, but for Florence, who glances at a magazine as she appears to tidy the room, home means ever-solicitous care. The tabletop scarves and the curtains bear witness to her decorating responsibilities; she has taken lengths of bordered fabric and draped them creatively to form curtains. Her pose as well as her demonstrated vigilance reinforces her well-defined role within the family.

The photograph of the Avant house in South Texas shares certain features with that of the West Texas home of the James Milton Frame family (fig. 3.10). Cultural and photographic conventions have created remarkably similar compositions. The Frames express identification with family less by the decorative use of photographs than by

3.9. Parlor, Robert Fletcher Avant house, South Main Street, Dilley, 1908 (Courtesy Niny A. Massey).

3.10. Sitting room/bedroom, Mr. and Mrs. James Milton Frame house, Monahans, ca. 1909 (James Milton Frame Collection, Permian Historical Society Archival Collection, The University of Texas of the Permian Basin, Odessa).

the room's function and use. The family poses in a room that serves many functions — music room, bedroom, and sitting room. While the room looks modest and crowded to late-twentieth-century viewers, with its piano and wallpaper it was probably considered quite fashionable in Monahans in 1908. (Ward County, of which Monahans is county seat, was then only sixteen years old.)

Presumably the photographer has arranged the Frames according to convention: the sitters, grouped by age, pursue traditional gender-related activities; only Frame, his wife, and their friend (identified as "Ma" Gray) merit chairs. The head of the household reads (even though his glasses and the only lamp are across the room) as he sits in a rocking chair, while his wife and friend sit in rockers and sew. Daughter Thelma is posed at the piano spread with sheet music, a sign of accomplishment, but she watches her friend play with a doll; sons Paul and Pete work a puzzle on the floor.

The room displays a number of homemade embellishments, such as the wall plaques. Mother or daughter has sewn the matching window and bookcase curtains. Store-bought portières hang on the room partition, which serves as a shelf to hold the boys' train set. The small segmented space beyond them accommodates a colonial revival rocker and a sewing machine.

Beneath the beaded wooden ceiling trimmed with decorative molding, the Frames have chosen a solid wallpaper topped with a wide frieze in an art nouveau design. Matting covers the floor wall to wall, while smaller rugs indicate areas of activity and wear: piano, stove, bookcase, and threshold.

The view reveals other information about the Frame family: the banner for William Howard Taft, Republican president, 1909 – 1913, documents Frame's political sentiments. The concentration of decoration around the piano — scarf, ceramics, portrait, album, and books in addition to the music stand — indicates the instrument's importance to the family even though it is not emphasized in the photograph.

Besides the magazines on the lower shelf and cards or matted photographs, reading glasses, and a kerosene lamp on the top, the center table displays a card receiver, which holds a starfish. Despite the distance from style centers and the informality of this scene, the Frame family is aware of the ritual of calling. While the tray is probably rarely, if ever, used, its presence communicates that the family knows the rules of polite behavior.

A different sort of family group is documented in another photograph of an East Texas home (fig. 3.11). Built three to four years prior to the photograph, the Thomas Earl Singletary house was a one-story structure in the small community of Alto, about twenty-five miles west of Nacogdoches. The 1906 interior view provides a generational portrait of a family: Thomas Earl Singletary, his mother, Jane, who lived with her son and his pregnant wife, Laura. Jane Singletary's crayon portrait hangs behind her; on the other side of the window hangs the companion portrait of her late husband, George.[13]

A family portrait taken in the bedroom/sitting room is unusual and intimate. Public spaces, especially the parlor, were deemed the appropriate setting for family portraiture, but some homes had fewer differentiated spaces, and rooms often combined functions. The Singletarys obviously thought this a decorous enough setting for a photograph.

The horizontal wallboards and floorboards are unpainted, the grain of the plentiful East Texas pine providing the wall pattern. The bedspread, lace curtains, fringed window shades, homemade wall pocket, splash cloth, mirror scarf, and mat marking the dresser area make a

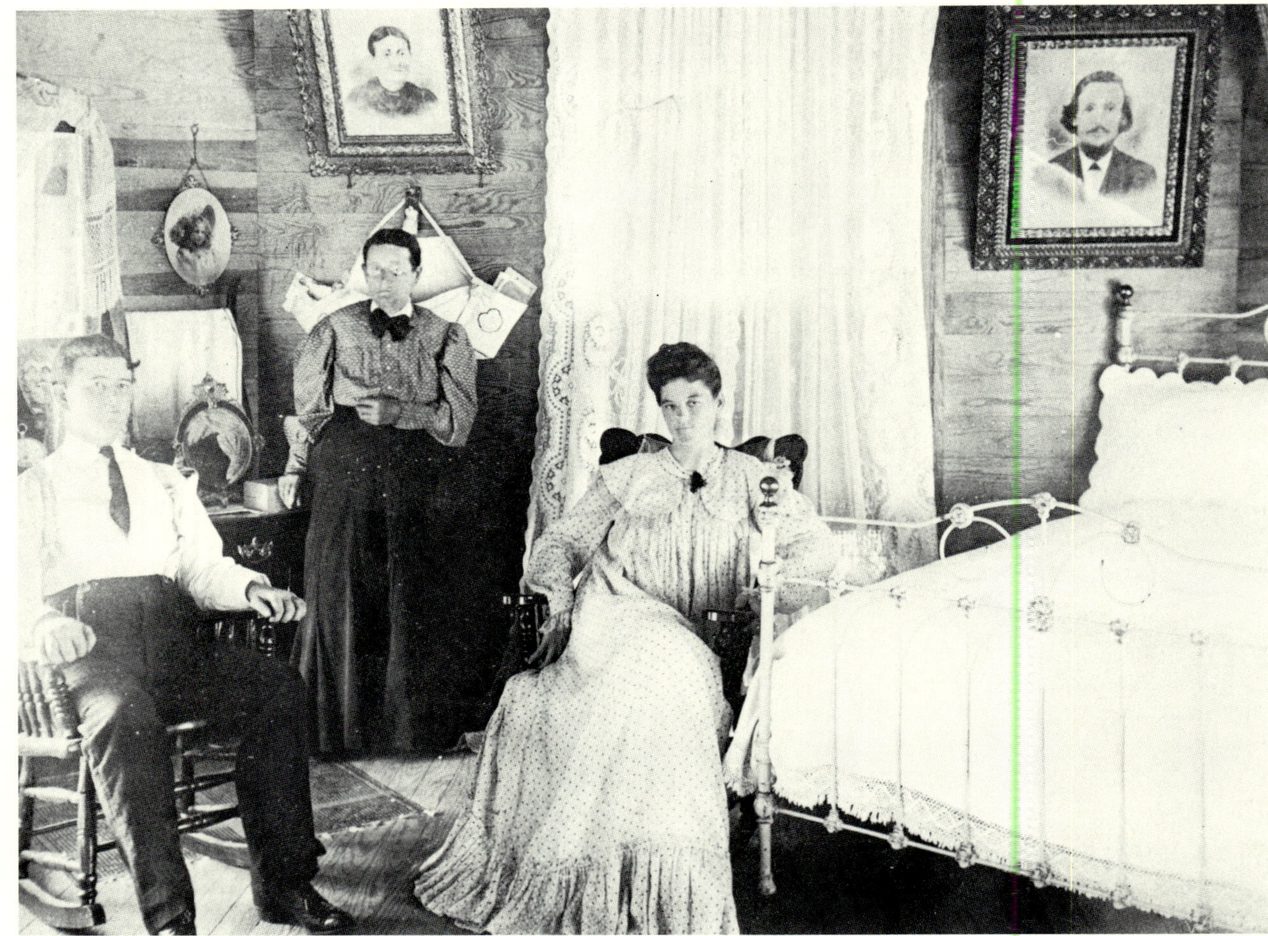

3.11. Bedroom/sitting room, Thomas Earl Singletary house, Singletary Street, Alto, August/September 1906 (Courtesy Beverly Singletary Perdue).

lavish effect on the unfinished surfaces. The enameled iron bedstead, dresser, and matching rockers fill the room.

About 100 miles east southeast of Alto in Calvert, three generations of the Conitz family wedged themselves into the family parlor: Hulda; Rudolph; Edward; Louise; Emil; Emil, Jr.; his wife, Hermena, and their baby, Marvin; Paul; and Gustav (fig. 3.12). Born in Posen, Prussia, in 1845, the elder Conitz immigrated to Sterling, Texas, as a young man and married Louise Meier, a native of Berlin, Germany. Moving two miles east to the new town of Calvert, which had been laid out on the Houston & Texas Central Railroad in 1871, Emil expanded his business interests. Trained as a cobbler, he ultimately owned a retail grocery store, a cattle ranch, and a dairy, had part ownership in a lumber company, and held stock in the Citizens State Bank.[14]

In the Conitz parlor, colonial revival and wicker furniture is placed along the perimeter so that all the family members are visible for the camera. The family circle is mirrored by a ring of family portraits, the only wall-hung

3.12. Parlor, Emil Conitz, Sr., house, Corner of Browning and Railroad streets (201 Browning Street), Calvert, 1909 (Courtesy Thelma Conitz and Cecelia Conitz Heinrich).

accessories in the room. A photograph album, which probably normally rests atop the table, is the toy for the youngest Conitz.

This family photograph reveals other interior details typical of early-twentieth-century Texas houses. Fashionable rope portières, sold in catalogues of the period, hang from the entry into the room, while the piano angles the viewer into the space. Since the room lacks a fireplace, the draped piano and the covered table provide settings for tabletop ornaments. Lightweight cotton curtains, folded to create a valance, hang in two panels at the windows. A medallion-pattern paper dominates the walls, and a large rug with a garland design covers the center of the floor. The rug, fashioned of halves inexactly sewn together, appears to be placed on top of another carpet. The gasolier hangs in the center of the room, ornaments dangling from its arms.

Thus far we have seen how several households exhibit identification with family in a single room. The following seven images of an Abilene home (figs. 3.13 through 3.19) demonstrate how identification with family can become a ruling principle of decoration in several rooms. The Digby-Roberts home was occupied by Frederick Charles and Fannie Torrey Digby-Roberts, Fannie's widowed mother, Jane Torrey, and later, in 1902, their son, Frederick William. The Torreys had moved from Philadelphia to Abilene in 1883, attracted by the sale of railroad lands.

Digby-Roberts and an uncle arrived from England in 1885. Frederick entered the lumber business in Abilene and had yards there and in nearby towns. He married Fannie Torrey in 1891 and built this home soon after. An amateur photographer, Frederick has taken the interior views of the house, documenting both the furniture the Torreys brought with them from Philadelphia in 1883 and the family's tendency to keep familial bonds visible in their new home.[15]

A corner in the Digby-Roberts home (fig. 3.13) shows a space used for a variety of family activities. As was typical even in the 1880s, the area doubles as dining room and study, a cane-seat dining chair serving as a desk chair. But the space functions in another way: to the right of the small cuckoo clock is a piano.[16] The Digby-Roberts family made a portrait gallery of the desk top and have crowded upon it matted portraits and snapshots. Other framed cabinet cards featuring family members hang above the desk. An oval-framed portrait of a deceased family member and an oval floral print hung from the paper border bring further attention to this crowded corner between two windows.

The family has embellished the manufactured sideboard using scarves, wedding presents, and family heirlooms, including an English silver cream pitcher, French wine bottles, and silver tea- and coffeepots inherited from the Digby-Roberts family. The sideboard also features a portrait: centrally placed is a photograph of Fannie taken in 1891. In addition to the dining table, a bamboo stand set for tea provides a serving surface. The style of the stand and the objects necessary for the tea-drinking ritual demonstrate the family's knowledge of and participation in the traditional Japanese custom, so much a part of post-Centennial American life and household decoration.

The Japanese detail is matched by other elements in the popular aesthetic style. The wallpaper features a crossed branch design; a matching frieze is bordered at the top with a guilloche design and at the bottom with a row of stars that serves as picture molding. The curtains, which appear as straight-hung panels in a later photograph, are here draped in a manner considered artistic. A small birdcage, a popular room detail during the 1890s, dangles from a wall bracket. The floor covering features scrollwork; countless designs like it sold via mail-order catalogues at the turn of the century. The banded table cover hints at aestheticism. The cloth appears to be felt and was probably embellished at home since the seamstress appears to have stretched the rickrack to make it run the length of the last side. The pitcher of water and stemmed glass on the white table scarf, like silver-plated tilting water pitchers in Texas entry halls, offer refreshment and a gesture of hospitality to visitors.

In order to take the view of the bedroom, Digby-Roberts stood behind a renaissance revival bedstead and captured a host of family images hung against a background of C and S scrolls that cover floor and walls in complementary patterns (fig. 3.14). The view documents Jane's use of the space. With the rattan rocking chair and the armchair pulled up to the center table, over which hangs the electric light with a carbon filament bulb, Jane could spend evenings reading the books stacked on the table. A ceramic vase, box, clock, Bible, and Valentine card adorn this table, which is draped with a fringed cover embroidered in a ribbon design. The nearby dresser provides a surface for personal accessories — clothes brush,

3.13. Dining room, Frederick Charles Digby-Roberts house, Southeast corner of North Second and Hickory streets, Abilene, 1892 (Courtesy Mr. and Mrs. Frederick W. Digby-Roberts and Justine Digby-Roberts Grisham).

3.14. Bedroom, Frederick Charles Digby-Roberts house, ca. 1892 (Courtesy Mr. and Mrs. Frederick W. Digby-Roberts and Justine Digby-Roberts Grisham).

scissors, hair receiver, hatpins, and pincushion. The dresser serves as a focal point for a constellation of homemade wall-hung items, including a wall pocket. The bureau is draped with a light linen cloth decorated with edged drawnwork.

The mantel shelf, like the bureau top, projects strong family affiliations. Draped and adorned with family photos, mementos, the obligatory center clock, and flanking vases, the mantel is overhung by paired portraits of Jane's deceased father and mother. As in other homes, photographs serve memory and family identity. The altarlike appearance of the hearth is in part seasonal: the bench blocking the draped fireplace opening indicates summer.

The wall pocket, a popular decoration in bedrooms in Texas at this time, holds photographs of family members. Decorated with cherry blossoms and fan-shape pockets, the hanging displays cabinet cards and cartes de visite. The popularity of these banners, or "bannerettes," was enhanced by the appearance in several books and magazines of instructions for making such holders from fabric or paper and in advertisements for ready-made pieces women could embellish at home.

Three of the photographs of the Digby-Roberts house provide a rare opportunity to view almost 360 degrees of an early Texas room (figs. 3.15, 3.16, 3.17). In Fannie and Frederick's bedroom, matted photos rest casually on the mantel, and a large portrait of William Torrey, Fannie's deceased father, hangs above. The formal mantel features an arrangement of ewers, candelabra, and a clock, the symmetry reinforced by the lavish draping of the shelf and hearth. Positioned for this interior view, an Eastlake stand atop a dyed animal-skin rug — the two serving as a minishrine — displays the image of an unidentified family member. Nearby is a small wardrobe, its crest partially concealing the small suitcase above. As was typical of some turn-of-the-century bedrooms, the wall and floor colors are lighter and the patterns less bold than in other rooms of the house. Strips of matting run wall to wall; the ceiling and walls are papered.

Figure 3.16 shows activity in the hallway. A woman, probably Fannie, sits in a rocker by an open door. The transom windows are curtained. A hallstand holds a coat and straw hat adjacent to a wall pocket of cards and photographs. In the bedroom, family photos line the walls. Below the horizontal photo gallery of four women, the dresser is draped with a long tasseled scarf. On it sits a predictable array of pincushions and hair receivers; a clothes brush and a commemorative ribbon hang on the mirror arms. Standing diagonally across one corner, a dressing table has portrait photos wedged in the mirror frame, while the mirror itself reflects Frederick's image. Figure 3.17 shows portraits of unidentified family members on the wall behind the bed.

The visual references to the Digby-Roberts family in the fashionable bedroom of Fannie and Frederick indicate the strength of a decorating strategy. The young couple selected bird's-eye maple furniture. Stylish during the 1890s, bird's-eye maple bedroom furnishings are used in combination with animal-skin rugs and an enameled bedstead, this one covered with a summer-weight voile bedspread. Exterior shutters, roller blinds, and ruffled curtains cover the bedroom's five windows.

Above the bed and patterned bolster, facing the fireplace wall, hangs a familiar horizontal still life (see figs. 6.4, 8.20); suspended from its frame is a small landscape. Portraits of a family matriarch and patriarch share the important position over the bedstead. On the adjacent wall, another horizontal composite features an anthology of Digby-Roberts family members, below which stands an oil lamp, the room's only lighting fixture. The nearby easel displays a print, the pairing accented by another animal-skin rug that defines the area.

3.15, 3.16, and 3.17. Bedroom, Frederick Charles Digby-Roberts house, ca. 1895 (Courtesy Mr. and Mrs. Frederick W. Digby-Roberts and Justine Digby-Roberts Grisham).

Compared with other spaces in the Digby-Roberts home, the parlor (fig. 3.18) has only a few family references in the form of photographs. The family uses the parlor to display its taste and refinement. In the absence of a fireplace mantel, the piano top is the point of visual interest in the room. The mantel-like arrangement features a scarf to which a photo has been pinned, a few small, matted family photographs (several of Fannie), vases, and a spray of dried grasses. The large landscape print and floral still lifes hanging above the piano resemble those that usually adorn mantels.

Propped up on the sofa pillows is a mandolin. As if to highlight the musical function of the room, an easel holds a popular print of a child listening to her mother play the piano. The other draped easel in the parlor displays a print that attests to the family's awareness of Japanese taste.

The parlor photograph was taken during summer. Slipcovers conceal the plush upholstery of the Eastlake parlor suite. The simple window treatments, fringed roller blinds in a medium shade, represent accommodations to the heat. The curtain hardware remains in place during the warm months, ready to support the return of the curtains and poles.

Three years later the Digby-Roberts parlor was again photographed in a different season (fig. 3.19): the slipcovers are absent, the sofa is banished, and curtains once again hang at the windows. Despite these changes, many of the same elements are present. The piano has been moved across the room. The Japanese print stands in the same position on the same easel, but the other easel along with its print now sits in front of the windows. Tabletop accessories stand in new configurations on the piano, center table, new bookcase, and music stand: the vase and dried grasses once on the piano now are displayed on the center table with a different drape, and the ceramic plate rests on the music stand. These rearrangements do not indicate radical changes in taste, but periodic or seasonal reordering of an interior and a conscious effort to make an artistic photo.

Effectively framing the parlor composition, the portières have been pulled back, much as a theater curtain is drawn for a performance. Although there was a kind of "performing" in the rituals of early-twentieth-century parlor culture, real people, not actors, inhabit this space. The family has placed a bordered rug on top of the carpet, and the upholstery on the family's well-worn armchair has frayed from years of use. Although images of family members are relegated to the bedrooms as some late-nineteenth-century writers recommended, the family shows its presence in other ways — by periodic changes in the parlor, by photographs of those changes (no other room being sequentially documented), and by their use of the space (not much time has elapsed since the house was constructed and the furniture was new, yet the parlor shows considerable wear). The folding bed in figure 3.18 at the right behind the rocker, and possibly in figure 3.19 on the right behind the portière, blurs sharp distinctions between formal or public space and intimate or private space.

Finally, in Pecos the mission-style living room of the W. L. Ross house shows that in about 1920 some Texans were still decorating their interiors to express family identification. A rancher, Ross died in September 1915, just five months after completing this home; his widow and children continued to occupy the residence. An oak library table, piano, and three leather-upholstered rocking chairs crowd into the living room, but the decorative accessories announce the Ross family identity. Photographs of relatives rest on the piano, just below family portraits hung from the picture molding. To the right of the French doors, an oval-framed photograph of three of the six Ross children is blind hung on the wall; a framed photograph of an earlier family home hangs from a straight cord like that

3.18. Parlor, Frederick Charles Digby-Roberts house, ca. 1892 (Courtesy Mr. and Mrs. Frederick W. Digby-Roberts and Justine Digby-Roberts Grisham).

3.19. Parlor, Frederick Charles Digby-Roberts house, ca. 1895 (Courtesy Mr. and Mrs. Frederick W. Digby-Roberts and Justine Digby-Roberts Grisham).

from which two of the three family images by the piano are suspended from the molding. The only other visible wall-hung item in the room manifests a patriotic identity; not quite centered over the interior doorway is a panoramic view of San Pedro Harbor, which the American fleet visited after World War I.[17] All these accessories stand out against the plain background. Light paint accents the ceiling and extends down to the picture molding; below is a slightly darker colored wall.

Besides the family photographs on the piano, there are other noteworthy elements. The electric table lamp is powered by means of a cord from the ceiling fixture. Dried grasses and a mandolin top the piano. Nearby a bamboo music stand, draped by a floral scarf with a conventional pattern, displays an art pottery vase.

Textiles are used sparingly. In contrast to the plush or silk lambrequins, tasseled and fringed, that adorned parlor pianos in Texas houses a decade or more earlier, the Rosses' piano is covered with a white scarf. In the reform style, the window covering consists of short white curtains with a dark valance and drapes. Shades alone provide privacy at the French doors. In the foreground at the top of the photo are mission portières, fashioned of bands of fabric edged with tassels, popular in Texas houses circa 1905 – 1915. The geometric-pattern carpet is sewn in strips and may extend wall to wall.

★ ★ ★ ★

Photographs of family members and friends contributed to the visual exuberance of late-nineteenth-century taste, adding variety to rooms. The Ross house in Pecos shows that some householders continued to incorporate these images into their homes, identifying with family, long after the "newness" of photography waned and after exuberance in house decoration fell from fashion.

Photography provided the means by which people could retain visual and emotional ties to others. It served memory. Texans, always hailing from someplace else, heartily embraced photography to help conquer the distances of time and space. Through the photographic image, the "absent" family was present in Texas homes.

3.20 (facing page). Living room, W. L. Ross house, 607 West Third Street, Pecos, ca. 1920 (Courtesy Callie Bevill).

4.1. Bedroom, P. J. Agerskov Petersen house, Danevang, ca. 1900 (P. J. Agerskov Petersen Collection, Institute of Texan Cultures, San Antonio).

4

"Madonnas upon Log-Walls"

ETHNICITY

PHOTOGRAPHS document the expression of ethnic identity among Texans of Danish, Hispanic, German, Wendish, and English origins. Other groups settled in Texas — the Japanese, the Italians, and the Polish, for example — but photos of their home interiors do not survive in large numbers. Still other groups — the Scottish and to a lesser extent the Irish — took a great many interior views judging from this sample, and yet their ethnic identity is not generally announced in household decoration.

Why Scottish immigrants (who accounted for only .097 percent of the total state population in 1890) and Irish immigrants represent almost 10 percent of those in this survey is not known.[1] But families with Scottish names — McKee, Campbell, Bowie, McGregor — and Irish names — McLean and Landergin — make a strong showing; some even gave their homes "old world" names — Glen Eden and Brawn Sheling (Beautiful Home). Nor is it known why German families were more likely to take and keep photographs than Tejano families, even though the Germans were a numerically smaller group in Texas.[2] It is easy to attribute this to economics and class, but other factors may have played a role. The act of photographing one's home may have been related to ethnicity.

Anthropologist Robert Thomas Teske in his study of living rooms of Greek Philadelphians observes that families' ethnic identity is manifested in two ways: by including objects suggesting the classical, modern Greek, or both heritages of their owners and by using the color scheme of blue and white, the colors of the Greek flag.[3] He notes that in the homes of upper- or upper-middle-class, second-generation Greek Philadelphians expressions of ethnic identity are rarely on display. The same may be said of prosperous Scottish families living in turn-of-the-century Texas. We will probably never know whether

Scottish Texans decorated their homes using the colors of the Scottish flag since our record survives in black and white. Further, colors alone can be ambiguous indicators: red, white, and blue were used in the Union Jack as well as the United States and the Texas flags. The Bowie family of Weatherford did not display a Scottish flag for the photos of their home, nor did the McGregors exhibit any tartans. Yet the Petersen house in Danevang sports a Danish flag, and in Pampa the Brown residence flies the Union Jack.

In other households, the occasion of picture taking may suggest ethnicity. In ethnic households, families often chose to have photos taken at the time of a religious celebration or family event, like Christmas or a wedding (see figs. 4.2, 4.11 through 4.14). In still other households, a decidedly conservative decorating scheme becomes a feature expressive of ethnicity.

An interior view of the P. J. Agerskov Petersen home (fig. 4.1) exemplifies how domestic environment could manifest ethnic identity. Some seventy Danish families settled Danevang in Wharton County in Southeast Texas during 1894.[4] Several years later, the Petersen family arrived and posed in front of an oak bureau in a bedroom or perhaps a multipurpose room in their Danevang home. An American flag, a popular decorative device at the time of the Spanish-American War, hangs above the bureau. More as a display of their ethnic allegiance than as a decorative convention, the Petersens have placed two small Danish flags, each with a white cross on a red field, at the top corners of the mirror.[5]

Placement of such artifacts in a position of importance establishes householders' identity. The Petersen house probably lacked a fireplace, and in the absence of a mantel, which typically functioned as visual and symbolic center in a room, the bureau top serves as the focal point. It supports the main art grouping of images, while the chair rail protruding from the board wall serves as a shelf for additional decorative items. The bureau's largely symmetrical arrangement includes a central horizontal card resting on a small easel, flanked by two bud vases and two matted vertical photographs; three books complete the symmetry. The Petersens' walls are decorated in a manner popular at the turn of the century: small objects are suspended from larger ones. A cotton boll dangles from one of the crayon portraits (cotton was a major crop grown in the fertile Wharton County soil); two rabbit feet hang from the American flag.

West of Wharton County a decade later, a Tejano father and daughter posed in their South Texas parlor (fig. 4.2) on the occasion of her *quinceañera*, or fifteenth birthday celebration, the rite of passage into womanhood. On the table next to them are a man's hat and a woman's fan, objects reinforcing the gender roles the *quinceañera* celebrated. The young girl stands eye level with a calendar girl who probably decorates a promotional calendar for a Tejano business in Brownsville. Her father sits in a chair draped with handmade crocheted lace. Their respective poses echo those in formal portraits of husbands and wives.

This Tejano home resembles other turn-of-the-century middle-class interiors. For example, the side chairs lining the walls and the fringed rug covering the wide-plank pine floor were probably purchased via mail-order catalogue or from a local furnishings store. A store-bought lace curtain panel and fringed window shade adorn the window with exterior shutters. The wallpaper is a fashionable arts and crafts design that covered the walls of other middle-class houses throughout the country. Partially obscuring the paper at eye level, prints in matching frames line the wall, their bases aligned. More decorations are attached to the corners of one print, while the pins securing the bottom of another become hooks for suspending smaller circular

4.2. Living room, Unidentified house, Brownville, ca. 1910 (Texas State Archives, Austin).

4.3. Multipurpose room, Unidentified house, Big Bend area, ca. 1920 (Photography Collection, Harry Ransom Humanities Research Center, University of Texas at Austin).

items, possibly religious medallions or commemorative pins.

Circa 1920, photographer W. D. Smithers took a photograph of the two-room dwelling of a Tejano family somewhere in the vast desert of the Texas Big Bend, just north of the Mexican border (figs. 4.3, 4.4).[6] One of the rooms featured an elaborate religious shrine with crucifixes and statuary expressive of Roman Catholicism. Veiled behind the lace curtains are probably two prints with religious themes. The family has used machine-made textiles to drape the walls, "altar," and table; the ceiling sprouts mass-produced paper bells dangling from outlines of beads.

In the second room ethnicity is less apparent. In this space, wood, scarce in the area, provides the ceiling, finished and unfinished beams, shelving, and furniture; even a paneled wooden door has became part of the dwelling. A piece of worn canvas covers one of the room's windows.

According to Smithers, Tejano families living in the area sometimes benefited from U. S. Army discards; the family likely acquired their large stove from salvage at Polvo, near Redford. He speculated that they traded goats for the Singer sewing machine. The machine and the stove demonstrate the influence of mass-produced and mass-marketed goods in some unlikely and remote areas. As acculturation and accommodation occurred, what was distinctly ethnic about the abode has become diluted.

The house may have been remote and the region lacking in some natural resources, but the family did not lack resourcefulness. They used food crates for shelving and fashioned a table, shelves, and a bench from recycled pine. The textiles on the bench and the sewing machine and the wealth of cooking and eating utensils suggest a family that provided for its own home needs.

By contrast, photographs of the Edward Steves house in San Antonio (figs. 4.5, 4.6, 4.7) show an upper-middle-class German interior during the late nineteenth century. In San Antonio in the mid-1870s, prosperous lumberman

4.4. Multipurpose room, Unidentified house, Big Bend area, ca. 1920 (Photography Collection, Harry Ransom Humanities Research Center, University of Texas at Austin).

4.5. Entry hall, Edward Steves house, 509 King William Street, San Antonio, 1879 (San Antonio Conservation Society and Institute of Texan Cultures, San Antonio; probably Doerr and Jacobson, Photographers).

4.6. Sitting room, Edward Steves house, May 1878 (Courtesy Mrs. Charles C. Bush, III, and Institute of Texan Cultures, San Antonio; Doerr and Jacobson, Photographers).

Steves, at the height of his career, built himself an imposing residence. Born in Germany in 1829, he had immigrated with his parents and siblings to the predominantly German-settled Hill Country of Texas in 1848. After finishing school in New Braunfels, he went into farming with his family and in 1857 married Johanna Klapper. The couple moved to Kerr County near Comfort, an area "infested with Indians," where they lived for nine years; while there, Steves laid the foundation for his lumber business, which grew into a large and successful operation.[7] In 1866, the couple and their three children moved to San Antonio; eight years later construction began on their King William Street home.[8] Today the residence is a showplace of the King William Historic District, an area along the San Antonio River settled primarily by Texans of German descent. Containing features of the second empire and the Italian villa styles, the residence is attributed to English-born architect Alfred Giles and may be his earliest work.[9]

The Edward Steves house proved a source of pride for the lumberman and his family. Stereographs of the parlor, produced in the city and presumably sold, have found their way into several collections. Steves even commissioned the photographer to produce a montage of views of his home. The composite image appears in the Steves family records and contains the earliest dated interior photographs in Texas. Labeled "Our Home in 1878," the montage features a large circular frontal view of the exterior with small corner disks of the sitting room, dining room, and library and another exterior view with family in their phaeton.[10]

Visitors to the Steves home in the late 1870s were greeted in the entry hall (fig. 4.5), a space finished with plaster walls and a walnut staircase. An exotic sentinel on the newel guarded and lighted the area. These newel gaslights were almost always exotic figures; this one may have been made by Cornelius & Company of Philadelphia or some other large eastern lighting manufacturer.[11] Instead of a hallstand, a pair of serviceable chairs and a marble-top sideboard line the passageway. The pictures to the right appear to be matching portraits; to the left are souvenir views of the 1876 International Centennial Exhibition in Philadelphia.

To the left of the entry hall, the sitting room contains furnishings that could have been assembled twenty or more years earlier (fig. 4.6). Popular since mid century, the pattern on the borderless, wall-to-wall Brussels or Wilton carpet features large alternating geometric shapes. The fourteen-foot walls are covered with plain plaster, to which decorative painting was later added. At the windows, Louis XVI-style walnut cornices and tiebacks trim the lace curtains.

Along with a Gothic revival pier mirror, the Steves sitting room contains furniture in the rococo revival style. Horsehair fabric, or haircloth, upholsters the sofa, armchairs, and probably the balloon-back chair behind the center table. The gasolier is of the latest fashion and provides illumination above the covered table, which displays a photograph album. The shells adorning the draped table and the mirror shelf were common decorations in houses of the second half of the nineteenth century, valued because they connoted travels to distant places and picturesque landscapes. A parian or porcelain compote offers grapes to visitors in a gesture of hospitality and abundance.

On plant stands, Johanna has placed a geranium and a coleus plant. Those who profiled the "Mother of the Lumber Industry" (her three sons followed in their father's business) rarely failed to mention her gardening talents. Long after her husband's death in 1890, one observer wrote of "the homestead on King William Street . . . [in which] Mrs. Steves has lived with her music, flowers and laughter for more than fifty years."[12]

The same carpet that covered the sitting room floor extended into the adjacent dining room (fig. 4.7). As in the sitting room, the ceiling and walls are finished with plaster. In the dining room, paneled doors of pine have been grained to look like black walnut.

The light, simply designed cane-seat chairs are counterpoint to the renaissance revival sideboard, which holds a rich display of silver and glass: pots for coffee and tea, tureens, compotes, and liquor decanters. On the dining table are cruets, condiment containers, and turned-over glasses ready for a meal. Only three photos hang on the wall surrounding the sideboard: one of a woman, proba-

4.7. Dining room, Edward Steves house, May 1878 (San Antonio Conservation Society and Institute of Texan Cultures, San Antonio; Doerr and Jacobson, Photographers).

bly a family member; one of the couple and their three sons; and one of an unidentified structure (possibly the Steves Lumber Company). These images and the display of silver and glass reinforce a sense of family and prosperity.

The 1878 – 1879 interiors show contentment with furniture forms and styles long popular. The Steves family had occupied the home for at least two years before the interiors were documented, so they had time to decorate in whatever manner they wished. These images may testify to a personal and aesthetic conservatism reinforced by their (especially his) advancing years. Similar conservative tendencies appear in the images of other German families, the Faltins and the Wulffs, indicating that such habits were very much a part of these families' ethnic identity as well as associated with age.

August Faltin (1830 – 1905) and Clara Below (1835 – 1929) married in 1856 and soon after emigrated from Germany. Faltin, the son of a Danzig merchant, and his bride entered the United States through New Orleans, traveled to Galveston, and settled in the German Hill Country town of Comfort where they prospered, operating a general merchandise store and raising stock.[13] Shortly after his retirement from business in 1889, he and his wife posed with their grandchild, Albert Faltin, in their portière-framed parlor (fig. 4.8).[14]

Frederick Law Olmsted, who traveled to Texas in the 1840s, remarked upon visiting the homes of German settlers, that there were "[m]adonnas upon log-walls; coffee in tin cups upon Dresden saucers; barrels for seats, to hear a Beethoven's symphony on the grand piano," suggesting unexpected signs of culture in simple surroundings, an odd juxtaposition of necessity and luxury.[15] The elegance of the Faltin parlor in a second-story apartment over a general store in rural Texas, even some forty years later, is

4.8. Parlor, August Faltin residence, Corner of Main and Seventh streets, Comfort, 1891 (Courtesy Helen Faltin Martin; Albert Glock, Photographer).

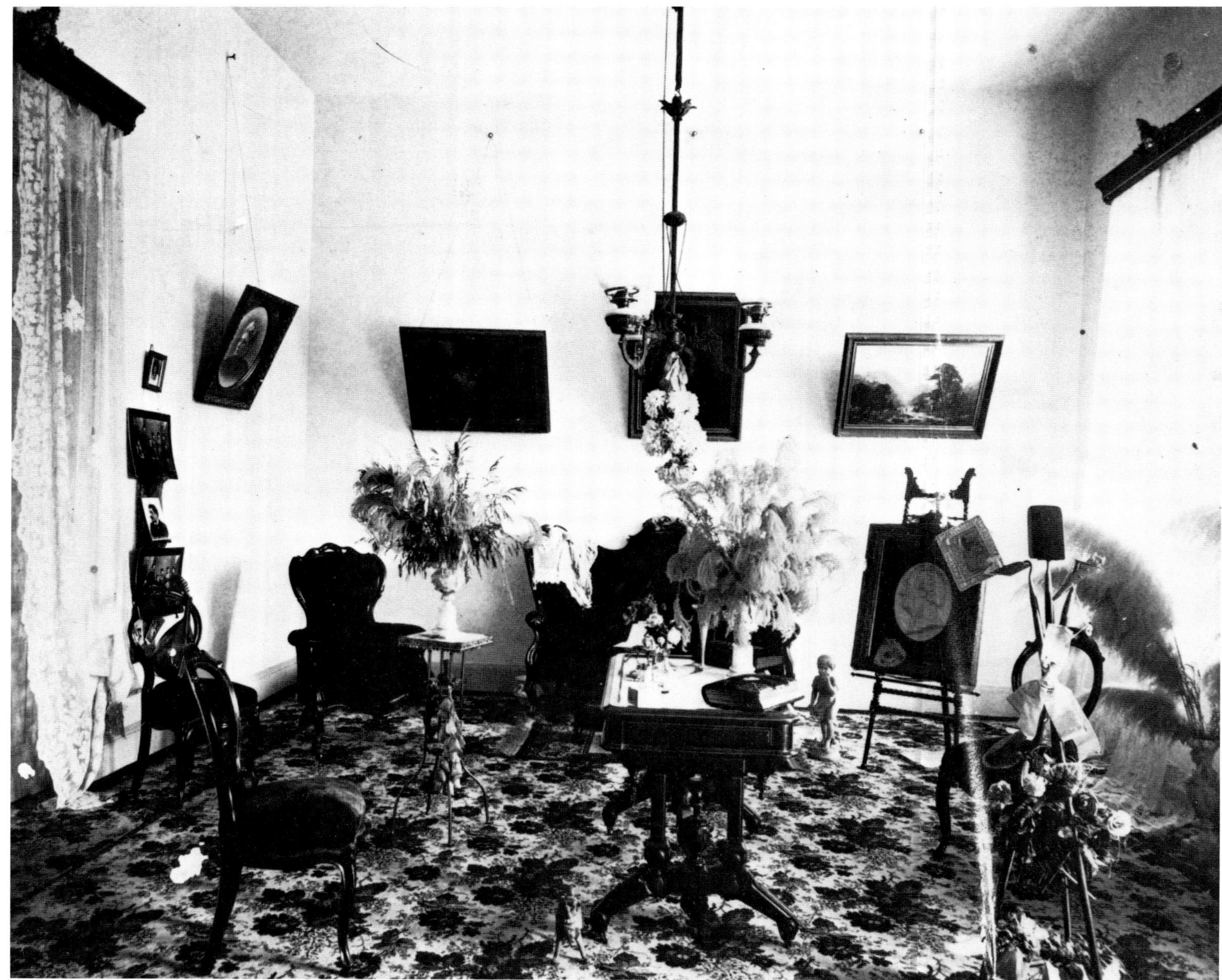

4.9. Parlor, Anton F. Wulff house, 107 King William Street, San Antonio, 1892 (Howard Paveglio and Institute of Texan Cultures, San Antonio).

remarkable. Their store, a two-story stone structure, was designed in 1879 by the Steves house architect, Alfred Giles, in an era when few rural stores were designed by professional architects. An exterior photograph of the store is to the right of the large family portrait photograph above the sofa.

The dense aggregation of framed paintings and photographs is common in homes of emigrant Germans, especially those who decorated their first houses at mid century. They continued to use the plan into the new century. According to family history, the Faltins brought the oil paintings with them from Germany along with numerous family portraits of relatives who remained in Germany. Through the paintings and photographs, the room speaks of a connection to their past as well as to their former homeland. As in many interior views expressing householders' ethnicity, the Faltin parlor shows the strong connection between family and ethnicity.

In addition to the paintings, the family brought with them from Germany the piano, the textiles, and the case piece in the corner — an organ. Lonn Taylor, coauthor of *Texas Furniture*, has observed that as experienced travelers, the Anglo settlers in Texas traveled "light," whereas Germans traveled "heavy."[16] The Faltins' furnishings support that notion. The family purchased newer, fashionable items once they had settled in their home: the kerosene fixture, the marble-top center table, and the Louis XVI-style sofa date from the 1870s; the wicker rocker probably dates from the 1880s or the 1890s; and the carpet dates from the 1890s.

The Wulff home in San Antonio was photographed a year or two after the Faltin residence. Anton F. Wulff, born in 1822 in Altoona, Germany, near Hamburg, was a traveling salesman who immigrated to the United States about 1848. Working his way through New York, Cincinnati, New Orleans, and Indianola, he settled in New Braunfels, obtaining a job as a store clerk. By 1852, Wulff had married Paula Olivarri and settled in San Antonio, where he operated a freight business, running wagon trains from San Antonio to Chihuahua, Mexico.[17]

Although the photograph of the Wulff parlor dates from 1892, the interior decoration reflects a much earlier taste (fig. 4.9). The house was built circa 1870, but some of the furnishings like the horsehair-upholstered rococo revival parlor suite that was marketed in the 1850s and 1860s may have been purchases the Wulffs made soon after their marriage at mid century. The marble-top table, the easel, and the onyx stand date from the 1870s and 1880s.

A portrait of Paula hangs on the plaster walls (no doubt a companion portrait of Anton decorates the wall to the left of the interior doorway). The curtains and cornice of the interior doorway to the left match those at the window and exterior door, an unusual mirroring in Texas homes. Between the portrait of Paula and the doorway, a line of photographs — two similar studio family portraits, cabinet cards, and cartes de visite — climb the wall. Three symmetrically placed romantic paintings adorn the far wall, reinforcing the symmetrical arrangement of sofa, armchair, and easel. The overall restraint of the room is alleviated by the exuberant puffs of dried grasses and cattails as well as by the floral pattern of the bordered wall-to-wall carpet.

Family identity emerges in some of the objects. For example, Henry Wulff, one of the two sons, crafted the medallion resting on the easel and possibly the statue on the floor. An artist, Henry was eventually required to participate in the family business. In the foreground, a tripod of gardening tools has been arranged into a decorative stand. The arrangement relates to Anton's position as first parks commissioner of San Antonio. He was responsible for the

4.10. Parlor, Anton F. Wulff house, 1892 (Howard Paveglio and Institute of Texan Cultures, San Antonio).

design of Alamo Plaza, the completion of which was commemorated in 1891, shortly before the photograph was taken.[18]

A close-up of the Wulff parlor (fig. 4.10) provides a portrait of a family friend (an unidentified member of the Madero family) who plays a mandolin, a then-popular parlor instrument, which at other times sat on a rococo revival chair by the doorway (fig. 4.9). This image shows the ceramic spittoon peeking out from behind the sofa; household advisers considered it déclassé to include a spittoon in the parlor, and yet the articles do appear in a number of Texas interiors (see figs. 5.5, 9.3, 11.20). The metal dog chained to the center table was a popular nineteenth-century visual "trick" that amused the Wulff grandchildren.[19] On the tabletop rest a card receiver, a photograph album, and a vase with ceramic flowers in relief that echo the cut roses in it. The chrysanthemums that hang from the fashionable kerosene fixture also appear in another Texas home (see fig. 3.4), probably photographed within a year of this one, indicating a popular decorative detail rather than ethnic or regional preference.

The aesthetic conservatism of the Wulffs was not shared by Gustav and Magdaline Duerler, who also lived in San Antonio. Born in 1841 at St. Gallen in northern Switzerland, Gustav A. Duerler and his parents left their homeland in 1849, journeying three months before reaching San Antonio. After completing school there, young Duerler worked in a local confectioner's firm for three years before serving in the Confederate army, Third Texas Infantry. In 1866, he married Magdaline Werner, daughter of San Antonio contractor Christian Werner, who had emigrated from Germany in the early 1850s; the next year he founded G. A. Duerler Manufacturing, a pioneer candy manufacturing business in Texas.[20]

Like the Faltins, the Duerlers lived in an apartment above their business (fig. 4.11); however, unlike the

4.11. Parlor, Gustav A. Duerler residence, 220 West Commerce Street, above Duerler's confectionery, San Antonio, 1889 (Mrs. Faulkner Heard and Institute of Texan Cultures, San Antonio).

Faltins, the Swiss-German Duerlers first set up housekeeping in Texas and were sensitive to changing taste in furnishings. In 1889 their parlor was smartly up-to-date, in contrast to the Faltins' more traditional one. Decorated for the November 16, 1889, wedding of their daughter Minnie to August A. Herff, the parlor exhibits elements of the aesthetic style, which had become popular among the wealthy in the mid-1870s. An Anglo-Japanese paper covers the walls below the fine plaster molding, the gasolier hangs from a center medallion, and a bordered brown-and-gold carpet stretches wall to wall.[21] To the right are bentwood chairs based upon those made popular by German-Austrian cabinetmaker Michael Thonet and probably distributed in San Antonio furniture stores via Thonet Brothers, New York City. Rococo revival chairs from an earlier parlor suite are scattered at the room's edges; a newer parlor suite trimmed with banded plush provides most of the seating.

A fine Eastlake table supports a cluster of small floral arrangements at one side of the temporary wedding altar; a large ewer dominates a smaller scarved table on the other side. Large banana trees, popular plants in San Antonio where the humid climate encouraged their cultivation, stretch to the ceiling, while fall flowers bloom in window and floor pots. Above a potted palm, a floral horseshoe provides the centerpiece of the wedding decorations. A popular American image of good fortune, the horseshoe appears in the homes of other newlyweds (figs. 9.2, 9.19), as well as on the exterior of the Wulff house above certain windows. Use of the horseshoe may be related to ethnicity.[22]

Figure 4.12 illustrates the interior of a Wendish house, an ethnic group related to Germans. Charles Simmang, Jr., was born in the Wendish colony of Serbin, Lee County, Texas, in 1874.[23] His father, an immigrant blacksmith and wheelwright, married Anna Paulo, also Wendish, in Serbin in 1870. The Simmang and Paulo families were among a group of some 500 Slavs who had emigrated in 1854 from an area southeast of Berlin, Germany, in search of religious freedom; they formed communities in the Lee County area in southeastern Central Texas.[24]

With their five sons and one daughter, the Simmangs moved to San Antonio in 1880. There, Charles Simmang, Jr., apprenticed with Charles Stubenrauch, a German die sinker and artist who had studied at the Papal Mint in Rome. Simmang eventually took over Stubenrauch's engraving business and began to produce commercial items such as seals and stencils. He continued to execute artistic medals for special events and by private commission, including numerous portrait medals of local people. A member of the American Federation of Arts, Simmang gathered around him many of San Antonio's artistic community including Robert and Julian Onderdonk, José Arpa, Ernst Raba, Tom Brown, Rolla Taylor, and Alois and Joe Braun.[25]

Historians of the Texas Wends profile a somber, religious, hard-working, and frugal people who formed deep and lasting family ties, keeping largely to themselves, intermarrying and socializing with their German neighbors rather than with Catholic Czechs or English-speaking "Americans," as they called the native inhabitants. Although they were closer culturally to the Germans than to their other neighbors, there were subtle differences between the two groups. The Wends had fewer comforts and improvements in their homes and on their farms. Typically, the homes were "unpainted, and the furnishings included only bare necessities. The Wends, with their innate desire to accumulate savings for old age, were slower than their German neighbors to make improvements on their property. Some of the furnishings of their German friends were called 'German luxuries' by the Wends."[26]

Perhaps the Simmangs' move to cosmopolitan San An-

4.12. Parlor, Charles Simmang, Jr., house, 918 Avenue B, San Antonio, 1903 (Josephine Simmang Jones and Institute of Texan Cultures, San Antonio).

tonio blurred distinctions between the domestic material culture of the Wends and the Germans. The room's strong signals of occupational identity obscure those clear-cut differences. The interior of the Simmang parlor is comfortable and up-to-date, although it lacks the fine interior finishes characteristic of some German families (compare fig. 4.12 with figs. 4.8, 4.9, 4.11).

Simmang had lived for a time with his mentor. After Stubenrauch's death, circa 1900, Simmang purchased his house. According to a note on the original photograph, the occasion for this 1903 picture is a family celebration welcoming cousin Karl Simmang who stopped in San Antonio en route to St. Louis where he was to represent the German government at the Louisiana Purchase International Exposition in 1904.

The aesthetic wallpaper provides the backdrop for a variety of artwork produced by the professional and amateur artists who lived in and visited the home. Medallions by Stubenrauch and Simmang rest on identical wall brackets hanging beside the makeshift mantel. Fringed, tasseled, and embroidered lambrequins, the work of the Simmang women, provide the decorative background for the shelf accessories. The same "lady amateurs" may be responsible for the still-life paintings hanging high on the wall. A romantic landscape hangs prominently in the center, and a similar one hangs to the right; the winter landscape to the left has a near-twin print on the adjacent wall. The sheer quantity of framed items and their symmetrical arrangement is reminiscent of the Faltin parlor. The artwork shows a powerful connection between ethnicity, occupation, and refinement.

The Seele house in San Antonio displays artistry of another sort (fig. 4.13). The tabletop Christmas tree, a German tradition, dominates a holiday photograph and presents an elaborate village of toys — dollhouses, castles, bridges, trains, wagons, and pens for horses and sheep. Both the tabletop and the family's cedar tree are festooned with decorations: strings of popcorn, glass balls, paper cutout figures, and lanterns. An angel floats above, suspended from the ceiling.

Like his father, Frederick H., Harry Seele enjoyed creating fantasy worlds for children. The elder Seele, a lawyer, educator, and historian, was widely known for the annual masque he organized for the children of New Braunfels beginning about 1857. The celebration encouraged the schoolchildren of the German Hill Country community to dress in costume derived from "Fastenzeit" or "Fastnacht," a Germanic post-Lenten festivity, lasting several days, during which the entire town celebrated, going from house to house dancing and feasting.[27] Probably inspired by his father, son Harry, a bookkeeper who had moved to San Antonio by 1880, created a complete Christmas village, a miniature fantasy world for children. Frederick's crayon portrait hangs on the wall adjacent to the display.

Aside from the seasonal decorations, the parlor contains familiar furnishings — an Eastlake-inspired upholstered lounge, a matching armchair, and a reed rocking chair, all draped asymmetrically. Covered with a dark plush scarf embroidered with conventionalized flowers, a small table or stand displays framed baby pictures and photograph albums. Crayon portraits hang from cords and pins at the customary picture molding level, even though the Seele parlor has no such molding only a ceiling paper border extending for several inches down the side walls.

As in many Texas houses, a kerosene parlor lamp with a spring extension for raising or lowering it hangs in the parlor, long after the city had electricity. The small glass bulb has been suspended from the lamp; its function is probably decorative, but it may have been used as a

4.13. Parlor, Harry Seele house, 433 East Crockett Street, San Antonio, ca. 1900 (Hermann Seele and Institute of Texan Cultures, San Antonio).

handle to pull down the kerosene lamp for lighting. A similar bulb appears in another German home, that of the Villarets in nearby Comfort (see fig. 4.17).[28]

Johanna Maria Elizabet Flato Jersig of Cat Spring, a German community in Central Texas, married Paul Gustav Villaret in Flatonia on September 5, 1883. Soon after, the couple and two of her five sons from an earlier marriage moved to Comfort. Paul Villaret, a native of Danzig, Germany, had emigrated in 1879 when he was about thirty years old. He worked as a banker, eventually becoming an officer of the Comfort Bank. After the births of Alexander and Paul, the family moved to the residence pictured here (fig. 4.14), which had been built by Joseph Heinan in 1885.[29]

At the turn of the century, the Christmas tree was placed on the dining room table, which was moved into the parlor for the holiday season (see fig. 4.16). The painted wooden floors are nearly bare, covered only by a machine-made rug featuring a Jean-François Millet-style pastoral scene, a popular arts and crafts reference. Similar images appear on pillow tops and in prints (see figs. 6.8, 9.12). The Christmas tree is a Texas cedar, then and now plentiful in the Hill Country. (In East Texas the pine was more commonly used; see figs. 8.11 and 8.12). Its tabletop position is Germanic. The tree is decked with colored paper chains and cutout paper or wood animal silhouettes. At least one decorative pinecone hangs from a ribbon near the top of the tree; cornucopias and a pocket watch dangle from other branches.

Although the four children pictured here are male — Paul Villaret, Jr., half brothers Rudy and Walter Jersig, and Alex Villaret — the presents at the base of the tree and

4.14. Parlor, Paul Gustav Villaret, Sr., house on Cypress Creek, Comfort, ca. 1891 (Courtesy Catherine Villaret Spinks).

table represent both masculine and feminine toys. Along with the pistol and rifle on the table, a child's tea set, a small kitchen, and boys' tool chests sit on the floor. The gifts for a young girl were presents for Johanna's niece, a daughter of then-widower August Faltin, Jr. (whose parents and son are pictured in fig. 4.8 in 1891). The presents are material bonds of the German family, as the Villarets share their celebration and extend gifts to members of the larger family.

The German family communicates its respect for tradition and family in this Christmas photograph. Johanna sits in one of the parlor chairs, a pose reinforcing her position of honor as wife and mother. She holds the hand of her youngest child, their clasped hands resting on the Bible, signifying her charge over the family morals. Villaret's pose suggests both authority within the family and control of its material well-being — his extended right arm lays claim to the Christmas array.

Three years later, the Villarets and the two younger boys again posed in front of the bay window (fig. 4.15). The center table has been strategically placed in the bay and becomes a sort of family altar displaying cabinet cards honoring Johanna's parents, a silver-plated pitcher (a familiar sign of hospitality, but also practical in this summer scene), and the watch that was a recent Christmas present: all treasures of family. The Villarets pose in conventional, if idealized, postures: he reads, and she sews — her handiwork is visible in the chair tidies and the fringed table scarf — and their sons stand by attentively.

In this photograph, furnishings have been moved and added. For instance, the large desk and bookcase has been removed, and the corner whatnot now takes its place.[30] The horn footstool, a new item, is prominently placed between the couple. Horn furniture, popular in the 1890s, could be expensive or not; thus, a small object like a footstool might demonstrate a family's knowledge of current fashion but not require a large expenditure. This example could have been either an inexpensive, locally made product or a more costly item crafted by cabinetmaker Wenzel Friedrich of San Antonio, widely known for his furniture made from the horns of Texas longhorn cattle.

The photographer has snapped the image of the Villaret family on a summer night, evidenced by the darkness at the windows and the shadows cast by the photographer's flash. The lighting fixture and its cover confirm that it is summer. Without wire window and door screens (developed by the 1880s but not universally available), Texas houses were plagued by insects that could destroy the finish on paintings and mar lighting fixtures. When not in use, the lamp was covered with netting to protect it from fly specks; to prevent a fire, the netting was removed when the kerosene lamp was lit.

The corner of the Villaret parlor opposite the bay shows a sofa and side chair, constituting a small conversational group, typical of late-nineteenth-century furniture arrangements (fig. 4.16). This stiff corner grouping has been made slightly more convivial by the addition of a spittoon and the small gallery. Portraits of Alexander Paul and Agnes Reinhardt Villaret, who remained in Germany, and Frederick William and Charlotte Welhausen Flato, Johanna's parents, are featured in the gallery. These images of family figure prominently in the decoration and introduce a third generation of family into the home.

The parlor suite, embellished with carving and upholstery tufting, was probably purchased from a San Antonio furniture retailer soon after the Villarets' 1883 marriage. The wallpaper resembling a textile with a narrow border would have been a current style when it was applied in 1885 at the completion of the house. A draped center table and a side table, the latter probably standing beneath a pier mirror, complete the furniture in this niche.

The dining room, with embossed wallpaper and painted

4.15. Parlor, Paul Gustav Villaret, Sr., house, ca. 1894 (Courtesy Catherine Villaret Spinks).

floors, is visible through the doorway. The cloth-covered dining table, which provided the base for the tree at Christmastime, stands without chairs around it. The format of the original photographs suggests that figures 4.15 and 4.16 date from approximately the same period, although the latter was taken during the daytime. Like figure 4.15, this picture was probably taken during the summer since the flue cover is in place and the stove is not; however, the parlor lamp is not protectively draped.

Figure 4.17 provides the most complete view of the Villarets' "Eastlake" parlor suite: three side chairs, a platform rocker, and a center table. Seating pieces are arrayed around the center table like sentinels. In the absence of a fireplace and mantel in this southern Central Texas parlor, tabletop groupings provide visual and emotional centers. Books and scarves top the draped center table; on the round and rectangular side tables, also draped with fringed cloths, are cabinet cards on easels, photographs, and prints. Framed items overflow onto the walls. The top tier of wall-hung items features large gilt frames holding portraits of Johanna's parents, tipped out at the top and secured by ceramic-headed pins at the bottom. The size and placement of these items relate to figure 4.16 where large framed items hang high on the wall and smaller ones beneath. Another display form, the corner whatnot, has been shifted to the other side of the bay window.

The dominant architectural feature of the room, the bay window, serves as the backdrop for the parlor views and offers a chronology of window treatments. The lace curtains in the 1891 view are probably the same ones visible in the 1894 photograph, but the natural light streaming through the windows in the daytime has obscured details. In figure 4.14, a curtain pole and rings are ready to receive a heavier winter curtain, but in figure 4.15, all curtain hardware has been removed for the summer. The curtains

4.16. Parlor, Paul Gustav Villaret, Sr., house, ca. 1894 (Courtesy Catherine Villaret Spinks).

resemble those in other Texas houses of the period, heavily embroidered with floral and foliate designs.

By the time the 1898 photograph was taken, roller blinds cover the windows, while dotted swiss curtains line the opening to the bay window and cover the one visible side window. The curtain hardware has returned; from it hangs a fringed flat valance of the type pictured in pattern books circa 1890. This view of the parlor is a winter scene, suggested by the heavier window treatment and the presence of outdoor plants, mostly geraniums, filling the bay.

In addition, the kerosene parlor lamp has its summer netting removed. As in the Seele parlor decorated for Christmas (see fig. 4.13), the lamp dangles a light bulb. The object may represent a fashion at the turn of the century, or it may be an ethnic-related or even a seasonal item, since both examples appear in parlors decorated for the winter.

After the 1894 Christmas portrait of the family in their parlor, the ethnic features of the house become less pronounced. Possibly the family, along with other German families living in Comfort, was rapidly assimilating.

Decidedly English themes decorate a room in the northwestern Texas residence of M. K. Brown (fig. 4.18). A native of England and a veteran of the Boer War in South Africa, Brown came to the United States in 1903 to work for the White Deer Land Trust Company, which owned 613,000 acres of the Texas Panhandle. In 1916, he became co-manager of the operation, and several years later he was photographed in his apartment above the offices.[31] The building had been constructed in 1916, and the apartment shows characteristics of both the reform and the colonial revival styles then popular.

4.17 (facing page). Parlor, Paul Gustav Villaret, Sr., house, ca. 1898 (Courtesy Catherine Villaret Spinks).

In the photograph Brown relaxes in a rattan armchair, a Navaho rug on the floor and his scarved gateleg table strewn with papers and books. His finely detailed wooden bookcases with beveled glass door panels stand oddly empty. A United States flag marks each end of the mantel, which is filled with images of uniformed friends and family members; another flag drapes the corner of the stuffed sofa positioned diagonally across the room. A large Union Jack hangs from a bookcase behind Brown. A string of Allied Forces banners links the flag display, while a pair of sconces flanking the mantel mirror dangles patriotic lanterns. The lighting fixtures, the built-ins, and the interior finishes show prairie-style architectural details mingling with patriotic and ethnic elements in a single space.

★ ★ ★ ★

In a perfect world, a sample of images devoted to ethnicity and home decoration in Texas houses from 1878 to 1920 would include images from all ethnic groups, in all regions of the state, at regular intervals over the forty-two-year period. Even without such a sample, some generalizations are still possible. The extant photographs illustrate that householders expressed ethnic identity in a variety of ways — from an obvious display of flags to a subtle aesthetic conservatism. Families with ties to other countries may also have expressed their backgrounds in the mere act of taking pictures, even in the occasion of taking pictures.

The overt elements of ethnic identification do not typically dominate house decoration, as the Petersen interior documents. And yet, conservative decorating strategies inform the furnishing of an entire room, as in the Wulff, Steves, or Faltin houses; however, some of the conservatism may be age related, as the heads of these households

4.18. Living room, M. K. Brown apartment above the offices of the White Deer Land Company, 114 – 116 South Cuyler, Pampa, ca. 1918 (Carson County Square House Museum, Panhandle).

were born in 1822, 1829, and 1830 respectively. Ethnic identity is often combined with occupational identification, as in the Simmang and Wulff houses, or with familial identification, as in the Villaret house.

Apparently, many families remained in ethnic enclaves — Danes in Danevang, Tejanos in South Texas, and Germans in the Hill Country or in a predominantly German area in San Antonio. It may have been more comfortable for the Petersens in the homogeneous community of Danevang to express their allegiance to homeland than it was for the Simmangs living in San Antonio. But even in such enclaves, first- and second-generation ethnic families were engaged in new circumstances; their house decoration shows a response to time and distance from homeland. Some of these photographs suggest a dilution of ethnicity related to establishing residence in larger cities with heterogeneous populations.

5

Home Away from Home

SOCIAL GROUP

PEOPLE who lived away from home had a number of choices including cooperatives, hotels, boardinghouses, and dormitories, each of which had public and private spaces. The interiors of these shared dwellings were distinctively different from those of private residences. Photographs reveal that the public rooms in these facilities shared certain features: since space was at a premium, the public areas often had multiple functions, and the decorations in these rooms were diffuse and additive. In the private spaces, the inhabitants often made an attempt to personalize the anonymous space; especially in dormitory rooms, they created individual compositions that identify the occupants as members of social groups.

The relatively new phenomenon of the working woman, or the "business girl" as she was known, prompted the establishment of safe, chaperoned housing for middle-class women who left their families to live near job markets (much like New England mill girls generations earlier). Figures 5.1 and 5.2 suggest curiosity on the part of Americans about the business girl and her surroundings. The photographs assured a skeptical society that the young women would live in decent, safe environments.

Rebecca Sparks of Waco had founded such a haven for local women by 1910.[1] A then-popular song proclaimed, "Heaven Will Protect the Working Girl," but Sparks gave heaven considerable assistance.[2] Her tenants socialized in an impersonal room filled with unmatched chairs, a game table, a piano, and a record player (fig. 5.1). The furnishings bespeak the nature of the space: it was not for comfortable, intimate chats with members of the same or opposite sex, but for more decorous discussions. The mantel, looking bare and unattended, supports a glass vase of roses and fern fronds, which almost block the picture, *Light of the World*, while a small image of a bewigged religious leader rests nearby. With these two images, Sparks

5.1. Sitting room, Rebecca Sparks Co-operative House, 1118 Franklin Street, Waco, ca. 1910 (Texas Collection, Baylor University, Waco).

communicates to her boarders that hers is a Christian home.

Other decorative items in the room, primarily wall hung, differ from the planned, picturesque groupings of homes. They appear to be lost in the space, standing out on the solid field of wallpaper, without purpose or focus. The diffuse placement of some of the objects reinforces the room's function as an area that must serve a variety of unrelated people rather than a single family. There is no distinctive decorating hand. In the lack of a personal or familial identity, the room expresses its accommodation to a social group, residents of the co-op.

A single covered electric bulb hangs from the pale papered ceiling over the game table. The photographer's flash may be the only other light illuminating several areas of activity for the women; without it they would sew, share a magazine, and play the piano in relative darkness. A paper inspired by the arts and crafts movement covers

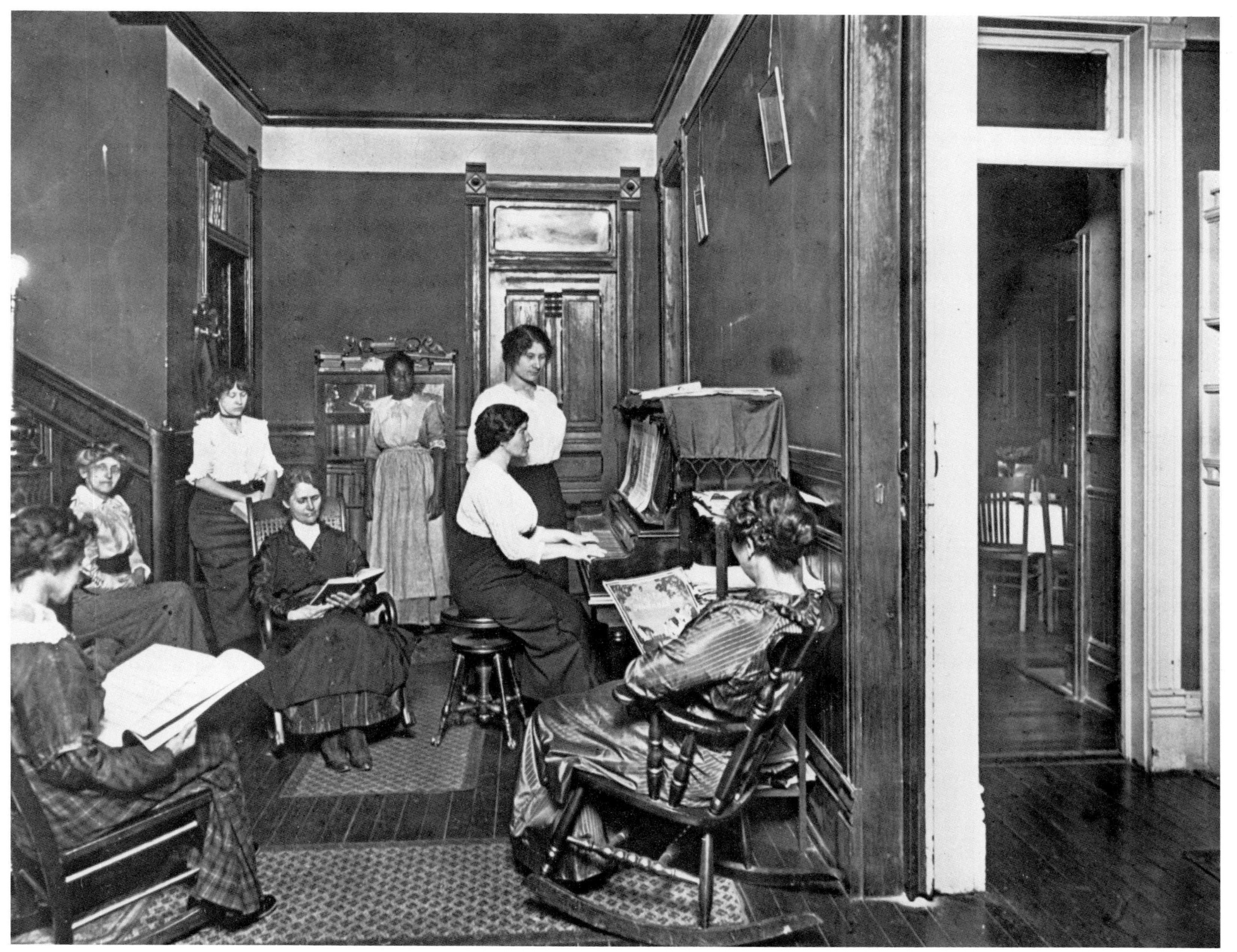

5.2. Entry hall, Unidentified house, Houston, ca. 1910 (Harris County Heritage Society, Houston).

the wall above the paper border, its pattern complemented by the geometric and medallion motifs in the twin rugs (see fig. 10.20).

Other group houses were created in residences. In figure 5.2, the young women play the piano and read while their chaperone sits with a proprietary air on the stairway and a maid stands in the background. (The poses imply that the photographer has positioned the subjects: the three women attired in dark clothes sit in the rocking chairs, while those wearing the lighter colors are in the middle ground to brighten the dark hallway.) The house was built some twenty-five years before the photograph was taken; its interiors have been recently outfitted in the colonial revival style. Some room details — lengths of stair carpeting used as mats — suggest modest expenditures on furnishings, characteristic of group housing. The residents may have gathered in the hall, much as families used their halls for informal sitting rooms, or the women may have assembled there since space was at a premium.

Hotels offered another alternative to individual living. The parlors of the Cottage Hotel and of the Hereford House, also a hotel, look like places where many people deposited things — no single hand has arranged the interiors featured in figures 5.3 and 5.4 .[3] In the Cottage Hotel the wall calendar featuring an image of a horse hangs askew above a crowded corner where transient boarders propped frames on the floor and pictures on the chair rail rather than attaching them permanently to the wall. The room's decoration is an accidental, additive grouping that differs from the distinctive decorating strategies found in a single-family dwelling of 1900 – 1910. The stained ceiling paper and the tattered frieze indicate a lack of attention or means.

The bay window serves as a niche for the piano, the rustic music shelf nailed beneath the chair rail demonstrating that the piano is in its permanent location. Details of the bay show that the season is summer: shades hang alone at the windows; bare curtain and portière poles indicate that the openings are draped during winter. Despite the season, the window screens have been removed and rest on the floor behind the piano.

The photograph does not provide reliable information about the placement of other furnishings. For example, the chairs serve the purposes of the photograph rather than as an index of daily social interaction among the occupants. The electric light cord drops from the center of the ceiling where early electric fixtures were fed through gas pipes or where by tradition a fixture would have been. Here the light has been looped over the curtain pole to illuminate the desired area by the piano.

Across the state, in the Panhandle, the Hereford House parlor also exhibits a diffuse, additive quality in its decoration (fig. 5.4). Instead of being arranged in picturesque groupings, the wall-hung accessories appear to float around the room, aligned unevenly on the boldly patterned wallpaper.

Some of the wall decorations draw attention to the piano and the shelf of the folding bed; each in turn provides a centering force in this stove-heated room that lacks a traditional hearth and mantel. The piano top is lined with portrait photographs, a shell, and a kerosene lamp, the only visible lighting device in the room. A large paper butterfly spreading its wings above the draped piano is flanked by a crayon portrait of a young man and a print of a stag in a winter landscape As if to emphasize the image of the stag, a trophy of a small animal dangles from the frame of the print. When the hotel parlor is not the setting of a chaperoned party, the table by the piano probably sits in the room's center topped by the kerosene lamp, near a more convivial grouping of chairs.

5.3. Parlor, Cottage Hotel (Calvert Hotel), Corner of Railroad and Mitchell streets, Calvert, ca. 1905 (Courtesy Reba Alsup).

The other visual focus, the shelf of the folding bed, displays a richly framed cabinet card portrait at its center and a horizontal row of matted photos connected by ribbons. The surface is transformed into a makeshift mantel over which looms the image of an unidentified man.

While the parlors depicted in figures 5.3 and 5.4 show an additive and diffuse quality in their decoration, Ella Moore's boardinghouse parlor, circa 1900, expresses a strong decorating voice (fig. 5.5). Moore has carefully ordered room details, if only for the photograph: neatly positioned record cylinders on the center table, precisely placed books and scarves in the combination case, and strategically mirrored live and pictorial palms. The room's arrangement conveys control and planning. Moore was a boardinghouse manager by profession; Fort Worth city directories show that she set up several different houses at the turn of the century.[4]

In the boardinghouse parlor, Moore displays an anthol-

5.4. Parlor, Hereford House, Dewey Avenue, Hereford, December 1, 1902 (Deaf Smith County Historical Museum, Hereford).

ogy of styles typical of the period's eclectic taste. Native American themes inspire the pillow top; oriental motifs, the carpeting; and Mexican designs, the rug. A pair of Moorish busts rests on the piano top, and a print in the tradition of French landscape painting hangs on the wall. The most remarkable feature of the room is the use of multiple patterns of wallpaper: a paper of conventionalized Japanese-inspired palms and one of naturalistic cabbage roses are paired on the side walls; a matching rose-motif frieze borders the walls; the ceiling paper continues the rose motif. Moore and her niece peek out from behind string portières.

The room accommodates various activities within its walls, with Moore as social director. Her boarders can enjoy the player piano, rolls resting on the bottom three shelves of the music stand across the room, or listen to records on a Victrola that sits on the center table bedecked with a cover complementing the rose-pattern wallpaper. For those who chew tobacco, Moore provided a spittoon. Should they want to read, boarders could choose from the stacks of books. The combination case stands in front of portières blocking passage into an adjacent room, a frequent occurrence in communal homes.

A Brenham home that housed students of Blinn Acad-

5.5. Parlor, Ella Moore's boardinghouse, "6th & Houston over Fair Department Store," Fort Worth, ca. 1900 (Bess Hornbeak and Amon Carter Museum, Fort Worth; Swartz, Photographer).

5.6. Dining room, Unidentified boardinghouse, Blinn Academy (Blinn College), Brenham, ca. 1895 (Barker Texas History Center, Austin).

5.7. Sitting room, Howe house, Blinn Academy (Blinn College), Brenham, ca. 1895 (Barker Texas History Center, Austin).

emy shares features with boardinghouses and hotels (fig. 5.6). A photograph showing one room suggests the multiple functions of the space: a dining room, a storage area, a sewing room, and a study area. An assortment of chairs in various styles encircles the extension table. The corner cupboard appears to be a mass-produced piece from a nonlocal factory, but the walnut wardrobe was probably made by a local cabinetmaker.[5]

The interior view shows a sitting/dining room in a boardinghouse, used exclusively by women, continuing the earlier tradition of using second parlors for these combined functions. The women have decorated the area with a Berlin-work motto; possibly two others hang above the doorways. Nevertheless, the arbiters of taste in this room have refrained from "parlorizing" and fully feminizing the room, possibly as a concession either to the multifunctional nature of the space or to prescribed taste. A medallion-pattern paper with a matching frieze covers the walls; an ingrain carpet stretches wall to wall. Braided rugs top the floor covering, and a piece of linoleum indicates the entrance to a service part of the house, probably the kitchen. By the stove, an older woman sits with her arms crossed in a rocking chair, looking like a stern but benevolent house mother.

In another image of a house occupied by students of the Blinn Academy (fig. 5.7), a Best stove, parlor organ, rocking chair, bureau, and locally made space-saving drop-leaf table are in view. Here, too, the variety of furniture forms suggests multiple uses of the room, from studying and dining to musicmaking and dressing. School-age children and young adults use the area as a sitting room, for playing games and reading popular magazines like *Harper's Weekly*. Wall-hung decorations are placed high on the walls or are suspended from the low ceiling. The windows are covered with commercially stenciled blinds; between them hangs a print of a wreath of paper flowers that encloses a sentimental poem; the frame is decorated with sprigs of cedar wedged behind it. The photographer's flash has momentarily illuminated the readers' papers, which were otherwise lit only by the light of a single kerosene lamp.

The images thus far in this chapter have represented the public spaces of group living homes; other photographs show the private areas of these facilities. In 5.8, a boarder poses in the sitting area of his room with two captain's chairs, a Boston rocker, and a table topped with a plant, books, and magazines. A spittoon rests nearby. The dressing area, illuminated by an electric light, is marked by a concentration of embellishments: an impressive string of ties, dresser scarves, and portrait photographs of women. The sleeping area has been set off by a screen, behind which the canopy of a bed is just visible. Selling for about $1 in 1905, the fabric screen separates social from private functions; in addition to serving as a barrier, it acts as a hallstand for the boarder's umbrella and hat. The apparent lack of storage and space has induced creative solutions; besides the wall decoration of ties and the screen/hallstand, the mirror reflects a rack of clothes hanging behind a fabric-curtained closet. What appear to be a commercial print and a calendar adorn otherwise bare walls.

5.8. Bedroom/sitting room, Unidentified boardinghouse, La Grange, ca. 1905 (Fayette Heritage Museum and Archives, La Grange).

In contrast to the bedroom in the Digby-Roberts house (see fig. 3.14) in which sleeping, dressing, and relaxing activities also occurred, this boardinghouse room is vastly different. The decade between the two images accounts for only part of the difference. The boarder probably has no place to entertain other than the communal parlor, and so the screen blocks his bed from visitors' view; his niche serves public and private functions. But the Digby-Roberts family had a number of other rooms for entertaining;

there was no need to shield the bed within the room. A family could and did lavish decorating energies on their bedroom, selecting and purchasing wallpaper and floor coverings and creating family shrines of sorts; by contrast, a boarder is a transient tenant, and the owner of the building has no reason to lavish attention on the room's finishes. While a tenant may make a valiant attempt to express his identity, he usually brings only a limited number of personal objects, so no distinct statement of taste emerges in his decoration.

In another rented room (fig. 5.9) in an unidentified structure, an older woman tries to keep warm in December 1914 in Dallas. Her lap blankets are in place, a heating stove is nearby, and a supply of wood is under the corner table. With a dog as a companion, the woman sits in the small space not occupied by her disheveled bed (a slop jar or chamber pot showing beneath it), pine nightstand, side chair, and table. She rests her feet on a small rug, the only floor covering visible on the unfinished pine floors.

The popular medallion-pattern wallpaper falls away from its canvas backing, now poorly fitting the corners of the rented room. The woman has, nevertheless, personalized the room with artistically arranged wall-hung accessories — trade cards and fans of paper and straw advertising the goods and services of the marketplace.

Not all inhabitants of boardinghouses were single adults. Photographer Ed Irwin may have captured the scene of his children at bedtime in an unspecified house (fig. 5.10). Two of the youngsters stop their pillow fight just long enough to pose for the camera, while a third child seems to sleep on the quilt-covered bedstead. The anonymous look of the room's decoration and its multiple beds support the notion that the space is in a boardinghouse. The room is filled with inexpensive furnishings: the wooden bedstead, for example, simply decorated with a crest and incising, is similar to those available through

5.9 (facing page). Bedroom, Unidentified boardinghouse, Dallas, December 1914 (Dallas Historical Society). **5.10 (above).** Bedroom, Unidentified Texas boardinghouse, possibly Fort Worth (believed to be room of photographer Ed Irwin and his family), ca. 1905 (Amon Carter Museum, Fort Worth).

mail-order catalogues for $3. Rag carpets and animal-skin rugs (the latter often photographers' props) cover the floor. The only other visible furnishings include a child's colonial revival rocker and a child's fancy chair, both lined with dolls and toys. A man's leg, visible behind the stove, suggests that a lounge or other "adult" seating is just out of the camera's view.

An entire family apparently lives in this room (or rooms). They have hung two large, framed, family crayon portraits, a promotional poster, a map, and a commercial

5.11. Unidentified dormitory room, A&M College (Texas A&M University), College Station, ca. 1900 (Author's collection).

calendar in an effort to personalize their temporary quarters.

Dormitory rooms were often distinctively personalized by their inhabitants. In one turn-of-the-century view, two pipe-smoking Aggies, the picture of urbanity, sit in their Texas A&M College quarters (fig. 5.11). The light walls, dark window shades, picture molding, and radiator serve as backdrop for a collection of collegiate banners. The interior decoration of the room attests to the occupants' strong identification as college students, fraternity brothers, and team members. The enthusiastic use of banners and photographs belies the restraint of the posed pair.

Clad in smoking jackets and sitting amid their picturesque items, the men read and write under a shaded, clear electric bulb, at least for as long as it took the photographer to snap the photo. The two are inventive in using their Corps epaulets as window curtain adornments and wall decorations; one epaulet even supports a photograph. The pair's connections to other people are visible around the room — from the group photograph of the football team hanging above the dresser to the two group photos hanging on the curtains. The fashionable young woman in Japanese garb posed in front of a Japanese screen may have made the decoupaged oval wall plaque of a Gibson Girl playing golf or embroidered the pillow with "AMC Rah! Rah! Rah!" Only a few commercial prints find space in the crowded corner; photographs of friends and family adorn the dresser and tabletops.

Women decorated their dormitory walls with different strategies, as the room of Carrie Hofer and May Virginia Warden shows (fig. 5.12). The young women have transformed their small space into a convivial and visually coherent room. They have segregated the wall-hung pictures according to gender: photos of men, mostly baseball players, occupy one wall; group portraits of women, probably fellow Nazareth Academy students, share the wall with

5.12. Dormitory room, Nazareth Academy, 206 West Convent Street, Victoria, 1910 (Nazareth Academy, Victoria, and Institute of Texan Cultures, San Antonio). The back of the photograph is inscribed: "Carrie Hofer and May Virginia Warden's room in 1910 — at Naz. as a boarder / afterwards May Va. became sister Loyola — and Carrie died on Feb 27 — 1910."

the window; homemade wall pockets and commercial prints of women fill the third wall. Other decorations cluster on the dresser, including a fan, strings of cards and bags, photographs, a pincushion, a hair receiver, jewelry boxes, and a photograph of a mother and child juxtaposed with a print of a madonna and child. The effect of all the decorations is to deemphasize the small floor space crowded with seven pieces of furniture — colonial revival rocking chairs, side chair, washstand, table, dresser, and bed. Unlike figure 5.11, this room has only a kerosene heater and bare light bulb.

Another photograph of an A&M student snapped in

5.13. Dormitory room, Harvey Perrin's room, A&M College (Texas A&M University), College Station, ca. 1912 (Beulah Margaret Perrin Hoch and Institute of Texan Cultures, San Antonio).

1912 reveals limited personalization of space (fig. 5.13). Harvey Perrin, an engineering student, presents himself as a surveyor, ready for fieldwork.[6] His room reflects his temporary and changing condition. This candid shot indicates that he normally keeps a fringed throw (an anomalous affectation in his spartan room) on the table that functions at once as a desk and a dining, kitchen, and parlor table. The flooring is of unfinished and uncovered pine planks; the painted walls are embellished with only a few unframed pictures. The bare washstand contrasts with the slim, overburdened wardrobe/hallstand on which Perrin uses all available space: books are piled on top, a clothes bag hangs to one side, and an overcoat, a jacket, and a shoe caddy obscure its front. A side chair, a stove, and a bed complete the furnishings of the single occupant's room.

From this modest abode, Perrin went on to become president and manager of the Southern Cement Products

5.14. Dormitory room, Henry J. Lutcher Stark's room, University of Texas campus, 1903 Whitis Avenue (or 311 West 21st Street), Austin, 1905 – 1910 (Nelda C. and H. J. Lutcher Stark Foundation, Orange).

Company of San Antonio. His company supplied "art stone" for Smith Brothers Hotel, Westmoorland College and dormitory, San Pedro High School in San Antonio, the Highland Park Church of Christ in Dallas, and the De George Hotel in Houston.[7]

"Collegiate cosmopolitan" describes the decor of Lutcher Stark's dormitory room of a few years earlier (figs. 5.14 through 5.17). Both while a student at the University of Texas from 1905 to 1910 and later as an alumnus, Stark was an enthusiastic booster.[8] Banners of the universities of Wisconsin, Cornell, Lehigh, Bowdoin, and Michigan, among others, show that he identified strongly with collegians. On the 1905/1906 campus of 1,991 students, Stark found a niche for himself within Phi Gamma Delta fraternity — banners and flags announce his membership; formal group photographs and individual portraits of fraternity brothers adorn his walls.[9]

Figure 5.14 shows the view that greeted Stark's visitors.

GAMMA DELTA
TEXAS

A mission bookcase and a piano, the latter perhaps relating less to refinement than to conviviality, flank the entrance. Figure 5.15 is taken from the other end of the room. Figure 5.16 provides a closer look at the piano wall and documents that for the photograph Stark has decorated the only unadorned surfaces in the room, placing an illustration of collegiate athletes on one window shade and an additional banner of his fraternity on the other shade. Figure 5.17 shows a doorway leading to his bedroom.

A flamboyant Japanese parasol "floats" above the library table, almost concealing the moire ceiling paper. Stark has combined the oriental parasol with Native American motifs that were part of the arts and crafts style. Navaho rugs cover the room's wooden floors; a portrait of an "Indian" painted on leather hangs in the corner by the stove (fig. 5.15). The furnishings — leather-cushioned armchair, rocker, bookcases, library table, table lamps, candlesticks, desk, and sofa — are all in the mission style.

Few university students could afford such fine furnishings, but Stark was not an average student. His grandfather had come from Pennsylvania to Texas where "he found a fortune in the pineys of southeastern Texas."[10] The family's prospering lumber business allowed grandson Lutcher to live well, as this room attests. The room displays no overt family identity; the presence of his wealthy family is conveyed by the quality and "newness" of his furnishings.

The UT booster was a sportsman of sorts. Fellow students and alumni of the University of Texas recall his fashionable and expensive sports car, a Stutz Bearcat, but his enthusiasm for automobiles appears earlier in the sports car image tacked to his college-room closet door (fig. 5.17). A hunting enthusiast, Stark displays several tripods of rifles, pictures of sportsmen, and a pyrography plaque of a hunting scene.[11]

5.15 (facing page) and 5.16 (above). Dormitory room, Henry J. Lutcher Stark's room, University of Texas campus, 1905–1910 (Nelda C. and H. J. Lutcher Stark Foundation, Orange).

PHI GAMMA DELTA
TEXAS
TEXAS

★ ★ ★ ★

The nature of shared living space affected the use and decoration of rooms. Photographs indicate that public spaces of shared living quarters, such as boardinghouses or hotels, served various functions; this is reflected in their furnishings and appearance. Many such rooms exhibit a diffuse, additive quality in their decoration. In private spaces of group housing, photographs of bedrooms show that inhabitants made an effort to personalize the rooms; sometimes the efforts were successful, but often they were not. Dormitory rooms are in a different category. In personalizing their space, students identified with their families, but they also identified with those in the group with whom they lived, studied, and socialized.

5.17 (facing page). Dormitory room, Henry J. Lutcher Stark's room, University of Texas campus, 1905 – 1910 (Nelda C. and H. J. Lutcher Stark Foundation, Orange).

6

The Alamo, the Lone Star, and the Confederacy

REGION

REGIONAL identification was often indicated by furnishings, decorative motifs, building materials, and accommodation to the climate. Louis Melcher of LaGrange fashioned settees and center tables from the horns of Texas longhorn cattle and filled his parlor with the furniture — the room asserts its cattle-country origin. Elements in a landscape — the Piney Woods of East Texas, for example — were used as decorative motifs in the McLean house in Crockett and the Robinson house in Rockhill. Pine lumber was an essential building material in the Marsh house in Livingston. The manner in which architecture and furnishings accommodate the climate is also a regional clue.

6.1 (left). Living room, King Ranch house, three miles west of Kingsville, 1915 (King Ranch Archives).

Patriotic objects in a room often indicate loyalties associated with place. For example, some Texans who served in the Confederate army during the Civil War and some who did not expressed allegiance to the Lost Cause by using icons of the Civil War in their parlors and offices decades after the conflict (see figs. 6.2, 6.3, 7.14, 10.1, 11.18, 12.2, 12.6). In the late nineteenth century, the cult of the Lost Cause, developed as former Confederate states nostalgically reinterpreted the Civil War, was one element of the search for a national past that occupied many Americans. Further, the King Ranch house living room in South Texas — its rug emblazoned with the Texas flag and a painting of the Alamo prominently displayed over the hearth — is unlikely to be home for anyone living in Minnesota or New York.

In the living room of Santa Gertrudis, or the King Ranch house (fig. 6.1), against a backdrop of "gray and cream" walls, rattan chairs, leather-seat side chairs, and cane chairs hover at the perimeter. The furnishings leave bare the geometric-border rug, woven in Austria, that features the Lone Star flag. Overhead, the barrel vault creates an openness in the room. Pargetry of intersecting lines and connecting squares with corner fleurs-de-lis and central paterae decorate the ceiling. Adorned with deep red hangings, the window cornices echo the bend of the ceiling arch, as they shape rather than block the entry of the South Texas sun.[1]

In the foreground, a fireplace with a cast-stone mantel provides a visual focus for the large, long room that opens expansively to the out-of-doors. The mantel holds silver trophies won by the Santa Gertrudis breed of cattle, introduced, raised, and made famous by the ranch. Over the mantel hangs a painting of the Alamo, one of several Spanish missions that appear in Central and South Texas houses (see figs. 2.12, 10.24).

When Alice King, youngest daughter of Captain Richard King, the founder of the ranch, married Robert Justus Kleberg in 1888, their union combined two old Texas families. The Klebergs had emigrated from Germany to Galveston in 1834 seeking political freedom; New York native Captain King had begun to build his "mesquite fiefdom" in Texas in 1852 starting with a not-so-modest 75,000 acres. Under King's and later Kleberg's direction, the King Ranch flourished, with 90,000 head of cattle grazing on its 1.2 million acres at the time this photograph was taken.[2]

When the family's Italianate house burned in 1912, they hired San Antonio architects Carlton W. and Carl C. Adams, of Adams and Adams, to build a Spanish villa on the same site, three miles west of Kingsville. They selected the Tiffany studios of New York to provide art glass windows and to supply most of the "hardware, lighting fixtures, interior decorations and furnishings."[3] Located close to Mexico, the house draws upon Spanish colonial architectural sources. The open vistas of the interior space complement the flat country outside and subtly relate to the Texas landscape.

Robert E. Lee once told Captain King, "Buy land and never sell."[4] Since the family eventually accumulated more than 1.5 million acres, the general's advice was well-taken. The Texas family kept a framed oval portrait of Lee on the office desk (fig. 6.2). When discontent in Europe presaged the outbreak of the "war to end all wars," Lee's portrait perhaps reminded users of the office of an earlier war and a general's sage advice.

Lee's image is not the only reference to that lost war nor the most central in this room. On the cast-stone mantel sits a framed picture of crossed flags: the national flag of the Confederacy and the Stars and Bars, the Confederate battle flag.

Harking back to a still earlier conflict, a 1906 photograph of the survivors of the Texas battle for independence (1835 – 1836) rests at the far right of the mantel.[5] During a reunion in Goliad, photographer C. A. Major made the image; he reproduced it and sold souvenir copies for $1 each. The picture kept alive the memory of San Jacinto, the eighteen-minute battle of April 21, 1836, that became a symbol of the Texas victory over Mexico, avenging the defeats at the Alamo and at Goliad.

When Kleberg's parents, Robert Justus and Rosa von Roeder Kleberg, emigrated from Germany, their early years in Texas coincided with the Texas struggles with Mexico. Robert Kleberg and the von Roeder brothers fought at the battle of San Jacinto. Rosa lived through the Runaway Scrape, later writing a compelling account of the flight of families around Harrisburg (now Houston) from the oncoming Mexican army.[6] The younger Kleberg's identification with family and the vision of Texas' romantic past was strong.

Robert Kleberg was largely responsible for the prosper-

6.2. Office, King Ranch house, 1915 (King Ranch Archives).

ity of the King Ranch during the late nineteenth and early twentieth centuries.[7] Not only a supporter of the Confederacy and a Texan, Kleberg identified with his family, joining his two brothers Rudolph and Marcellus in a portrait photograph prominently displayed on top of the mantel clock.[8] He was also part of the King family, whose identity is expressed both in the wooden or plaster medallion flanked by garlands and on the wreathed cast-stone reproduction of the King Ranch brand, the Running "W," which simultaneously announced his occupational identity as a cattleman.

The well-finished room features wainscoting, medium field and picture molding topped with a lighter painted frieze and ceiling blended by a graduated molding. Shades

6.3. Multipurpose room, Lavonia Archer house, Mount Calm, April 1904 (Barker Texas History Center, Austin).

cover double-hung sash windows and screens; Kleberg could draw the shades at the transoms by pulling the routed cord hanging at the sides of the windows. Navaho rugs cover the floor. A leather-cushioned mission rocker matches the leather-covered daybed.

Kleberg's desk is cluttered with a predictable array: a map under glass — probably of the King Ranch itself — books, small boxes, tray, ruler, file, calendar, whisk broom, letter holder, message spike, ledger, electric lamp, and bullet mold. He is reading in his office, the fireplace cleaned and outfitted with its summer garb, newspapers spread beneath the andirons. His spittoon is across the room — too far away to be immediately functional and apparently too distant to catch Kleberg's toss of crumpled paper.

In the northern Central Texas community of Mount Calm a decade earlier, another interior includes items that signify the occupants' identification with a political region (fig. 6.3). Photographer Joseph E. Taulman has pictured his mother-in-law, Lavonia Archer, in a setting expressive of the Southern identity of both sides of the family. Two framed prints flanking the mantel clock demonstrate Archer's Southern sympathies during the Civil War. One print depicts Robert E. Lee and his horse, Traveller, the other, Lee surrendering to Ulysses S. Grant at Appomattox. Taulman himself subscribed to the Southern journal, *Confederate Veteran*, and so shared Archer's loyalties.[9]

The presence of the spinning wheel relates to a turn-of-the-century interest in the past, as do the colonial revival decorations. Across the nation, Americans alluded to the nation's colonial past by displaying candlesticks and setting out cradles; the spinning wheel proved the most popular and enduring of all colonial items. Taulman, who took the photograph for a competition in London, was capitalizing on the interest in the past — a past that included an idealized version of colonial life and the heroes of the more recent Civil War.

Taulman's image, a sort of Whistler's Mother (*Arrangement in Black and Gray*, 1871) of the southwestern frontier, has been frequently reproduced on educational posters and in Texas history books to illustrate a much earlier period in the state's history.[10] He unwittingly created an image of the archetypal pioneer Texas woman of the 1830s or 1840s, or at least fed the myth. The wall and floor finishes and the use of the fireplace for cooking might recall the colonial past, but other elements — such as the store-bought broom and the milled floorboards — indicate a later date as surely as the April 1904 calendar on the wall.

The mantel treatment especially points to the late nineteenth or early twentieth century. A lambrequin has been pinned to the shelf and embellished with embroidered flowers. The mantel supports dozens of glass bottles, and a stenciled shade covers the window. Other objects — handmade ladder-back chairs with hide seats, walking cane, *Farmer's Almanac*, shotgun, and old notions box — are less easily dated.

Region and style combine with occupation at Archer's carding cotton. A spinner and a weaver, she may have made the floorcloth using her own cotton crop.

Familial and occupational identities of the photographer also emerge from the motives of the picture taking. Taulman posed the sitter to achieve an exhibition-quality image. The photographer therefore is more "present" than in many other interior views. He labeled this image "Home," and the reverse side specified:

> Printed on Aristo Platino paper in sunlight. After washing through a number of waters to get the free silver out, all these Platino prints were toned in a gold bath, then into a "short stop" of water, then in a platinum bath to get the desired color, then another wa-

ter bath, then a "fixing bath," then wash, wash, wash, in clear water — and *that is not all!*

Another aspect of regional identity was expressed in the Texas Governor's Mansion. In Austin, the state capital, Thomas M. Campbell of Palestine served as governor of Texas from 1907 to 1911, during which time he, his wife, Fannie, three daughters, and one son occupied the Governor's Mansion. Two interior photographs show the home as it was decorated for a New Year's reception held by the Campbells as first family (figs. 6.4, 6.5). The rooms exhibit a political identity: a bust of Sam Houston — romantic political leader and certified hero — sculpted by German Texan artist Elisabet Ney, presides over this space from its pedestal in the corner.

To the left of the fireplace, Governor Campbell added a trompe l'oeil still life, a newspaper fragment of the *Dallas Morning News* of August 17, 1906, which expresses his personal political identity and achievement (fig. 6.4). Artist Bernhard Gordon based his image on a headline announcing "The Campbells Have Come"; the accompanying article relates how Campbell won the nomination of the Democratic party for governor.[11] The painting may also represent the Campbells' attempt to give the room a sense of family identity. Most other furnishings were provided with the dwelling. Governor and First Lady of Texas from 1899 to 1903, Joseph D. and Orline Sayers had selected many of them. The piano, typically a valued family object, was a new Starr baby grand "on loan for advertising."[12]

Bernhard Gordon's painting is balanced by an unidentified picture and a popular horizontal floral still life sold through mail-order houses at the turn of the century for about $1. This popular still life appears in photographs of several Texas homes, above fireplace mantels and bedsteads (see figs. 3.17, 8.20). Both original works of art and inexpensive mass-produced prints were used in decorating Texas houses.

A moire wallpaper covers the wall above and below the picture molding. The crown molding of anthemia and a central heraldic emblem were added to the mansion during Sayers' tenure, as was the grille above the doorway (visible in the mirror reflection) separating the double parlors.[13]

The windows are draped with lace curtains, each framed with an asymmetrical festoon, probably fashioned of silk. The panel is an unusually formal window treatment for Texas homes, yet it is suitable for the Governor's Mansion.[14] Holiday decorations include wreaths hanging at the windows. Vines of smilax trim the picture molding and trail down the combination gas-and-electric fixture. A bank of calla lilies fills one corner, their bases camouflaged with pillows and tissue paper; palms are clustered in the opposite corner. Cut flowers adorn the piano and small center table, and potted azaleas line the mantel. If the plants were removed, the room would look fashionably bare.

Fannie Campbell gained favor with Texans by the manner in which she spent appropriations to improve the Governor's Mansion. She felt that the people's money should be spent in beautifying the grounds of the mansion — for Texans to enjoy — rather than the interior that would be seen only by the family, declaring that the mansion's interior decoration was already "good enough for anybody."[15] The civic-minded First Lady was undoubtedly influenced, as were many other Americans, by the City Beautiful movement that was peaking at this time. The same impulse prompted the landscaping of the nearby Capitol grounds.

The interior of the Governor's Mansion was quite elegant and certainly "good enough for anybody." The sofa, chairs, and table were relatively recent purchases. The so-

6.4. Parlor, Governor's Mansion during Thomas M. Campbell's tenure, Northeast corner of Mesquite (Eleventh) and Colorado streets, Austin, 1908 – 1911 (Courtesy Mr. and Mrs. Drew Wommack).

6.5. Library, Governor's Mansion, 1908 – 1911 (Courtesy Mr. and Mrs. Drew Wommack).

called art pieces, the light table and the chair by the fireplace, as well as the other more ponderous seating pieces in "period" styles were less than a decade old.

For the holiday the bust of Sam Houston is bedecked with a cedar necklace after its relocation to the library to preside over the less formal space (fig. 6.5). A small framed print of a camel, the Campbell family totem, rests by the fireplace. The sturdy leather-upholstered rocking chair and armchair and the American Empire center table contribute to the room's decoration. The library walls and floors are covered with bold patterns. An art nouveau-inspired paper lines the walls above the chair rail, and a sunflower pattern, possibly embossed, covers the walls below. The carpeting features a conventionalized floral design and the sinewy lines of art nouveau.

Decorated for the same New Year's reception as the parlor, the library is also brightened with calla lilies. The flowers define the fireplace and, in a jardiniere on a Moorish stand, or taboret, mark a passageway leading to the adjacent dining room. A ribboned wreath hangs in front of lace curtains framed by overcurtains with matching borders and tiebacks. Flowers decorate the mantel and overmantel with its paired columns and spindled gallery.

The style of some of the room's furnishings suggests recent purchase; the seating pieces and the pedestal table date to the turn of the century, and the gas-and-electric ceiling fixture is also new. Other objects, however, seem to have long furnished the mansion. An earlier neo-Grec pier mirror (partially concealed by a plant, jardiniere, and stand) hangs between the windows.

In addition to expressing regional identity by incorporating political displays, householders also expressed identification with place by using indigenous materials for the construction and decoration of houses. Often, using native materials was merely pragmatic. But in some instances it was a self-conscious celebration. Craftsman Louis Melcher used the horns of Texas longhorn cattle to fashion a variety of forms — inkstands, footstool, bud vase, table, and settee — to decorate his home. He introduced variety by adding the racks of Central Texas deer to large wall plaques (fig. 6.6).

One interior view of Melcher's house, too poor an image to reproduce, shows a bay with a furniture "gallery" of sorts. The space is filled with horn objects against a backdrop of patterned ceiling, frieze, wallpapers, and wall-to-wall carpet. Melcher's exuberant wares included hallstands, armchairs, clockstands, and picture frames. The numbers on many objects suggest that the photograph served as a catalogue from which buyers could place orders.

For Melcher, photography and making furniture complemented one another; he used the former to promote the latter. Crafting horn furniture was a moneymaking effort, a sideline to his photography business, but in addition he furnished his home with the objects he created. Their advertising potential aside, Melcher's horn furniture suggests an expansive spirit intoxicated with the abundant natural resources of the Texas land.

In his parlor Melcher's horn furniture mingles easily with manufactured goods from distant factories: the horn couch with its plush upholstery sits next to the platform rocker with its patchwork upholstery. Since mid century middle-class Americans favored the mix of store-bought with handmade objects. The room features other contrasts. Cut flowers join dried grasses in glass vases. A mundane object like a hearth brush hangs near a highly ornamented, although badly fitted, mantel lambrequin.[16] Late-nineteenth-century Americans enjoyed contrasts that gave the decorated spaces movement and play, causing occupants visually to sort such juxtapositions.

Few, if any, rooms in Texas houses resembled Melcher's parlor, and few Texans embraced wholeheartedly his brand of regionalism. Instead, families sought other forms of regional expression. Two East Texas homes, those of the McLeans and the Robinsons, show how residents appropriated a strong feature of the area's geography into their house decoration. Daniel and Jennie McLean built their Crockett home in 1903, ordering stock house plans from an advertisement in a magazine, a relatively common practice at that time. A merchant, McLean frequented the St. Louis market, selecting items for his general store. On buying trips, he purchased many of the furnishings — carpets, wall coverings, and furniture — for his home.[17]

In 1908, McLean posed with his nephew in the entry hall (fig. 6.7). They sit against a backdrop of a boldly outlined landscape wallpaper. According to family tradition, the pattern made the paperhanger so homesick that after completing this job, he returned to Germany; the wallpaper is one of the landscape papers so popular between 1905 and 1915.[18] This and other tree-filled wallpapers may have recalled German landscapes, but they also mirrored timbered East Texas. That East Texas residents favored such papers suggests a regional preference — an attempt to recreate the out-of-doors inside their homes. Especially in an entry hall, the landscape paper marks the transition between natural forests outside and the areas of culture, the parlor and dining room, inside.

The McLeans' boldly patterned paper almost obscures the framed prints, which in stair-step formation mark the ascent of the stairway. Also nearly lost in the wallpaper forest are small, matted and framed scenes and the large print of a stag, a favorite subject for halls and other traditionally masculine domestic spaces, including the dining room. It is no accident that the men are positioned beneath the stag image on the dining room side of the hall, while McLean's daughter sits at the piano on the parlor side of the hall (fig. 6.8).

The original of figure 6.7 was labeled to explain the pairing: "Dan & 'Buster' he is a beautiful child but you cant tell a thing about his picture. He stays with us as much as at home." The comment reveals a strong family identity. The photograph reveals another identity — the pillow, topped with a fabric in a shamrock design, recalls the ethnic identification of the Irish McLeans.

Frequently in Texas houses (as well as in those of other states) during the period 1890 – 1910, the pairing of stands and plants at doorways mark a transition between differentiated space (see figs. 6.5, 7.2, 8.3, 8.20). In the McLean house, the stands and potted plants signal the entrance to the dining room and the living room; they relieve the angle of the door and create "picturesque" thresholds. This practice probably occurred more often during the summer months, when there were no portières at the doorways to soften the angles.

The McLeans furnished their dining room in a combination of styles. The sideboard, dining table, and chairs were considered colonial revival; the wallpaper features a grapevine design above the plate rail and an arts and crafts muted stripe below. Although many of the portières and draperies have been removed for the summer, the dining room curtains remain, fastened asymmetrically at each window but forming a symmetrical wall grouping with the china cabinet. A bordered medallion rug covers the floor, and a striped fabric serves as tablecloth. While the McLean family is not celebrating any obvious occasion, a crepe-paper bell dangles from the electric fixture above the table.

The view into the parlor (fig. 6.8) shows important furnishings typical of some late-nineteenth- and early-twentieth-century entry halls: a hallstand, holding umbrella and hat, and a table with a card receiver, hat, shell, and vase. The view also reveals some of the parlor's furnishings: piano, pedestal, armchair, two rocking chairs in the

6.6. Parlor, Louis Melcher house, La Grange, 1893 (Barker Texas History Center, Austin).

6.7. Entry hall into dining room, Daniel McLean house, 1105 East Houston Avenue, Crockett, 1908 (Courtesy Mr. and Mrs. Wilson E. Hail, Jr.).

colonial revival style, plant, and stand. The machine-woven pillow-cover design, a pastoral scene based on Jean-François Millet's painting *The Angelus* (1855 – 1857) is a reference to the arts and crafts movement. Romanticizing the life of peasants and elevating the role of handcrafted work were prominent themes in the ideology of the arts and crafts movement; similar images appear in other Texas interiors (see figs. 4.14, 9.12).

The parlor wallpaper consists of a wide and subtly shaded striped background in an overall moire pattern. The floor covering differs from that in the other two rooms, contrasting with the large, dark hall rug, which has a medallion border and probably a center medallion in the solid field, and with the overall pattern of alternating large and small medallions with a matching border in the dining room. The parlor carpet features a bouquet design on a light background, not an unusual choice. But the way it is installed is unusual, with a portion of the body of the

6.8. Entry hall into parlor, Daniel McLean house, 1908 (Courtesy Mr. and Mrs. Wilson E. Hail, Jr.).

carpet laid over the threshold on the other side of the border.

At the windows, dark shades are drawn and bare curtain rods bespeak lace curtains that inevitably were rehung every autumn and winter. The back of the photo notes: "The front windows in parlor and dining room do not show in pictures and they add so much to the looks of the rooms. I have all my curtains and draperies down for the summer too so the rooms do not look their best."

Also in East Texas was the home of Kentuckian Joe E. Robinson, who served in the Union army during the Civil War and afterward settled in Rockhill near Carthage. He prospered in the lumber business and owned several sawmills by the time he and his family posed for the photograph (fig. 6.9). In a room that functions as both a bedroom and a sitting room, Robinson is pictured with his wife, Irene Hays Cordray Robinson, and his daughter, Jo, from a previous marriage.[19]

6.9. Bedroom/sitting room, Joe E. Robinson house, Rockhill Community, 1905 – 1910 (Courtesy John W. Cordray).

A textile-pattern frieze, modeled on moire, encircles the room and probably covers the ceiling. A landscape wallpaper lining the walls beneath the frieze makes the space distinctive. With forests surrounding them, the family might just as well be sitting outside their home in deep East Texas. While showing the family's fashionable taste, the paper recreates the woods that were Robinson's stock-in-trade.

Irene has pinned the guilloche-pattern lace curtains directly on the wall above the window; fringed shades hang below. In addition to the crayon portraits, a railroad map of Texas and a commercial calendar compete with the landscape paper. In contrast to the boldly patterned paper, strips of grass matting cover the floor, interrupted only by a small rug at the organ.

The room's furniture includes an oak bedstead with shallow-carved leaf and scroll designs applied to the flat surfaces of the bedstead. Robinson reads the newspaper in a leather-upholstered rocker, while his daughter sits primly in a side chair and his wife poses in a Morris chair. Placed diagonally across a corner in the room, the parlor organ displays two curled elk horns, symmetrically positioned. Juxtaposing nature and artifice, the Robinsons embellished the organ, a symbol of refinement, with animal trophies.

Using the plentiful natural resources of East Texas, the Manton Edward Marsh family fashioned a log structure in the heart of the area's Piney Woods (fig. 6.10). The same trees that provided the McLeans and the Robinsons with decorative motifs supplied this family with the material for the structure and the room finishes. Unpapered, unpainted, and unvarnished ceilings, walls, and floors define the dwelling. Located near what is now the Sam Houston National Forest in southern East Texas, the house was built in 1853.[20] Members of the family occupied the log cabin between the time it was built and the time of this circa 1905 photograph.[21]

Local woods also provide the household furnishings. The ladder-back chairs with hide seats and the bed in the far corner were locally made; the mirrored bureau, turned bedstead, and rocking chair may also be of local manufacture. The pine tables covered with oilcloths in the adjacent "shed room," which functions as a kitchen and dining area, were also probably locally made.

6.10. Bedroom/sitting room, Manton Edward Marsh house, Livingston, ca. 1905 (Special Collections, Ralph E. Steen Library, Stephen F. Austin State University, Nacogdoches).

With the exception of the bed linens, the room appears devoid of textiles: the window on the fireplace wall, lacking both glass and textiles, is covered only with a hinged panel. Light streams in through the windows and down from the brick-and-stone chimney, which is short and open.

The mantel clock, given its position and size, appears to be a valued artifact, sharing a shelf with medicine bottles, books, and boxes. More accessories cluster on the bureau than on the mantel, including a crayon portrait of Cinthia (or Cynthia) A. Marsh and a print of grazing cows, the latter in a handmade frame of unfinished tree bark. Wall pockets of tin, leather, and wood hang by both the bureau and the bed providing storage and decoration. The *Farmer's Almanac* is a ready reference pinned on the wall (see fig. 6.3).

In contrast to the wide-plank pine floors, ceiling, and walls of the Marsh house in East Texas, the Charles Otis and Minnie Mae Finley house in wood-barren far West Texas is finished with plaster walls over adobe and narrow wooden boarding on the floor and ceiling (fig. 6.11). Without the wood from which to fashion furniture, imports were necessary. The Finleys purchased two unmatched rocking chairs, a piano, and a stool. Despite its small size, the room accommodates the upright piano. Partially blocking the doorway, the piano is positioned under a crayon portrait of Finley's parents. Its double drape consists of a decoratively patterned and fringed scarf under a heavier cloth that protects the instrument from the dust of West Texas.

6.11 (facing page). Parlor, Charlie Otis and Minnie Mae Finley house, near Valentine, September 1902 (Archives of the Big Bend, Alpine).

Within the spartan room, the mantel holds a comparatively elaborate assemblage. A sawtooth-edge, marble-pattern oilcloth lambrequin provides the shelf cover upon which rest medicine bottles, a kerosene lamp, shells, ceramic vases, and matching frames with photographs of daughters Zora and Florence. A decorative figure of a dog stands atop the neoclassical-revival-style mantel clock, similar to those advertised by Sears, Roebuck as ornaments suitable "for mantels or the tops of mantel clocks."[22] The 1902 calendar features a dog and a cat, reminiscent of the sentimental *Dignity and Impudence*, a print based on an English genre painting by Sir Edward Landseer.[23]

There is nothing sentimental about the skull hanging over the mantel. A favorite southwestern motif, the animal skull served as a naturalistic reminder of the desolation of the desert, prized as the animal trophies that hung in homes in other areas of the state and the country. This particular skull may have originally belonged to the only grizzly bear ever killed in Texas. Finley wrote about the results of a bear hunt which took place in the Davis Mountains in the autumn of 1900: "The head I took home and put in a big old washpot and boiled all the meat off of it. I scraped and cleaned it up good and hung it over our front door outside and never did expect anything to be done with it other than to be seen and admired by all guests." It was later accessioned by the Smithsonian Institution. Given the shape of the skull, the dates of the hunt and the photograph, and the pride that Finley took in the event, that bear's skull may have been included over the mantel.[24]

Three interior views (figs. 6.12, 6.13, 6.14) have been tentatively identified as the lodgings of photographer Otis A. Aultman, who settled in El Paso in 1908 and whose famous images document the Mexican Revolution.[25] Figure 6.12 features a cozy corner set off by Mexican serapes

6.12. Sitting room, Unidentified house (believed to be house of photographer Otis A. Aultman), El Paso, ca. 1910 (Southwest Collection, El Paso Public Library).

on top of which hang skins of rattlesnakes and a wildcat, a girth strap, and a print of an "Indian chief." Within the "walls," the occupant has picturesquely arranged a Mexican loom model, small Pima baskets, tomahawks, a blackware pitcher, and a flintlock pistol above a plush-covered trunk topped with pillows. The display gives the space a decidedly southwestern air. The theme is continued outside the cozy corner, with Pima baskets to the left, a miniature Apache carrying basket above the combination case, and a bow and sotol to the left of the case. A colonial revival rocking chair and the case piece, jammed with photos and statuary as a mantel might have been, fill the rest of the image.

In the second view (fig. 6.13), Navaho rugs continue the southwestern theme; a Mexican blanket covers the bed. Photographs, probably Aultman's, provide visual interest. Both textiles and photos emerge as strong decorative elements against the solid-color walls and wooden floors. Another colonial revival rocking chair, an oak library table with twist-turned legs, and two leather-seat side chairs fill this side of the room. Unlike the darkened cozy corner, natural light streams through the windows fitted with shades and short curtains. The partially visible electric ceiling fixtures provide artificial light for the sitting room; a cord from one of these powers the table lamp. In addition to the tabletop grouping, the wall space between the two windows displays an artistic arrangement of portraits and plaques. A silver-plated chafing dish on its stand bespeaks the multifunctional nature of the room.

The third view (fig. 6.14) shows a piano positioned diagonally across the corner opposite the cozy corner. Also treated like a mantel, the piano top is adorned with portrait photographs and scarves, over which are hung other accessories. The occupant has contrived an arrangement of prints and photographs between two windows. Above the

6.13. Sitting room, Unidentified house (believed to be house of photographer Otis A. Aultman), ca. 1910 (Southwest Collection, El Paso Public Library).

radiator and the coleus plant, photographs hang by ribbons, including a ladder of matted snapshots.

The adjacent room may have served as both bedroom and dining room, containing dresser, wardrobe, table and chair. Perpendicular to the sliding doors, the wardrobe possibly partitioned a sleeping area from the rest of the room. The dresser may have been shifted by the photographer to reflect his image in the mirror.

Accommodations to the climate can also be considered

6.14. Sitting room, Unidentified house (believed to be house of photographer Otis A. Aultman), El Paso, ca. 1910 (Southwest Collection, El Paso Public Library).

6.15. Entry hall, T. F. Harwood house, known as Walnut Ridge, 405 Saint Joseph Street, Gonzales, ca. 1900 (Courtesy Helen Rugeley).

regional features. J. F. Miller equipped the classical revival house he built for the T. F. Harwood family in southern Central Texas with detachable interior screen doors.[26] The screens were an accommodation to the Texas climate. Bare at the time of the photograph, the hinges on the doorjamb to the right in figure 6.15 stand ready for screens during the summer when the windows and exterior doors would be left open. With these conveniences, the Harwoods, like many families living in South and southern Central Texas and in other warm parts of the country, could take advantage of the breezes and prevent the entry of troublesome insects.

The absence of the interior screen doors in this view suggests that the photograph was taken during the winter. The silver-plated pitcher, which presumably held water during the summer, here serves a ceremonial welcoming function.

From the hall, family members and guests can enter the library to the right of the staircase or the dining room to the left. The door to the service area of the home, the kitchen, remains closed.

The entry hall has a wall-to-wall carpet with a border. Metal stair rods hold a matching runner in place. Plaster covers the upper part of the wall. The pine woodwork features egg-and-dart molding, square paterae, inset panels of curly pine, wainscoting, and parquet paneling. The dark hall is illuminated by two gas-and-electric fixtures. Sparsely furnished, the entry hall is architecturally impres-

6.16. Dining room, T. F. Harwood house, ca. 1900 (Courtesy Helen Rugeley).

sive. An arched window to one side and an oval window on the landing unify the space visually. A spreading palm, inside for the winter, tops the newel in place of statuary or a newel light.

The dining room (fig. 6.16) features long windows, arched on the outside and covered on the inside by wooden venetian blinds. The two "windows" perpendicular to the camera extend to the floor and provide passage to porches. Like the screen doors of the entry hall, the windows provide ventilation. During the winter, the dining room was heated by the radiator, probably a recent addition, given the exposed pipes; the flue cover high on the adjacent wall indicates that a stove once stood near the sideboard.

Unadorned plaster walls top the wainscoting, which encircles the room as does a picture molding. As counterpoint to the bare walls, a bordered wall-to-wall carpet provides pattern in the space. Cane-seat dining chairs line the walls. Horticultural enthusiasts, the Harwoods have placed glass and ceramic vases with fall-blooming roses from their gardens on the extension table along with a servants bell. The china cabinet supports a potted ivy plant with tendrils trailing the array. On the opposite wall, a sideboard display contrasts and complements the cornucopias of nature with rich arrangements of silver, the top shelf adorned as a mantel, with a clock, a figurine, and a pitcher. The message of this dining room is abundance.

★ ★ ★ ★

Only in parts of Texas — southern, eastern, central, and western — did a regional symbolism emerge. In many areas of the state, residents exhibited few ties to their subregion or even their political region — the state of Texas — while in other areas they perceived themselves as denizens of a distinct and desirable locale. Some symbols were worked in as background elements; others were focal points of rooms. In yet other instances the distinction between regional and occupational identities was blurred by self-conscious individual statements as in the Kleberg, Campbell, Melcher, and Aultman residences.

7.1. Parlor into sitting room, W. A. Fletcher house, "East side of W.A. Fletcher home Calder Ave. foot of Pearl Street, Double Parlor looking North," Beaumont, ca. 1900 (Courtesy Florence Fletcher Dessart).

7

Art Good Enough for Texas

REFINEMENT

IN A 1921 issue of the New York journal *Arts & Decoration*, art critic Forbes Watson related an anecdote about a woman from Texas who some twenty-five years earlier had been impressed with the *Winged Victory*. Seeing a plaster cast of the famous statue in Boston, the naif reportedly exclaimed: "There's a gal with some go, and I want to tell you right now that if that's what you all call art then art is good enough for Texas!" She promptly sent her "western village" a carload of *Winged Victorys*. "They tell me here in Boston that we haven't any art in Texas," she is supposed to have said, "but I'm going to show them that we have." Watson concluded that she represented a typical breed of Texans "seeking quick culture," who thought "that art could be canned and delivered like any other sweet preserve."[1]

Watson used the tale to establish Texans as stereotypically untutored in matters of art, but photographs reveal that, as was common across America, reproductions of artworks were popular household art in Texas throughout the 1878 – 1920 era. The gauche Texan reportedly shipped copies of the Nike of Samothrace wholesale to Texas because she identified with "a gal with some go." The *Winged Victory* may have made it to Texas, but photographs show that it was the serene *Venus de Milo* who met a readier reception in Texas houses (figs. 7.1 through 7.4).

In addition to incorporating reproductions of works of art in their interiors to signify gentility and refinement, women throughout the country decorated houses with emblems of their own musical and artistic accomplishments. Many Texans, especially women, sought to excel at the piano. As women were agents of culture in the West, so pianos functioned as marks of civilization. It is hard to overestimate the importance of the piano during this period. The instrument was often the most expensive item a householder purchased, costing $200 and more in the 1880s. The average late-nineteenth-century middle-class wage was $2.50 to $3.00 per day (or between $600 and $700 per year), so a piano represented a considerable investment.[2] Besides its monetary value, a piano had great symbolic worth, especially to frontier Americans. Many communities regarded the arrival of the first piano as a benchmark of civilization. Authors of historical monographs argue over when and who brought the first piano to Texas, and early travelers and settlers frequently noted the presence of pianos in homes visited. Amelia Barr lamented that in 1856 she knew "of only two pianos in the city of Austin."[3]

Pianos defined the space where "refined" activities took place in a home. In the parlor or a space designated as the "music room," a piano signified prosperity, accomplishment, and taste. But pianos were not the only emblems of wealth and culture. The late nineteenth century was the age of leisure: having money meant that one had time to learn to play the piano, to paint china, to practice artistic needlework, and to pursue a variety of other amateur arts. To show their refined sensibilities in the visual and textile arts, Texas women often engaged in a variety of amateur art activities like panel painting and fancy work. Cultural critic Thorstein Veblen decried what he termed "conspicuous leisure," disdainful of those who flaunted their "pecuniary ability to afford a life of idleness."[4] Nevertheless, women embraced instruction in everything from lacemaking to pyrography. And as part of domesticity, most of these skills resulted either in objects created for home display or in talents for home performance.

The W. A. Fletcher house contains many of these elements — a piano, amateur artwork, art pottery, and statuary (including the *Venus de Milo*). A pair of photographs shows the parlor and sitting room of the Fletcher family home in Beaumont near the turn of the century (figs. 7.1, 7.2). Born in 1839 in Louisiana, Fletcher served in the Confederate army and later wrote *Rebel Private, Front and Rear* about his war experiences.[5] Like his father, he was a millwright. Fletcher sold his prospering lumber business to the East Texas Kirby Lumber Company in 1901.

Objects expressive of occupational and Southern affiliations do not adorn the Fletcher parlors; instead these rooms project feminine grace and refinement. Fletcher's wife and his daughter, Valentine, were largely responsible for the appearance of the rooms. Nicknamed "Vallie," his daughter was the artist who produced some of the decorative items in the main parlor and acquired others.[6]

The Fletcher parlor features the *Venus de Milo* poised on the overmantel. On the wall facing the mantel arrangement, a canvas with a life-size figure of a spring maiden holding a flute and adorned with flowers was painted by Vallie. She may also have decorated the pillows that dot the floor, leading the viewer's eye into the space.

The decorator's hand may also have marked the interior of the Fletcher home. Like other prosperous Texans with an interest in fashion, the Fletchers may have hired a professional decorator to provide the wall, window, and floor coverings as well as other fabrics in the room. The stylish themes and matched selections of wreaths and banding in the wallpaper, carpeting, and window treatments suggest the influence of a design professional, probably from nearby Houston. The room resembles an illustration of the empire style, described by the *Decorator and Furnisher* in 1893 — some seven years before this photo was taken — featuring the wreath as an important motif.[7] Vallie and her mother may have selected the gilt chairs, called art pieces, and the colonial revival seat.

Framing each end of the parlor, the portières are the most striking feature of the room. The casual draping of the moire hides the intricate construction and careful

7.2. Parlor, W. A. Fletcher house, "Front Parlor facing Pearl Street," parlor and sitting room, Beaumont, ca. 1900 (Courtesy Florence Fletcher Dessart).

placement of the portières beneath the two grilles, as a darker shade of the fabric creates the symmetrically swagged ball-fringe valance above the side panels.

The portières demarcate the transition to spaces beyond the main room, in this instance to a bay window at one end and a sitting room at the other. The bay displays a symmetrical arrangement of potted plants, the vines trailing upward with some assistance. The sitting room or informal parlor features a piano and a Japanese screen in the fireplace. There are distinct differences between the more formal parlor and the less formal sitting room, which features a series of rugs on a hardwood floor, a simpler mantel, and a less ornate lighting device.

In the sitting room of an Austin house on Whitis Avenue near the University of Texas, another *Venus de Milo* seems to float above the heads of members of the Saturday Evening Conversation Club (fig. 7.3). Two images of a madonna and child and two floral still-life paintings dwarf a small horizontal wall hanging depicting American patriots that is almost lost amid the sprigs of the floral wall-

7.3. Sitting room, Saturday Evening Conversation Club, Whitis Avenue, Austin, 1901 (Barker Texas History Center, Austin).

paper. Like many rooms that signify refinement, this is a feminine domain both in imagery and in attendance.

Posed in a Morris chair, an upholstered sofa, a wicker rocker, and two colonial revival rocking chairs, the women have gathered around a colonial revival library table covered with the books and magazines that presumably stimulated their discussions. A wire descending from the unseen fixture electrifies the table lamp. The vase, hand decorated with a conventionalized floral design, attests to the women's artistic taste and accomplishments.

The thriving North Texas community of Honey Grove also boasted a number of impressive turn-of-the-century houses that testify that the language of refinement was spoken in smaller Texas communities as well as cities. The B. O. Walcott home in Honey Grove was built in the Queen Anne style. Photographed within several years of the Fletcher house in Beaumont and the Whitis Avenue house in Austin, the Walcott house also displays a statue of *Venus de Milo*, highlighting the piano positioned diagonally along one corner of the parlor (fig. 7.4). The Greek goddess rests on a tasseled scarf next to a cupid print. The arrangement effectively announces the artistic and musical aspirations of the Walcott women.

Across the doorway, a colonial revival armchair with

7.4. Parlor into Entry hall, B. O. Walcott house, North Fifth Street, Honey Grove, ca. 1901 (Courtesy John Black).

7.5. Parlor, B. O. Walcott house, October 18, 1904 (Courtesy John Black; Foster of Bonham, Photographer).

deeply tufted silk damask upholstery is prominently displayed; both the upholstery technique and the fabric are signals of expense. Popular wreath-pattern portières hang in the doorway, framing the view of the entry hall. The long, paneled settle is cushioned with a half-dozen pillows; over it hangs a large painting executed by a friend of the family. Like *Venus de Milo*, the painting symbolizes a refinement with which the Walcotts identify: the statue shows their appreciation of art; the tapestry signifies their connection to a network of artistic talent.

Other photographs of the Walcott home document the interiors decorated for a wedding (figs. 7.5, 7.6). In her

7.6. Entry hall, B. O. Walcott house, October 18, 1904 (Courtesy John Black; Foster of Bonham, Photographer).

1978 best-selling novel, *A Woman of Independent Means*, Elizabeth Forsythe Hailey fictionalized the life of her grandmother Bess Walcott Kendall. The real Bess Walcott married Joe Kendall in her parents' Honey Grove home on October 18, 1904. In the novel, Bess marries in 1909 and in anticipation writes: "I would like to be married in our front parlor. It is more splendid than any church in Honey Grove and I have been happier there. I imagine it will be many years before Rob and I can afford a house as fine, but I want him to know what is expected of him."[8] These photographs show the home in which Bess had grown up.

An altar of plants — palms, ferns, and geraniums —

7.7. Library, B. O. Walcott house, ca. 1900 (Courtesy John Black).

provides the backdrop against which the Walcott-Kendall wedding ceremony will take place, under an electric fixture from which three cupids dangle and netting is draped in ceremonial maypole fashion (fig. 7.5). But beyond the temporary trappings of nuptial festivities are the symbols of refinement. On the wall are prints of women and flowers: a print of Baron François Pascal Simon Gérard's *Madame Récamier*, a print of a parlor scene, a china plaque, and a woman's profile in a pyrography frame. The placement of these elements suggests that a chair, sofa, or divan normally stands in this corner. As the furniture has been rearranged to accommodate the wedding, so, too, have the mantel adornments — vase, bust, and candlestick — been shifted to make room for the clusters of vases holding cut flowers.

The Walcott parlor indicates a conscious decorative strategy, probably carried throughout the rest of the house: matching frieze and wallpaper in a medallion pattern with complementary ceiling paper, unbordered wall-to-wall carpeting, and a combination of French and colonial revival details. The family heeded critics' advice to use light colors in the parlor (and bedrooms) and darker ones in entry halls and dining rooms.

For the wedding the Walcotts moved the piano into the entry hall (fig. 7.6). Greenery climbs the balustrade, decorates the grille, and frames the keyhole arch at the end of the hallway. All the ceremonial adornment is overlaid on a space that incorporates elements of exoticism then popular in home decoration: a conquistador tops the newel, a Turkish bust sits atop the piano, and a Japanese figure is the subject of a small framed print.

The entry hall displays a pastiche of medallion-pattern wallpapers: the side paper extending up the stairs becomes a visual wainscoting, the frieze of the hall serves as a rail on the stair landing, and another pattern hangs above the border. The dark passageway is illuminated not so much by the small electric hall fixture as by the light entering the space both at the front door and at the window on the stair landing.

Another photograph shows the progression of spaces in the Walcott home — from library to parlor to sitting room (fig. 7.7). The medallion-pattern wallpapers and the distinct patterns of unbordered wall-to-wall Brussels carpeting reinforce the differentiation of spaces. Even the passageways display distinct draping: a fringed valance stretches across the top of the foreground opening, facing into the parlor; in the background doorway a symmetrical hanging of rope portières faces the parlor, while side panels drape the inside of the far room.

Yet the spaces blend because the patterns of the wall and floor surfaces are similar. A small rug covering the seam of two carpet patterns at the threshold blurs an abrupt intersection. Lace-border scarves also link the two rooms, along with the trail of pillows, if only for the purposes of this photograph. The colonial revival chairs and the table, probably placed at the doorway for the picture-taking event, serve to frame the entrance to the last room in which a leather-upholstered récamier sofa is prominently featured.[9]

The photographer shot the niche in the library at the time of Bess' wedding, evidenced by smilax topping the window and doorjambs and tucked behind a seascape print (fig. 7.8). As on the newel, a conquistador stands guard at the door into the parlor. Hanging over the shade, lace curtains have been carefully draped. Photographer Foster must have thought the corner "picturesque" since it is not the main area of wedding activity. The wall-hung accessories are satellites around the chairs. Above the fancy chair, a photograph and several prints of women punctuate the large medallion-pattern paper, while the image of a Native American stands out in a leather frame with beaded fringe.

Many Texas houses featured Native American themes, frequently introduced by means of pillow tops. In the late nineteenth and early twentieth centuries, people of northern European heritage were especially interested in and curious about exotic cultures, including Native American culture. Victorians saw simpler, "primitive" man as the antithesis of their own civilized state, which was increasingly viewed as complex, inequitable, and bellicose. The newly created academic discipline of anthropology was studying "cultures" scientifically; popular curiosity about these cultures prompted the creation of a "tame Indian" suitable for framing or decorating pillows.

7.8. Library, B. O. Walcott house, October 18, 1904 (Courtesy John Black; Foster of Bonham, Photographer).

Perhaps the most widespread sign of cultivation and leisure in homes was music. Mary Bell Stratton and Lily Moore Field, identically dressed, pose in their Waco home with four musical instruments: guitar, violin, mandolin,

7.9. Parlor, Unidentified house (probably the house of Mary Belle Stratton or Lily Moore Field), Waco, ca. 1895 (Barker Texas History Center, Austin).

and piano (fig. 7.9). Field's casual pose may be misleading; her musical ability was probably hard earned.

Decorated with shallow carving and incised panels, visually reinforced by the draping of the tasseled scarf, the piano is positioned across the corner. Ceramics adorn the adjacent mantel. A recently fashionable silk-shade kerosene floor lamp stands at the far end of the piano to illuminate the musicians' score. Photographer Joseph Taulman captured the room in the summertime: a framed portrait blocks the fireplace, a pleated lambrequin hangs low on the painted mantel, and only lace curtains drape the windows (the worn, stenciled roller blind is drawn to regulate the light for the picture-taking session). Typical of parlors, light colors pattern the walls and floors: wallpaper of floral pinwheels connected with scrolling vines covers the walls, and a conventionalized leaf-pattern carpet extends wall to wall, over which a fringed rug is placed under the piano.

Clearly a valued family possession, the piano is the primary subject of the next photo (fig. 7.10). Irish settler Michael Whelan built his house circa 1848; it was demolished in late 1901 or early 1902.[10] This photograph was probably taken in 1900. Whelan's granddaughter, Josephine O'Brien Mitchell, husband, Oscar, and daughter, Madie, lived in the home. The Mitchell family's square piano, recently inherited from Josephine's parents, was then about forty or fifty years old. Its placement against an interior door was thought to keep the instrument in tune longer, but the position may reinforce the piano's importance: the family arranged the small parlor to accommodate it and hung the pier mirror, dating from the 1870s, to help conceal the passageway. However, an accommodation to cold weather, suggested by Madie Mitchell's shawl, provides another explanation for the furniture arrangement. Like many families, the Mitchells may have closed off rooms to minimize drafts and to heat zones rather than the entire house.

The room's interior finishes consist of an unfinished

7.10. Parlor, Oscar and Josephine O'Brien Mitchell house, Southwest corner of Commerce and Empresario, Refugio, ca. 1900 (Estate of Jamie Lambert Hynes and Institute of Texan Cultures, San Antonio).

7.11. Parlor, Robert Bruce Barclay house, Beaumont Highway (one block from courthouse), Wharton, ca. 1900 (Wharton County Historical Museum, Wharton).

7.12. Sitting room, Unidentified house, possibly Galveston, ca. 1905 (Texas State Archives, Austin).

wooden floor and a painted board wall. A light animal-skin rug with a dark border (possibly dyed at home by Josephine or Madie, who may have followed suggestions to dye borders of some animal-skin rugs for a dramatic effect) is placed under the renaissance revival piano stool. Tipped out and anchored by pins, framed crayon portraits of John and Johanna O'Brien flank the door. Framed portrait photographs and a photograph album resting atop the fringed piano cover suggest strong identification with family as well as with feminine accomplishment.

A crested shadow box features a wooden cross decorated with wax flowers, which Josephine Mitchell made at the Nazareth Academy in nearby Victoria.[11] Instructions for such items were widely published during the 1880s. The photograph hints at another "female accomplishment" — playing the guitar. The picture's arrangement also bespeaks artistic skill. (The photographer, incidentally, is a woman, her skirt reflected in the mirror.)

In the photograph of the Robert Bruce Barclay parlor, the piano becomes an altar, ceremonially set apart by a bank of pillows (fig. 7.11). Since the stool is occupied by a large oriental vase and the pillows hide the pedals, this piano is meant to be seen and not heard, as a paean to refinement.

The hanging cutout paper bells and smilax indicate a wedding celebration. Roses dangle from the ceiling fixture; geraniums bedeck both the center table and the hearth. The low mantel draping and the sheer curtains at the windows suggest summertime.

In an unidentified Texas home (fig. 7.12), the piano and

a suite of wicker furniture provide the reason for picture taking. This scene is also a paean to the piano. The prominent pillow top features a bard singing and strumming to an Elizabethan lady, reinforcing the musical theme. Only a framed landscape interrupts the bold medallion-and-stripe wallpaper, a pattern that adorns the walls of many turn-of-the-century Texas interiors. The chairs are positioned atop rugs of various styles and patterns.

Refinement is not always signified by the presence of a piano. The decorative arrangements of other household objects were also important indexes of accomplishment. Circa 1900 John Henley Hill and his two daughters, Bertha and Olive, had their pictures taken in the parlor of their 1878 home (fig. 7.13). According to family tradition, the Hills purchased much of their furniture from the Huntsville penitentiary, which, having closed after the Civil War, reopened in the late 1870s about the time that Hill would have been furnishing his newly constructed house.[12] The two rocking chairs, side table, and bookcase may well have come from the prison manufactory.

The boards of the parlor's unpainted pine walls are aligned vertically rather than horizontally. The kerosene lamp is the only visible source of artificial light in the room; natural light enters through the window covered by lace curtains and a window shade. A summer floor covering — matting sewn in strips — extends wall to wall and lightens the room.

The Hills have boarded the rock fireplace for the summer and symmetrically arranged the decorative items on the unpainted mantel shelf. The large portrait of the late Susanna Hill is flanked by vases and prints framed in shellwork.

Bertha and Olive, active amateur artists, were responsible for the shellwork frames and some of the unframed landscape and still-life paintings placed below the mantel shelf and pinned to the wall. They composed the picturesque wall grouping — a trio of shellwork frames topping a "ladder" of floral prints — that extends from above eye level down to a bank of pillows.

Another sign of refinement in 1895 was the ritual of serving and drinking tea. "If there is a tea-table in the room set out with cups and saucers, banish it. The maid can bring all in from the pantry if it is the custom of the house to have afternoon tea, and if it is not the custom, no longer put up with such a ridiculous sham," wrote household decorating expert Mabel Tuke Priestman early in the new century.[13] Both Priestman's comment and this interior view of an unidentified house in Victoria, taken some ten years prior to Priestman's pronouncement, testify to the popularity of the tea-drinking ritual (fig. 7.14). A woman prepares to engage in this ceremony of polite behavior in her parlor, although she clearly has more cups than people in the room. A call button to her left allows her to summon a maid. The woman's companion displays his mark of accomplishment — a violin.

This summer view shows that the adjacent room houses the piano. The two rooms share a common wall treatment, painted plaster walls over wainscoting, and similar electric ceiling fixtures. The string portières invite rather than inhibit a peek into the adjacent room. The doorway provides a glimpse of a piano, metronomes, and a music stand as well as an architectural overmantel asymmetrically draped and adorned with small statuary.

A pair of bamboo side chairs painted white and gilded and another pair of bamboo armchairs with rush seats furnish the sitting room. A tripod, its legs "tied" with a bow and its top twice draped, stands near the center of the room. In one corner, a silk-shade kerosene floor lamp adds light to a room primarily illuminated by an electric fixture. In the left corner, a plush-upholstered armchair, asymmetrically draped, sits by the window; nearby a twist-turned pedestal supports a statue of a female figure,

7.13. Parlor, J. H. Hill house, Trinity, ca. 1900 (Courtesy Elizabeth Cauthan).

7.14. Parlor into music room, Unidentified house, Victoria, ca. 1895 (Victoria College, Victoria).

7.15. Parlor into entry hall, Alexander Rossy house, 208 Crockett Street, San Antonio, ca. 1890 (Mrs. Kenneth Terral and Institute of Texan Cultures, San Antonio).

a draped plant stand holds a palm, and a renaissance revival easel displays the portrait of an unidentified man. An image of Jefferson Davis hangs on the wall behind the easel, expressing continuing Southern loyalties.

Lace curtains in a stylized foliate design partially conceal the interior shutters. Suspended from a curtain pole mounted above the window, the single lace panel artistically trails the floor. The mantel is draped with a sunflower-pattern scarf, a reform-inspired motif. Art pottery tiles frame the fireplace. The arched art glass window above the mantel has been cut out of thick plaster walls.

Refinement could be attitude as well as activity, as seen in the pair of interior views of the Rossy house in San Antonio (figs. 7.15, 7.16). Alexander and Maria Rossy's three daughters were teachers in the city schools.[14] Two of these daughters pose in the family's parlor; the third looks

7.16. Parlor, Alexander Rossy house, ca. 1890 (Mrs. Kenneth Terral and Institute of Texan Cultures, San Antonio).

into the entry hall from the parlor, poised on the stairs, a kind of mirror image of Eastman Johnson's painting *Not at Home* (circa 1872 – 1880).

In the entry hall, a rustic plant stand and silver-plated water pitcher and glass greet visitors. To these, the Rossys have added a drape of Spanish moss, juxtaposing the "naturalness" of the stand and the moss with the "artificiality" of the manufactured pitcher and glass. In the parlor the center table arrangement echoes the same combination: on its marble top, cut flowers are placed beside a plate decorated with hand-painted morning glories.

As the presence of the piano and music cabinet suggests, the parlor is the place of refinement for the Rossy family. Both pieces block the entrance into an adjacent room, the sliding doors having been closed; the passageway is covered with festoon-pattern and fringed ready-made portières. A romantic landscape hangs above the piano on wallpaper with a foliate pattern on a dark ground. The floor covering reverses the pattern; dark flowers appear on a light field. The rug covers most of the wooden floor, exposing a foot or so around the room's perimeter.

The books, artwork, and decorating expertise exhibited in figure 7.16 attest to the women's refinement. The book on the center table is matched by another being read by one of the Rossy daughters. A large framed landscape is highlighted by its position on the easel and further distinguished by an asymmetrically draped scarf and an animal-skin rug at the base of the easel. Its decorative effect aside, this display also hides the stove. Gilt-framed landscapes and a crayon portrait adorn the wall; under these are smaller ornaments, including a small shovel tied with a satin ribbon. At the windows, lace curtains with foliate designs over lace-border roller blinds brighten and lend pattern to the Rossys' parlor. The women pose seated on their parlor suite, one of the sets of matching furniture still available circa 1890.

A decade or so later, a reflective Carrie Little sits in the parlor of her family's Victoria home, and sister Janie stands at the mirror flanking the hearth (figs. 7.17, 7.18). Neither is photographed at the piano, which is just out of view. In this pair of cabinet cards, the Court Studio photographer emphasizes portraiture of the well-dressed young women, carefully poised in the feminine domain of the parlor — they might seem out of place in a library.

Besides capturing two of Victoria's refined young ladies, the photographer has documented the Littles' dramatic scrollwork wallpaper and complementary wall-to-wall carpet. To increase the light, the photographer has folded back the linen shade underneath the lace curtains. Surprisingly, the family's furnishings resemble a photographer's props: in Carrie's photograph, the table seems less a recent purchase than an object needed to achieve an attractive composition; in Janie's picture, a silk-damask-covered side chair balances the composition. But the setting is the Littles' home and not the photographer's studio. Janie's photo shows family treasures placed on the mantel — shells, statuary, a formal wedding portrait set on a rustic easel — and a vase of roses on the mantel scarf. The room expresses fashion in both the dress and the poses of the young women.

In contrast to photos illustrating the many ways householders exhibited their identification with refinement, the 1905 photo taken in the Meredith A. Benton home in Fort Worth demonstrates two young women's efforts to debunk that aspiration (fig. 7.19).[15] They sit on a bedroom floor, exposing their legs and petticoats in what, for the time, was a rather bawdy pose. To enhance the indelicacy, the women are reading novels, a dubious pastime for young ladies. Like humorous stereographs of boudoir scenes, this image is misleading. Behind their posturing is conventional decoration that undermines the women's attempt to shock. When not reading novels, they have been

7.17. Parlor, Henrietta A. Little house, Northeast corner of North Victoria and Power streets (502 North Victoria Street), Victoria, ca. 1898 (Institute of Texan Cultures, San Antonio; Court Studio, Victoria, Photographer).

7.18. Parlor, Henrietta A. Little house, ca. 1898 (Institute of Texan Cultures, San Antonio; Court Studio, Victoria, Photographer).

engaged in culturally prescribed activities. Homemade wall plaques hang on the pale medallion wallpaper, and typical corner-draped drawnwork scarves cover the side table and the dresser. The girls have only temporarily left the rattan rocking chair in favor of a stack of pillows on the floor.

★ ★ ★ ★

In spite of a few Texans' lighthearted attempts to shock, many sought to identify themselves as cultured and accomplished: prominently displayed reproductions of great works of art, pianos, and amateur artwork helped them to do so. This aspiration reached people who lived in cities — Beaumont, Austin, San Antonio, Waco, and Victoria — and those in smaller communities like Trinity and Refugio. More signs of cultural adornment — pianos and artwork — are found in the homes of prosperous businessmen, especially those with daughters, than in the homes of less prosperous farmers; it may be, however, that successful businessmen, especially those with daughters, were more likely to photograph their rooms.

Since women were largely responsible for creating refined domestic settings in the late-nineteenth- and early-twentieth-century home, gender is a critical issue. Charged with such a mandate, women are primarily the sitters who are identified as artists or musical performers, and the objects signifying refinement are positioned in rooms considered feminine domains.

7.19 (facing page). Bedroom, Meredith A. Benton house, 1730 Potter Avenue (Sixth Street), Fort Worth, ca. 1905 (Courtesy Lois Harvey).

8

From Art Galleries to Sears, Roebuck

CLASS

PHOTOGRAPHS in this chapter illustrate that a householder's socioeconomic level was a critical variable in the decoration of domestic interiors. Many interior views show extremes — high or low income levels — which represent the range of choices people had based on their financial resources. Between these extremes, middle-class families, equally influenced by the size of their pocketbooks, identified status with their new economic circumstances as they outfitted their homes to demonstrate their inclusion in the monied ranks. Arranged for comparison and contrast, the images here date from 1892 to 1915 and explore the similarities and differences among Texas interiors.

Nineteenth-century Americans had a great range in the quality of goods available to them. Prosperous city dwellers in Houston, for example, might have access to furnishings and art objects from Europe, either because they purchased them while traveling abroad or because design professionals they hired — architects and decorators — or furniture stores they patronized had access to such furnishings. Less expensive goods from midwestern and local furniture manufacturers were available to many more Texans. And mail-order catalogues offered low-price household goods to the widest audience.

Even among these numerous sources, there were choices to be made. Furniture manufacturers carried different lines of goods of varying quality and cost. Even catalogue items could be "customized." For example, in 1897, Sears, Roebuck sold a four-piece upholstered parlor suite with prices varying according to the fabric used: $23.00 for cotton tapestry; $25.50 for crushed plush; $29.50 for silk brocatelle; and $34.00 for silk damask.[1]

Families who occupied the high end of the socioeco-

8.1 (facing page). Art gallery, William L. Crawford house, 3709 Ross Avenue, Dallas, ca. 1905 (Dallas Historical Society).

nomic scale were more likely to identify consciously with their class. The William L. Crawfords were such a family. Their home featured an art gallery, which occupied the second story of the house on Dallas' fashionable Ross Avenue (fig. 8.1). The room shows that the Crawfords did not identify with other Texans so much as with other Americans who had the money to devote such a conspicuously large space solely to leisure and "culture getting" (as opposed to "money getting").

The room does not resemble other rooms in Texas houses photographed circa 1905. Instead it shares similarities with "picture-galleries" shown in *Artistic Houses* and approximates those spaces in the homes of wealthy Americans Mrs. A. T. Stewart and John T. Martin, for example. Published nearly two decades before, *Artistic Houses* highlighted the homes of J. Pierpont Morgan and W. H. Vanderbilt, among others.[2]

Born in Kentucky in 1839, William Crawford served in the Civil War, becoming lieutenant colonel and commanding the Nineteenth Texas Infantry. After the war, he "began the study of law at home in a log cabin and on Saturday he would go to town to be examined in his progress." Crawford and his brother began a law practice in Jefferson, Texas, and by 1880, they had moved to Dallas forming the firm of Crawford & Crawford, which did "the biggest commercial business of any law firm in the city."[3] In 1896, after his first wife died, Crawford married the widow, Katherine Lester Lamar, originally of Oxford, Mississippi. The second Mrs. Crawford had led a charmed life. As the wife of L. Q. C. Lamar, Jr., and daughter-in-law of L. Q. C. Lamar, secretary of the interior during Grover Cleveland's administration, she had lived in Washington, D.C., and traveled throughout Europe, studying art in Paris.[4]

Soon after the Crawfords' marriage, the couple installed this gallery "of over three-hundred splendid canvasses, and a collection of statuary and antiques." European artists like Anthony Van Dyck and Rudolph Christian Schade were represented in their collection, as were Texas artists Julian Onderdonk and Hale Bolton.[5] The setting for the art collection was a long gallery with a beamed ceiling, a central skylight, and Ionic columns lining the length of the room. Visitors could admire the painting highlighted at one end of the room, sit and contemplate the "sweetness and light" of the overall grouping, or enjoy a private viewing in the small spaces created along the right side of the gallery.

Ten years later and 300 miles west northwest of Dallas, in Crosbyton, Pink and Bessie Parrish pose with their children at their dining table (fig. 8.2). They lived in one of the many C. B. Livestock Company-owned houses lining Main Street. The rented house exudes a certain anonymity. Minimal finishes, fashionable plain paper, and pine woodwork contribute to the effect. The family has outfitted the adjacent room with a single table and positioned a shell on the floor by the entrance into the dining room. A kerosene lamp hangs over the table, and a china cabinet is in the background. (Compare this light fixture with the lavish use of electric bulbs in fig. 8.1.) While the room seems spartan, it was a fine home compared with the family's earlier half-dugout, near Lubbock, that had to be bailed and dried out after rains.[6]

Design was not paramount in the minds of those who constructed company housing, but most homeowners demanded good design in the houses they built for themselves. Albert A. Van Alstyne and his widowed mother commissioned Galveston architect Nicholas J. Clayton to design their house, one of many elaborate mansions that once lined Houston's Main Street. The premier Texas architect at the time, Clayton fashioned for the Van Alstynes an Italianate villa costing $20,000. Judge James Masterson bought the house circa 1890, and John F. Dickson pur-

8.2. Entry hall into dining room, Pink L. Parrish, Sr., house, Main Street, Crosbyton, ca. 1915 (Crosby County Pioneer Memorial Museum, Crosbyton).

chased it at the turn of the century, hiring Clayton to redesign the parlor and make other interior changes updating the function and appearance of the house. The Dickson family lived in the home until it was bought by the Humble Oil Company and demolished in 1918.[7]

Although the emerging arts and crafts movement advocated simplicity, the Dicksons chose another fashionable option: purposefully unrestrained and randomly organized quantities of objects creating a dizzying array (fig. 8.3). The Dicksons filled their entry with a pastiche of exotic elements and a virtual zoo of styles, from the Moorish stand marking the entrance into an adjacent room, to coolie hats and a Chinese hall chair and settee, to a neo-Grec pier mirror. A Japanese screen blocks the service areas of the house. The stuffed crane perches in the background; a moosehead and an elk join the menagerie.

Weaponry, armor, and statuary stand guard around the hall, while a figure in the tapestry on the far wall welcomes guests. The weaponry and the heraldic references seem to look back to Eastlakean Gothicizing and forward to the American renaissance, a turn-of-the-century design movement spurred, in part, by a desire for a usable past and its images (see figs. 8.6, 8.7).[8] A double eagle thronelike chair at the right stands by ceremoniously; heraldic motifs, continued in the pillow covers by the stairs, lend the pedigree of a past to the space.

The visual diversity is set against a richly patterned stage and backdrop. The wallpaper features a dark field

8.3. Entry hall, Van Alstyne-Dickson house, 1216 Main Street, Houston, ca. 1900 (Houston Metropolitan Research Center).

8.4. Dining room, Van Alstyne-Dickson house, ca. 1898 (Houston Metropolitan Research Center).

patterned with medallions. Woods in intricate borders and fields compose the original parquet floor, which is covered by oriental rugs, adding still more pattern to the reception space.

Figures 8.4 and 8.5 are photos of the dining room probably taken before and after Clayton redesigned the parlor, his work changing this space as well. The renaissance revival furnishings depicted in both views represent expensive furniture available to the wealthy during the 1870s and 1880s. An impressive gasolier, possibly from Mitchell, Vance & Company, a New York lighting manufacturer, hangs above the dining table, its circumference matched by that of the table. A plush cloth covers the table, which is unextended, the typical position when not in use for guests. In figure 8.4, the large sideboard displays on its draped shelves a careful arrangement of ceramics and silver. The covered side table is positioned to keep dishes convenient during dinners. In the foreground a neo-Grec cabinet with wood inlays and hand-painted china plaques commands attention.[9] Atop the cabinet rests a sentinel flanked by a pair of Egyptian revival busts.

In the second photograph, the gasolier, carpeting, and

8.5. Dining room, Van Alstyne-Dickson house, ca. 1900 (Houston Metropolitan Research Center).

wall treatments remain the same (fig. 8.5). The neo-Grec slate mantel, part of the original design of the house, frames a hearth tiled in art pottery. A pair of bronze candelabra and a clock compose the mantel garniture made doubly impressive by their reflection in the large mirror. But the photograph also documents changes and refinements. The cane armchair, presumably part of the dining set, has been replaced by a set of chairs exhibiting Georgian scroll pediments and twist turnings. The configuration of paintings has also changed. Instead of marching around the top of the room with an occasional vertical drop carefully spaced above and below the picture rail, the pictures are arranged in relation to the furniture; at least one painting ignores the picture rail. The grillework at the end of the room is probably one of Clayton's modifications. Flanking the opening into what appears to be the library stand two large wooden carvings of the hunt, which are unlike dining room statuary in any other Texas house photographed during this period.

More fashionable than any other interior in this sample, the Dickson drawing room exemplifies the American renaissance (figs. 8.6, 8.7). In Europe by the 1870s a renewed interest in the Renaissance had been stirred by the publication of such works as Walter Pater's *Studies in the History of the Renaissance* and John Addington Symond's *Renaissance in Italy: The Fine Arts*. People wanted to experience the best of civilization; many writers and artists argued that Renaissance Italy had attained the pinnacle of cultural achievement. Of course, the Renaissance had been inspired by classical Rome; a liberally interpreted classical style named "American renaissance" by its practitioners became a recognized manner of decoration during the late nineteenth century.[10]

One of the signs of the Dicksons' familiarity with the Italian Renaissance is their inclusion of the print or painting hanging above the cabinet. The image is based upon Guido Reni's *Aurora*, a ceiling fresco for Casino Rospigliosi in Rome, executed in 1613. The image was often reproduced and found its way into American houses of this period and earlier. William Young's *Town and Country Mansions and Suburban Houses* (London, 1874) featured this image over a cabinet, displayed much as the Dicksons showed it a quarter of a century later.[11] Flanking *Aurora* are two nineteenth-century landscape paintings, possibly executed by Italian artists.

Architect Clayton classicized the room architecturally. Classical statuary encircles the room, and the arch at the window area is marked by paired Ionic columns and pilasters standing on plinths decorated with garlands. The ornamental plaster frieze and Adamesque ceiling molding continue the classical motifs, although they differ from the frieze motifs executed on Clayton's drawings of the parlor's redesign. His drawings indicate that above a pier mirror would rest a shield bearing the letter *D* for Dickson; this may or may not have been executed.[12] (The fixture, its electrically powered globes camouflaged to appear as lighted candles, obscures the view.) The allusions to pedigree and the past are nevertheless conspicuous.

The room contains a pile carpet, woven in the late nineteenth century to imitate a mid-eighteenth-century Axminster carpet; a renaissance revival parlor set; and a neo-Grec cabinet that dates to at least two decades before the room was photographed. The parlor suite has been newly upholstered with silk damask. In a stylistically catholic interpretation of renaissance design, the Dicksons have incorporated a mother-of-pearl folding chair — a so-called Savonarola chair — probably acquired in the 1890s, as an exotic element. American interpretation of renaissance design permitted reproductions of antique furnishings; the Dicksons' chairs in Chippendale and Sheraton styles were probably recent purchases.

Finally, the room's symmetry speaks of its debt to clas-

8.6. Drawing room, Van Alstyne-Dickson house, ca. 1900 (Houston Metropolitan Research Center).

sical design. Everything has been meticulously planned from the hanging of the curtains to the arrangements of the wall accessories — all contributing order and unity to the style. It is an impressive and beautifully appointed room, but it is not functional. The Dicksons created a "room as art" in which guests admired their hosts' wealth and taste but were not encouraged to interact with each other.

In contrast to the imposing Dickson drawing room, the Alfred James Taylors created a more convivial middle-class parlor (fig. 8.8). In 1909 rancher Taylor, his wife, and two children lived in a relatively new single-story home in Karnes City. The parlor is adjacent to a bedroom, continuing a rural tradition reflected in A. J. Downing's pattern books of 1842 and 1850. The space accommodated multiple functions: sleeping (a large mantel folding bed stands between the windows); playing (a toy piano stands by the hearth); and receiving guests. Family portraits are scattered around the room. Like images included in Chapter 3, the Taylor house shows that in both imagery and use, the space belongs to the family.

It is easy to concentrate on the many differences between the Van Alstyne-Dickson house and the Taylor house and consequently overlook what a fine dwelling the Taylors had. They probably selected what they liked and believed was fashionable from a mail-order catalogue. The wall treatment is quite stylish: ceiling paper suggesting trompe l'oeil plasterwork and bordered arts and crafts-inspired paper. The pair of matching rocking chairs, inspired by Chinese design, were enormously popular in Texas. The jute carpet has a stamped design, a new offering of the mail-order catalogues that found its way into other Texas parlors. The table and mantel display seashells, glass vases, family photographs, a mantel clock, a kerosene lamp, and a virtuoso piece of drawnwork. The Gibson girl on the pillow top belongs in the Taylor parlor

8.7. Drawing room, Van Alstyne-Dickson house, ca. 1900 (Houston Metropolitan Research Center).

as much as the gilt footstool belongs in the Dickson drawing room. While it is easy to dismiss so-called catalogue furnishings, there was a decided contemporary excitement about access to such items that current decorative arts historians sometimes dismiss.

A photographer documented the interior of the Marlin home of William Jones circa 1895 (fig. 8.9). Like the Taylor house, the room suggests family activity — piano playing and reading — and has an informal, inviting quality: at the left, a cat curls up on a side chair; an opened bookcase door beckons readers; conveniently near the pi-

8.8. Parlor, Alfred James Taylor house, 512 Johnson Street, Karnes City, 1909 (Karnes City Library).

ano, a bench is piled high with sheet music. But unlike the objects in the Taylor home, those in the Jones sitting room have been accumulated over time and are not recent purchases from mail-order catalogues. For example, the marble-top walnut center table, which holds a card receiver, a kerosene lamp, cut flowers, and vases, was a wedding present to the Joneses and dates to the 1880s.[13] The colonial revival rocking chair appears relatively new, but the wicker platform rocker is at least a decade old. The quality of some of the objects — the piano, the mantel vases, and the decorative screen, an example of panel painting executed by the couple's daughter — suggests a prosperous middle-class home.

Besides the quality of the furnishings, the sitting room shows typical decorating strategies found in images of many homes of middle-class families throughout this book. A framed print covers the fireplace opening, an indication that this is a summer view. Instead of matting on

8.9 Sitting room, William Jones house, Oakland Place, Marlin, ca. 1895 (Courtesy Martha Hartzog).

the floor, the Joneses leave their stained and varnished hardwood floor uncovered, save for mats at the hearth and under the center table. A light window treatment includes fringed roller blinds and lace-border sheer curtains, tied back; the portières still hang on poles at the entrance to the room, as shown in their reflection in the mantel mirror, but stand fully open.

Two potted palms mark the fireplace wall; shells, ceramics, and glassware decorate the mantel and overmantel. Anthemia and fleurs-de-lis embellish the wooden mantel, complementing the scrollwork pattern of the wallpaper. A madonna tops the arrangement over the hearth, while a crayon portrait of patriarch Churchill Jones hangs prominently above the piano.

Thirteen years later in deep East Texas, music teacher Hattie Eakin stands by pupil Carror Gillaspie in the young girl's home (fig. 8.10). The furnishings are uniformly inexpensive: a rug covers most of the unfinished pine floor;

8.10. Sitting room and bedroom, Gillaspie house, 313 West Wellington, Carthage, ca. 1908 (Panola County Historical Commission, Carthage).

photographs serve as the primary wall decorations. Photographs of the Gillaspie children, parents, and grandparents are clustered around the piano, which is partially concealed by a heavy tasseled drape, embroidered pillows, and a basket filled with sheet music.

Despite the modest furnishings, including a piano stool with a worn upholstered seat, the image is one of aspiration toward refinement, primarily because of the piano, although it is at least fifty years old. Worn objects do not keep the student from her music exercises.

The furnishings show that the room serves many purposes. The table with twist-turned legs functions as a music and book stand; the chair is a type usually found near a dining table or in a kitchen or office; and the painted iron bedstead indicates the sleeping section of the space. The utilitarian stove is topped with a decorative finial, much as the serviceable, multifunctional room has its own embellishments.

Multipurpose rooms were common in East Texas houses built in the late nineteenth and early twentieth centuries (fig. 6.9). So, too, was landscape wallpaper, this pattern featuring a matching border of linked medallions, each framing alternating tree-lined landscapes (see figs. 6.7, 6.8, 6.9).

Taken within a few years of the view of the Gillaspie house was this interior view of a Southeast Texas house (fig. 8.11). The photograph shows how a Houston family relinquished the use of the parlor during the holiday season to showcase a large pine Christmas tree, which stands on the floor rather than on a table as in figures 4.13 and 4.14. A sheet provides a base for both the gifts and the tree and protects the carpet from the pine needles. The tree is decked with gifts, like the handkerchiefs and toy drums, and decorations — strings of tinsel, glass ornaments, pinecones, candles, and small American flags (a popular decorating device at the time of the Spanish-American War; see fig. 4.1). Under the abundantly decorated tree is an array of gifts including ceramics, matching glass vases, children's books, and other toys. The azalea at the right, probably grown in a hothouse, was a favorite in southeastern Texas. Although it normally blooms in early spring, potted versions appear in several homes photographed at Christmastime.

Judging from this room, the householders are middle class. They can afford to employ a professional photographer to document their home on this special occasion. They own a piano and silver candelabra. The bordered rug and the wall covering are in a medium-price range. The wallpaper's bold pattern of medallions with rose centers on a field imitating a textile was a popular style at the beginning of the century, which indicates it is a recent purchase. The family is also aware of popular colonial revivalism as seen in the painted mantel; its style dates the house to ten or fifteen years before this photograph was made.

Taken about five years after figure 8.11, the image of a corner in a dining room in another Houston home (fig. 8.12) captures another pine Christmas tree and a pyramid of gifts. The size of the space and the room's finishes and furnishings suggest an upper-middle-class household. The wealth of gifts, too, indicates either a prosperous or a large family, perhaps both. In fact, so impressive is this array that when one compares it with figure 8.11, the two images seem to share only the azaleas. If wealth is a measure, this Christmas must have been a happy one for the children who received this abundance: tool chest, dresser set, tea set, toy village, fire truck, and dolls. The gifts spill over the relatively bare tree and onto a tabletop.

The walls of the dining room are covered with a dark paper and panels of a striped damask, unique in this sample. Gilt molding in a bellflower design outlines the panels, which are topped with a wreath motif and marked with corner paterae. A hunting scene hand painted on a large china plaque, typical of the era, hangs in the middle of one of the panels. Above the door heads, a print marks the entry into the service area and a valance marks the entrance to public spaces of the house.

The sideboard to the left predates the photograph by twenty years; the server to the right is a more recent purchase. Both case pieces feature impressive displays of ceramics and cut glass. Scarves and doilies lend service and ceremony, protecting the wood and decorating the sideboard's marble top.

Another pair of photographs (figs. 8.13, 8.14) records

8.11. Parlor, Unidentified house, Houston, ca. 1905 (Harris County Heritage Society, Houston). **8.12 (facing page).** Dining room, Unidentified house, Houston, ca 1910 (Harris County Heritage Society, Houston).

8.13. Dining room, E. M. Carter house, Seventh and El Paso streets (513 West Seventh), Plainview, ca. 1910 (Courtesy Jack Oswald; R. E. Cochrane, Photographer).

how decorating strategies differ in families of varying means. Figure 8.13 documents the dining room in the home of Plainview's prominent land- and store-owner E. M. Carter, who in 1909 built a house combining elements of colonial revival and beaux arts classicism. The floor plans were drawn by his wife, Lela Taylor Carter, and the structure was erected by builder Ben Mitchell between March and November 1909. Fond of gardening, Lela Carter designed a conservatory just off the southwestern corner of the dining room; this interior view provides a glimpse into that space.[14] Lela's horticultural interests were part of a national trend that peaked during the late nineteenth century. Many prosperous households had special rooms, light-filled spaces adjacent to dining areas, in which plants could thrive (see figs. 13.23, 13.47). R. E. Cochrane has photographed Lela and her friends as they pause during preparations for a party. The dining room's decoration consists largely of Lela's plants and flowers. Asparagus ferns top the door head, the fireplace, and the electric lighting fixture; potted plants and cut flowers decorate the tables and floor.

The mission style reigns in the Carter home. Oak ceiling beams, door and window jambs and heads, plate rails, and mantels and overmantels with cabinets constitute the trim. An unusual stenciled Shaker-motif wallpaper covers the dining room's walls below the plate rail and complements the design of the large oriental rug. The straight lines of the electric fixture and the dining table pedestal are counterpoint to the ornate curves of the German-inspired novelty chair. Hand-painted china plates, probably the work of Lela or her friends, rest on the plate rail; the large art pottery vase on the sideboard represents studio- or factory-decorated wares.

Built about 1898, the McKees' one-story house had no room designated as the conservatory (fig. 8.14). Instead, Jack and Sydney McKee transformed the bay window of their parlor into a living screen, an improvised solution to the need for space to accommodate and display their plants. Framed by ruffled organdy curtains, the well-lit bay features ferns, palms, geraniums, and wandering Jew, which thrived whether hanging from the ceiling, sitting on the window seat, or resting on the floor. In addition to more than a dozen clay pots, the McKees have used enameled pots and recycled tin cans for their plantings.

Compared with the Carter dining room, the McKee parlor features less expensive but nevertheless fashionable finishes and furnishings: the wooden ceiling is beaded, a medallion-pattern paper covers the walls, and the windows have varnished frames and stylish curtains. The scarved case piece on the left, the only piece of furniture visible in the image, displays some of the household's treasures — a kerosene lamp and a jewelry box. Resting on a shelf is a pinecone, possibly the heir to the pineapple as a sign of hospitality in dry West Texas. The pinecone may represent the fruit of one of the few plants that even the McKees could not successfully nurture.

On the Gulf Coast in Galveston in 1859, transplanted New Yorker James Moreau Brown built an Italianate villa constructed of bricks made at his own brickyard.[15] A family room was added in the late nineteenth century and photographed in 1901 (fig. 8.15), showing a small tabletop feather Christmas tree standing near the window.

The family room has a rather baronial scale, resembling a "living hall" filled with a pastiche of furnishings. Located at the back of the house, this room was used by the family as a kind of sitting and family dining room. A massive fireplace, almost one-story high, dominates the space. The furnishings are an eclectic mix: a suit of armor stands in the corner, a "Turkish" portrait and valance hangs above a doorway, a Mexican blanket is draped over a colonial revival rocker, an animal trophy floats above the fireplace, and a variety of vases and mantel figures line the shelf above the fireplace.

Some of the furnishings have been relocated to this room as newer objects replace them in more public areas of the house. For example, the large mirrored hallstand probably formerly served the front hall. Other pieces, such as the Morris chair, the colonial revival rocking chair, and the hanging electric fixture are newly purchased. The warming kettle on the hearth is a colonial revival element.

A bridal dinner given for a family friend occasioned another photograph in 1913 (fig. 8.16). The dining room is the picture of abundance — the table overflows with

8.14. Parlor or "front room," Jack W. and Sydney O. McKee house, Avenue E, Ozona, 1898 – 1905 (Courtesy Mrs. W. H. Savage).

glassware, ceramics, and silver, with chairs from several sets encircling it. Despite the lavish display on the table, the china cabinets are filled with dishes. Plaster walls are nearly obscured behind the tapestry wall hangings, case pieces, wall plaques, and pictures. Windows are crowned with cornices dating to the 1870s (although the bay was added in the 1890s) and covered by lace curtains, overcurtains, and interior shutters. The entry into the pantry is marked by portières matching the dark curtain panels.

In 1908 the Arthur C. Hoovers of Ozona in West Texas set their dining table for a more modest Thanksgiving feast: one photograph shows a turkey, a loaf of bread, bowls of mashed potatoes and cranberries, and a platter of sliced layer cake (fig. 8.17). The view of the Hoovers'

8.15. Family room, James Moreau Brown house, known as Ashton Villa, 2328 Broadway, Galveston, 1901 (Galveston Historical Foundation and Rosenberg Library, Galveston).

8.16. Dining room, James Moreau Brown house, Galveston, April 20, 1913 (Galveston Historical Foundation and Rosenberg Library, Galveston).

Thanksgiving suggests that the food itself represents plenty, while in the Browns' celebration the furnishings convey abundance. The Browns possess objects that allow them to elaborate the act of dining. Servants will bring a succession of courses served on functionally specific plates and eaten with functionally specific utensils; the Browns' guests will be experienced in dining rituals. Such practice was common in upper-middle- and upper-class households. By contrast, the Hoover photograph indicates that diners will partake of a simple feast without such ceremony.[16]

In the Hoover dining room, with unfinished and uncovered pine floors, pine wainscoting, chair rail, and plaster walls, a sideboard has been positioned diagonally across the corner. The case piece holds serving items needed for the meal. The oilcloth-covered dining table is set for six. The unmatched plates, each crossed with a knife, rest near unmatched drinking vessels. The chairs are also not part of a single set.

Several years earlier in Kaufman County, food has been set out on the dining table (fig. 8.18). The plates are face down. The black woman standing in the kitchen may be the cook/housekeeper; the man who helps himself to coffee is probably the head of the household. Humble as the interior appears in comparison with the Brown or the Van Alstyne-Dickson house, this family has the means to hire household help.

Cane-seat chairs and a child's high chair encircle the cloth-covered table. Draped and scarved, with the requisite display, the sideboard is positioned below a framed still life. A practical geometric-pattern linoleum covers the floor. Even in this lower-middle-class dining room, there are distinctions, however small, between the dining room furnishings and those in the adjacent kitchen — distinctions between the public and the service areas of the house. The kitchen wallpaper is less ornamental, and a worn, unfringed window shade covers the window. (The kitchen paper may have been "sanitas," a washable wallpaper used in bathrooms, kitchens, and pantries. "Sanitas" has a dull finish and mimicked patterns of wallpaper designed for the parlor and other public spaces.)[17] The dining room walls are covered in a decorative garland-pattern paper,

8.17. Dining room, Arthur C. Hoover ranch house, Ozona, ca. 1908 (Crockett County Museum, Ozona).

8.18. Dining room into kitchen, Unidentified house, Kaufman County, ca. 1900 (Courtesy Edward Cave).

and the fringed window shade is in good repair. A serviceable kerosene wall sconce hangs in the kitchen and represents the only example seen in this survey of interior views. But the differences between the two rooms are not as great here as they frequently are in more elaborate houses that used decorative screens to block service areas from the dining room.

Style is of little concern to the people who furnished the multipurpose room in Brenham (fig. 8.19). The couple in the photograph may have been boardinghouse owners serving the needs of Blinn Academy.[18] Unfinished pine floors and painted horizontal wallboards define the space; however, the occupants have created an artistic corner wall grouping of four identically framed cabinet cards, two commercial calendars, and other printed items. A floral still life hangs above the desk, a match holder of tin beside it.

The photograph illustrates the mingling of the work of individual cabinetmakers and that of large manufacturers in some late-nineteenth-century Texas homes. The com-

8.19. Bedroom/office/kitchen, Unidentified house (may be associated with the Howe house, Blinn Academy [Blinn College]), Brenham, ca. 1895 (Barker Texas History Center, Austin).

mercial wall decorations are at home with the pine desk; its paneled doors and interior details suggest it is of German Texas origin. The chairs and the table are probably locally made; the oilcloth and the fringed roller blind are store bought.

The image is both posed and candid. The photographer has taken the picture at night, using a flash to illuminate the room; the couple is posed reading, and yet we see her dirty apron and the tin bucket and shoe box littering the desk top. The window glass reflects a dresser mirror.

Style is of considerably more concern in the Crockett home of Andrew H. Wootters circa 1905 (fig. 8.20). Exemplifying a fashionable middle-class parlor in the French taste, the room conforms to the preference for light colors, floral motifs, so-called fancy furniture, and ruffled and fringed textiles. The owners selected appropriate furnishings and decorations: floral cascade-pattern wallpaper, scrollwork carpet, a mantel with gilt detailing, fancy chairs, and textiles — fringed portières rather artfully draped and a silk lampshade covering the figural kerosene lamp. The mantel adornments — ceramic mantel clock, vases, and pitcher — are also in the French taste.

The parlor features a catalogue-purchased element appearing in other turn-of-the-century Texas homes, especially in parlors and sitting rooms: the horizontal floral still life. The still life over the mantel may be the popular 8-by-34-inch study of roses advertised in the 1902 Sears, Roebuck catalogue.[19] Sears, Roebuck offered other studies in flowers and fruits, which — judging from their appearance in photographs — were less popular than the rose study.

Several features of the Wootters parlor are reminiscent of another Texas house, the W. A. Fletcher house in Beaumont (see figs. 7.1, 7.2) which was constructed at approximately the same time as the Wootters house. These houses offer a contrast in the way taste was interpreted, depending upon socioeconomic status. Both the Fletchers and the Wootterses display pillows on the floor; in the Fletcher house they trail on the carpet to link parlor with sitting room. In both houses a taboret marks the doorway from room to room. Both parlors are furnished with a seat or bench, a rocking chair, and numerous chairs. The two families have used similar decorating strategies, but the professionally coordinated Fletcher house is a more expensive dwelling: its rooms are larger, its finishes finer, and its furnishings more costly.

The McVities used a professional decorator to transform their Galveston parlor to the French taste (fig. 8.21). In 1891, William A. McVitie's lot at 1305 Tremont was estimated for tax purposes at $1,200; the following year, at $8,000.[20] McVitie, a prosperous cosmopolitan shipping-firm owner from New York, employed an unnamed decorator to create his family's fashionable Louis XV-style parlor, which featured cove molding, gilt rococo relief designs, and a gilt-and-white pressed-metal cornice.

The wall decoration consists mainly of the elaborate molding, while the tabletops exhibit a good array of decorative objects. A white mantel, highlighted with gilt, frames a pink-tiled fireplace that displays English, French, and German ceramics, as do the stand, pedestal, and Louis XIV-style center table. The gilt fauteuil and side chair continue the French theme, which is accented by a Roman-inspired curule stool and chair.[21]

The parlor opens off an entry hall illuminated by electric globes camouflaged by a bronze winged figure. The library is opposite. The rooms share the same rich parquet flooring, on which small oriental rugs are strategically placed.

Just as the decorator chose the prevailing French revival style for the parlor, he exhibited conventional taste in selecting the English style for the dining room (fig. 8.22). Suggesting a grand English dining hall, the large room accommodates a server, sideboard, china cabinet, trestle table, and screen—pieces inspired by renaissance design. In keeping with the convention that the dining room is a male space, an all-male dining and drinking scene hangs above the china cabinet. The few textiles used in the room protect the furniture and frame an interior doorway. Oriental rugs and runners dot the parquet floor. The overall effect is one of richness, created by the patterned rugs, the ceiling and wainscoting woods, and the shining silver, glass, and china.

The wooden wall plaques flanking the sideboard appear in several other upper-middle-class houses along the Texas Gulf Coast, including the James M. Brown house in Galveston. Made in Switzerland around 1890, the walnut sculptured trophies feature game, suggesting man's role as hunter and provider, his mastery over nature, and control of its bounty.[22]

Sconces in an arts and crafts design, new to Texas in

8.20. Parlor, Andrew H. Wootters house, 500 South Seventh Street, Crockett, ca. 1905 (Courtesy Nancy Land).

8.21. Parlor, William A. McVitie house, 1305 Tremont Avenue, Galveston, ca. 1892 (Courtesy June S. Holly).

8.22. Dining room, William A. McVitie house, ca. 1892 (Courtesy June S. Holly).

1892, provide peripheral lighting; an electric ceiling fixture complementing the room's English themes illuminates the dining table. Reflecting the light are the mirrors of the china cabinet and sideboard, the latter showing a decorated plate rail (or mantel) on the opposite wall. On the left wall, a portière-covered doorway leads to other public spaces of the McVitie home, while the door on the right opens to the pantry and kitchen, which are physically and "psychologically" blocked from the dining room.

* * * *

Socioeconomic status mixed with personal taste and availability of goods to determine the appearance of a home. Those families who could afford opulence tended to identify with trendsetters in the northeastern United States. Residents of larger Texas cities — Dallas, Houston, and Galveston — were more likely to spend money on fashionable and expensive house interiors than residents of more remote or recently settled areas.

Photographs reveal that while some wealthy Texans had access to professional designers who decorated their homes in newly fashionable styles, a theme that will be more fully developed in the following chapters, others of more modest financial means decorated their homes themselves. Moderately prosperous householders sometimes developed strategies for expressing their stylishness, approximating the efforts of the upper classes; even households of modest means exhibited knowledge of some prevailing fashions.

9.1. Parlor, Francis Newberry and Julia Macy Holbrook house, Third and Santa Fe streets, El Paso, 1885 (Southwest Collection, El Paso Public Library).

9

Aesthetic, Mission, and Colonial Revival

STYLE

MANY Texans sought decorating models beyond those that evolved from their occupation, ethnicity, or region. The desire for a recognizable style became a major criterion for house decoration, and acceptance of various styles linked Texas homes and interiors to national decorating trends. Many householders tried to achieve a stylistic "purity" in their home interiors and whatever style they chose — aesthetic, mission, or colonial revival — was embraced wholeheartedly.

The images here are in chronological order according to the date of the photograph rather than the date of the structure. They provide a view of some of the major styles popular several decades before and after the turn of the century. Some of the photographs were taken when the domestic settings were newly in place; others were not.

In 1885 Francis and Julia Holbrook had their parlor photographed (figs. 9.1, 9.2). Their adobe dwelling was built near the intersection of Third and Santa Fe streets in downtown El Paso. Scenes of the neighborhood in 1885 show dirt streets and burros. Within the walls of their home, the newlyweds from New York, who had moved to El Paso so the groom could accept a position as a mining and construction engineer, styled an oasis of fashionable taste.[1]

Soon after the Holbrooks arrived, they had photographs taken of their up-to-date interiors. The objects shown in the vertically oriented view seem an odd mélange photographed at an unusual angle. In the absence of a hearth, the wide windowsill functions as the family altar; with the table, it provides a display surface for wedding gifts. A pair of fashionable matching ewers flank a mantel clock topped with a classical urn-and-anthemion finial. Doilies provide draping; a woven basket introduces a southwestern Indian theme; framed and unframed cabinet cards recall distant family members. Hanging above, the horizontal print is styled after French artist François Boucher,

9.2. Parlor into bedroom, Francis Newberry and Julia Macy Holbrook house, 1885 (Southwest Collection, El Paso Public Library).

whose classical cherubs in horizontal rows had only recently become a motif for amateur art, amounting to a kind of Boucher "cult."[2]

The tabletop grouping reinforces the fashion consciousness of the Holbrooks; accessories clustered on a table with twist-turned legs are a crowded assemblage of materials and forms. Joining the ceramic and glass items is a filled silver-plated card receiver, which indicates the Holbrooks knew and practiced the ritual of calling.

The second photograph provides another view of the couple's aesthetic parlor (fig. 9.2) and a glimpse of the adjacent bedroom. One of the elements identifying the public space as "aesthetic" is the powerful pattern of the wallpaper's stylized floral forms. The art groupings, above and around the doorway and at the easel, continue the style. At the threshold a pair of Boucher-style prints and a print of classical figures demonstrate the current interest in classical civilizations. The print within the asymmetrically carved and painted frame at the right embodies aestheticism. The asymmetry continues in the draping of the easel, which features a Japanese-inspired print. Below it are several examples of southwestern Indian basketry; the larger basket is from the Chemehuevi tribe. The parlor also features a colonial revival banister-back chair overlaid with an asymmetrically draped scarf, embellished with unmatched bands, typical of the aesthetic style. As was fashionable, the Holbrook home accommodated classical, oriental, Native American, and colonial revival themes.

At the left in this photograph is another view of the "mantel" window. A horseshoe hangs on the window frame, a familiar sign of good luck for a newly married couple. The table arrangement has been simplified, its composition subordinated to the wall-hung accessories. The card receiver and newly fashionable umbrella stand in the corner suggest that, although the Holbrooks lacked an entry hall to receive guests, they maintained the requisite forms.

The Holbrook house does not have many rooms and differentiated spaces. The bedroom is adjacent to the parlor; the same wallpaper is used in both rooms. Only portières in a foliage-and-bird pattern separate the spaces. This narrow view of the not-so-private area offers a glimpse of a bed, possibly a daybed, a crazy quilt, a framed picture on the floor waiting to be positioned on the wall, and a dresser in the popular Eastlake style.

Aestheticism also appeared in a fine parlor in coastal South Texas (fig. 9.3). The fashionable tripartite wall division helps to identify this room as an aesthetic interior. The wallpaper is a Western interpretation of Japanese design that became popular among middle-class householders during the 1880s.[3] Like other papers in the style, the fill paper in the Thomas and Mary Reeves Fleming family parlor consists of asymmetrical groupings of conventional floral designs and vases imposed upon an irregular grid. The wide frieze contains a design of encircled pages of sheet music, making a literal reference to the "art" of the artistic interior and reinforcing the musical aspect of the room.

During the 1880s, American wallpaper manufacturers produced many inexpensive small borders that outlined larger borders and framed ceilings.[4] Such narrow edgings allowed more modest households to approximate the Flemings' remarkable frieze and dado paper. Theirs is printed with bands and borders that create alternating panels and make material the aesthetic philosophy of art for art's sake — every object appears within a frame and is thus treated as something worthy of contemplation.

In the room, framing operates at all levels. The tabletop picture frames — themselves covered with surface decoration — enclose artistic images. The upholstery of the Eastlake chair and sofa is accented by bands of solid plush; the back of the platform rocker features alternating light and dark bands of color. A wall-to-wall carpet border frames the floor. But on the walls, the paper is sufficiently "aesthetic" to preclude the necessity for framed pictures.

In the foreground a kerosene fixture is suspended from a pale ceiling. A small cupidlike figure, a putto, flies beneath it. At the window, exterior shutters block the sunlight. Lace curtains hanging from rings and poles drape the floor, tied back low, in an "artistic" manner.

As is characteristic of aesthetic interiors, the emphasis is on surface decoration. The Flemings have embellished the room's surfaces with patterns and two-dimensional designs rather than three-dimensional objects. Few tabletop accessories are visible. In addition to the simple drape on the piano and the more elaborate one on the table, there are two tabletop easels, one displaying a framed portrait, the other a decorative book and a small cylindrical ceramic vase. The surface decoration of the photograph's frame, the vase, and the larger easel — rather than the grouping itself — provides the visual interest. At the base of the table, a decorated ceramic spittoon only slightly belies the stylishness of the Fleming parlor.

The family had always traveled "heavy." Between 1849 and 1852 Fleming's parents moved their piano from Mobile, Alabama, to Green Lake near Port Lavaca, Texas. Federal troops burned their house in Green Lake during the Civil War, but the family saved the piano. Their home destroyed, they retreated to their plantation home on the

San Antonio River; later when they moved to Victoria and built this home in 1881, the family piano accompanied them.[5]

A piano also angles into the Taulman parlor, and, as in the Fleming parlor, a boldly designed wallpaper defines the style of the room (fig. 9.4). Mr. and Mrs. F. A. Taulman pose for their son, photographer Joseph E. Taulman, as he experimented with night photography, the shadow cast on the wall behind Mr. Taulman documenting the use of a flash. For Joseph Taulman, the photograph is both a portrait of his parents and an attempt to practice and perfect his craft; thus, the image relates to his occupational identity as well as to his participation in the culture's interest in the medium. But Taulman has also captured a picturesque backdrop (resembling a photography studio vignette) that is a stylistic gesture, expressive of his parents' embracing and identifying with a particular manner of room decoration. The Taulman parlor represents one of the few and certainly the purest example of a middle-class room decorated in the Anglo-Japanese style collected in this survey.

British design reformers had admired certain features of the Anglo-Japanese style: its "abstraction, two-dimensionality, and refinement in treating natural and geometric forms." Unfortunately, American wallpaper factories frequently produced "garish popularizations" of the style that featured "realistically shaded pictures of Japanese and Moorish objects — buildings, vases, fans — that appeared to reside in three-dimensional spaces." Decorative arts historian Catherine Lynn notes with irony that in Japanese prints, blank spaces are sensitively balanced with visually active areas; Western interpretations were quite

9.3. Parlor, Thomas Newton Fleming house, Northeast corner of Slayton and North Victoria streets (508 West Slayton Avenue), Victoria, ca. 1888 (Estate of Roger Fleming and Institute of Texan Cultures, San Antonio).

the reverse, with unrelieved crowding of elements.[6] The Taulmans' wallpaper is one of these inexpensive interpretations: the shaded vases of swirling roses occupy Moorish archways and blend with fan motifs, while a variety of geometric shapes punctuate the already crowded paper.

As if the Japanese element is not strong enough in the wallpaper, the Taulmans have pinned to the wall a dark Japanese fan decorated with a half-moon and blossom design. Above the platform rocker hangs a plush Japanese kakemono featuring calla lilies, a favorite floral motif of the aesthetic movement. Objects of Japanese design were believed to be well suited to the aesthetic style and frequently appeared together in house decoration.

Other furnishings in the Taulmans' room are only partially visible: a grand piano, sewing basket, animal-skin rug, and ottoman. Probably if we could see them fully they would appear incidental to the overwhelming oriental visual themes.

Although photographed after figures 9.1 through 9.4, which show styles popular during the 1880s and 1890s, the rooms documented in figures 9.5 through 9.8 illustrate fashionable interiors of the 1870s that remained for the most part intact into the 1890s. These four views show the Epperson house in Jefferson, which many Texans know by the fanciful name of the House of the Seasons, so called for its four-sided cupola, each side featuring windows of a different color glass: green for spring, amber for summer, red for fall, and blue for winter. Built in 1872 by an unknown builder or architect, the Italianate residence was photographed some twenty years after its completion; the interiors display many features that date to its original construction.

9.4. Parlor, F. A. Taulman house, Hubbard City, ca. 1890. The back of the photograph reads "Made at Night, Mamas" (Barker Texas History Center, Austin; Joseph E. Taulman, Photographer).

Benjamin H. Epperson, a native of Mississippi, settled in Texas in 1841 at the age of seventeen. Six years later, the Princeton-educated lawyer was elected to the second legislature of Texas from Red River County and served as a state official for the next twenty years. From his first Texas home in Clarksville, Epperson moved to Jefferson where he built this house. He occupied his new home for only six years before he died in 1878; his widow and children continued to live in the house until it was sold to the Marion Taylor Glass family in 1906.[7]

The parlor floor is covered wall to wall with strip carpeting, patterned with large connected geometric shapes, each enclosing a realistic floral spray, typical of carpet styles popular during the 1860s and early 1870s (fig. 9.5). It may be a so-called velvet carpet, also known as a tapestry Wilton. A fresco paper of banded uprights creating panels around an abstract design diaper on a light field covers the walls. Fresco papers consisted of different printed elements combined to simulate paneling. Ornate examples imitated marble or wood; the paper in the Epperson house represents a simpler pattern, suggesting panels edged by moldings. Popular in stylish eastern and southern homes of the 1850s, fresco paper, also called *décor*, appears in this sample only in the Epperson house partly because the popularity of the paper predates the construction of many of these structures and photographs.[8] Nevertheless, in Texas in 1872 this paper and other furnishings in the room remained available in large furnishings stores and paint and paper stores, possibly in Dallas or New Orleans, where the Eppersons probably purchased them.

Also unusual in this sample is the tasseled and symmetrically shaped lambrequin at the window; the fixed panel hangs over sheer lace curtains at the parlor window. The window treatment would also have been found in fashionable eastern and southern houses at mid century. The

9.5. Parlor, Benjamin H. Epperson house, Delta and Alley streets (409 South Alley), Jefferson, 1890 – 1895 (Courtesy Richard and Susan Collins).

spare use of textiles reflects, too, an earlier taste rather than decorating ideas current at the time the photographs were taken. The undraped marble mantel shelf supports a restrained display of small ceramics; there are numerous wall-hung accessories, including an original landscape painting, above the mantel. In a popular 1870s and 1880s arrangement, some framed items are double hung; a large gilt-framed print hangs above the square piano; another hangs across a corner.

Few other furnishing choices that the Eppersons made for their parlor are visible. In one corner an older sofa is hidden behind a more recent purchase, a leather-upholstered rocking chair; at the center of the room a kerosene table lamp and a gasolier provide lighting. As in the Fleming parlor, putti dangle from the ceiling fixture.

In the mid-1890s, the Epperson dining room looks as it did in 1872, with the renaissance revival furnishings still in use, their heyday having passed (fig. 9.6). Typical of that style, the sideboard is architectural in scale and detail. Its oval panels enclose carved fruit suggesting the bounty and function of the dining room. The draped side shelves and marble top of the sideboard support a rich display of glass, silver, and ceramics. And yet in this upper-middle-class Texas home, relatively inexpensive cane-seat chairs encircle the covered table and line the walls by the window.

The dining room floor is bare and the exterior shuttered windows are covered only by dark roller blinds. The light use of textiles might suggest summer, but the family left the stove in place. The walls are embellished in a manner similar to that in the living room. The fresco paper, a vertically striped wallpaper border with a medallion on the uprights, placed at the same level around the room encloses a plain paper. Unceremoniously, the stovepipe interrupts the decorative paper. The hearth's composition — paneled wall, prints, and a pair of glass vases atop the marble mantel — is curiously undermined by the indecorous, but practical, placement of the appliance that has supplanted the fireplace as the source of heat.

For lighting, the Eppersons have retained the original gasolier. Its glass shades have been removed; a paper parasol serves as a decorative shade, documenting the taste for the exotic that became fashionable after the International Centennial Exhibition in Philadelphia in 1876. That exhibition sparked interest in Japanese-style objects, much as a fire might have been sparked if the gas flame touched the paper and straw of the fashionable parasol.[9]

Through the dining room doorway, a corner of an adjacent room is visible. The space was probably originally planned as a sitting room because of its position opposite the front parlor, just across the structure's central hallway. Circa 1890 – 1895 it functions as a bedroom and features a corner washstand with a reeded pitcher and bowl. It is possible that the space was originally used as a bedroom by the Eppersons, following the Deep South practice of having a bedstead in a front room, or the rural tradition of having bedrooms adjacent to public areas of the house. The room also may have been converted to a bedroom during Epperson's lifetime or later as his widow became infirm.

The half-tester renaissance revival bedstead is the subject of the photograph in figure 9.7. Massive and grand, like many pieces of furniture of the period, it could be "knocked down," or separated into parts for shipping prior to assembly (noted in furniture orders and receipts as "kd."). It stands on matting, which further suggests that the photographs were taken during the summer, against a backdrop of a diamond-diapered wallpaper. The paper is edged at the baseboard with a decorative border featuring an anthemion motif that matches the bedstead's crest.

A globed gasolier with a drop light, a central element that can be pulled down, illuminates the room. A dining room side chair stands by the window where the rococo

9.6. Dining room, Benjamin H. Epperson house, 1890 – 1895 (Courtesy Richard and Susan Collins).

revival side table probably stood. For this photograph the marble-top table has been placed decoratively at the foot of the bedstead; on the table a stoneware jug displays dried grasses. The jug, a colonial affectation popular at the time of the picture taking, was likely a product of the famous Marshall Pottery located twenty miles south of Jefferson.

The furnishings in the Eppersons' wide upstairs hallway (fig. 9.8) are less unified stylistically than the downstairs furnishings. The space features the original stenciled floor in imitation of tile or marble, but by the time this photograph was taken, the floor was quite worn, the animal-skin and bordered rugs having done little to protect the stenciling. The wear patterns provide useful documentation of activity in the hallway: many people traveled through the door at the right, paused in front of the hallstand mirror, and used the stairs at the left down to the first level or up to the cupola; family members probably often sat on the lounge, for the floor pattern has faded in front of it. That the floor is so heavily worn suggests this well-lit and well-ventilated hall replaced a downstairs room as the family sitting room.

Comfortable and worn seating pieces fill the informal space — three cane rockers, three matching cane armchairs, and a covered lounge. Near the rococo hallstand, which may have been replaced in the downstairs entry hall by a later and more fashionable one, are several objects — a spittoon, a woman's hat, and a kerosene lamp.

Painted or papered, the walls of the space imitate stone and are topped by a decorative border. Wallpaper mimicking marble or stone was popular for entry and stair halls from the middle of the nineteenth century to the 1880s. Framed pictures are hung on the walls well above eye level

9.7. Bedroom, Benjamin H. Epperson house, 1890 – 1895 (Courtesy Richard and Susan Collins).

but tipped out at various angles. Punctuating the painted ceiling, a pair of gasoliers flanks the circular opening to the cupola.

Unlike the Epperson house, the Frank W. Ball house, located in Fort Worth, presents an au courant room at the time of the photograph (fig. 9.9).[10] Identified on the front of the original photograph as "Interior of one of Aunt Freddy's parlors," the view documents a fashionable room of the 1890s filled with light wicker furniture. If ever there was a room done in "the wicker style," this is it, the only one represented in the sample.

Ease in shaping the wicker, reed, and rattan material allowed manufacturers to produce a host of outlines and designs, the variety of which evidently appealed to the Balls. The wicker twists, crisscrosses, fans, and curls, forming the fancy chairs that face the camera, arranged as if for some sort of performance. This movement is echoed by the frieze, ceiling border, and medallion-applied moldings that swirl and circle in fleur-de-lis and anthemion motifs, blending French and classical designs. Music stand, easel, and table in the gardenlike space exhibit similar exuberance.

Floral and foliate themes reverberate throughout the space — from the easel painting to the floor covering; they entice visitors to enter the adjacent room, they cushion chair seats, they pattern curtains that lengthen the window, blurring the distinction between interior and exterior.

In Houston some six years after the Ball house was photographed, the Benjamin Charles and Rebecca Wheeler Simpson house showed the persistence of the aesthetic style even after the turn of the century (figs. 9.10, 9.11, 9.12). Their home, an impressive Italianate residence, stood at 144 Main Street at the corner of Rusk Avenue. From Rochester, New York, Simpson, a twenty-one-year-old machinist, moved to Texas at the urging of a fellow New Yorker who had settled there. Along with his friend James A. Cushman, Simpson worked in Houston until the Civil War, during which he served in the famous Company A, Fifth Texas Infantry, Hood's Brigade. For almost a decade after the war, Simpson was a partner in the Phoenix Iron Works of Houston. Soon after his marriage to Rebecca Wheeler in 1873, he organized Simpson & Hartwell (later Simpson, Hartwell & Stopple), an equipment agency that handled "machinery and implements" at 10 – 12 Commerce in Houston.[11]

9.8 (facing page). Upstairs hall, Benjamin H. Epperson house, 1890 – 1895 (Courtesy Richard and Susan Collins).

The Simpsons built their home circa 1880 on what was known as the Wheeler block, bounded by Main, Rusk, Fannin, and Walker. The architect or builder is not known. Rebecca Wheeler's family was prominent, "one of the first-settled families of the city"; her father, wharfmaster at Harrisburg during the Republic period, owned the entire block. When his house burned, the block was divided among the five Wheeler daughters.[12]

At the turn of the century the Simpson parlor was still decorated in the aesthetic style (figs. 9.10, 9.11) that had been especially popular between the International Centennial Exhibition and the World's Columbian Exposition in Chicago in 1893, during which time the house was completed. The paper covering the side walls of the parlor resembles that in the Holbrook parlor (see figs. 9.1, 9.2). The frieze, patterned with flat, stylized leaf-and-sunflower forms, is bordered at the top by a line of connected diamonds, at the bottom by the same line along with a wide, solid dark band, the same that marks the bottom edge of the side-wall papers. Only the ceiling, covered with a light paint, remains an unembellished surface.

9.9. Parlor, Frank W. Ball house, 324 Summit Avenue, Fort Worth, 1895 (Fort Worth Public Library).

Like the wall treatments, the floor covering and window treatments conform to aestheticism. A conventional floral and fern-leaf design on a light field stretches wall to wall, edged by a border. At the side windows, a flat valance banded with openwork and fringe hangs from stained wooden rings and poles. A paneled frieze and dark drapes tied back near the floor distinguish the bay window. Inside the heavier fabric hang lace curtains, their large fern-leaf design complementing that in the carpet.

Other room finishes and furnishings fit the aesthetic standard. The Eastlake-inspired mantel is decorated with incised, highly stylized leaf and floral designs sprouting from Greek vases along with shallow carved conventional flowers. Reflecting the gasolier and the box camera, the gilt mirror above the mantel features a sawtooth crest, another element associated with the Eastlake style, while the gilt pier mirror features its own Eastlake details, trefoil and bellflower designs. The renaissance revival parlor suite consists of a sofa, three side chairs, an armchair, and a platform rocker, all upholstered in the same bouquet-pattern fabric.

The piano (fig. 9.10) is positioned diagonally across the corner holding a measured display resembling that of both the mantel and the pier mirror shelves. The tabletop decorations consist mainly of ceramics, favorite accessories in aesthetic interiors. The pier mirror displays a turn-of-the-century art pottery vase. One of the two Simpson children, Fannie Wheeler Simpson, was a talented china painter; evidence of her work and the popular taste for hand-painted china and art pottery is seen in the framed china plaque on the piano, the vases on the pier mirror and mantel, and the pitcher on the hallstand.

A view of the Simpson parlor provides the only photographic clue to the decoration of the entry hall. From this vantage, the photographer captured a wallpaper of medallions and stripes, a popular pattern for entry halls in the

9.10. Parlor, Benjamin C. Simpson house, 144 Main Street, Houston, ca. 1901 (Courtesy Fannie Simpson Carter).

1890s, a hallstand displaying a hat, cane, and hand-painted ceramic pitcher, and a wall-to-wall carpet topped with mats.

Less formal and less restrained than the parlor, the Simpson sitting room shows an identification with family in a setting defined by the aesthetic style's emphasis on embellished surfaces (fig. 9.12). Whereas the parlor had only one portrait over the piano, the sitting room displays clusters of family photographs at the mantel and desk, contributing to a more personal atmosphere in this space. A portrait

9.11. Parlor, Benjamin C. Simpson house, 144 Main Street, Houston, ca. 1901 (Courtesy Fannie Simpson Carter).

of Benjamin Simpson, who had died in 1888, hangs over the mantel, similar to the shrine in the Maxey library (see fig. 2.11). Images of Simpson's son (Benjamin, Jr.), daughter, and wife also decorate the room. But even in the placement of family images, the Simpsons may have been following the advice of household critics who by the 1880s were urging readers to place family mementos in the sitting room and master bedroom.

The relative informality of the sitting room is evident in the furniture forms: there is no parlor suite here; seating is supplied by the unmatched rocking chairs and a pillow-strewn rattan lounge. The colorful pillows soften the lounge, adding to the patterned decoration of the room. One is identical to the sofa cushion in the parlor; another features a popularized image of a Native American. By the turn of the century, Sears, Roebuck was selling lithographed sofa-cushion covers stamped with an "Indian Head" design.[13] This cushion, like the popular Jean-François Millet pastoral print hanging by the Simpsons' hearth, is a reference to the arts and crafts movement, which influenced house interiors around the time of the photo.

Other textiles figure prominently in the sitting room. Geometric-pattern portières hang at the interior doorways leading to an adjacent bedroom. While the portières block the view as well as entry into other rooms, they also beckon, for they are tied back to permit both view and entry; the combined functions of hiding and enticing can also be seen in the decoratively embroidered fire screen. The mats, too, serve several functions: they protect areas of frequent use and herald passageways — important in late-nineteenth-century houses because different rooms frequently demanded different comportment. These and larger rugs of oriental inspiration cover the matting that stretches wall to wall. The textiles contribute surface patterns in the room as do the wall and ceiling papers.

Unlike the patterned surfaces of the Simpson house, a circa 1908 Dallas interior projects "plainness"; in contrast to the swirling outlines of the finishes and furnishings of the Ball house, it displays the rectilinear quality equated with arts and crafts design and mission furniture (fig. 9.13). The interior replaces the use of textiles, multiple patterning, dense groupings of objects, and rococo lines — precepts of late-nineteenth-century house decoration — with beamed ceilings, solid-color wall surfaces, wooden floors punctuated with oriental carpets, and rectilinear tables and seating pieces covered by leather cushions.

The windows are fitted with short curtains; the wooden trim of the windows is deliberately exposed. Although oak was popular for interior woodwork and furniture in these houses, in this, as in many middle-class houses, a stained pine has been substituted for the ceiling beams and probably for the mantel shelf in the living room and the wainscoting and plate rail in the dining room. The mission furniture in the living room is oak, and the pedestal table and Queen Anne revival chairs in the dining room are probably also oak.

Little about the room seems personal other than a few tabletop accessories. Occupational, familial, and ethnic identity has been subordinated to the stylistic statement of the room, which suggests that the occupants were well-educated and middle- to upper-middle class.

The Alexander Thompson house is another straightforward middle-class example of a popularized interpretation of art and crafts design (figs. 9.14, 9.15), yet it is more personalized than the Dallas interior. The family chose the same option of design reform as did the householders whose room was photographed in figure 9.13: both exemplify the ideas of Frank Lloyd Wright and Gustav Stickley who advocated "simple" and "honest" domestic environments and both feature rectilinear furniture and interior finishes, sparse use of textiles at the window, co-

9.12. Sitting room, Benjamin C. Simpson house, ca. 1901 (Courtesy Fannie Simpson Carter).

9.13. Living room into dining room, Unidentified house, Dallas, ca. 1908 (Dallas Historical Society).

ordinated rugs on a wooden floor, tempered wall and tabletop adornments, and an open atmosphere.

Like the interior decoration, the multiple functions of the flowing space bespeak reform. The living room is an entryway, a room in which family relaxes, friends socialize, and Thompson works. This is not the highly structured, specialized use of space in late-nineteenth-century houses with an entry hall, parlor, sitting room, and library, as in the Fleming, Epperson, or Simpson homes.

Despite the direct statement of style, the Thompson living and dining rooms convey the personal identities of the occupants. The reform wallpaper of naturalistic leaves (fig. 9.14) suggests Thompson's occupation as lumber merchant in East Texas.

In 1908 the Thompson home — a two-story transitional structure combining elements of the Queen Anne and the bungalow styles — was the finest house in a row lining the railroad tracks in Doucette. A more modest late-nineteenth-century *L*-shaped one-story vernacular residence stood next to it. Other houses, unvarying rectangles with front porches, completed the row of dwellings that paralleled the tracks. This was company housing. As vice-president and general manager of the Thompson Brothers Lumber Company, Alexander Thompson lived in the largest and finest of the homes. His employees occupied the row of houses set slightly apart from his, in descending order of their rank within the business.

Born in Kilgore in 1883, the son of pioneer lumberman John Martin Thompson, Alexander was educated in Kilgore, at Austin College in Sherman, at Cornell University where he was graduated from its college of law in 1905, and at Eastman College in Poughkeepsie, New York, where he studied business. Having spent time working in his father's lumber mills during his youth, Alexander quickly achieved positions of authority in the company. In July 1905 he married Gladys Walsh of Sherman; after several months in New York the couple returned to Texas where he worked briefly at Willard, another lumber-mill site owned by his family, before moving to Doucette.[14]

The photographer, whom we see reflected in the dining room sideboard mirror (fig. 9.15), has done more than photograph two rooms; he has documented the floor plan of the Thompson home. The first-floor rooms are separated only by portières; each of two curtain poles suspends a pair of portières, a solid ball-fringe fabric for the living room and a floral-border one for the dining room. The dining room shows its arts and crafts inspiration: a patterned paper above and a solid paper below the plate rail, a geometric-pattern rug, a light window treatment, and a measured display of ceramics, glass, and silver. Mission furniture and the panelized wainscoting continue the rectilinear elements of the style.

The Stoner family dining room (fig. 9.16) in the South Texas town of Victoria resembles the Thompson dining room in East Texas — in the wall and floor coverings, the sparing use of textiles, the presence of a plate rail, and the overall rectilinear quality of the space. While Evelyn, the cook, stands by the sideboard, George Overton Stoner and his wife, Zilpa Rose, and their grandson, Kemper S. Williams, sit at the dining table.

George Stoner began his Stoner Pasture Company in 1876 "with but a few head of cows, and no money" and through hard work became one of the most successful and prosperous stockmen in South Texas. George (born in 1847) and Zilpa Rose (born in 1850) were elderly when they posed in their newly renovated dining room in 1912. It seems unusual that an older couple would remodel so late in their lives, but they were raising their motherless grandson and had recently decided to take advantage of the comforts of town living.[15]

The house is in the classical revival style, probably built

9.14. Living room, Alexander Thompson house, (Two blocks east of State Highway 69), Doucette, ca. 1908 (Texas Forestry Museum, Lufkin).

9.15. Dining room, Alexander Thompson house, ca. 1908 (Texas Forestry Museum, Lufkin).

circa 1905. According to family history, the structure was begun by gambler Pink Reed who, because of "bad luck," was unable to complete it. The Wood family occupied the house until the Stoners purchased it in 1909, about three years before this picture was taken by the two photographers who are reflected in the sideboard mirror.

In remodeling, the Stoners combined arts and crafts and colonial revival details. Popular moire paper adorns the ceiling and frieze, and a paper patterned with large stylized floral and foliate motifs covers the wide space above the plate rail. The light fixture and the curtains reflect the arts and crafts style. As in the Thompson dining room, a solid paper extends below the rail, and a geometric-pattern rug covers the floor. But the Stoners have selected colonial

9.16. Dining room, George Overton Stoner house, 106 North William Street, Victoria, ca. 1912 (Courtesy Margaret Stoner McLean).

revival furniture for what is essentially a room finished with arts and crafts details.

Colonial revivalism was the focus of a photograph Duncan Caldwell Crooks took in the entry of a house in Galveston (fig. 9.17). The young woman at the spinning wheel is probably his sister. She is dressed in a colonial costume such as other American women wore when they attended Martha Washington or colonial theme parties. Like the woman who poses rather than works, the spinning wheel is decorative, not utilitarian; bolls of cotton were very likely not spun on this wheel — they merely adorn it.

For late-nineteenth- and early-twentieth-century Americans, the spinning wheel was one of the most popular

9.17. Entry hall, Duncan Caldwell Crooks house, probably 1519 24th Street, Galveston, 1909 – 1912 (Rosenberg Library, Galveston).

objects for conjuring up images of past. Decorative arts historian Christopher Monkhouse charts the use of the wheel in this country from the seventeenth century to its decline by the early nineteenth century, when it was supplanted by more efficient spinning devices. Interest in the spinning wheel renewed at mid century when various New England towns celebrated their bicentennials. This attention was increased by colonial themes in certain installations at fairs, expositions, and historical displays — the most famous and far-reaching of which was the Farmer's Home and Modern Kitchen (known as the New England Kitchen) at the International Centennial Exhibition. The kitchen featured a spinning wheel.[16]

In Texas the pattern developed differently from the East Coast. The spinning wheel's evolution was necessarily compressed in time. Far from waning in importance in the early decades of the nineteenth century, the spinning wheel was a necessity for many women living on the Texas frontier. Mary Rabb, for example, describing her peripatetic life in early Texas, told of moving about the land in the late 1820s and created a strong image of domestic life at that time: all the family's possessions were packed on their horse with the spinning wheel on the very top of the bundle and two chickens tied to its spokes.[17] Rabb's wheel was prized neither because of its decorative value nor because it moored the chickens. It was used to create fabrics essential to the family's existence.

As New England towns heralded two centuries of history, Anglo Texas was battling to remove itself from Mexico's rule. In the eyes of these settlers, Texas did not have a past to celebrate. Because of this historical difference, the colonial revival style was not as self-conscious or far-reaching in Texas as in New England, the Crooks photograph notwithstanding. Nevertheless, Texans did acknowledge the colonial revival style with a candlestick on the mantel, moire ceiling paper, contrasting color schemes, or catalogue-ordered furniture with vaguely colonial motifs, thereby appropriating a past and recognizing a popular style.

In the Crooks entry, much of the woodwork has been painted white or a light shade and contrasts with the dark balustrade and floor. Colored glass windows and fabrics introduce patterns and colors to the room. A stair carpet and a bank of pillows top the steps; two small rugs dot the dark hardwood floors, marking spatial transitions, as does the palm in an art pottery jardiniere.

There are few pieces of furniture in the entry hall. Earlier a mirrored hallstand might have reflected the appearance of family and guests, received cards, and held coats, hats, and umbrellas, but in this photograph, a simple rectangular beveled mirror in an oak frame with clothes hooks partially fulfills these functions, suggesting the wane of the ritual of exchanging calling cards. Imposing chairs have here given way to a dainty colonial revival hall seat that usually holds pillows with unmatched and eclectic tops; the needlework of the pillow tops probably exemplifies the householder's skill with the needle.

In addition to the aesthetic, mission, and colonial revival styles, some Texans embraced the advice of decorating authority Elsie de Wolfe. Among the additions to the Maxey family's 1868 Italianate residence in Paris, Texas, was a breakfast room (fig. 9.18; see fig. 2.11). Remodeled between 1911 and 1913, the informal space reflects the changes popularized by de Wolfe in the early years of the twentieth century: less clutter, light colors, and colorful fabrics, especially cretonne and chintz. In fact, her advocacy of the latter fabric earned de Wolfe the nickname "The Chintz Lady."[18]

It is difficult to overestimate the strong influence Elsie de Wolfe (1865 – 1950) had upon American decorating

9.18. Breakfast room, Sam Bell Maxey house, Southwest corner of Church and Washington streets (812 East Church Street), Paris, ca. 1915 (Texas State Archives, Austin).

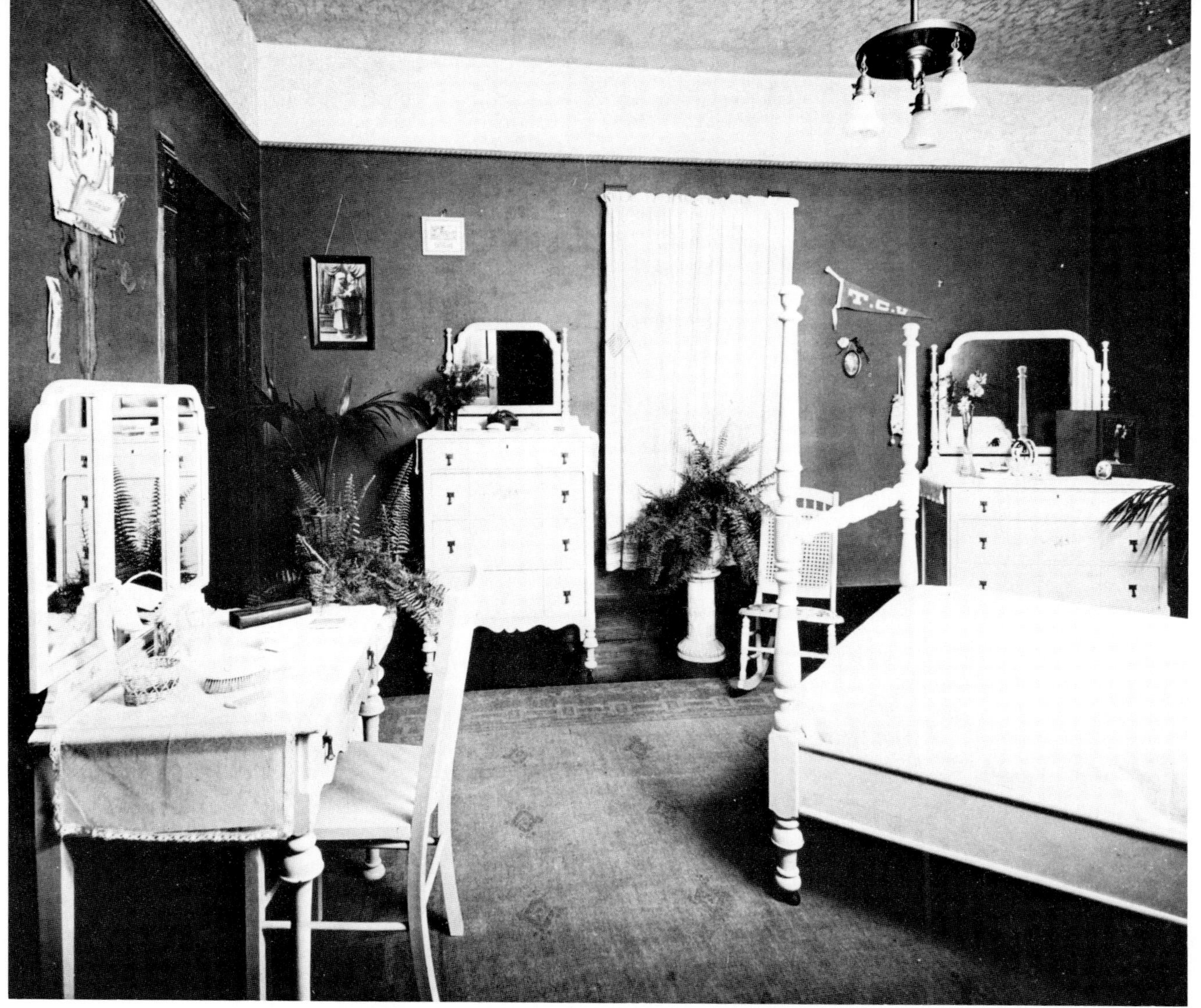

9.19. Bedroom, Urban S. and Ella Maye Bumpass Russell house, 206 West Mulberry Street, Sherman, ca. 1920 (Sherman Historical Museum).

taste. Her magazine articles were collected in a manual for style, *The House in Good Taste* (1915), which carried her popularized reform message to the middle classes. She is credited with leading Americans out of the Victorian darkness into the light of the twentieth century and publicizing the ideas originally set forth by Edith Wharton and Ogden Codman in *The Decoration of Houses* (1897). She further earned the reputation of founding the profession of interior decoration, secured when she completed the Colony Club commission in New York City, a result of Stanford White's recommendation. In Texas, her influence was seen in Galveston; she was chosen to redecorate the

9.20. Dining room, Urban S. and Ella Maye Bumpass Russell house, ca. 1920 (Sherman Historical Museum).

George Sealy Mansion designed by McKim, Mead & White.[19] More important, her influence was widely disseminated in the popular press. The Maxey addition resounds with de Wolfe's tenets — simplicity, suitability, and proportion — and documents the pervasiveness of her advice, linking the Maxey house in North Texas to a national taste.[20]

The table, armchair, and three side chairs are in the Elizabethan revival or cottage style. Like the walls, they are painted a light color. Instead of the heavy draping that characterized the spaces of earlier houses, the textiles follow the de Wolfe canon, here including only a light runner on the side table in a sheer, loosely woven fabric embellished with palm leaf designs, and pale dining table runners decorated with birds and floral patterns, reminiscent of Japanese design. A chintz curtain covers a built-in storage compartment; the seats and backs of the dining chairs are covered in a matching floral print fabric. Flowers — daisies probably grown in the Maxey family's extensive flower gardens — decorate the ledge of the window and the center of the dining table and fill the hanging basket near the entrance to a service area.

The bedroom of the Urban S. and Ella Maye Bumpass Russell house (fig. 9.19) in the North Texas town of Sherman, near Paris, is also a statement of style, an elegant middle-class example of the de Wolfe manifesto. An image of the newlyweds hangs by the bureau; the same photograph sits on the dresser near a ceramic horseshoe, the traditional sign of good luck to the couple (see figs. 4.11, 9.2). A Sherman schoolteacher and graduate of Texas Christian University in Fort Worth, Ella Maye displays her loyalty to her alma mater with a collegiate banner fastened to the plain wallpaper.[21] Another wall-hung accessory, a United States flag, testifies to the Russells' patriotism during World War I. Over the dressing table, the top section of a commercial calendar, a promotional advertisement for a Sherman business, partially hides a water stain on the wallpaper.

The Russell bedroom makes a clear statement of the colonial revival style. The bedroom suite was a recent purchase from Sherman's Taliaferro Furniture Company, where Russell worked as a bookkeeper.[22] The pieces adhere to de Wolfe's preference for furniture painted in light colors; their turned decoration evokes the William and Mary style of the late seventeenth century. And the light furniture against the dark wallpaper background contributes the element of color contrast.

The Taliaferro Furniture Company also provided "period" furnishings for the dining room (fig. 9.20). The Russells chose oak furniture combining elements of late-seventeenth- and early-eighteenth-century styles to create a fashionable colonial revival setting. In accordance with de Wolfe's philosophy, the room exhibits a sparseness that dining rooms furnished a decade or more earlier did not; if the ferns and palms were removed, the room would be quite bare.

⋆ ⋆ ⋆ ⋆

These images share an enthusiasm for stylistic unity as a decorating goal, while the householders ignored or suppressed expressions of personal identity. The images demonstrate an awareness of and eagerness to accept national home-decorating trends, a desire to have the styles that were fashionable throughout the country. Because the families included here were of at least middle-class means and had financial access to the furnishings market, they could achieve this goal.

10.1. Parlor, Gregor Carmichael McGregor house, Corner Columbus Avenue and North Eighth Street (725 Columbus Avenue), Waco, 1896 (Courtesy William M. and Frances P. Harris).

10

Houses of Many Rooms

MULTIPLE IDENTITIES

THROUGH the decoration of their homes, people expressed their identity as residents of a region and as members of families, various social and ethnic groups, and economic classes. In many cases such identification was visible throughout a room and occasionally through several rooms. And while other identities may be alluded to in some spaces, they are generally subthemes. But only in images of several rooms in the same house do rooms express an assortment of identities that reflect the way a household defined itself for friends, relatives, and even family members.

Some of the following rooms were photographed at the same time; other images were taken at various intervals from 1896 to 1920. In both cases — within any period of time, range of styles, or geographical area — the houses illustrate how families fashioned different spaces in personally expressive ways and thus made their homes distinctive.

Consider first the Waco residence of Gregor and Annie McGregor (figs. 10.1, 10.2, 10.3). Born of immigrant Scottish parents in North Carolina, McGregor had moved to Texas after his 1852 graduation from medical school at New York University; he founded a small colony whose members, mostly his Scottish North Carolinian relatives, settled across Washington and Austin counties during the next eight years. In 1859, McGregor married Annie Portia Fordtran, daughter of a pioneer German emigrant and Austin colonist, Charles Fordtran, who was one of the largest landowners in the county. McGregor, too, had prospered — both as a physician and as a land speculator. He purchased big tracts of land in Washington, Austin, and Fayette counties, subdivided them, and then sold parcels to Germans and Czechs who were arriving in large numbers at that time.[1]

When McGregor gave up his medical practice in 1872, he and his family moved to Waco, where he continued to

10.2. Sitting room, Gregor Carmichael McGregor house, 1896 (Courtesy William M. and Frances P. Harris).

manage his land interests.[2] In 1873 he built an Italianate residence. Its interior was photographed twenty-three years later as the McGregors introduced their new daughter-in-law, Mrs. Will (Irene) McGregor, into Waco society. As the local newspaper announced, "a handsome young bride was to be ushered into matrondom, and her welcome was to be greeted in no commonplace way." More than 300 guests were formally received in the parlor where

> the florist's smilax formed scarf draperies for every window, caught in graceful festoons by American Beauty buds. The piece de resistance here was an artist's triumph in a magnificent jardiniere, [?]y over-

> flowing with the Beauty roses. The smile of the American Beauty, the queen among flowers, and the American woman the queen among women, was never better illustrated than in the handsome group that surrounded the hostess.[3]

The "pièce de résistance" is the jardiniere highlighted in figure 10.1 at the center of the piano top. The jardiniere itself is painted with a rose motif that is echoed around the room in stencil-decorated panels.

The equation of flowers and women was not just the product of the imagination of the Waco newspaper reporter; in nineteenth-century America, flowers, part of the sentimental culture, were the province of women. Women nurtured flowers, and in so doing, embodied the virtues inherent in "womanhood." As if to mark a feminine domain, flowers provided motifs for carpeting and wallpaper mills that produced countless floral patterns for room decoration. In Annie McGregor's parlor, for example, flowers define floor, walls, and ceramics. Floral themes also embellish the elaborately draped scarf that renders the piano exclusively decorative because the hostess had arranged for that day to have "music [steal] down the stairway from an unseen source."

In a corner of this feminine room is a copy of *The Greek Slave*, originally sculpted life size by Hiram Powers. This sculpture, which Henry James remarked was "so undressed, yet so refined," inspired countless casts that found their way into homes across the country, renewing the legitimacy of the nude as a vehicle of artistic expression.[4] A recent art historian has said that during the late nineteenth century "no house was really properly and tastefully furnished without at least a little bisque version of the statue."[5]

Amid these and other images of womanhood gracing the parlor, a painting of Robert E. Lee riding Traveller hangs behind the piano and expresses Gregor McGregor's Southern identity and his sympathy with the Lost Cause. His brothers both fought in the Civil War: physician Malcolm lost an arm as a result of an injury received during the battle of Chickamauga, and John died from exposure after the fall of Arkansas Post.[6]

Although the newspaper reporter contended that the "luxurious old home with its high ceiling and immense window niches was made to fairly lose itself under a tangle of smilax, a jungle of palms and a bower of roses," Annie made sure that important elements were not masked. Stenciled cove molding encircles the room, and a gasolier hangs from a circular medallion centered on the painted ceiling. Naturalistic themes on the lace curtains continue the floral motifs at the windows; swags of a striped fabric create a valance. Silks asymmetrically drape the piano and the mantel, and silk damask upholsters the suite of furniture that was considered Eastlake when purchased.

In the sitting room (fig. 10.2) "a punch bower suggestive of the winter home of woodland sprites toying with aurora carnations" was presided over by Geraldine Garland and Nell Symes, "themselves resembling the white robed fairies told by legend as the inhabitants of woodland haunts." Like the bower, palms encased in ball moss seem to spring from the sitting room floor, and according to one reporter, "were everywhere through these rambling rooms."

Unlike the parlor, the sitting room walls are covered by papers — a dark side-wall paper, a conventionalized floral frieze, and a ceiling paper featuring a field of astronomical motifs bordered by a guilloche design. The windows of the sitting room are more simply treated, with roller blinds and sheer curtains trimmed in complementary guilloche. Instead of wall-to-wall carpeting, a bordered rug in a foliate pattern tops the wooden floor. Framed paintings and prints help decorate a room that looks quite bare, the

10.3. Dining room, Gregor Carmichael McGregor house, 1896 (Courtesy William M. and Frances P. Harris).

furniture having been pushed to the walls so that the guests at the gathering could more easily navigate the spaces near the bower.

Like those in dining rooms in many fashionable Texas houses, most of the McGregor furnishings are remarkably plain (fig. 10.3). Simple, cane-seat dining chairs from at least three sets line the walls, and a fabric screen masks entry to kitchen and pantry. The sideboard, however, is impressive and unusual in its large storage and display area, functioning in part as a china cabinet. The linen-scarved shelf displays silver and glass; a crumb sweeper hangs nearby. For the party, "the table [is] a study of purple and yellow in a broad oblong of satin strewn with Parma violets fresh from the green house . . . while mint and almond trays were at irregular intervals."

A rug in a floral and geometric design spreads across much of the parquet floor. As in the sitting room, the walls are covered with unpatterned paper topped by a floral frieze and complementary ceiling paper, enhanced by framed paintings and prints, some of them possibly executed by amateur artist Annie McGregor. Illuminating the entire composition, a gasolier hangs over the table, and a banquet lamp sits on the small table in one corner.

The interior views of the McGregor public rooms show an identification with region, refinement, class, and style. The occasion for the picture taking suggests the McGregors' identification with family.

The Bowie house in Weatherford was photographed soon after its completion (figs. 10.4 through 10.8).[7] Born in Scotland in 1846, George Morland Bowie came to the United States in 1868. After his 1875 marriage to Margaret Armstrong, daughter of a Texas rancher, Bowie joined another prominent Scottish Texan, William Cameron of Waco, in the lumber business, an affiliation that lasted nearly twenty years.[8]

George Bowie first managed the Weatherford yard then became a partner in a division of William Cameron & Company whereby he supervised the Northwest Texas interests of the firm. Assigned to take charge of the company's cypress lumber and shingle mill, Bowie moved his family, his wife and six children, to White Castle, Louisiana. In 1900 William Cameron died, the Bowies' White Castle home had burned and been rebuilt, and Bowie decided to retire from the lumber business at the age of fifty-four. The family resettled in Weatherford where Bowie built a twenty-four-room Queen Anne house on a large corner lot.[9] According to daughter Ellen, Margaret Bowie was upset when her husband presumed to rebuild the White Castle home "without the guiding eye of a woman." Margaret made sure she was on site during the construction of the house in Weatherford, even though the family could afford to hire both architect and professional decorator. At the time, Weatherford lacked the "services of erudite interior decorators," so Margaret fashioned the interiors herself, probably relying on the stockrooms of Weatherford, Fort Worth, and Dallas furniture stores.[10]

> The [family's] French furniture had gone up with the ghosts in smoke, when our house in White Castle burned, so now new furnishings must be had. Bird's-eye maple was popular for bedrooms, and wicker pieces were new and "important." Our house seemed always to be full of pretty guests, and if there is a prettier sight than a lovely lady, in a sprigged summer frock, seated in a lacy wicker chair, I don't know what it is. . . . Of course wicker chairs had wicked ways and could catch and tear yards of cloth from one's dress.[11]

The furnishings exhibit no great temporal range. There are two of every item in the entry hall (fig. 10.4). Twin colonial revival chairs sit side by side. Two silver-plated water pitchers sit on identical tables, identically draped, each with a lower shelf used to store magazines. Two similar hearth rugs appear in front of twin fireplace mantels, each with a center figurine, the one in the foreground a bronze image of the Three Graces, a New Orleans purchase according to family history. The wicker armchair in the foreground is matched by its twin on the near side of the fireplace in the background. In fact, the fireplace walls are mirror images of one another, leading us to believe another armchair is positioned to the left of the foreground fireplace, just out of the camera's view. Multiple copies of similar or identical household objects may suggest a limited selection of goods or an efficient decorating strategy; possibly their purchase signaled the socioeconomic status of the Bowies.

The impressive entry area is unusual among Texas houses for its openness and spaciousness. It was "well planned for a large and active family." The walls are of plaster, the ceilings of tin; fashionable grilles and monumental mantels embellish the hall. The wainscoting "of selected burl cypress which Father [Bowie] had been stashing away for this purpose" bespeaks his occupation.[12] Less personal are the hallway objects that appear in many other interiors: the animal trophy above the fireplace and the water pitchers near the front door. Just out of view stood another typical feature, the hallstand, which Ellen described:

> A hatrack was a very articulate piece of furniture. From the conglomeration hanging on it, at a glance, you could tell if Uncle Harry, Cousin Frank or the Misses McGruders were being entertained — and it was exciting to see a strange flowered hat, a city derby, or a feather boa. Our hatrack was the biggest, ugliest piece of furniture made since they divided all Gaul into three parts. But we didn't know it. It was simply accepted as a necessity. It was of oak and around a mirror bristled six fancy double brass prongs. The lower part was an armed seat and the top of the seat was hinged like a chest. It opened and when we came home we dumped our extra fribbles into it. Whenever anything was lost someone would say, "Have you looked in the hatrack?"[13]

The camera skipped the billiard room, two rooms with walls of mirrors "*à la* Versailles," the bedrooms, and the bathrooms, one on each floor, and the "round glassed-in conservatory, full of thriving pot plants, which was Mother's [Margaret's] special pride," but it captured snatches of the three parlors (fig. 10.5).[14]

The passageway linking these and a fourth room is filled with variously styled wicker, rattan, and bamboo chairs and side tables and stands topped with statuary, vases, and lamps. A floral-and-scrollwork motif wall-to-wall carpet spreads throughout the rooms. Similar if not identical electric lighting fixtures convey a sense of unity. The foreground space and adjacent room are "rhymed" — a crocheted butterfly is attached to the portières, while a butterfly-back chair appears in the photograph's middle ground. The chairs are positioned to invite the viewer into the rooms.

As in the entry hall, the parlor furnishings reveal Margaret's efficient decorating solutions. She purchased multiple copies of several items. Although many decorating strategies were available in 1901, she knew what she wanted — painted walls, uniform carpet, tin ceilings, and electric fixtures. Details were often consistent in rooms connected by open doorways, but within each room, specific themes might dominate. The glimpse of the Bowie sitting room in the foreground shows, for example, the influence of exoticism. The objets d'art include prints and

10.4. Entry hall ("Living room"), George Morland Bowie house, 1539 Fourth Street, Weatherford, 1902 (Panhandle-Plains Historical Museum, Canyon).

10.5. Parlor, "Looking from sitting room through library into back parlor," George Morland Bowie house, 1902 (Panhandle-Plains Historical Museum, Canyon).

statuary of Moorish design and a classical pedestal stand; portières of oriental inspiration hang in the doorway. The next room has a wicker theme; and the third and fourth rooms show curule chairs of Roman inspiration.

Another downstairs room was Bowie's study, termed "Father's domain" (fig. 10.6).

> He really liked for all of us to stay out of there and to loosely impress us with this craving, he usually kept the door closed. Against the east wall was a large roll-top desk and its pigeonholes were crammed with all manner of stuff. He never used it for anything but a receptacle and it was fascinating to look at. Another wall had book shelves and along a third wall there was a tufted leather couch. One end of this couch was raised in an inquiring curve and it looked like a fat caterpillar about to inch forward. In the center of the room there was a spacious table where he wrote his letters. There were old drawings on the walls, and a large globe stood between two windows.[15]

The camera has captured part of the room — the library table, the tufted couch, a rocking chair, an armchair, a Morris chair (behind the palm), and bookcases. The table has Elizabethan twist- and ball-turned legs and stretchers, baroque brass drawer pulls, gargoyles at the corners and on the drawer, and paterae. Typical in libraries, most of Bowie's seating pieces are upholstered in leather. Art pottery decorates both bookcases: the larger, with its pierced gallery, incising, and size, suggests Eastlake inspiration; the smaller one detailed with twist-turned molding complements the library table.

Although the room seemed formidable to a young Ellen, the comfortable objects in it belie the impression. The businessman may have periodically excluded his children from his private domain, but their images were nearby. The room expresses Bowie's identification with family: photographs of his wife line the smaller bookcase, while those of his six children surround him in the room. A portrait photograph of Bowie hangs near the window. By 1902 the fifty-four-year-old man had achieved success in business and was prosperous enough to build this house and support a large family. The sign on his private office in downtown Weatherford best sums up his attitude: "G. M. Bowie, Office Hours, Now and Then."[16] This seemingly casual attitude and his early retirement from the lumber business did not preclude his serving as vice-president of the First National Bank in Weatherford, or investing money as a stockholder in numerous local and statewide enterprises, or serving as a booster of the Chamber of Commerce.

In the dining room, the members of the family exhibit an awareness of style and an identification with Bowie's social group (figs. 10.7, 10.8). Figure 10.7 was photographed with the rest of the public spaces of the home in 1901 or 1902; figure 10.8 dates eight or nine years later. The earlier photo shows a dense display typical of the late 1890s and early 1900s: china cabinet, server, sideboard, and dining table, all featuring glassware, silver, and ceramics, including a large fish service, one of the specialized serving sets popular between 1890 and 1915. These rich materials are highlighted against a painted wall, which rises from chair rail to ceiling. Suspended from gilt picture molding just below a gilt cornice, two similarly framed pastoral landscapes flank one window, and a more decoratively framed still life hangs above the china cabinet. Pressed tin covers the ceiling, and a bordered wall-to-wall carpet in a medallion-and-diamond pattern conceals the wooden floor. Lace curtains cover the window shades. As in the library, the curtains are asymmetrically pulled back in an "artistic" fashion. In the center of the room, an electric fixture hangs well above diners who will sit in bentwood chairs and a colonial revival chair.

10.6. Library, George Morland Bowie house, 1902 (Panhandle-Plains Historical Museum, Canyon).

Less than a decade later Margaret made substantial changes to update the dining room and its furnishings. Her husband, at the left corner of the view in figure 10.8, hosts a meal and a meeting. An extension table accommodates sixteen members of this unidentified group, which is attended by a Tejano servant standing at the back of the room. At the windows, lace curtains have given way to straight-hung center panels framed by patterned panels. A monumental bowfront sideboard has replaced both server and sideboard. The china cabinet with its ball turnings has been moved. A new plate rail displays ceramics, including several steins and mugs decorated by decalcomania with pictures of stags. A different still life and a new heraldic wall plaque decorate a corner beneath the plate rail. On the table, a plateau supports the fern-filled loving cup, which like the stein sets may relate to the social club Bowie appears to be entertaining. Above the group hangs the same lighting fixture as in figure 10.7; for this photo-

10.7. Dining room, George Morland Bowie house, "1901 or 1902" (Panhandle-Plains Historical Museum, Canyon).

10.8. Dining room, George Morland Bowie house, ca. 1910 (Panhandle-Plains Historical Museum, Canyon).

graph it is lit but draped so that the photographer could illuminate the group portrait.

Moving from North Texas to the southern tip of the state, Brownsville, the next series of images (figs. 10.9 through 10.15) show the Mary Hune Waltgenbach house, a middle-class dwelling built about the same time as the Bowie house. A cosmopolitan port, Brownsville was home for many emigrants from Germany, France, and Italy in the nineteenth century. German-born Carl Waltgenbach married Mary Hune, daughter of a German emigrant, in 1889. The couple built a one-and-one-half-story brick house on Elizabeth Street after the turn of the century, shortly before he died in one of the yellow fever epidemics that plagued Brownsville during the nineteenth and early twentieth centuries.[17]

Having assisted her husband with his photography business for nearly twelve years, Mary took over the enterprise after Carl's death, stamping the back of mounted photo-

10.9. Sitting room, Mary Hune Waltgenbach house, Southeast corner of Elizabeth and Thirteenth streets (1300 Elizabeth Street), Brownsville, ca. 1904 (Courtesy Barbara Bates Mills; Mary Hune Waltgenbach, Photographer).

10.10. Sitting room, Mary Hune Waltgenbach house, ca. 1906 (Courtesy Barbara Bates Mills).

graphs, "Mrs. Mary Waltgenbach, Photographer."[18] In the following years, her extended family — brothers-in-law Arthur Bates and Vicente Tamayo and sisters Adele Hune Bates, Henrietta Hune Tamayo, and Antoinette Hune — sometimes lived with her.[19]

Most of the photographs displayed in the room interiors of the home are Mary Waltgenbach's work. She identified with her occupation, her family, and her social group. Photographs of her family and friends decorate the corner whatnot and fill the wall pockets; gifts that they made embellish the rooms. Often in these photographs familiar room objects appear rearranged, in different configurations, much as the people are grouped in slightly varying poses.

Figure 10.9 also expresses the family's aspiration toward fashion. At the time the photograph was taken, theme parties were popular in Texas as well as around the country. Men and women outfitted themselves in costumes for colonial theme parties, they donned recreations of clothing from the classical age for pageants, and they dressed in "exotic" garb for gypsy parties. But most popular of all were Japanese theme parties.

Americans had been enthusiastic about Japanese objects since the International Centennial Exhibition in Philadelphia in 1876 at which many countries displayed their native art and technology. Impressed with the ingenuity of the Japanese and inspired by their exhibits, middle-class Americans began to incorporate Japanese-style adornments into their homes. Fans adorned mantels and parlor walls; paper parasols and lanterns hung from lighting fixtures; screens embellished with Japanese-style flowers and birds stood in parlors and dining rooms.[20]

Showing their passion for Japanese taste in both home decoration and social life, Antoinette and Adele Hune and three friends staged a Japanese party during which they had their picture taken. Positioned on a mat, or small rug, spread over what appears to be tatami grass matting, the women are ready for tea and hold paper fans and an Autoharp. The corner is inventively assembled — some of the Japanese-style articles have been added for the party; others were not just temporary room elements. The kimono-clad group has added the parasol and the paper fans to the painted horizontal boards of the interior walls, but the kakemono is a year-round feature in the room. Similar to those shown in other Texas houses, the banner is embroidered on silk with abstract floral and bird designs and has a contrasting dark plush top and bottom border. This decorative hanging was probably fashioned by one of the Hune women using widely published instructions for such home adornments. Like the kakemono, two bamboo stands suit the theme of the party but will continue to display a collection of glass and ceramics and to support an aspidistra plant long after the group disbands.

Two years later the same room was photographed from a slightly different perspective, providing an index of changes within a brief interval (fig. 10.10). The floor and wall treatments remain the same, as does the dark shade trimmed with a lace border. But the earlier curtains have been replaced, and some of the wall-hung accessories and furniture have been shifted. The Japanese banner has been joined by two portrait photographs; a landscape topped by a stuffed bird sits in one corner, and a whatnot occupies the other. Next to it are decorations alluding to the women's social and artistic identities. A portrait of one of the sisters is hung above a photograph album resting on its own stand. Nearby, a studio portrait has been turned into a wall pocket holding still more photographs. The plush, ball-fringe wall hanging painted with roses and topped with decorative paper circles, attests to the activities of the Hune women and their friends.

While documenting overlapping family, social, and artistic identities, the images in the left corner also express photographer Mary Hune Waltgenbach's occupation, skill, and activities. One of her images appears twice in the two cartes de visite featuring a family friend dressed and posed as the Statue of Liberty.

Over time a series of parlor photographs (figs. 10.11, 10.12, 10.13) provides a partial chronology of decoration, including small changes made expressly for picture taking. As in the previous two images and as was common at the time, sitters are posed against a picturesque interior backdrop — the bay window hung with curtains of large-pattern naturalistic designs.

Chronologically first in this parlor series, figure 10.11 features two of Waltgenbach's sisters, Antoinette and Adele, and Valentine Tamayo, Henrietta's husband and

10.11. Parlor, Mary Hune Waltgenbach house, ca. 1906 (Courtesy Barbara Bates Mills).

10.12. Parlor, Mary Hune Waltgenbach house, ca. 1907 (Courtesy Barbara Bates Mills).

Brownsville's chief of police. Behind them hang two July 1904 wedding portraits of Henrietta. In addition to the framed images suspended by dark cords, several examples of blind-hung wall art executed by the Hunes and friends are displayed: the utilitarian metal flue cover has been decoratively painted with yellow roses and signed A[ntoinette] Hune; a family friend painted the landscape, a snow scene.[21]

Soon after Waltgenbach photographed the trio, she posed a larger group by the window (fig. 10.12). This view shows more detail about the manner in which a floral-patterned and asymmetrically hung fabric drapes the recess as a kind of valance. The curtains are new, but many of the room details are not: a crayon portrait of Casiminao Tamayo, Henrietta's father-in-law, is again featured on the easel; wall-hung accessories remain in place; and one of the family's most treasured — and photographed — artifacts, the photograph album, stays in view.

By 1910 the parlor walls are covered with a colorful

10.13. Parlor, Mary Hune Waltgenbach house, ca. 1908 (Courtesy Barbara Bates Mills).

10.14. Bedroom, Mary Hune Waltgenbach house, ca. 1908 (Courtesy Barbara Bates Mills).

wallpaper in a floral design (fig. 10.13). A boldly patterned matting has replaced the earlier plain matting. The fabric valance has disappeared, unnecessary in this wallpaper garden; some wall-hung accessories have been replaced by portrait photographs of family.

A bedroom reveals the occupational and artistic identities of the owner (fig. 10.14). Two picturesque groupings, one at the fireplace and the other at the washstand, are evidence of an interest in decoupage, embroidery, wood carving, and pyrography. Waltgenbach sold frames she decorated, along with other household adornments, in addition to her photographs, but she kept some artwork to embellish her bedroom. Using pomegranates as a motif, she has decorated various frames, including an elongated

10.15. Sitting room, Mary Hune Waltgenbach house, ca. 1910 (Courtesy Barbara Bates Mills).

frame containing photographs of dogs, visible above the mantel. A popular subject in commercial prints, dogs were also important to the photographer; her album reveals labeled pictures of her own pets. She has also lavished her time decorating the plant stand, fashioning a fire screen from surplus wallpaper, and embroidering the stenciled mantel scarf with designs of fans and butterflies.

The other picturesque wall group surmounts the draped washstand on which is placed a toilet set; a splash cloth detailed with bow designs protects the wallpaper. Waltgenbach has included another of her favorite photographic subjects — the cemetery, scene of outings with her sisters and friends who posed among the monuments and gravestones. A print of a crane, the Japanese symbol of long life, hangs on the adjacent wall above the homemade wall pocket.

In a corner of the redecorated sitting room, both sitters and objects project an identification with family and social group (fig. 10.15). Waltgenbach captured her sister Antoinette "revealing" to the camera a pair of hearts and one of spades as she discards an unmatched club. The card-playing trio sits among adornments made by friends and family. For example, a second snow scene was a hand-painted wedding gift to Henrietta, and the carved stand and decoupaged image of a Saint Bernard represent more artistic talent.[22] In spite of their Hispanic and German heritage, the Hunes embellish their room with cosmopolitan images of Oriental and Dutch women.

In the Texas Panhandle, the Hill family hired a professional photographer to document their new home (figs. 10.16 through 10.21). Merchant, stock farmer, and businessman, Frank H. Hill was born in Connecticut in 1858 and grew up in Illinois. He began working for the Santa Fe Railroad in 1885; two years later when the railroad was completed as far as the town of Panhandle, Texas, Hill came with the first train. He served as the railroad agent for the town but soon decided that Panhandle, the rapidly growing regional business center, offered a greater variety of opportunities.[23]

He established the F. H. Hill Mercantile Company, which sold dry goods and clothing, and became co-owner

10.16. Entry hall, Frank H. Hill house, Panhandle, ca. 1910 (Courtesy Betty O. Ellis).

10.17. Parlor, Frank H. Hill house, ca. 1910 (Courtesy Betty O. Ellis).

of Hill and Sellars Hardware Store and Hill-Hoffman Lumber Company. A member of the Panhandle German Coach Horse Company, Hill bred fine horses and raised cattle on his 1,000-acre property, "a model fancy stock farm, equal to any in the north or east."[24]

In 1903 Frank and Lucille Stanhope Stone Hill built their house, the Armitage (named after his mother's family), on their stock farm on the outskirts of town. A trio of decoupaged prints of horses, trimmed with horseshoes at the corners and topped by a bit, hang in the entry hall (fig. 10.16). As the name of his homestead bespeaks his identification with family, so this wall plaque expresses his occupational identity.

The entry hall also attests to the Hills' stylistic identity. Lucille has selected the mission style for the armchair, clock, portières, and curtains. A small screen and a bamboo stool contribute Japanese elements. Called diaphanie, translucent, colored paper on a small window at the landing achieves the effect of art glass, a popular arts and crafts finish. (The sunlight entering the diamond-shaped window burned out the details in this photograph; the photographer has manipulated the print to regain those de-

10.18. Sitting room, Frank H. Hill house, ca. 1910 (Courtesy Betty O. Ellis).

tails, at the cost of the pattern on the wallpaper.) Built-in benches or hall seats on both sides of the staircase show an awareness of early-twentieth-century architectural reform.

Animated patterning of the floor and wall surfaces provides the most impressive feature of the space. A large rug conceals much of the wooden floor; mats mark the transition into the adjacent room; a diapered stair carpet held in place by metal stair rods covers the steps. An unusual wallpaper in a classical design with panels topped by a border of anthemia covers the wall below the dado rail. A bold medallion-pattern paper adorns the walls above the rail, while a matching frieze blends the color of the side walls into the light geometric-pattern ceiling paper that crowns the room.

The Hills' entry hall illustrates the preference among turn-of-the-century householders living in the Texas Panhandle for wallpaper. Businessmen, too, preferred this wall treatment, as was the case in 1902 when George Tyng of nearby Pampa instructed partner F. de P. Foster in New York to choose paper for their hotel, the Pampa Inn. "Paper should be strong, pretty & cheap. Patterns to reflect light as much as possible without too gaudily dis-

10.19. Dining room, Frank H. Hill house, ca. 1910 (Courtesy Betty O. Ellis).

playing dirt, tobacco juice etc. It can be ordered (when wanted) from here or selected from samples at N.Y."[25]

The Armitage was "probably the finest and largest residence in the Texas Panhandle, an imposing looking place, furnished and finished in splendid style and with a liberal hand, such as one will not . . . find outside of urban communities."[26] The Hills often entertained there, frequently in the parlor (fig. 10.17).

This 1910 view of their colonial revival parlor shows a family displaying its knowledge of the new restraint in home decoration, especially in the more formal rooms. High color contrast, so much a feature of the colonial revival, is articulated in the light wall and floor coverings, which form a pale backdrop for the dark mantel and furniture. The paneled folding doors, painted a dark color and set within light woodwork, are an unusual feature in Texas houses documented in this survey. Other elements typify Texas middle-class tastes, like the framed landscapes, seascapes, and madonnas that adorn the parlor walls.

Without electricity or gas, the Hill home relies on kerosene lamps for illumination. The decorative candlestick on the mantel is a hallmark of a so-called colonial room, and the ornate candelabrum on the music cabinet adds to the formality of the room. The candles contribute to the room's artificial lighting, but the major source of light remains a kerosene lamp, sitting on the large table along with a card tray.

Mission portières similar to those marking the door from the entry hall into the parlor hang at entrance to the sitting room (fig. 10.18). The sitting room walls and those of an adjacent room contrast with those of the entry hall. Instead of displaying highly patterned papers, the walls are covered in a solid, medium-shade paper; a lighter solid ceiling paper extends to the frieze. Only a mirror and prints interrupt the papered walls. The entrance into the smaller room provides some variety as its doorjamb is hung with portières of beads or shells beneath a transom decorated with paper patterned in imitation of art glass, or diaphanie.

The large bold outlines of the rug provide pattern in this room. The rug appears to have been laid on matting suggesting that it is winter, an impression heightened by the reflection of a heating stove in the mirror. In full view are a leather-upholstered armchair and rocking chair, a piano used by Lucille and daughter Florence, and a child's rocking chair.

Like the parlor, the dining room was the scene of entertaining (fig. 10.19).

> Quite an elaborate affair was given at the home of Mr. and Mrs. F. H. Hill Monday noon, when Governor O. B. Colquitt, his private party and a number of Panhandle citizens were entertained at dinner. A slow rain was falling, it was rather chilly and the beautiful home presented a very pleasant effect with its big fireplaces all aglow. The home spoke the spirit of welcome and the governor seemed truly "at home" in his big easy chair. . . . Governor Colquitt expressed his delight for being so warmly received in this home and took his leave for [the town of] Claude.[27]

Despite the Hills' prosperity, their dining room seems hardly a notch above middle class (see figs. 10.3, 10.35). Nevertheless, in this area of the state, far removed from large commercial and cultural centers, the Armitage served as trendsetter. In 1910 the wallpapers were in the "newest styles" — a ceiling paper in a moire pattern, an appliquéd frieze of boldly outlined pomegranates over solid paper that may be an oatmeal or ingrain paper, and below the plate rail, a geometric-pattern paper.

Ceramics decorate the room: art pottery fills the china

cabinet; a cut glass punch bowl shares the sideboard with ceramics; game, naturalistic florals, and figures embellish the china displayed along the plate rail. In the foreground at the left, Deldware plates from the Buffalo Pottery occupy the rail. Made in Buffalo, New York, and distributed as "premiums" in soap purchases, the forms often featured hunting scenes, here reinforcing the idea that in the Hill household in 1910 the dining room was still a male preserve.[28]

Other room details include a kerosene lamp hanging from the ceiling and suspending a dinner bell over the oak pedestal dining table. A large rug occupies the center of the room, placed over wall-to-wall matting. Two metal child's chairs stand at the edge of the rug, while a china cabinet, a sideboard, and cane-seat side chairs line the walls. In the right corner, a telephone hangs on the wall between the kitchen door and the outside door. Above it is perched a punkah made of peacock feathers.

In an upstairs bedroom daughter Florence created a personal space (fig. 10.20). Patterned with a wallpaper featuring floral clusters, matching frieze, and ceiling paper, the walls are hung with imaginative groupings of prints and photographs. In places, the dense arrangement overlaps itself: for example, in the pair of unframed commercial still lifes at the head of the bed, and at the bay, portraits of young women, Florence's contemporaries, jump over a group photograph of a choir, achieving an unbroken frame-to-frame line. On an adjacent wall, prints and photos appear as satellites to the oval mirror. The imagery is overwhelmingly feminine, a mix of portraits of friends and family combined with commercial images of women and children.

On the matting and rugs, the brass bed is positioned to take advantage of the natural light and to catch breezes during warm weather. Florence selected bird's-eye maple furniture: the lady's desk and armchair occupy one corner, along with a ceremonial minimantel, clothes bag, and wastebasket; the draped washstand holds a toilet set, including a slop jar to the side. A colonial revival rocking chair, table of geraniums, birdcage, and trunk complete the furnishings.

The unusually constructed curtains — wide valances and side panels — appear homemade and top dark fringed window shades. The fabric is hung low on the outside of the window frame so that the corner fan motifs can be seen. In the symmetrically treated bay, the center window uses a curtain tieback or portière rope as adornment.

The Hills' bedroom projects family and stylistic identities (fig. 10.21). Crayon portraits of family matriarch and patriarch hang on the long wall and flank a wall plaque featuring a popular image of horses based upon Rosa Bonheur's work and a colonial revival reference — a portrait of George Washington.[29] Washington rises above the symmetrically arranged plate rack, the top shelf serving as a symbolic mantel in this stove-heated bedroom. The top of the desk is likewise treated as a mantel, adorned with various ceramic forms and surmounted by one of the crayon portraits. Above the washstand, women dominate: a calendar girl adorns the month of February and a trade card promoting Antikamnia Tablets for "Women's Aches and Ills" hangs in the cluster of images.

The furniture suggests that the space was used as an informal sitting area. The couple's pine bedstead is set diagonally across a corner, and a Morris chair is placed by a window and near the only artificial light source in either of the upstairs bedrooms — a kerosene lamp.

While figures 10.16 through 10.21 document the circa 1910 home of a merchant and farmer living in a region distant from commercial centers, figures 10.22 through 10.28 show the 1910 interiors of a prosperous and cosmopolitan family in Austin. Entrepreneur Ira Hobart Evans was a New Englander and Union soldier who came to

10.20. Bedroom, Frank H. Hill house, ca. 1910 (Courtesy Betty O. Ellis).

Texas after the Civil War and decided to stay. He became a cattleman, an official in the Reconstruction government, a state legislator, and a land speculator and railroad developer. Much of his prosperity came from his twenty-six-year presidency of the New York and Texas Land Company, Ltd. (NYTLC), one of the largest privately financed land companies to operate in the state. Evans lived in South, East, and Southeast Texas before settling in Central Texas in the mid-1880s.[30]

In Austin, Evans bought Bellevue, a chateauesque resi-

10.21. Bedroom, Frank H. Hill house, ca. 1910 (Courtesy Betty O. Ellis).

dence built in 1874; later, prominent San Antonio architect Alfred Giles spent two years on extensive remodeling of the house, and in 1894 the Evans family took up residence there.[31]

Some of Evans' occupational and regional identities are on view in the 1910 photograph of his library (fig. 10.22). Evans sits with Thomas B. Yale, brother-in-law, fellow Union officer, and manager in the NYTLC. Yale holds the *Vermonter* in his lap, signifying their shared heritage. A framed certificate announces Evans' membership in the Sons of the American Revolution. Other certificates probably document membership in military and historical societies, including the Military Order of the Medal of Honor, which he earned for his performance at Hatcher's Run, Virginia, in 1865. His Union sympathies are further indicated by the image of Abraham Lincoln above the bookcases. It may be a print of the widely circulated engraving by Alexander Hay Ritchie after a painting by Francis B. Carpenter, *The First Reading of the Emancipation Proclamation before the Cabinet.*[32]

This space is clearly a masculine retreat, albeit a fashionable colonial revival one. A deer trophy hangs high

10.22. Library, Ira Hobart Evans house, 708 San Antonio Street, Austin, ca. 1910 (H. Leslie Evans and Institute of Texan Cultures, San Antonio).

252 **10.23.** Entry hall (south), Ira Hobart Evans house, ca. 1910 (H. Leslie Evans and Institute of Texan Cultures, San Antonio).

above the mantel, lending an air of rusticity, as does the horn chair that resembles the one in the library of Sam Bell Maxey of Paris (see fig. 2.11). As in the Maxey house, the horn chair is an accent, not part of a suite, as in the Louis Melcher parlor (see fig. 6.6).

The Queen Anne and Chippendale styles of the eighteenth century have inspired most of the furniture visible in this view of the Evans library. The arts and crafts movement influenced other room elements: brightly colored curtains of a coarsely woven fabric hang at the windows, and a large geometric-pattern rug covers the floor. Detailed with classical motifs, the electric-and-gas fixture above the desk supplies gas via a flexible hose to the table lamp, the shade adding an oriental element to the room.

Visitors originally entered the house through a room the Evanses made into a comfortable sitting area — at least for the duration of the photo session (fig. 10.23). During the remodeling, they added a fireplace here when the front of the house was reoriented to the east and the architect designed the impressive new entry hall to the right of this space. The adapted area seems to carry out the motto carved on the colonial revival fireplace surround — "Olde bookes to rede, Olde woode to burne, Olde frendes to talke." A filled bookcase is close at hand, a supply of wood is ready to burn, and comfortable chairs promote leisurely conversation.

The room reveals a family who identifies with region, aspires toward refinement, and possesses knowledge of popular styles. Mantel ornaments and framed pictures, the primary decorative accessories, are clustered symmetrically around the central arch. A landscape painting of a nearby locale, Enchanted Rock, executed by artist Hermann Lungkwitz, is centered above the mantel, flanked by two seascapes, double hung over English genre scenes. The variety in the sizes of these pictures contrasts with the standard height of the paired mantel adornments — teapots, candlesticks, and vases — all elements of the colonial revival style.

Framing the fireplace are two stained glass windows, which were added during the remodeling (possibly located in the old doorways). According to contemporary design theory, the windows provided gently colored light to play upon the polished woodwork and create thought-provoking artistic compositions.

The entry hall, added in the 1890s, is impressive (fig. 10.24). The room's finishes include an embossed wallpaper in a fleur-de-lis pattern, very likely gold on white. The ceiling appears to be Tynecastle, canvas hand pressed into wooden molds, which after drying was removed and stretched across a surface; or it may be a less expensive embossed paper.[33] The scrollwork designs are repeated in a cherry stair screen and grille and even in the radiator, which is highlighted with gilt. Polished dark mahogany woodwork, oriental rugs, and a multi-tiered gasolier add to the richness and formality of the space. The fixture resembles that in the dining room of the Van Alstyne-Dickson house in Houston (see figs. 8.4, 8.5); both may have been purchased from Mitchell, Vance & Company, a New York lighting manufacturer and importer-exporter that supplied prosperous householders.

The original oil paintings testify to the Evanses' aspiration toward refinement and their economic status. The family commissioned the Hermann Lungkwitz painting of the San José mission that hangs above the radiator. Two framed pastoral landscapes flank the hall mirror; the dado rail holds other paintings, prints, and plaques. The radiator and table are adorned with other accessories. The table below the large mirror holds a card receiver and functions as a hallstand did decades earlier. The ubiquitous stand greets visitors, but its jardiniere is empty; flowers are seen only in the stained glass window and on the pillow of the window seat.

10.24. Entry hall (east), Ira Hobart Evans house, ca. 1910 (H. Leslie Evans and Institute of Texan Cultures, San Antonio).

10.25. Sitting room, Ira Hobart Evans house, ca. 1910 (H. Leslie Evans and Institute of Texan Cultures, San Antonio).

The comfortable sitting room (fig. 10.25) in the Evans house is also colonialized, with decorative candlesticks, a bed warmer, and teakettle, as well as a Queen Anne revival rocker (its mate is in the library), and a ladder-back chair. A plush-upholstered armchair, a painted fancy chair, and a sofa in a "period" style, probably considered colonial with its reference to the Elizabethan style, complete the room's furniture. A pillow on the sofa bears a silhouette of a cat, a design found in several Texas houses in these years.

Probably gold on white or a light background, the embossed wall covering with its matching border complements the radiator's raised decoration and resembles the paper in the entry hall. In the same shades as the side-wall papers, the ceiling paper consists of connecting circles, of varying sizes, astronomical in design. A solid rug covers the oak parquet floor.[34]

The Evanses used the sitting room to read and to play the piano and records. They also displayed their china collection on nearly every flat surface in this room. Collecting ceramics was a fashionable pastime during the late nineteenth and early twentieth centuries. Evans' wife, like many other American women, may have succumbed to "chinamania."[35] Wall-hung accessories include paintings — another Lungkwitz landscape in the corner — and prints.

The ensemble is well lit by the central fixture that has been wired for electricity and piped for gas. The odd burner with the clear glass chimney appears to be a Welsbach burner for producing gaslight. The table lamp burns kerosene, while the wall sconce is fitted for both gas and electricity.

In the dining room (fig. 10.26) brown and orange encaustic tiles decorate the floor under the bordered rug; pressed tin panels form the ceiling; and the walls combine the finishes of wainscoting and paint.[36] Small globes do little to illuminate the space, but above the table an electric fixture with an art glass shade provides effective lighting. Within this setting, the Evanses have placed a reform sideboard dating to the 1880s, inexpensive leather-seat side chairs, and a colonial revival table.

The doors at the left lead to the south porch; their transoms feature stained glass representing the seasons, in effect, mediating between indoors and outdoors. Prominently displayed in the dining room, a Japanese screen evokes the natural world, as does the romantic landscape painted on a china plaque hanging above a built-in display of hand-painted plates. In addition to blocking the view of and entry into the service area, the Japanese screen indicates the family's identification with style and class since similar ones were used in prosperous households. As in other dining rooms in this sample, this is not the most finely furnished room in the house nor the most expressive of the householders' identities.

Photographs of two bedrooms give an idea of the Evanses' stylistic, familial, and regional identities. Figure 10.27 shows a room decorated in a popular combination of colonial and French styles. Colonial elements include sharp color contrasts between the light woodwork and darker furnishings and the candelabrum-type light fixture. The dark side-wall paper is in a strong landscape pattern — a columned trellis in perspective surrounded by floral motifs — a colonial revival reproduction paper. A partially visible chair influenced by art nouveau design stands between an empire revival dresser and a matching French bedstead, both of which were considered colonial at the time. The window shades hung with the rod toward the window are covered by curtains in a fleur-de-lis pattern. The unbordered wall-to-wall carpet features rococo scrollwork and may have been "recycled" from a prerenovation room downstairs, given its design and household reuse patterns.

Through the open doorway, furnishings in the adjacent area are barely visible: a brass bed, a lady's desk positioned diagonally across the corner, a side chair, a nightstand, landscape prints, wallpaper patterned with light festoons on a dark field, and a semicircular, bordered rug with floral motifs on a dark field.

The colonial revival style pervades the other bedroom (fig. 10.28). The contrasting light and dark color scheme is most notable on the fireplace wall: the white woodwork stands out against the dark wallpaper, foil to the light moire ceiling paper. The contrast is continued in the foliate designs decorating the dark field of the bordered rug and on the small carpet rectangles marking the closets.

The room's furniture is an eclectic mixture of styles: a renaissance revival bedstead, a small Elizabethan revival desk, a colonial revival bird's-eye maple rocker, a popular and inexpensive renaissance revival cane-seat side chair, and a side table on which sits a homemade shellwork box and an oil lamp.

Delft tiles frame the fireplace, and an oval mirror tops

10.26. Dining room, Ira H. Evans house, Austin, ca. 1910 (H. Leslie Evans and Institute of Texan Cultures, San Antonio).

10.27. Bedroom, Ira H. Evans house, ca. 1910 (H. Leslie Evans and Institute of Texan Cultures, San Antonio).

10.28. Bedroom, Ira Hobart Evans house, ca. 1910 (H. Leslie Evans and Institute of Texan Cultures, San Antonio).

the mantel shelf. Ceramics, prints, paintings, and photos rest on and above the closet door heads, including a large photograph of a Union soldier (possibly Ira Evans), an image representing family and regional identities.

Photographed a decade after the Evans house, Henry F. and Louise Kraemer Hodde's Italianate residence in Brenham housed the couple and their ten children (figs. 10.29 through 10.37). Henry Hodde emigrated from Germany to Texas in 1859, at the age of twenty. After service in the Confederate army, including capture by Union forces and escape, he returned to Brenham at the close of the war. There he worked as a clerk for four years before he formed a partnership in a general merchandise store, Hodde & Werner. In 1870, he married Louise Kraemer, another German emigrant, and eight years later the couple built their home.[37] Although the photographs of the house date to circa 1920, the decorating choices the Hoddes made some forty years earlier are plainly in evidence.

Henry's business may explain some of the home's fashionable furnishings.[38] As partner in a general merchandise store, he may have been knowledgeable about and eager to acquire new and stylish items available from large markets. As a buyer for his company, he had ample opportunity to purchase merchandise outside local markets. Family history records that Henry and Louise bought their furnishings in New York.[39]

With its elaborately adorned surfaces, the Hodde parlor is an interpretation of the aesthetic style (fig. 10.29). According to the dictates of this style, artistically embellished domestic goods — furniture, textiles, and wallpapers — enrich the home. Large, stylized florals in rose and beige shades pattern the wallpapers.[40] A banded frieze encircles the room above the wooden picture molding (see figs. 9.3, 9.10, 9.11, 11.15). The floor covering lends more pattern to the space. Sewn strips form the wall-to-wall foliate-pattern carpet that extends into the bay. A wide floral border meets the strips at right angles on two sides; a narrow floral border frames the room excluding the bay. The windows are covered with a sheer material topped with a valance of fringed, stamped plush, similar to that of the Simpson parlor in Houston (see figs. 9.10, 9.11). Decorative textiles, including an embroidered spiderweb on both a table scarf and a nearby pillow, may show the handiwork of one of the Hodde daughters.[41]

The room shows further evidence of the women's amateur pursuits in the two identical floral still lifes painted by eldest daughter Katie Hodde that hang on either side of the bay.[42] Such handiwork expressed refined artistic identity, as prescribed in amateur art publications of the late nineteenth and early twentieth centuries.

A second photograph of the parlor documents the hearth (fig. 10.30). The mantel is made of marbleized slate with incised decoration; its shelf is noticeably lacking adornments. The spare mantel treatment may reflect a lingering reform taste or the sparseness of the 1920s, or it may be a consequence of an earlier tendency to place the strong, fixed embellishments above the mantel. The panel immediately behind the shelf has been created out of a pastiche of wallpaper patterns and borders, the same motifs that create the remarkable ceiling: a row of light and dark chrysanthemums is framed by a narrow border of stylized daisies. The molded panel above, unique in Texas houses in this sample, approximates the shape of the ceiling's four corner medallions. Instead of family portraits above the mantel and on the mantel shelf as we might expect, the featured position above the hearth relates to the aesthetic style embraced by the Hoddes.

The room is illuminated by an electric bulb that drops inelegantly into the otherwise empty center of the room. On the onyx-top brass stand sits a new electric lamp influenced by arts and crafts design. The stand and the lamp

10.29. Parlor, Henry F. Hodde house, Corner of Gilder and Market streets (113 Market Street), Brenham, ca. 1920 (Courtesy Norman and Loretta Hodde).

10.30. Parlor, Henry F. Hodde house, ca. 1920 (Courtesy Norman and Loretta Hodde).

10.31. Parlor, Henry F. Hodde house, ca. 1920 (Courtesy Norman and Loretta Hodde).

are among the few new items in the house; well chosen, they complement the original style of the room.

Figure 10.31, another view of the parlor, reveals many details about the structure's first-story floor plan, with a view across the entry hall into the dining room. Leaving the parlor, we see an image of Henry, its frame awkwardly abutting the doorjamb, and an old crayon portrait of Louise, which has been removed from its frame and placed well below eye level. In these positions, both images are incidental rather than central; family identity is subordinated to style.

This third view of the parlor shows the enduring aesthetic of the late 1870s. The parlor suite dates from at least the 1880s. In the right foreground corner, a chair features carving of stylized foliate designs with a sunflower, a popular motif of aestheticism. The renaissance revival pier mirror also dates from the completion of the house and documents that the Hodde family was remarkably up-to-date in their initial decoration of their home.

The ceiling paper in the Hodde parlor is the subject of an amazing fourth photograph (fig. 10.32). The geometric-and-floral banding forms an intricate pattern culminating in the center medallion or trompe l'oeil cupola. The corners are marked with female figures, each in a diagonally positioned panel. Members of the family recall that the figures were painted, not paper, and that the garments were shades of red and green. This ceiling paper is an example of a nondirectional pattern that appears the same from all points in the room.[43] If the room is halved in either direction, the result is a pair of mirror images. The panels and the paper create an effect that appealed to Americans with aesthetic goals in house decoration.

Typically, decorative arts historians consider wallpaper a less expensive, and less valued, option than decorative wall painting. The Hoddes lived in an area where there were a number of talented German decorative painters who could have embellished the entire ceiling, using stenciling, infill, and freehand painting techniques, rather than painting only the figures for the ceiling corners. Yet the Hoddes, possibly with help from wallpaper store personnel, chose what was probably for this locale a more costly and "foreign" strategy for adornment. Perhaps in Brenham, paper may have been considered more desirable.

Unlike the parlor, the entry hall has been updated, possibly because it received more use (figs. 10.33, 10.34). Although Hodde died in 1901 and Louise did not maintain the family's earlier prosperity, there were resources for a limited redecorating project around 1905, the results of which are evident in the entry hall, dining room, and bedroom. For example, the hall's wallpaper — strips of solid paper topped by an arts and crafts-inspired applied border—dates to the remodeling. The simply shaded electric lighting fixture is an updated feature, and a telephone hangs outside on the enclosed porch wall. Regardless of the new backdrop and new technologies represented, much remains from the 1878 furnishing effort. Evidence of Louise's earlier taste is seen in the screen, rug, and seating pieces from the aesthetic parlor suite.

The furniture arrangement of the entry hall suggests a convivial space outside the powerfully styled parlor. Some of the seating pieces may have been moved to fill the room for the picture-taking event, but some pieces, especially the piano and sofa, are permanent features in this space. Not only is the piano positioned where it really does not fit "to increase the sense of the house as a place for entertainment and enjoyment," but a more practical reason prevailed.[44] During hot Texas summers families gathered in an entry hall because it was a breezeway, a longstanding southern architectural practice. The rest of the year the informality of the space drew sitters.

Framed by an archway, the vestibule is furnished with a diagonally placed hallstand and three leather-upholstered chairs. As one entered the house, the arch, repeating those at the front door and transom, framed the stairway, blocking the awkwardness of the stairway trimming the corner of the entry into the dining room.

The sparing use of light textiles in these rooms suggests either the summertime, the restraint of the late date, or both. Only muslin panels, with top and bottom hemmed and shirred on rods, hang at the door; the window is covered in the same fabric with a short valance. The hardware visible at the entry to the parlor (fig. 10.34 *right)* shows that during the colder months portières hang in front of sliding doors. Movable transient objects are relocated for each photograph — the fern and the aspidistra plant, for example.

Like other middle- and upper-middle-class dining rooms in Texas, this one in Brenham is unadorned and relatively modest (fig. 10.35). The room's spareness expresses both the late date of the photograph and the finances of the elderly Louise Hodde. Nevertheless, the dining room was also redecorated. The wallpaper, an alternating stripe with an applied border of poppies, dates to 1905, as do the cane-seat side chairs. The dining table, however, is the original extension table that seated the twelve Hoddes, even though the composition of the fam-

10.32. Parlor, Henry F. Hodde house, ca. 1920 (Courtesy Norman and Loretta Hodde).

10.33. Entry hall, Henry F. Hodde house, ca. 1920 (Courtesy Norman and Loretta Hodde).

10.34. Entry hall, Henry F. Hodde house, ca. 1920 (Courtesy Norman and Loretta Hodde).

ily is much changed by 1920. (Typically when dining rooms were photographed, tables remained uncovered unless set for a celebration or meal. The cloth here may hide forty years of use by the large family.) The marble-top sideboard is probably positioned as it has been for four decades, while a kitchen table has received a new coat of paint and functions as a server, near the door to the service area of the house.

There are few decorative objects; the same bowl that adorned the piano now rests on the uncluttered mantel. There are few textiles, as in other areas of the Hodde home. In addition to the table covers, only small scarves adorn tabletops; a bordered rug covers the hardwood floor. Cornices dating to the completion of the house look unnecessarily heavy for the lightweight curtain panels that cover the windows over the interior shutters.

The family has solved the problem of lighting the dining room with an uncovered electric light bulb that hangs over the table, slightly off center. The fireplace is rendered anachronistic (as were most fireplaces long before this time) with a small heating stove. The long stovepipe dramatically crosses from the fireplace wall to a far corner,

10.35. Dining room, Henry F. Hodde house, ca. 1920 (Courtesy Norman and Loretta Hodde).

10.36. Bedroom, Henry F. Hodde house, ca. 1920 (Courtesy Norman and Loretta Hodde).

10.37. Bedroom, Henry F. Hodde house, ca. 1920 (Courtesy Norman and Loretta Hodde).

the pipe serving as a radiator. The style of the stove with its Gothic arches and houselike form indicates that the stove was probably the original heating source for the dining room.

A pair of photographs provides a look at Louise's bedroom (figs. 10.36, 10.37), which had access to a large porch through a floor-to-ceiling window to the left of the fireplace. (Figure 10.30 documents that the parlor opened onto this porch; both rooms' windows show identical curtains.) The focal point for this first-story bedroom is the marbleized slate surround at the hearth and its restrained display of portrait photographs of her children, now adults. Compared with many houses in this sample, this is hardly an effusive display of family identification; yet, in the context of this one house, it is significant. Photographs of the children do not decorate the mantel in the public parlor, but rather the one in the private space, the bedroom.

The paint, paper, and carpeting show wear. With the exception of the colonial revival rocking chair, which represents a relatively recent purchase, around 1905, most of the furnishings date to the period of the dwelling's construction. The incising on bedstead and bureau, the veneer, and the matching crests of anthemia reveal their 1880s renaissance revival origins. Likewise, the upholstered armchair, possibly fashioned by Chicago furniture manufacturer Joseph Zangerle, and the small leather-seat and cane-back rocking chair at the hearth represent purchases made at the time the house was completed.[45]

★ ★ ★ ★

These well-documented houses invite exploration of the ways family members expressed various identities in different rooms. The interior views show that the expression of identity was in part prescribed. Certain rooms were inherently more likely than others to include objects relating to specific identities. Libraries generally accommodated statements of occupational identity; parlors often invited items displaying the refinement and artistic skills of women occupants; bedrooms frequently contained items relating to family and social group.

Prescriptiveness might suggest uniformity; yet there is a great variety and diversity in the appearance of these rooms. Because the circumstances of these families' lives differed and because the ways in which they expressed their identities differed, so, too, did their rooms.

JOSEPH W. RICE. VICTOR J. BAULARD. G. W. OUTTERSIDE.

RICE, BAULARD & CO.

DEALERS IN

PAINTS, OILS

—AND—

VARNISHES,

Window Glass,

Wall Paper,

Wax Flower Materials

—AND—

PAINTERS' SUPPLIES

In Any Quantity, constantly on hand, to Suit the Trade.

PAINTERS

HOUSE, SIGN AND ORNAMENTAL

Painting,

GILDING,

GRAINING, GLAZING,

Wall Paper Decorating

FRESCOING

—AND—

PAPER HANGING.

73 TREMONT STREET,

Bet. Strand and Mechanic,

GALVESTON.

Manufacturers of Galveston Paint Co.'s Ready-Mixed Paints.

11.1. Advertisement for paint and paper store, Rice, Baulard & Co., Galveston, 1888 (*Directory of the City of Galveston, 1888 – 89*, p.9).

11

"Interior Decorators Were Not Yet With Us"

ADVICE LITERATURE

EVEN Texans who created the most idiosyncratic interiors also sought to approximate national decorating trends. That pursuit introduced elements that effected the way Texans shaped their domestic environments once they were aware of the cultural marketplace — broadly defined as ideas, advice, expertise, and goods. Such influences were clearly *outside* one's personal identity. How did these sources of advice and goods contribute to the look of Texas homes? And what happened when builders were consulted in the process of building and making a home?

Late-nineteenth-century Texans had wide ranging options for decorating advice and furnishings. They wholeheartedly embraced the spate of magazines with pages full of information on home decoration, child rearing, food preparation, and beauty tips. Women's magazines such as *Ladies' Home Journal* and *Woman's Home Companion* were enormously popular in Texas judging from their numbers in the collections of women's papers in museums and libraries around the state. Some Texas women participated in the magazines' exchange columns that offered advice on a range of subjects including home decoration: Mrs. T. M. Paschal of Castroville told readers how to secure a waterproof fiber cloth, while Mrs. C. L. H. D. of Castell in Llano County shared her technique for crystallizing grasses for use in decorative vases.[1]

Texas had an important general ladies' journal in *Holland's Magazine*, published by Farm and Ranch Publishing Company in Dallas. Marketed throughout the Midwest, *Holland's* focused on topics of regional interest, included articles by writers who contributed to national magazines, and featured essays on home decoration elsewhere in the country. While serving Texas, the magazine promoted nationalism and helped to dissolve geographical barriers.

A host of periodicals devoted their contents to matters of household art and decoration, suggesting a readership of women with leisure, more than middle-class means, and a seriousness of purpose. The *Art Amateur*, the *Art Interchange*, the *Decorator and Furnisher*, and the *Household* made up a fraction of this advice literature. Many Texans often subscribed to or read more than one. Nannie Fulton Holden of Fulton subscribed to both the *Art Amateur* and the *Art Interchange* whose design studies inspired her hand-painted china.[2] J. E. G. of Sherman queried the *Art Amateur* editors for a preparation to "render impervious to the weather paintings or pen-drawings 'on fair or russet leather.'"[3]

But in 1889 another reader, Mrs. L. M., fretted about a larger dilemma. Her concerns centered on which "aesthetic" colors to paint her interior, and she reveals how fashionable she was — or was at least pretending to be. The inquirer lived in San Diego, seat of Duval County, which, although more than 1,800 square miles in size, had fewer than 8,000 inhabitants.[4] She wrote:

> We are so isolated in this place that it is impossible to procure skilled labor; but I have thought out a simple plan of decoration for four rooms which I wish to submit to you for correction or approval. As is customary in this climate, the walls and ceiling are ceiled, and it is very difficult to know how to relieve their "woodiness." The parlor and adjoining bedroom are 14 feet square, ceilings, 10 feet. I thought of having the walls of each painted a light buff brown, with ceiling of a lighter tone; predominating color of frieze in parlor red, in bedroom peacock blue or olive green. Two small rooms — library and dining-room — are 12 x 14 feet. The latter opens into a parlor and north gallery. It is rather dark, there being but one window, which opens upon a deep vine-covered south gallery. For this I thought of ivory or cream white, with a pretty bright frieze. The dining-room has east and south windows, the latter protected by the gallery. For the sake of coolness, I thought of having the walls of this sage green, ceiling soft light gray and frieze either red or pink. If the latter, I would paint clover in the two small panels below — glass in door. On the four panels of another door I thought of painting snow-balls. Would it do to have *all* the other wood-work, doors and casings painted ivory white, or what would you suggest for the different rooms? I have not determined about the friezes. I would paint them myself if the walls were more worthy.
>
> Would the ordinary wall-paper frieze be inappropriate? Where can I send for samples? Where can I get a good common burlap for portière? Can you tell me what colors will produce the buff brown, or brown buff rather, also sage green.[5]

More personal and more direct home decorating advice was available at local paint and paper stores, such as Rice, Baulard & Company of Galveston, Peg Bonney of San Angelo, or E. E. Thompson of Waco (Figs. 11.1, 11.2, 11.3). Thompson operated his store at 404 Austin Avenue from 1901 until 1919, providing many Waco matrons with paint, paper, and advice.[6]

Like paper and paint merchants, furniture store owners and salesmen dispensed informal decorating advice to consumers across the country. From the 1880s, in major Texas cities, wholesalers and retailers — T. Billington in Dallas, Galveston's H. Kauffman (fig. 11.4), M. Kreisle Company of Austin, and others — sold furniture and carpets, offering suggestions on their placement, use, and care.[7] By the turn of the century, residents of smaller communities like Panhandle and Sherman had access to similar advice and goods (figs. 11.5, 11.6).

In 1849, traveler William Steinert assessed the likelihood

of success for the various trades and professions in Texas and grimly predicted, "[p]aperhangers and upholsterers might starve."[8] At mid century the two trades were often paired: the person who covered walls was often the same one who recovered furniture. Other tradesmen also operated as carpet vendors, supplying floor coverings. Providing assistance in the decorating of Texas houses prior to the early twentieth century, these workers approximated the role of the interior decorators who would follow. The future for paperhangers and upholsterers in Texas may have looked bleak in 1849, but business was thriving by the turn of the century.

Just as advice literature and advice givers influenced house decoration, so did the range of available goods that could be supplied to homeowners across the nation, even those who lived far from manufacturing centers. The situation in Texas had changed considerably from the time the first Anglo and Tejano settlers brought what furniture they could carry with them by boat or overland, made the furniture themselves, purchased it from local cabinetmakers, or did without.

During the first half of the nineteenth century, elites could buy new furniture from markets outside the state. Between 1820 and 1840, a few Texans ordered furniture from Philadelphia. During that period, at least one ship carried seventy-eight boxes and twenty-five bundles, containing more than 300 pieces of furniture — cargo worth nearly $3,000 — from Philadelphia to Galveston.[9] By the 1850s very few Texans could travel to New York to buy household furnishings for their home; Lucadia Pease, wife of the governor, was one who could.[10]

By the 1880s, because of improved transportation and shipping, residents of cities and towns throughout Texas could examine and acquire goods at a variety of shops — general stores, furniture stores, department stores, and specialty stores, like china and jewelry shops. Mail-order

11.2. Interior of Peg Bonney paint and paper store, San Angelo, ca. 1900 (Fort Concho National Historic Landmark, San Angelo).

catalogues, too, reached Texas households. Many of the items shown in turn-of-the-century homes could have been ordered directly from the pages of Sears, Roebuck — the jute carpet in the parlor of the Taylor house in Karnes City (see fig. 8.8) or the box lounge from the Russell house in Pilot Point (see fig. 3.7) or the similar plush-covered lounge in the Jernigan house in Pecos (see fig. 11.9).

These mail-order catalogues are better sources for information about house furnishings in Texas than the *House Beautiful* or the *Craftsman* to which decorative arts historians might, from training and practice, turn. Although we might be dismayed to think turn-of-the-century Texans disposed of probable masterpieces of local cabinetmakers in order to buy the newest styles from Sears, Roebuck, reverence for so-called primitives must not bias a study of earlier Texans' enthusiastic acceptance of these newly marketed goods and enjoyment of access to a national market.

Texans relished variety and the ability to choose among several options. They could order a mantel clock from Sears, Roebuck or buy it locally from a jewelry or a furniture store. Framed prints for parlor walls could be purchased in general stores and furniture stores (fig. 11.7). Rural Texans could patronize the general store, go by rail to a larger town to visit a furniture store, even to San Antonio or Dallas to shop in a department store. Or, they could select furniture from a catalogue or place an order from a magazine advertisement. The markets and the choices seemed limitless.

Even families who hired a builder to supply the plans or to construct their home were ready to provide the interior furnishings, if not finishes, themselves (see figs. 6.7, 6.8, 8.13). J. O. Davis of Houston and U. G. Taylor of San Angelo ordered their house plans from builder George F. Barber of Knoxville, Tennessee, whose catalogues promoted his designs nationwide.[11] But builders like Barber left it to the individual owners to decorate their interior spaces appropriately and tastefully.

11.3. Interior of E. E. Thompson paint and paper store, 404 Austin Avenue, Waco, ca. 1905 (Texas Collection, Baylor University, Waco).

11.4. Advertisement for H. Kauffman household furnishings store, Galveston, 1888 (*Directory of the City of Galveston, 1888 – 89*, p. 16).

11.5. Interior of Whiteside & Sanford furniture store in Panhandle, ca. 1900 (Carson County Square House Museum, Panhandle).

11.6. Interior of Taliaferro Furniture Company, 516 North Grand Avenue, Sherman, 1908 (Sherman Historical Museum).

11.7. Llano Furniture Company, R. A. McInnis, Proprietor, Llano, 1907 (Photography Collection, Harry Ransom Humanities Research Center, Univeristy of Texas at Austin).

Some of the photographs in this chapter present houses with interiors that were decorated by their occupants in a manner that shows up-to-date advice gleaned from popular magazines, even in houses in remote areas of the state. Other photographs show that some residents clung to styles whose heyday had passed. A third group of images shows how householders updated their furnishings; pairs of images document evolving ideas. The last group of images shows two Texas houses, constructed by builders, with interiors that were decorated by their owners. The common denominator is that occupants rather than professional designers were responsible for the look of their interiors, although they were influenced by concerns beyond expressions of personal identity.

Despite its remote location, the Hartley County home of Albert Boyce shows a familiarity with fashion. Boyce was one of the great cattleman of the Southwest and a Civil War veteran. In 1887, he was hired to manage the

3-million-acre XIT Ranch, with operations stretching from the Panhandle to Montana.[12] Boyce and his family lived near the home ranch in Channing. Early in the last decade of the century a prospering Boyce, his wife, and grown children proudly posed in their parlor (fig. 11.8).

Fashionable animal-skin rugs top the wall-to-wall carpet; wallpaper and matching frieze adorn the walls; rattan rockers and a fabric screen furnish the room; stenciled roller blinds and artistic draperies cover the windows and makeshift mantel. In spite of all these elements, including a piano, the room does not look au courant. All the proper elements are present, but the composition is askew. The room functions both as parlor and as sitting room and, therefore, contains a mix of furniture. The presence of a center table and lamp would do much to focus the room. Further, the makeshift mantel displays an ill-proportioned array of objects. An oversize framed landscape is partially obscured by two pairs of large vases. Only the double framed cabinet cards, featuring two of the Boyce sons, are in scale with the shelf.

Although Mrs. Boyce and her daughter did not execute with finesse the decorating suggestions offered in the advice literature, they understood the more complex and subtle messages. Their parlor offered a respite from the business world, a place of relaxation for men, a haven where fathers, husbands, and sons would want to gather. The Boyce men appear comfortable: the head of the household sits at his desk smoking a pipe, taboo in fashionable urban households but admissible here, while his sons pose casually. The women's stance suggests propriety and the seriousness that comes from reading and piano playing, although the upside-down sheet music, "Happy Days," casts doubt upon Mrs. Boyce's immediate commitment to that occupation.

The Boyce women have fashioned a feminine room in making this place of comfort. The women blend into the space and are visually more "at home" here than the men. The gathers, tucks, and flounces of their clothing are echoed in the room's textiles. They perhaps took literally one mid century spokeswoman's comment: "The more womanly a woman is, the more she is sure to throw her personality over the home, and transform it, from a mere eating and sleeping place, or an upholsterer's show room, into a sort of outermost garment of her soul; harmonized with all her nature as her robe and the flower in her hair are harmonized with her bodily beauty."[13]

South and west of the Boyces' Channing home in the town of Pecos a druggist named Jernigan reclines in a plush-covered lounge, its top nearly obscured by pillows that spill over onto the floor (fig. 11.9). The decorations in this sitting room are reminiscent of the handmade adornments that women were encouraged to create from instructions included in popular publications such as George A. Martin's 1888 *Our Homes: How to Beautify Them.* Numerous periodicals, domestic economy books, and household art publications discussed the correct display of such elements.

Many fashionable items could be made for the home at very little cost, easily executed by those women who wanted to beautify their homes "with the labors of their own handiwork," and who had occasional "spare moments" in addition to "good taste and skill."[14] A picture frame could be fashioned from fungus or a key holder from an ear of corn. Inexpensive decorations such as these, despite Martin's claims for grandeur, were aimed at working-class and lower-middle-class housewives; judging from their presence in interior views, these women incorporated the ideas enthusiastically. Mrs. Jernigan, for example, followed Martin's directions for making a photograph frame from a fan. Her other homemade adornments include a ribbon-strung ladder of matted snapshots, a wall plaque featuring Native Americans, a circular photo

11.8. Parlor, Albert G. Boyce house, Corner of Fifth Street and Railroad Avenue, Channing, ca. 1890 (Barker Texas History Center, Austin).

11.9. Sitting room, Jernigan house, Pecos, ca. 1890 (Mrs. Hugh Roberson Collection, West of the Pecos Museum, Pecos).

frame, and inexpensive framed prints. All of these punctuate the garland wallpaper, which resembles the paper covering the walls in a dining room in distant Kaufman (see fig. 8.18). Like the wallpaper, the Jernigans' bordered rug and portières were stock catalogue items that may have been purchased by mail and delivered by rail.

Similarly remote was the late-nineteenth-century residence of rancher J. J. McAdams who bought for his wife and eight children a town house in Quanah, midway between Fort Worth and Amarillo on the Fort Worth & Denver City Railroad (figs. 11.10, 11.11). According to family history, the furniture arrived from Fort Worth, filling an entire railroad car.[15] The case pieces crowded into the McAdams bedroom give substance to the story: a folding bed, placed diagonally across one corner between two windows, a massive mirrored dresser, a combination case blocking an interior doorway, and a table and at least three chairs (fig. 11.10). That this furniture blocks windows and doorways and covers room decorations implies that the large case pieces were moved to be included in the photograph, although size and weight argue that the pieces are in permanent locations. Their positions also follow the

11.10. Bedroom, J. J. McAdams house, Quanah, ca. 1895 (Courtesy Bettie B. Gafford; stamped on photo, "S. E. Moore, The Elite, Quanah, Texas").

11.11. Parlor, J. J. McAdams house, ca. 1895 (Courtesy Bettie B. Gafford).

practice of placing a dresser with mirror or mirrors and bedstead to take advantage of breezes in warm months.

The McAdams bedroom is up-to-date with its colonial revival furniture and fashionable wallpaper of floral patterns with scrollwork. The family apparently escaped urban retailers who promoted out-of-date stock in rural areas. For example, it was rumored that Marshall Field Department Store routinely sent to prosperous Texans those out-of-style furnishings that had lost their market in fashion-conscious Chicago. Another explanation could be that merchants were willing to reduce the price on serviceable rather than fashionable goods.

In the parlor, floral motifs inspire the wallpaper, upholstery, piano drape, lace curtains, and wall-to-wall carpet (fig. 11.11). A cheval glass sits near the mirrored mantel. The spindled overmantel is adorned with carefully placed family photographs; nearby a photograph album rests on an onyx-top metal stand, and an easel displays a crayon portrait of Jim and Eudora McAdams. From the crayon portrait, we know what Eudora McAdams looked like, and from some of the objects in the room, we know something about her. Like other women, she fashioned table scarves and fringed seat, stool, and arm covers. Attentive to stylish details, she arranged her parlor and trimmed the standard curtain poles to fit the irregular shape of the room.

Some 200 miles east of Quanah, the parlor and the bedroom of another Texas house, Glen Eden, were documented circa 1900 (figs. 11.12, 11.13). Built sixty years earlier of split-log and clapboard construction, Glen Eden had two stories, each with a dog-trot or central passageway. The house had native rock chimneys, wide galleries, and plaster walls. The structure was home for bride Sophia Suttonfield Aughinbaugh and Holland Coffee, a famous fighter who led fifty men to drive out "marauding Indians" from North Texas in 1838. Holland was killed eight years later.[16]

Sophia remained in the house and married twice more. She was renowned for the hospitality of her home near Preston Bend; Ulysses S. Grant, Robert E. Lee, Albert Sidney Johnston, and Sam Houston were entertained there in the decades before the Civil War. During the war Sophia earned the title of the female Paul Revere when she forded the Red River to warn Colonel James Bourland of the approach of federal scouts; only late in the war did she briefly leave Glen Eden. In 1899 Captain John H. Williams inherited the home of Sophia Suttonfield Aughinbaugh Coffee Butt Porter. Soon after, he and his wife, Belle, who had been seamstress and companion to Sophia, had their picture taken in the parlor with an unidentified woman.[17]

By the turn of the century little of the original 1840s interior is visible; instead, this public space has been thoroughly restyled (fig. 11.12). New floral-pattern carpeting stretches wall to wall, and a paper with a trailing-vine design covers the wall. The floral motifs of both are echoed by the potted umbrella plant and the begonias, artistically arranged around the center table.[18]

The beveled mirrored panels of the whatnot hold cabinet cards and family portraits. The dresser top to the right is sparsely decorated, perhaps to minimize the presence of this form in the parlor. Rural Americans, especially southerners, were prone to combine the functions of sitting rooms and bedrooms. A practice that had begun of necessity in small, modest houses persevered long after larger dwellings had canceled the need.

The bedroom (fig. 11.13) contains recent crayon portraits of Belle and John Williams, but other room details reveal earlier dates. The fireplace mantel, for example, betrays fifty years of use with little modification. The large bedstead probably stood in this home or in the couple's

11.12. Parlor, Captain John H. Williams house, known as Glen Eden, north of Sherman, ca. 1900 (Sherman Historical Museum).

11.13. Bedroom into dining room, Captain John H. Williams house, ca. 1900 (Sherman Historical Museum).

former home for at least a quarter of a century. The cane-seat renaissance revival chair dates to about 1880 and resembles those in the dining rooms of the Edward Steves and the Benjamin Epperson houses (see figs. 4.7, 9.6). The colonial revival rocking chair, however, is probably less than five years old.

Similar wall treatments link bedroom and adjacent dining room. Possibly ordered from a catalogue, the wallpaper features a motif that indicates recent purchase and hanging: wide friezes above wreath and medallion patterns were popular with many turn-of-the-century householders. A new colonial revival extension table and a sideboard sit in the dining room.

In South Texas, the Edward LeGrand Dunlap house displays evolved interiors (fig. 11.14). Unlike the conscious selection of a variety of historic revivals to create a single "eclectic" style (see fig. 8.3), the Dunlaps' fashionable items were acquired over time, so their rooms achieved a kind of "evolved eclecticism" that demonstrated a ten-year effort to maintain stylishness.

Dunlap was born in 1846 in Kentucky of Scottish-French parents whose ancestors had long lived in America. Dunlap's father lost his money and property as a result of the Civil War and died soon after, leaving Edward responsible for the care of his family. Moving them to Kansas City, he succeeded in the real estate business but in 1882 decided to move to Refugio County, Texas, where he raised stock. Two years later he settled in adjacent Victoria County and combined his interests in real estate and cattle raising.[19] Soon after, he married Dolores "Dora" Welder, whose family had prospered in the Texas cattle business since the 1840s.

Dora's parlor was photographed circa 1895. The leather-upholstered renaissance revival suite incorporates details of the neo-Grec and Louis XVI styles and predates 1890 when construction on the house began. The parlor suite and the Eastlake-inspired center table and occasional chair may date to the couple's marriage in the mid-1880s or earlier. Other elements — interior shutters and the marbleized, incised slate mantel — are original to the 1890 house, as is the scrollwork wallpaper and frieze. The floor treatment — rugs over wooden floors — was fashionable, thanks to Eastlake and his American disciples, when the house was built. In earlier years, the Dunlaps would have illuminated their parlor with a kerosene table lamp, but by 1895 an unadorned electric light bulb, its cord tied to shorten it, dangles overhead. Unlike some houses where oil and kerosene gave way to gas, which, in turn, gave way to electricity, the Dunlap home seemingly missed the middle stage since no gas fixtures are visible in the rooms. The homes of many families who lived in small towns or rural areas were never serviced by gas since it required city gas works and lines.

The horizontally striped and fringed fabric that serves as window covering and mantel drape was an outgrowth of the British design reform movement. Charles Locke Eastlake advocated its use to his British audience in the late 1860s — "heavy ribbed material decorated with broad bands or strips of colour running transversely to its length, and resembling the pattern of a Roman scarf."[20] In America it became fashionable to use strips of this fabric as window curtains and portières in the late 1880s; the mode was popular in Texas especially during the 1890s, appearing early on in the Anson Ranch (see figs. 2.1, 2.2, 2.3) and later in the Wright house (see fig. 13.5).

Dora's mantel arrangement is one that had been popular in the 1880s and 1890s. One of her landscape paintings hangs above the ordered shelf, which features photographs of niece Bet Welder, husband Edward, and herself before her marriage. The screen that blocks the fireplace and the paper butterfly are Japanese-style items that middle-class Americans began incorporating into their homes in the 1880s.

The corner doorways beckon viewers to enter the room behind the parlor in which a parlor suite side chair, a picturesque arrangement of canes decorating the draped mantel, and a paired easel and print cluster on one side, while plants lead the eye to the other side of yet another doorway. That doorway may support heavy portières during the short winter season of South Texas, but for the summer it holds a swagged panel; or the treatment, colonial revival in feeling, may be a year-round one by the time of this photo. The view through the doorway frames details of the third room — a violin propped on a side table and a wall pocket of photographs hanging above it.

Like the Dunlap house in South Texas, the Magoffin house (fig. 11.15) in West Texas presents a view of a parlor in which the householders' tastes have evolved over a relatively brief period. Between 1875 and 1877, El Paso businessman and city official Joseph Magoffin erected this

11.14. Parlor, Edward and Dolores Welder Dunlap house, Northwest corner of North Victoria and Power streets (501 North Victoria Street), Victoria, ca. 1895 (Madeline Fleming O'Connor and Institute of Texan Cultures, San Antonio).

11.15. Parlor, Joseph Magoffin house, 1120 Magoffin Avenue, El Paso, ca. 1888 (Texas Parks and Wildlife Department, Austin).

large adobe house, a "palatial rural domicile," into which he, his wife, Octavia, and their two children — thirteen-year-old James Wiley, II, and four-year-old Josephine — moved in 1877.[21] A decade later, a newspaper article proclaimed, "The house is elegantly furnished and contains the beautiful, useful, and artistic of the leading American cities as well as of the great City of Mexico."[22] The following year, the same newspaper confirmed that "the interior of the house [is] richly furnished and supplied with every convenience of civilized life."[23] Photographed soon after the house was enlarged during the late 1880s, the parlor is a fashionable interior uninhibited by El Paso's distance from New Orleans or New York.

The Magoffins created an essentially aesthetic interior, a style popular at the time of the construction of the house and afterward in Texas. They then saw little reason to change it, although they updated specific elements. Onto the plaster interior walls of the original section of the adobe house the family applied fashionable aesthetic-style paper: a pale, patterned wallpaper crowned by a dark banded frieze. They added the ingrain carpeting that stretches wall to wall. The dark plush banding of the upholstery, the cut-out decoration, the veneered panels, and the incised decoration of the Eastlake-inspired furniture represent elements in sympathy with aestheticism. Japanese-style objects — matching kakemonos flanking the fireplace and three fans creating an asymmetric wall decoration — also complement the predominant style. Irregularity and asymmetry, so much a part of home decoration in the 1880s, are evident in the Magoffin home, as a fringed scarf asymmetrically drapes a chair, an asymmetric lambrequin decorates the mantel, and unmatched globes adorn the kerosene fixture.

Octavia's awareness of new decorating strategies is apparent in the way she has positioned small wall-hung decorations below larger items, the metal or ceramic plaque on the wall, and pampas grass in ceramic vases. Other visual clichés are the guitar in the corner, the photograph album on the table, and an ornament hanging from the kerosene ceiling fixture, in this case an unusual one — a blowfish. The workbasket by the hearth suggests that the Magoffin women did needlework. Octavia and Josephine may have sewn and decorated the table cover and mantel drape, or lambrequin.

On the other side of the built-in cabinet, a bedroom was added to the house by 1887 (fig. 11.16). Although the room is new, the renaissance revival mantel mirror, the Eastlake-inspired dresser, and the rocking chair may predate the addition by a decade. The bedroom and the parlor share fashionable details that belong to the late 1880s — dried grasses in ceramic vases on the mantel, asymmetrical mantel draping, and wall plaque.

The decoration of this room, particularly the mantel garniture, is like that in other houses. Like the Dunlap parlor in South Texas, the Magoffin bedroom displays cabinet cards featuring images of family members and friends. In this view the photographer snapped two unidentified subjects; the reflection of the box camera can be seen in the mirror behind the sitters.

Moving from West Texas, each of the following three pairs of images documents a South Texas house before and after the turn of the century. Two houses stood in Galveston and the other in Beeville. Each has been updated by its owners rather than by professionals.

Figures 11.17 and 11.18 document the interior of the home of Joel B. Wolfe, a wealthy commission merchant in Galveston. The pictures were taken before and after the Galveston storm of September 8, 1900, which killed thousands of residents and destroyed many commercial and residential buildings. The storm prompted a massive effort to raise all structures in the town by seventeen feet and to build a seawall. Besides its obvious impact, the storm

11.16. Bedroom, Joseph Magoffin house, El Paso, ca. 1888 (Texas Parks and Wildlife Department, Austin).

11.17. Music room, Joel B. Wolfe house, 1602 Ball Avenue, Galveston, ca. 1897 (Rosenberg Library, Galveston).

11.18. Music room, Joel B. Wolfe house, ca. 1905 (Courtesy Robert Clark).

served as a watershed for decorating tastes — necessity and choice prompted the changes that occurred after 1900. The disaster combined with the psychological benchmark provided by the turn of the century to catalyze change in Galveston.

The 1895 interior view of the Wolfe house was taken in the summertime — the piano blocks the fireplace opening. A surrogate mantel, the piano top displays a symmetrical arrangement of objects of African, Chinese, and Native American design. Foliate-motif chintz slipcovers bring seasonal color and pattern into the room.

The painted walls supply a neutral backdrop for the numerous framed items encircling the room, many hanging from gilt picture molding. Centrally positioned above the piano is a print of horses in the style of Rosa Bonheur's images following the enormous success of her painting *The Horse Fair,* which was heralded as the "World's Greatest Animal Picture."[24] Flanking the "mantel," cascades of framed objects descend the walls, the paired arrangements topped by images of women, the shapes and sizes leading the eye down the wall and along the alternating rectangular and oval frames. Above the sofa, picturesque groupings have likewise been carefully composed; a centrally positioned snow scene is flanked by identically framed portraits, below which hang clusters of smaller photographs of family members.

Mrs. Wolfe selected floor covering in the latest style — a solid, medium-shade strip carpeting stretching the width of the room and tacked down at the threshold to facilitate the movement of the sliding doors. The veneered, upholstered, midcentury sofa sits amid rocking chairs inspired by colonial and French styles — more recent, lighter seating pieces. The two tables are French: a Louis XV-style side table supports a potted palm by the window, while a marble-top rococo revival center table holds a kerosene lamp. A gas-and-electric fixture hangs in the center of the room.

In 1895, exoticism was indicated by wall-hung prints and tabletop accessories, especially vases. A decade later most of those objects are gone (fig. 11.18). The room has been "colonial revivalized." Its furniture makes it appear to predate figure 11.17. The Wolfes, having experienced a dramatic shift in taste, have "Americanized" their interiors.[25]

In place of ethnographic references, they have chosen references to America's Anglo-Saxon past. The "foreign" women have been replaced by George Washington and Robert E. Lee. The cult of the Lost Cause that found expression in other Texas interiors can be seen in this room. Lee figures prominently as a Southern icon, but Washington is here, too, perhaps because the Wolfes, like many Southerners, believed that as a Virginian, Washington would have sided with the South during the Civil War.

The taste for classicism that found expression in the World's Columbian Exposition in Chicago in 1893 supplanted the desire for exoticism among some American householders, including the Wolfes. Their parlor has been self-consciously "classicized." A mantel and overmantel have been installed. The Elizabethan revival table is set to serve tea. The rococo revival furnishings herald the middle of the nineteenth century — a usable past from the vantage of the turn of the century. While fewer objects decorate the walls and tabletops, some room elements have been elaborated and formalized. For example, the fine lighting fixture hangs above the new electric table lamp, and the window treatments have received a renaissance revival cornice above the same ball-fringe valances.

Although the rococo revival-style center table in the earlier view has been replaced, the style dominates the room. The seating pieces line the room's perimeter rather than impede movement about the room. Furniture placement harkens back to an earlier fashion when furniture was positioned to take advantage of natural light — and accommodates the picture taking.

Another prominent Galvestonian, real estate dealer John Hanna, photographed the interior of his parlor just one month before the 1900 storm and took another photograph more than three years later (figs. 11.19, 11.20). In a more modest setting than the Wolfe house, the Hanna parlor shows unremarkable finishes. Matting, sewn in strips, covers the hardwood floor wall to wall; paint or solid paper is used on the walls; and in the 1900 view, a decorative frieze encircles the room.

The 1900 furnishings are typical of other middle-class houses at the time. A piano, several small tables and stands, and unmatched chairs fill the room. Lacking a fireplace, the tops of the curtained bookcase and the piano hold decorative elements. Over the piano hang paired crayon portraits of Hanna's Irish father and his mother; symmetrically arranged wall accessories, including the United States flag, prints, photographs, and a homemade wreath flank the center window.

Three years later, details have changed (fig. 11.20). A fringed scarf drapes the piano top, now bare of accesso-

11.19. Parlor, John Hanna house, 1417 Market Street, Galveston, August 1900 (Rosenberg Library, Galveston).

ries. Simple shades cover the windows; the visible hardware indicates that curtains will cover them during colder months. Wall treatments, too, have changed. The removal of the wallpaper frieze as well as the replacement of the earlier picture groupings with small landscapes flanking the center window have created a less embellished appearance. A bookcase has replaced the side table in the earlier view. Some of the chairs are new in the later view, but the armchair by the spittoon is not. The artificial lighting devices as well as the floor treatment are the same in both photographs. The matting, typically a summer treatment, is still the floor covering for the Hannas' parlor in November.

The 1903 view adds a glimpse of the sitting room, which features a corner fireplace with tile surround. Matting topped with rugs covers the hardwood floor. A co-

11.20. Sitting room and parlor, John Hanna house, November 1903 (Rosenberg Library, Galveston).

lonial revival side chair, a rattan armchair, a gilt, bamboo-turned side chair, and an Eastlake-inspired center table furnish what we see of the room.

The Hannas modified the decoration of their rooms without the aid of professional designers. Instead, fortified by published decorating advice, making use of widely available sources for household goods, and motivated by reform taste and the 1900 storm, they implemented their own ideas about decoration. In the process they achieved remarkably "typical" middle-class parlors.

William H. and Julia Wood George in Beeville also redecorated their home near the turn of the century. In 1898, the Georges hosted a birthday banquet for members of their Anniversary Club. Eight years earlier, when decorating their late-nineteenth-century South Texas dining room, they had varnished the wainscoting and covered the walls with an aesthetic embossed paper featuring conventionalized floral patterns (fig. 11.21). For the 1898 dinner they selected a linen cloth, embellished with a drawnwork border, that extends over the long table and provides a base for the array: glass candelabra, a modest fern, a decanter, an olive dish, nut dishes, silverware, stemmed glasses, and tumblers. A small serving table holds a chocolate pot and cups. The number and variety of dishes and glasses suggest prosperous and refined occupants.

William George was born in Louisiana, the son of a plantation owner. The family moved to Texas and purchased a plantation in Washington County, but resided seventy-five miles away in Houston, which was connected by rail. William worked as a railroad conductor between Galveston and Houston and manned the first passenger train over the road from Houston to Victoria.[26] In 1884 he married Julia Wood and the couple built their Beeville residence in 1890.[27] In the dining room of their home they hung a pyramidal arrangement including a photograph of the train on which he worked, a photo of another family home, a still life, and a picture of an animal.

Just after the turn of the century, George and Julia remodeled their dining room in a colonial revival style, using dark patterned wallpaper and light painted woodwork. They added a plate rail and removed the wainscoting (fig. 11.22).

Earlier the room had highlighted George's career as a railroad worker; after remodeling, it highlighted cattle, the stock-in-trade of George's new enterprise, the basis for the fortunes of Julia's family, and the occupation of many Texans in this area of the state. A picture of two head of cattle hangs above the sideboard that is treated as a mantel.

The Reuben Anderson Cates and the John T. Price bungalow-style homes were constructed in Palacios, in 1906 and 1910 respectively, by a builder. The couples themselves, however, were responsible for the furnishings. In order to decorate in sympathy with the new lines, materials, and spaces of bungalows, the owners had to master a different vocabulary of suitable furnishings.

Palacios is located along the Gulf Coast midway between Galveston and Corpus Christi near Port Lavaca, an early cattle shipping point. The bungalow appeared in this region in the first decade of the twentieth century. A new style of house that had been winning favor since the popularization of British design reforms in the 1880s and 1890s, it had gained early popularity in the Midwest and California. These houses, too, were generally built without the use of architects and interior designers; the occupants chose the interior finishes and furnishings.

Decorating advice for these new structures was available from writers for national and regional magazines. About 100 miles from Palacios, the William A. Wilson Company issued *Homes*.[28] Like other periodicals, it illustrated dwellings outfitted in the new mode: furniture in the mission

11.21. Dining room, William H. George house, 801 North Adams, Beeville, ca. 1898 (Courtesy Mary M. Welder).

11.22. Dining room, William H. George house, ca. 1901 (Courtesy Mary M. Welder).

style, geometric-pattern area rugs leaving wooden floors partially exposed, dining room plate rails, brick fireplaces, iron bedsteads, built-in benches near the entry, walls covered with burlap or ingrain paper, and short madras curtains. Both the Price and the Cates bungalows resemble many builder-constructed houses of the first decade of the twentieth century.

After Opal Cates and lumber merchant/rancher John T. Price married, they built a bungalow overlooking Tres Palacios Bay on the Gulf Coast, twenty-five miles from Port Lavaca. Their home was completed in 1906 and photographed shortly afterward (fig. 11.23). The floor plan featured a flowing continuity, which the Prices reinforced with decorative treatments. For example, they chose the same fabric for valances in living and dining rooms and used a light green wallpaper topped with a frieze of peonies for the walls in both rooms.[29]

Line is emphasized. Alternating light and dark woods, probably pine and mahogany, outline the floor in patterns of decreasing rectangles. Strapwork decorates the fireplace

11.23. Living room into dining room, John T. Price house, Duson Street (later moved one block east to South Bay Boulevard), Palacios, ca. 1906 (Courtesy Helen Cates Neary).

cover, and the linear oak mantel shows its "honest construction." The simple lines of the door head and jambs are echoed in the Prices' dining room furniture.

Even the wall-hung and tabletop accessories conform to "simplicity," "honesty," and the handcrafted ideal. On the mantel, a narrow open shelf displays a single candlestick, an object of the colonial revival taste that links the space to the dining room's candle-motif fixture above the table. A plate rail encircles the dining room, supporting hand-painted plates, while the table displays a hand-painted ceramic pitcher. An exception to the arts and crafts aesthetic is the classical onyx clock with gold filigree above the mantel shelf; a family item, it matches the one that sat on Opal's parents' mantel.[30]

11.24. Living room, Reuben Anderson Cates house, Duson Street, Palacios, 1910 (Courtesy Helen Cates Neary).

11.25. Entry hall, Reuben Anderson Cates house, 1910 (Courtesy Helen Cates Neary).

11.26. Dining room, Reuben Anderson Cates house, 1910 (Courtesy Helen Cates Neary).

The Reuben Anderson Cates house was the second built on the Palacios site. The first, built in 1907, burned the night before it was accepted from the contractor, a Mr. Emerson. Beginning anew in 1908, Emerson finished rebuilding in 1910. The house was to be a winter home for the Cateses who lived in Tiptonville, Tennessee. They built it on property close to the home of their son-in-law and daughter, the Prices. The two houses sat at right angles to each other, overlooking the bay.[31]

Photographs of the house were taken in 1910, shortly after the Cateses moved in (figs. 11.24, 11.25, 11.26). The living room expresses the line and color of reform. Like the Price home, this one features the unembellished mission trim that builders and designers, trained or self-proclaimed, advocated. Builder Emerson provided a bench to the right of the fireplace suggestive of an inglenook recommended by many late-nineteenth- and early-twentieth-century "reform" architects; the fireplace tiles appear to have a fashionable matte finish. The Cateses added the set of reed furniture, piano, and leather-covered stool. One of the Cateses' children, Charles, attended the University of Virginia, and a commemorative pillow from that institution rests on the bench.

The woodwork, probably from Price's lumberyard, is pine stained to look like mahogany. Above the paneling, a "milk chocolate" colored paper covered the walls, topped with complementary stripes. The Cateses chose pinks and greens for most of the other room furnishings: green tiles frame the fireplace, a pink and green floral pattern covers the furniture cushions, and a geometric pattern in the same shades appears in the rugs.[32]

The Cateses were a mature couple by the time they decorated this coastal home. The interior architecture of the residence must have seemed avant-garde to them. Nonetheless, they embraced design strategies then being popularized by Frank Lloyd Wright, which blended inside with outside, as the photo of their entry hall shows (fig. 11.25). The continuous paint and paper scheme allows interior spaces to flow into one another, replacing the clearly defined and differentiated spaces of earlier houses.

Adorning the staircase, a statue of Sappho greets visitors to the house, while portraits of United States presidents decorate the far room. During the infrequent cold spells on the South Texas coast, the home could be heated by the corner fireplace or the furnace — two wall registers are visible in the photograph. The heating system may have been added at the request of the Cateses.

The dining room photo is unusually dark because the photographer pulled the window shades to prevent glare. The shadowy room is furnished with an oak pedestal table reminiscent of the empire style and four oak chairs in an arts and crafts version of Queen Anne. The Cateses' newly fashionable built-in storage cabinets have a dual purpose: displaying objects like a china cabinet and serving as a sideboard.

★ ★ ★ ★

Armed with advice offered in periodicals, household art manuals, and domestic economy books, Texans exercised their own sense of style and consulted local "experts" such as paperhangers and furniture store owners, as they tackled home decoration. They updated their rooms without direct help from trained professionals. Unlike owners of professionally designed houses, many householders were not reluctant to modify rooms as styles or their sense of fashion changed. Interiors, even in remote areas, show a widespread awareness and knowledge of recent fashions and national trends.

12

Toward Professional Decoration

A CASE STUDY

When householders began to use the services of architects and decorators, the result was standardization in house design. Some prosperous Texans wholeheartedly embraced the decorating advice of the professionals they employed, thereby subordinating indicators of their own occupational and ethnic identities. Professionally designed houses began to feature elements that expressed the financial resourcefulness of the owners and the occupational identity of the architects and decorators. And yet the very subordination of the owners' identity to that of the professional designers reveals a great deal about the householders' aspirations.

This new group of design professionals wrought many changes in the way some wealthy Texans furnished their houses. Twenty-five photographs of the interior of the Henry Thomas Staiti house in Houston, studied in chronological order, offer a revealing case study of the impact of the professional designer upon a dwelling, document the transformation in taste from 1905 to 1920, and illustrate the changing view of a house from an expression of the owner's individuality to that of the designer's talent.

Youthful Henry and Odelia Reisner Staiti built their Westmoreland Place home in 1905, soon after the discovery of oil at Spindletop increased their fortunes. Initially, they furnished it themselves. In August 1915, after they had lived for ten years in the substantial but unpretentious cottage, the house was damaged by a storm. From 1915 through 1918, it was renovated both inside and out by architect Alfred C. Finn and an unknown decorator.[1] Of the forty or more exterior and interior views documenting the house, four interior photos taken in 1905 at the time of the family's initial occupancy, three of a wedding held in the home in January 1912, and eighteen taken in 1920, after the remodeling, are included here. The earliest show that the interiors of this architect-designed house expressed the Staitis' personal identity and taste in decorat-

12.1. Entry hall, Henry Thomas Staiti house, Westmoreland Place 2, Houston (later 421 Westmoreland Avenue, at present located in Sam Houston Park), 1905 (Courtesy Lee Averill Lawrence, Carol Jackson, and Harris County Heritage Society, Houston).

ing. The latest reveal little about the residents but a great deal about the stylistic preferences of the architect and the decorator. The objects defining the Staitis' familial and regional heritage and occupational identity have been supplanted in 1920 by objects that show a careful but impersonal arrangement that has little to do with the occupants.

The absence of personal elements in the 1920 series of photographs may make them at first seem mere record photographs taken by architects, yet evidence indicates that the views were ordered by the Staitis. The couple liked to have their house photographed. More to the point, they posed in many of the exterior and in some interior views even in the third series; photographs taken by or for architects do not usually feature clients. Many copies of each series of photos have survived in the collections of the Staitis' descendants and in that of the photographer, but not in the collection of the architect. Photographs taken later in the 1920s (beyond the scope of this book) show that the Staitis changed little in their home. The sparseness and the absence of personalizing objects apparent in the 1920 views seem to represent a taste endorsed by the Staitis.

The original 1905 house is attributed to Charles P. Jones, who identified himself as an architect and superintendent. A few years later he joined John R. Tabor to form an architectural partnership, Jones & Tabor, and in 1910 they built a mirror image of the Staiti house for another Houstonian, Sam Randall.[2] The Staiti house, a two-story dwelling, may have been built on speculation.[3] Its design is probably not original and certainly not unique, but its construction is solid and its massing, substantial.

The dwelling, a hip-roofed cottage, was constructed on a fashionable street then known only as Westmoreland Place (later, as 421 Westmoreland Place). Henry Staiti purchased the house and lot in February 1905 for $5,400.[4] Henry's brother Grover also lived there after 1910 and Odelia's sister Leah was a frequent visitor, moving in permanently when she married Grover in 1918. After Grover's death later that year during the influenza epidemic, Leah continued to occupy the home, and other Reisner sisters, residents of Waco, visited Odelia and Leah frequently in the Houston residence. Henry's two other brothers, Charles and Albert, along with Charles' wife, Grace, joined the household at various times during the late 1910s and the 1920s.[5] Thus the house served as a kind of family compound for more than twenty years.

Purchased four years after the Staitis' marriage, the house was initially photographed within six months of their arrival.[6] Figure 12.1 shows the entry hall and staircase, with glimpses into the parlor and dining room. The entry features wall-to-wall carpet, described as "heavy Oriental Axminster," and a wallpaper patterned with stripes and medallions.[7] In spite of the rocker, brass spittoon, armchair, and built-in bench or hall seat (reminiscent of an inglenook), the arts and crafts-inspired decoration does little to encourage lingering.

Two framed items decorate the Staitis' entry hall. To the left, an image of a stag, placed at eye level for those climbing the stairs, expresses popular taste. To the right, positioned to catch the eye of those descending the stairs, a print of one of the many ruinous Spindletop oil fires (possibly that which began on September 13, 1902, and raged for a week) is personally expressive. To Henry Staiti, an oilman who made much of his wealth from Spindletop and nearby fields, the fire scene was no doubt a reminder both of his success and of potential catastrophe. The image appears in the entry hall where objects relating to men's activities were typically placed. Halls were places of passage, of activity, not of rest as were feminine parlors.

Decorating critics in the popular press recommended particular styles for certain rooms; "feminine" French

12.2. Parlor, Henry Thomas Staiti house, 1905 (Courtesy Lee Averill Lawrence and Jeanette Jackson King).

styles were considered well suited to the parlor. The Staitis agreed. In their "white and gold parlor," a tapestry-upholstered sofa and chair are liberal interpretations of the Louis XIV and Louis XV styles (fig. 12.2).[8] The carpet, patterned with ribbons and roses on a pale field, and the gas-and-electric fixture and curtains, both detailed with fleurs-de-lis, continue the theme (see fig. 12.6). The embossed wallpaper features floral clusters surrounded by scrollwork. The center table shows influence of both colonial revival and art nouveau.

One corner of the room features a fireplace; the other corner is softened by the sofa. Both have been marked by animal-skin rugs, probably goatskin or sheepskin. The mantel, undraped in accord with the growing sentiment for spareness, showcases family photographs.

Other aspects of family identity include *The Last Meeting of Lee and Jackson,* an image made popular by F. Halpin's 1872 print, which hangs next to the hearth.[9] Like many Texans, Henry Staiti's Confederate sympathies were probably rekindled in 1895 by the Confederate Reunion

12.3. Dining room, Henry Thomas Staiti house, 1905 (Courtesy Lee Averill Lawrence and Jeanette Jackson King).

hosted by the city of Houston; among the invited guests was Winnie Davis, the daughter of the late Jefferson Davis. Having been born in East Texas, which had ties to the Deep South, Staiti undoubtedly identified with the region's political affiliation and culture. Besides referring to the Lost Cause, the image of Lee and Jackson also relates to Staiti's identification with family. Henry's father, Santo Staiti, emigrated from Italy in 1848 for political reasons. Leaving his family, he settled in New Orleans and worked as a merchant. When the Civil War began, he joined the Ninth Louisiana Artillery. After the war as railroads were being built, Staiti followed the line of construction, working in Shreveport, Marshall, and Texarkana. He later became politically active in East Texas.[10]

No interior photographs survive of the home of Santo Staiti and his wife, Mary Jane. In the home of their Texas-born son, any allegiance to Italy as homeland is absent. Henry and Odelia expressed their identities as prosperous, style-conscious Southerners with oil interests.

Figure 12.3 shows the newly furnished colonial revival

12.4. Original master bedroom, Henry Thomas Staiti house, 1905 (Courtesy Lee Averill Lawrence and Jeanette Jackson King).

dining room. Queen Anne-inspired dining chairs line the curved and curtained bay window. An oak extension table stands in the center of the room below the gas-and-electric lighting fixture. A classically inspired sideboard, detailed with a large carved shell and acanthus leaves along with columns, displays an arrangement of cut glass. The oak sideboard is highlighted by a small oriental-style rug, laid atop a "heavy piled two toned green" wall-to-wall carpet in a stylized floral design and matching border.[11] In an unusual treatment, moire-pattern paper covers the ceiling and side walls above both the plate rail and the windows; a tapestry depicting a bounty of fruits extends below, while a matching border outlines the moire paper.

Unlike the dining room, Henry and Odelia's bedroom is a visually animated and personalized room (fig. 12.4). An abstract-pattern ceiling paper, a wallpaper printed with a classical design of a wreath encircling a stylized torch, and a wide matching border form the background. Wall-to-wall matting is covered by a boldly patterned rug complemented by the designs in the smaller rug and the upholstered footstool.

Sentimental decorations compete with the wallpaper design: cut-out hearts, pictures of romantic couples and idealized women, photographs of Henry, and a trade card for Antikamnia Tablets (featuring a Red Cross nurse and entitled "Confidence"), a popular remedy for a variety of "female complaints." The space also contains colonial revival furniture, including two rocking chairs; the chairs and the spittoon suggest that the bedroom was used as an informal sitting room by Henry and Odelia.

At the time of the January 1912 wedding of Odelia's sister Jeanette, the entry hall of the Staiti house remained essentially unchanged (fig. 12.5). For the ceremony, smilax encircles both the banister and the lighting fixture, a popular colonial revival hall fixture. The long, light curtains of 1905 have been replaced by shorter arts and crafts-inspired ones (this change occurs also in the dining room). The parlor center table to which gilding has been added functions as the reception table. A popular art nouveau plaque of a woman decorates the wall beneath a print of a stag. A wall telephone hangs at the end of the hallway. Wedding guests are directed by the placement of furnishings and decorations to enter the room at the right of the hall, the parlor where the wedding takes place.

The parlor additions are part of the wedding decorations: potted palms and roses, probably cut from the Staiti gardens (fig. 12.6). For the occasion, the Staitis have removed family mementos from most surfaces, although a few remain on the cabinet behind the chair. A window provides the backdrop against which palms arch gracefully. At the base of the steps, the bride and groom will stand on the animal-skin rug. Smilax decorates the altar and the combination fixture, while vases of cut flowers rest on the mantel, altar, and piano, which is set diagonally across the corner of the room.

Figure 12.6 introduces a custom that will be repeated frequently in later interior photographs — the frugal reuse of carpeting; here, the piano stool sits on a small remnant of wall-to-wall carpet cut from the excess as the rug was laid across the fireplace corner.

In the dining room, decorated with roses and lilies of the valley, the same moire paper and ceiling fixture embellish the space; however, several details have changed (fig. 12.7). Gone are the light curtains reaching the floor; the bay windows are covered with both an open weave fabric and curtains in a bold print. The furniture is the same, but the space is visually more active than in 1905. The curtain pattern contributes to the new sense of vitality as do the plate-rail decorations, which alternate hand-painted plates with a set of cups decorated by decalco-

12.5. Entry hall, Henry Thomas Staiti house, January 1912 (Courtesy Lee Averill Lawrence, Carol Jackson, and Harris County Heritage Society, Houston).

12.6. Parlor, Henry Thomas Staiti house, January 1912 (Courtesy Lee Averill Lawrence, Carol Jackson, and Harris County Heritage Society, Houston).

12.7. Dining room, Henry Thomas Staiti house, January 1912 (Courtesy Lee Averill Lawrence, Carol Jackson, and Harris County Heritage Society, Houston).

mania with images of friars. The sideboard still showcases family crystal that now complements the ceramics on the plate rail.

By 1920 architect Finn had dramatically changed the character of the Staitis' entry hall and living room by extending the same motifs, patterns, and colors throughout the downstairs area, thus creating a fluidity in the spaces (figs. 12.8, 12.9). The expansive effect is achieved by eliminating the walls that had separated living room from entry hall. This treatment alters the earlier sense of strictly differentiated spaces in the original plan of the house.

Bordered area rugs, all in the same pattern, cover the floors of the entry hall, living room, and dining room. Between the three large carpets and two long runners, the wooden floor is exposed in the newer taste. The solid wallpaper is topped with an identical art deco border in the entry hall and living room and a related border in the dining room. Matching electric fixtures and identically upholstered overstuffed furniture make the entry hall and living room seem a single space. To that end, both rooms dramatically juxtapose white woodwork and dark fabrics at doorways and windows.

The functions of the rooms have also changed. The entry hall no longer serves primarily as a passageway; instead, it is a minilibrary with oak bookcases and a small gateleg table and desk. Its open bookcases invite relaxed reading, as do the issues of *Popular Mechanics* and the *Saturday Evening Post* on the living room empire revival table.

Compared with figures 12.1, 12.2, 12.5, and 12.6, a pair of photographs (figs. 12.8, 12.9) does not reveal the identity of the owners. Gone are references to Staiti's business, family, or personal sympathies. By 1910 his success in the oil and gas business had earned him a regional reputation. He served variously as president of the Houston-Oklahoma Oil Company, the Oklahoma Exploration Company, and the Powhattan Oil Company, as joint owner with the Gulf Refining Company of major oil fields in East Texas, and as vice-president of Texas Exploration Company. He co-owned the Paystreak Oil Company, Johnson's Bayou Oil Company, Prairie Oil Company, Hop-Us Oil Company, Houston-Oklahoma Oil Company, Valley Oil Company, and Pathfinder Oil Company.[12] But in 1920 his prominence as an oilman is not apparent in the decoration of his house.

The side porch, just beyond the living room, has been transformed into an enclosed sun room (figs. 12.10, 12.11). The exterior wood facade and the beaded wooden eaves are now interior surfaces; the walls are painted a light color and trimmed with hinged panels below the dado rail. A single door opens to the front porch.

The cushions of the lacquered rattan furniture harmonize with the beige-and-brown chintz curtains and portières.[13] (Here portières are double hung; a dark, solid velvet faces into the living room; see figure 12.8.) The French doors also display popular paneled curtains. The art pottery is the Donatello pattern by Roseville; fluted in alternating beige and green vertical bands interrupted by a wide terra-cotta band with beige cupids, the jardinieres hold palms that, along with the ferns, thrive in this setting.

The remodeled dining room shows evidence of a decorator's hand in the use of textiles and the placement of decorative accessories (fig. 12.12). The rug, custom cut for the room, conforms to the shape of the space with a uniform border around the perimeter. At the bay window are shades, short curtains, and an appliquéd and fringed flat valance. The Queen Anne revival chairs remain, but their seats are now covered with a tapestry fabric.

The colonial revival china cabinet is new, as is the oak pedestal table of arts and crafts design. The polished oak

12.8 (above) and **12.9 (facing page)**. Entry hall and living room, Henry Thomas Staiti house, ca. 1920 (Harris County Heritage Society, Houston).

table matches the wood of the previously unphotographed mantel, which is embellished with columns and Greek key molding. The mantel is decorated symmetrically with a clock flanked by art glass vases with floral motifs that echo the freshly cut daisies on the dining table. The plate rail remains, now displaying a stein and hand-painted dessert plates. An English-style alabaster electric lighting fixture replaces the earlier gas-and-electric one.

The dining room is impressive for its professionally coordinated look: subtle backgrounds on walls and floor with measured details in the valance, frieze, and upholstery. But the space lacks a personalizing touch.

Wall coverings, window treatments, and floor coverings extend to the passageway that accesses second-floor bedrooms and the third-story billiard room (fig. 12.13). The view offers a rare look into the stair hall. Architect and

12.10 and **12.11 (facing page).** Sun room, Henry Thomas Staiti house, ca. 1920 (Harris County Heritage Society, Houston).

decorator have determined the look of the space; the Staitis have added the only embellishment, a small vase of the jasmine that probably grew in their gardens.

Figure 12.14 shows a bedroom that became the master bedroom after the Finn renovation. At the front of the house, the room has large built-in closets and a door to the newly created second-floor sun room. Its curtains resemble and its wallpapers match those in the old master bedroom (see fig. 12.17). The new rug is similar in character to those added to the first-floor public areas of the house during remodeling. The room's furniture includes rocking chairs resembling those on the porches upstairs and down.

The hand of the decorator is seen in the coordinated curtains, transom cover, and upholstery fabrics, although a few personal objects do intrude — a wall hanging of ties and scarves and a small oval photograph of Odelia. A portrait photograph of Henry rests on the dresser. This frequently published image appeared in the 1913 book of the Houston Press Club and the 1920 *Texans and Their State.*[14] The framed portrait looks oddly out of place here; too large for the dresser and framed to be hung, it may have been set on the dresser temporarily to identify the bedroom's occupants or as an afterthought.

Like the downstairs porch, the second-story eastern-exposure sun room was added during the renovation (figs. 12.15, 12.16). Bright blue-and-white chintz covers the windows (over white plissé undercurtains), cushions, and tabletops in this informal room. Other surfaces are painted white — the former exterior walls, the interior walls, and the wicker porch furniture.[15] A bordered area rug in a geometric pattern covers the floor, exposing the edges of the room's new wooden floor.

Figure 12.15 like figure 12.8 documents the new intercom system installed in their enlarged home. As in the room below, plants and a Donatello jardiniere made by Roseville Pottery accessorize the space. The upstairs sun

12.12 (facing page). Dining room, Henry Thomas Staiti house, ca. 1920 (Harris County Heritage Society, Houston). **12.13 (above).** Stair landing, Henry Thomas Staiti house, ca. 1920 (Harris County Heritage Society, Houston).

12.14 (facing page). New master bedroom, Henry Thomas Staiti house, ca. 1920 (Harris County Heritage Society, Houston). **12.15 (above left)** and **12.16 (above right).** Sun room, Henry Thomas Staiti house, ca. 1920 (Harris County Heritage Society, Houston).

room contains a tray, pitcher, and glass which also appear in the bedrooms. These items are functional but also serve as signs of hospitality. Figure 12.16 shows a rare glimpse into an early-twentieth-century bathroom added during renovation.

Figures 12.17, 12.18, 12.19, and 12.20 document secondary sleeping areas in the house. The former master bedroom photographed in 1905 is more restrained in 1920 and devoid of personal accessories (fig. 12.17). The new colonial revival furniture is positioned against the wall rather than placed diagonally across a corner. In remodeling this bedroom, the Staitis have used as an area rug the

12.17. Former master bedroom, Henry Thomas Staiti house, ca. 1920 (Harris County Heritage Society, Houston).

wall-to-wall carpet that originally covered the parlor floor. For its new location the carpet has been trimmed, although the border remains on the two visible sides.

The colorful fabric that forms the lampshade and the overcurtains also complements the wallpaper, detailed with a magnolia-blossom pattern. The undercurtains with their border trim and insertions relate to the bedspread's crocheted trim and insertions. Within this well-coordinated space, the only recognizable personal item is the portrait photograph of the late Grover Staiti, Henry's brother. As in figure 12.14, the photo appears awkwardly placed, perhaps a decorative afterthought. This room may have been the bedroom of Grover and Leah.

A third bedroom (fig. 12.18), not photographed earlier, in 1920 contains a dresser that had been in another bedroom when photographed in 1905 (see fig. 12.4). The wall-to-wall carpet pictured in both the 1905 and the 1912 views of the dining room (see figs. 12.3, 12.7) has been cut to become an unbordered area rug.

In later views the 1905 furnishings have been adapted and incorporated into the remodeled house either by Odelia or by the decorator who continued the frugal nineteenth-century custom. Although decorating tastes were changing in the period from 1905 to 1920, the recycled objects still served a function and were not worn beyond use. The changed placement is significant. Not only has the carpet been moved from public areas to private, but also there is a hierarchy among these private spaces. As noted, the master bedroom of 1905 (see fig. 12.4), for example, holds a then-new dresser that in 1920 is in a secondary bedroom (see fig. 12.18). The rose-pattern rug of the Staitis' 1905 living room appears in one secondary bedroom some fifteen years later (see fig. 12.17) when it might have better suited a still smaller bedroom that featured roses on the curtains and on wallpaper border (see fig. 12.18); perhaps a hierarchy of rooms and materials dictated that the carpet from the primary public room (see figs. 12.2, 12.6) become appropriate floor covering for the larger one. The new master bedroom (see fig. 12.14) received new carpet.

While the bed, chair, stand, and rocker in figure 12.18 may also date to the original construction of the house, the style of the nightstand indicates that it is a new piece. The lighting fixtures and the wall and window treatments are the recent work of the decorator who has selected a naturalistic frieze and baseboard border to line the striped wallpaper. These wallpaper borders were popular, especially in bedrooms, at the time of World War I; the decorator used them throughout the Staiti bedrooms. Also popular were matched paper and textile designs, but in this room the roses in the frieze complement, but do not appear to match, the patterned curtains.[16]

The fourth bedroom is small and narrow and barely accommodates the furniture (fig. 12.19). Several of the items in the room are familiar, including the rug from the entry hall (see figs. 12.1, 12.5) and the tray. The dresser is nearly identical to the one featured in the 1905 bedroom (see fig. 12.4) that is now in the other small bedroom (see fig. 12.18). The Staitis probably purchased both in 1905. The leather-seat mission rocking chair probably also dates to 1905. As in the other interior views of the renovated rooms, the wallpaper features the same subtle stripes and floral borders.

It is not known who occupied the smallest bedroom (fig. 12.19). Like the room pictured in figure 12.14, it contains a tie ring, which presumably kept clothing accessories handy for the occupant. But the room holds no clues to its occupant's identity even though bedrooms, as private spaces, typically served as arenas for the show of personal objects. The room might be a guest bedroom, yet

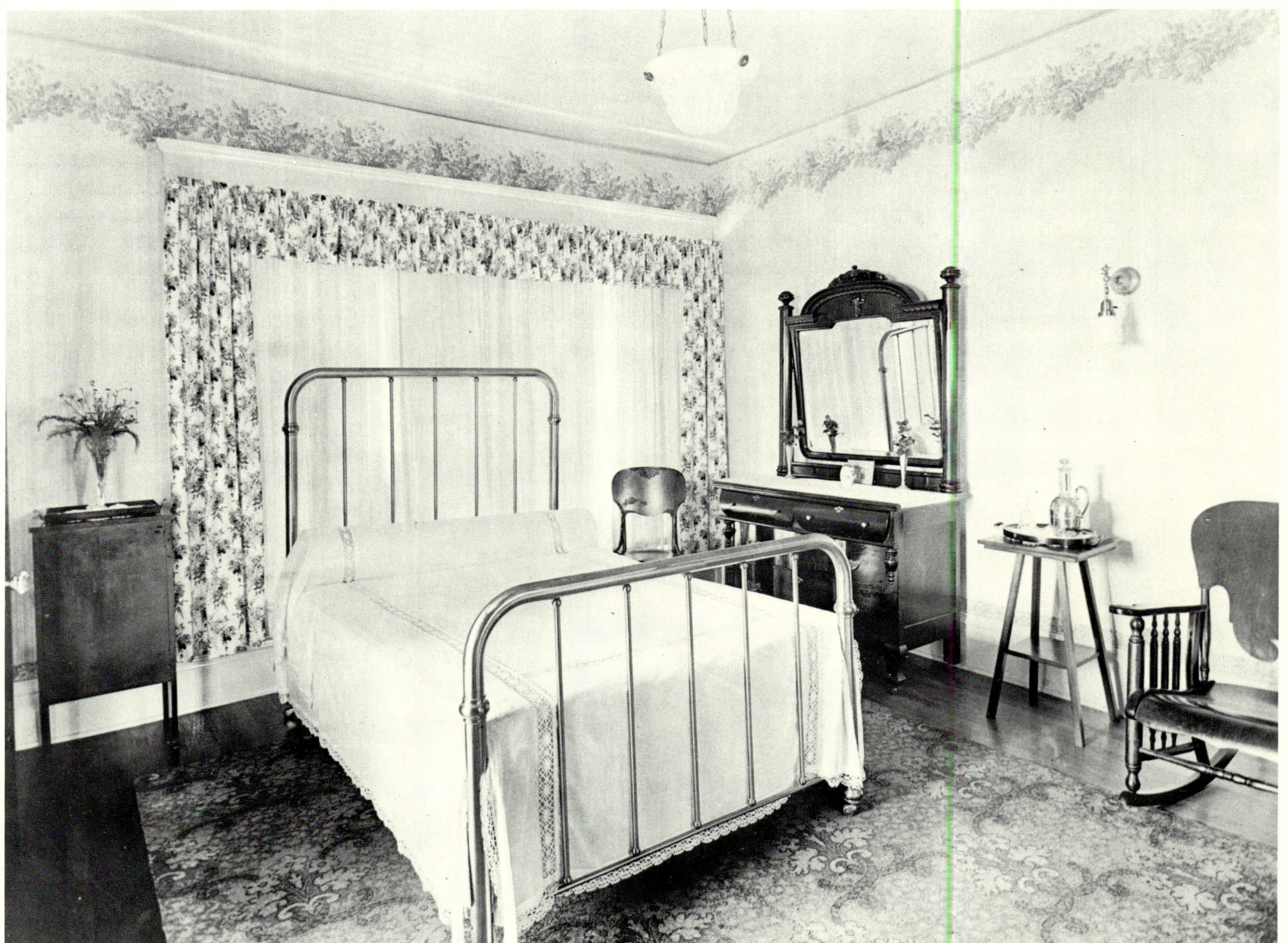

12.18. Bedroom, Henry Thomas Staiti house, ca. 1920 (Harris County Heritage Society, Houston).

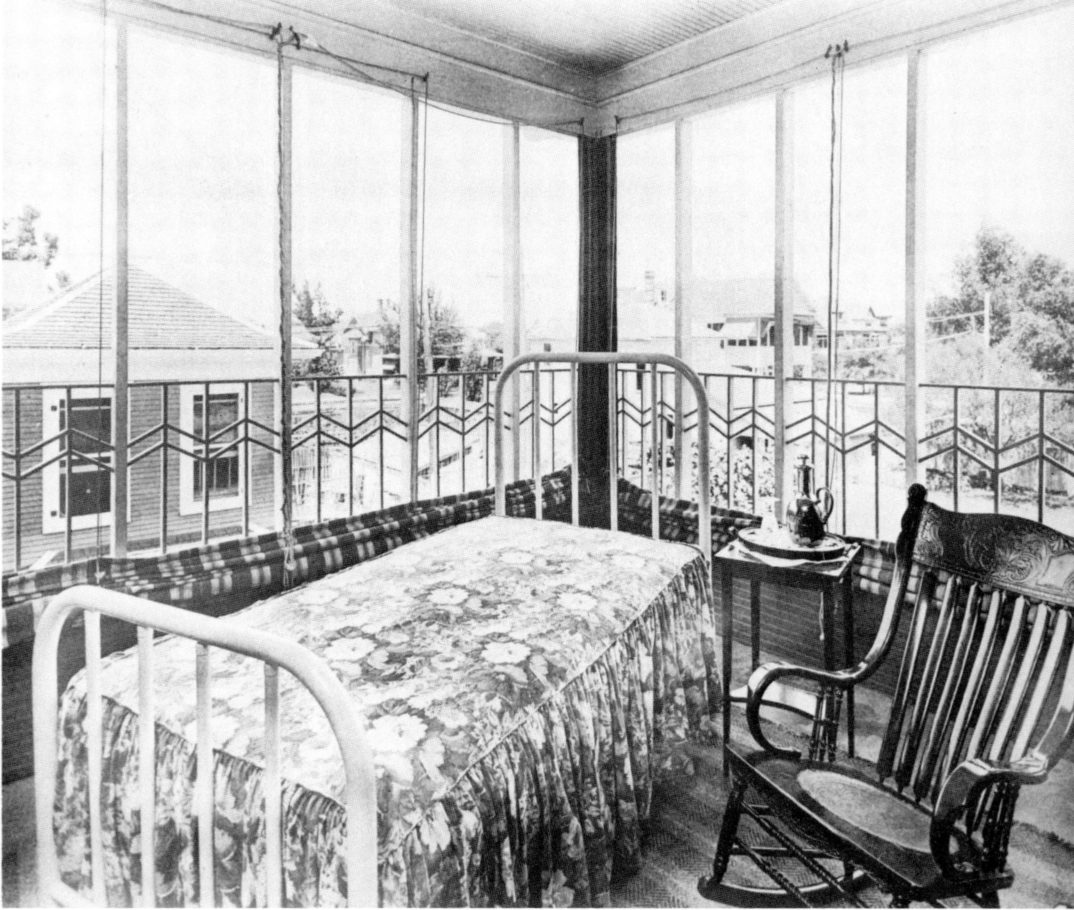

12.19 (above left). Bedroom, Henry Thomas Staiti house, ca. 1920 (Harris County Heritage Society, Houston). **12.20 (above right).** Sleeping porch, Henry Thomas Staiti house, ca. 1920 (Harris County Heritage Society, Houston).

the tie ring, accessories on the dresser, and the fan suggest that it was used permanently.

As an exterior view can reveal information about interior decoration (curtains through windows or hall furnishings through an open doorway), an interior view can offer information about the exterior. A photograph of the new second-story sleeping porch at the rear of the house captures a view of the grounds and neighborhood (fig. 12.20). The view includes one of the Staitis' outbuildings, the garden area, electric lines, and glimpses of nearby houses.

This addition to the original building features a wave-motif grille that resembles the woodwork detailing of the remodeled entry hall/library (fig. 12.9), and recalls details in the structures of Frank Lloyd Wright. The furnishings include the colonial revival rocking chair that in 1905 sat in a bedroom (see fig. 12.4); a stand holding a tray; another metal bedstead, this one with a colorful floral cover; a

12.21. Billiard room, Henry Thomas Staiti house, ca. 1920 (Harris County Heritage Society, Houston).

horizontally striped rug in a herringbone weave that echoes the grille; wire screens; and striped canvas shades that can be raised to become walls.

A billiard table, framed bar scene above the ball rack, and open cigar box confirm that the third floor is the men's retreat (fig. 12.21). The interior finishes used throughout the house fit in well here. Over an unpatterned wall-to-wall carpet is a rug mitered to fit the area of heavy use around the billiard table, in a pattern resembling that on the living and dining room floors. A ceiling fan hangs above the table. A pillow from the first-floor entry hall (see fig. 12.5), worn and with its ruffle removed, now

12.22. Breakfast room, Henry Thomas Staiti house, ca. 1920 (Harris County Heritage Society, Houston).

serves as an armrest. An intercom enables the billiard players to communicate with others on the lower floors of the house.

Adjoining the Staitis' pergola, filled with climbing roses, copper plants, and caladiums, is a breakfast room that blends indoors and outdoors (fig. 12.22). The merging is heightened by the screens and open windows that make it difficult to discern where the outside begins in a room created by framed voids and few solids. The tendency to blur the distinction between the interior and the exterior of a home is one of the "levels of ambiguity" scholars have recently noted about nineteenth- and early-

12.23 and **12.24 (facing page).** Kitchen, Henry Thomas Staiti house, ca. 1920 (Harris County Heritage Society, Houston).

twentieth-century American houses, especially architect-designed houses. Ambivalent about the type of life they want to lead in their homes, residents were at once attracted both to rules of etiquette — represented by interiors — and to a nostalgia for a simpler past, represented by nature.[17] This debate is made tangible in the design of their homes. Many of the spaces Finn redesigned for the Staitis deliberately blur indoors and outdoors, perhaps none more dramatically than the breakfast room.

The room is anonymous, revealing only the hand of its designers, not family members or their use of the space. The same decorating and furnishing strategies used elsewhere in the home have been applied here as well: coordinated fabrics for window treatments and cushions, rattan furniture, and art pottery accessories. Nothing but the cut flowers — gardening was a hobby of the Staitis' — refers to family.

The kitchen views demonstrate the premium placed on efficiency and cleanliness in kitchens of 1920 (figs. 12.23, 12.24). A practical linoleum floor, in a relatively expensive geometric design, introduces the primary decorative pattern into the otherwise white kitchen. In the pantry area, the glass panels of the cupboard doors have a dual effect — they exhibit the array of dishes, thus making work more efficient by disclosing the contents of the cupboard to household workers, but they also reveal the slightest dirt or disorder. Painted cupboards were easier to clean and created a sanitary and brighter look in this otherwise utilitarian space. A linen cloth under the objects in view appears more ceremonial than useful, marking an array of brand-name condiments made uniform and fancy by matching holders.

With the emphasis on cleanliness, the food preparation area (fig. 12.24) is white, as is a painted side chair identical to that in figure 12.18. Even the new A-B Gas Range is of white porcelain enamel.

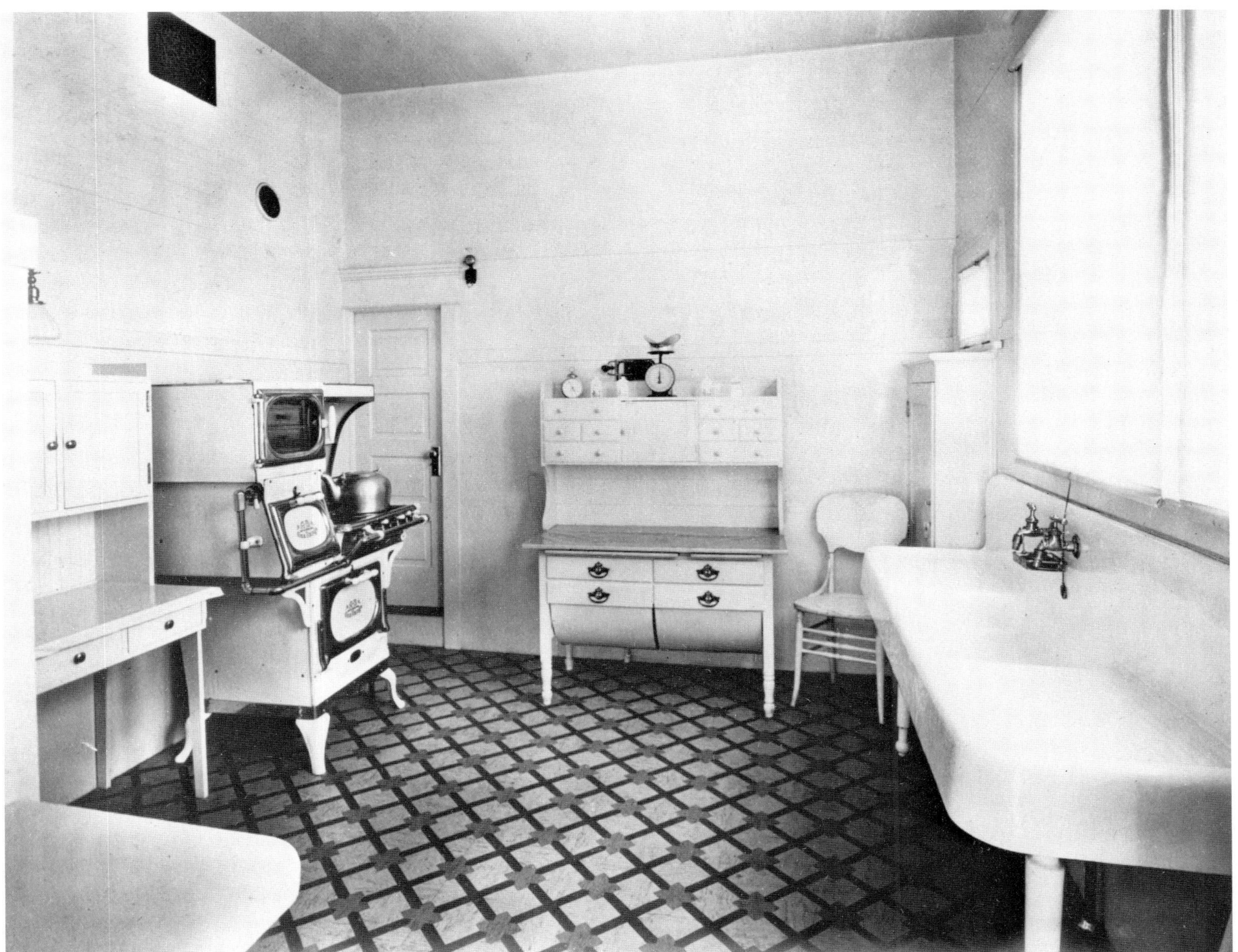

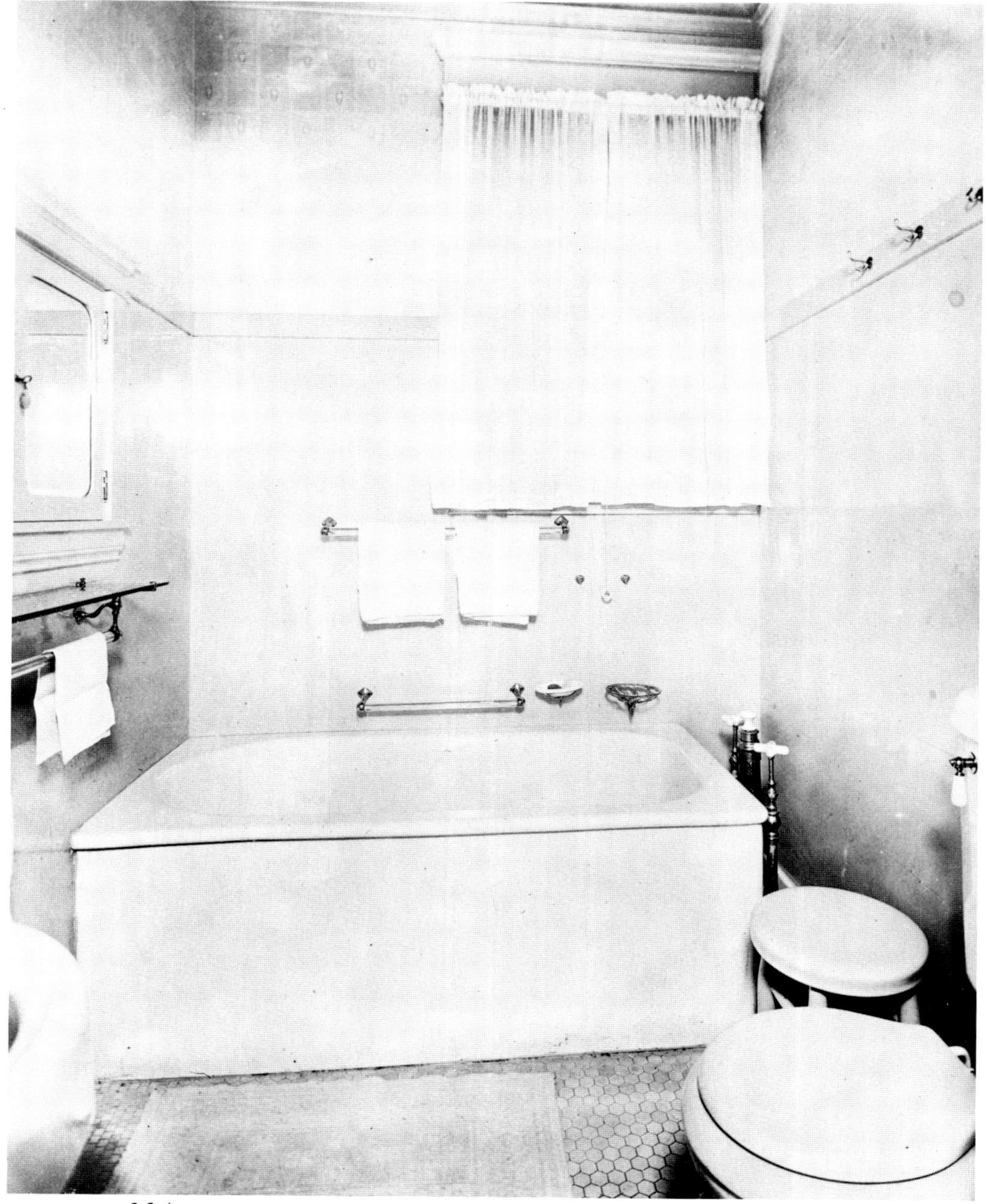

A rare glimpse into a bathroom shows another serviceable space (fig. 12.25): small white hexagonal tiles form the flooring; a painted wainscoting and waterproof paper, or "sanitas," cover the walls — all elements typical of early-twentieth-century bathrooms. The window is concealed by a shade and short curtains. A record of Finn's work on the house documents that a great deal of money was spent on the plumbing fixtures. In this bathroom, original to the house, the architect has updated the lavatory, tub, and toilet. Figures 12.16 and 12.25 show that in the late teens, Finn was approaching the compact bathroom that became standard in the 1920s.[18]

★ ★ ★ ★

Because of the 1915 storm damage to the Staiti house, the repair work undertaken by Finn was necessary; the extensive renovations were not. By the time of the remodeling, Henry and Odelia Staiti may have wanted a more impressive dwelling to match their new station in life. Embracing the new stylishness of the 1915 – 1918 period, the Staitis acquired a "new" home, choosing interiors that placed small premium on the expressions of personal identity.

Instead of personalized interiors filled with objects expressing occupational, familial, ethnic, or regional identities, the 1920 house exhibits efficient design strategies. One carpet pattern fills three spaces downstairs; in the up-

12.25. Bathroom, Henry Thomas Staiti house, ca. 1920 (Harris County Heritage Society, Houston).

stairs bedrooms the curtains are similar and the wallpaper designs are slight variations on a formula. Few personal items intrude upon the strategic coordination of all these elements.

In the decade and a half between 1905 and 1920 Houstonians alone had several interior decorators to choose from: Black Brothers Furniture Company, G. M. Kuhn & Company, Richard Kleine, and the Bullock Decorative Shops, all of which typically provided the wall coverings, floor coverings, window treatments, and furniture for their clients. These same services had previously been offered by various tradespeople, but the advertised expertise and interior decorating specialty promised a complete and packaged look appealing to certain homeowners. The new designers capitalized on the desire for "the professional look" and thereby effected major changes in household decoration for families like the Staitis who had the money to hire them and no strong inclinations about retaining expressions of their personal interests. Professional decorators implemented the new design ethic, "less is more."

The Bullock Decorative Shops

807 SAN JACINTO ST.
PHONE PRESTON 386

Designers and Makers of Homes and All That Pertains Thereto

ARCHITECTURE · BUILDING
DECORATION · FURNITURE · FITTINGS
FIXTURES · GROUNDS

WALTHER TAUSCHER

Designer and Decorator in Modern Frescoing

Painting in all Branches, such as Hardwood Finishing, Varnishing, Enameling, Graining, Etc.

DESIGNS AND ESTIMATES FURNISHED ON APPLICATION

Raw Seamless Canvassing a Specialty

REFERENCES: Dallas—Mr. Sidney Reinhardt, Judge F. M. Etheridge, Mrs. A. Silberstein, Mr. S. C. Baer, Real Estate—and many others

601 S. Ervay St. -:- **Dallas, Texas**

13.1 (above). Advertisement for the Bullock Decorative Shops, Houston, 1910 (*Directory of the City of Houston, 1910 – 11*, p. 94 [ads]) **13.2 (left).** Advertisement for designer Walther Tauscher, Dallas, 1910 (*Directory of Greater Dallas, Texas, 1910*, p. 74 [ads]).

13

Deep in the Heart of Anywhere

ARCHITECTS AND DECORATORS

To what extent were design professionals accessible to turn-of-the-century Texans? Ellen Bowie recalled that when her parents built the family's Weatherford home in 1901 "interior decorators were not yet with us."[1] Indeed, that house predated by four years Elsie de Wolfe's Colony Club commission in New York City, an event that some regard as marking the founding of the interior design profession in this country. Professional decorators were as rare in Texas as in many other areas of the country at the start of the twentieth century. There had been interior decoration and design activity in the East by such self-styled artists as Candace Wheeler and Louis Comfort Tiffany, but these were individual efforts. There was no large group whose members had design training and experience in implementing their plans for clients beyond those in the upper class. Although the 1910 census designated "decorator" as a new trade occupation, along with drapers and window dressers, recording 4,902 men and 439 women employed in that category, the label "designer" had been introduced in 1870. Grouped with "draftsmen" and "inventors," "designers" in 1910 numbered 9,211 men and 2,577 women; their activities ranged from designing textiles to designing house interiors.[2]

Some Texans had the financial resources to take advantage of the relatively new group of professionals. Initially they had to go outside the state for the kind of expertise they desired — to de Wolfe in New York City, to Mitchell & Halbach (also Mitchel & Halbach) in Chicago, and to Robert Keith and Company in Kansas City.[3] But Texas stores and newly trained decorators soon stepped into the breach.

Some furniture stores called themselves house furnishings stores, bringing attention to the range of domestic goods they had available and emphasizing their advisory talents. Large department stores like Wolfson's of San Antonio and Joske's of that city and Houston may have had decorators on staff early in the twentieth century. George M. Kuhn established his own interior decorating firm in Houston, while Samuel Schutz followed suit in El Paso.[4] W. F. Doyle opened his studio in San Antonio advertising that he could supervise "painting, wall decoration, the designing and manufacture of draperies, and [offered] works of art, fine rugs, fine furniture, and various home furnishings to those patrons who appreciate the unusual in home furnishing."[5] By 1910 Houston also had the Bullock Decorative Shops, "Designers and Makers of Homes and All That Pertains Thereto"(fig. 13.1).[6] Doyle Decorating Studio had "a corps of experts," and the Black Brothers Furniture Company of Houston had "more than sixty experienced people in the various departments," presumably some dispensing decorating advice.[7] Design entrepreneurs did not have to establish a company and employ others. Walther Tauscher advertised his services as "Designer and Decorator in Modern Frescoing" to Dallasites (fig. 13.2), and Houstonians could secure the services of R. Kleine, "Decorator, Fresco Painter, Paper Hanger."[8] Decorators may not have been available to the Bowies in Weatherford in 1901, but a decade later there were four to choose from in nearby Dallas.[9]

The level of sophistication, if it can be measured, had risen. Improved roads and railroads, increased literacy and travel, and prosperity in many endeavors — merchandising, cotton growing, cattle raising, and oil producing — fed the consuming impulse. Many Texans yearned to execute in their homes the latest styles advocated in the most recently published household decorating manual or to secure the skills of a builder. Wealthier Texans had another option: they could hire an architect and a decorator.

Decorators did not simply prescribe styles pictured in magazine articles; they actually implemented the furnishings plan. Typically they provided wall coverings, floor coverings, window treatments, and furniture, while the woman of the house chose the accessories for her home.

Some Texans hired architects to create an edifice whose presence would set the structure apart from others. Architects, too, were a fairly recent breed of professional. Several developments in late-nineteenth-century Texas opened this relatively new market for the skills of architects. The state's population had increased from 212,592 in 1850 to 3,048,710 in 1900.[10] Urban areas accounted for 17.1 percent of the population at the turn of the century.[11] Along with the growth in population, personal wealth had also increased.

By 1886 architects around the state had joined to form the Texas State Association of Architects (TSAA), designed in part to maintain and raise the standards of the profession but also to consolidate the power and legitimize the work of its members. State registration of the profession and new, "modern" designs would, in the eyes of these early organizers, serve to identify them as professionals and solidify their position in the economy.[12]

Significantly, they sought to distinguish themselves from those in the contracting and building trades. Their early organizational efforts were prompted in part by "the abuses and unprofessional methods employed by uneducated and unscrupulous pretenders."[13] Professional architects, the TSAA members maintained, were honorable men who had experienced "a long course of technical teaching, patient, laborious study of the master works of master minds, and constant application."[14] Anyone who lacked this training was "a bungling apprentice, copying here and imitating there, producing architectural monstrosities" and was an unsuitable candidate for admission into this emergent fraternity — with one possible exception. Drawing upon biblical sources to legitimize themselves, as late-nineteenth-century Americans were wont to do, the TSAA in 1888 pronounced, "our profession is as old as man," and although "the Savior of the World, . . . was not an Architect, . . . at least [he] was a carpenter."[15]

★ ★ ★ ★

James Riely Gordon's Wright-West house in San Antonio demonstrates that as early as 1890 Texas residences fashioned by architects and designers were more the expressions of skills and identities of the professionals than of the personal identities of the occupants. The Gordon pictures were taken as record photographs. But behind them is the ethic that the architect/designer had created a tasteful interior and had provided all necessary decorations and positioned them carefully, rendering objects of the family's personality unnecessary, indeed, out of place.

Born in Winchester, Virginia, Gordon was eleven when his family moved to San Antonio in 1874. By his early twenties, he worked for the civil engineering corps of the International & Great Northern Railway Company; he subsequently apprenticed in the office of architect W. K. Dobson of San Antonio for about two years before joining the staff of the United States Supervising Architect in Washington, D.C., where he worked with the designs of public buildings. By the mid 1880s, he had returned to San Antonio where he established his own architectural firm. During 1888 and 1889, he supervised construction of a San Antonio building that housed a federal courthouse and post office.[16]

These early experiences left Gordon well trained and well positioned to compete for architectural commissions for public buildings in the state. When the Texas legislature authorized the issuance of bonds to finance public works, it created a boon to the building business, and resourceful, ambitious Gordon capitalized on it. His designs won competitions for a variety of buildings including the Texas Pavilion at the World's Columbian Exposition in Chicago (1893) and the Cotton Palace in Waco (1895). A member of the TSAA, Gordon thrived in San Antonio and Dallas before moving his practice to New York City by 1902.

In Texas his reputation rested largely on the courthouses he designed. Still, he received private commissions as Texans prospering during the Gilded Age hired him to execute their residences. Indeed, his client list reads like a *Who's Who* of the Alamo City: B. F. Yoakum, Colonel William B. Wright, George H. Kalteyer, and Dr. S. T. Lowry. Gordon used some of the same design strategies for both public and domestic structures. In 1895 the architect copyrighted a design formula for a courthouse building that included a central ventilating shaft rising from the juncture of a cruciform structure. The A. P. Wooldridge house in Austin and the George H. Kalteyer house (see fig. 13.7) in San Antonio exhibit the same tower core; as in his public architecture, the shaft functioned as a ventilating mechanism in his houses.[17]

Gordon also involved himself with interior finishes and furnishings such as art glass, venetian blinds, skylights, hardwood finishes, frescoing, hard plaster, plaster ornaments, tile floors, electric lighting, and mantels. For the Yoakum house, Gordon specified an "antique oak reception hall and stairway, mahogany parlor, cherry library and oak dining room."[18] He also may have designed furnishings since later in his career he did so for his New York office. Gordon's interior spaces seemed to require a certain kind of furnishings. The Wright house furniture stayed with the house, and later occupants kept it in nearly the same position; parlor chairs, portières, an entire set of dining room furniture — all remained in their original context. The wall and floor coverings were not changed in more than a decade, although the second owner was wealthy enough to do so.

On March 22, 1890, lawyer and banker William B. Wright wrote a glowing letter of reference for "Mr. [James Riely] Gordon . . . the Architect who planned and superintended my building on Travis Park in this City [San Antonio], now nearing completion."[19] "My building" was Wright's residence, one of the first Gordon designed in San Antonio. This Richardsonian romanesque house overlooked Travis Park. Its interior was photographed shortly after completion, probably by Gordon or a member of his firm.

Of William B. Wright's home, a reporter wrote: "[the] new residence . . . is . . . one of the finest architectural gems of the South, built of St. Louis pressed brick, trimmed with stone and built upon a stone foundation, with a superabundance of griffin, capitals, columns, and other stone carvings, granite steps and polished columns, tile floors, a porte cochere, conservatory, elevator, electric bells, speaking tubes, burglar alarm and all modern conveniences to make a home comfortable."[20] The cost of this comfort was $17,000.

The parlor (fig. 13.3) features wallpaper that is vaguely aesthetic: stylized side-wall paper, banded frieze, and ceiling papers. Scrollwork patterns the bordered wall-to-wall carpet. Wall and floor coverings link the parlor and adjacent sitting room, which are separated only by fanciful Moorish grilles. Fretwork or grilles became increasingly popular during the decade, although few households had the elaborate ones Gordon was using in 1890. The room's appearance suggests that either Gordon or a professional decorator determined the furnishing program of the parlor. The textiles are custom made for the room, and the shape of the upholstered side chair echoes the motifs in the grille too precisely to be accidental.

A decade later, when the George Washington West family occupied the residence, they accepted both the decoration and the powerful interior spaces defined by architect Gordon. A former trail driver and cattleman who had recently become a real estate speculator, West was born in Tennessee and raised in South Texas. He earned his reputation at sixteen when he completed a contract to deliver 14,000 head of cattle to northern Montana "[t]hrough country infested by hostile tribes of Indians and swarming with herds of wild buffalo"; in doing so, he blazed what was then the longest cattle trail on the continent. Later in his career he bought a 200,000-acre ranch; in the first year a drought killed 22,000 head of cattle. Undaunted, "he forged ahead to success" and became "one of the most important cattlemen of the Southwest."[21]

At the age of fifty, near the turn of the century, West and his wife, Kitty, retired to the former Wright home in San Antonio. There, in a second-story office, he began orchestrating the building of towns in South Texas. During the next two decades, powerful, monied West transferred the seat of Live Oak County from Oakville to the town of George West and built a courthouse there, although Gordon was not the architect; he also named a town after Kitty.[22]

At the turn of the century, greenery adorns the Wests' parlor (fig. 13.4). The plant stands positioned back to back in the doorway hold cut flowers in decorative vases, shapes conveying the cosmopolitan quality of the "Moor-

13.3 (facing page). Parlor, William B. Wright house, Northwest corner of Navarro and Travis streets (603 Navarro Street), San Antonio, ca. 1890 (Architectural Drawings Collection, Architecture and Planning Library, General Libraries, University of Texas at Austin).

13.4. Parlor, George Washington West house, Northwest corner of Navarro and Travis streets (603 Navarro Street), San Antonio, ca. 1901 (Institute of Texan Cultures, San Antonio).

13.5. Dining room, William B. Wright house, ca. 1890 (Architectural Drawings Collection, Architecture and Planning Library, General Libraries, University of Texas at Austin).

ish" room. Similar embellishments and ceramics, including a Japanese vase, continue the theme above the art pottery fireplace surround, mantel, and elaborate overmantel. Aside from these details, little has changed. The portières in the grille are the same except that they face into the parlor. The fabrics of the portières hanging at the doorway to the entry hall and at the windows match the grille textiles. The chairs, upholstered and tufted and in the Turkish style, are probably original to the house. Few substantial changes have occurred during the Wrights' ownership or during the early years of the Wests' occupancy. The designs of Gordon and the decorator remain largely undisturbed.

Figure 13.5 shows the dining room during the Wrights' residence. It is furnished in an elaboration, scale, and quality uncommon in Texas. The walls are surfaced with a side-wall paper of medallions bordered with a scrollwork frieze; the ceiling is trimmed with an oak-leaf-pattern border, accented by corner disks of cornucopias. Abundance is the dining room's theme. The rich furnishings — sideboard, extension table, and dining chairs — were probably purchased from a midwestern furniture manufacturer.

13.6. Dining room, George Washington West house, ca. 1901 (Institute of Texan Cultures, San Antonio).

The architectural mantel and overmantel, detailed with art pottery tiles, dominate the aesthetic-style dining room.

Ten years later the dining room is basically unchanged (fig. 13.6). Even an overmantel ornament, a ceramic owl, perches in the same place. The china cabinet and the Japanese screen date to the construction of the house rather than to the date of the photograph. Only the window treatments are different — the Roman scarves have been replaced by dainty lace curtains over the interior shutters, possibly the summer treatment. In this large and expensively appointed room, the picturesque wall surfaces, carved dining furniture, and architectural fireplace wall express the design. The room is devoid of personalizing elements.

George H. Kalteyer also lived in an impressive early residence designed by Gordon. Kalteyer, founder and president of San Antonio Drug Company and president of Alamo Cement Company, had trained as a chemist. (His knowledge of chemistry helped him to recognize that the clay in the San Antonio area was suitable for making Portland Cement.) He lived in his polychrome brick and stone residence for less than a decade, dying in 1897 at the age of forty-eight. His widow remained in the home until she had another residence built at 332 King William Street in 1907. At both homes, she enjoyed the company of her neighbor and friend Johanna Steves (Mrs. Edward, Sr.), the pair taking turns serving afternoon coffee at their respective homes.[23] Figures 4.5, 4.6, 4.7, 13.7, and 13.8 provide us with the settings for these socials.

The Kalteyers' entry is an architectural tour-de-force, its archway framing a three-level central shaft, similar to Gordon's cruciform courthouse plan, his solution to the hot Texas summer. The Kalteyer house has a music room to the right and a parlor to the left; both doorways are draped by portières. The dining room sits behind the music room. Beyond the rotunda in the background is an arched opening, topped by a narrow grille from which portières are suspended; the arch leads to the service areas of the house.

Gordon has finished and possibly furnished the structure's interiors in a combination of French and colonial revival styles. The embossed and gilt wallpaper features a fleur-de-lis design enclosed in connecting medallions; the matching border paper uses a fleur-de-lis design on shields linked by scrollwork, while the ceiling paper introduces interlocking circles. Related papers in the adjacent spaces link the two areas. French styles inspired the design of the hallstand, while several colonial revival chairs decorate the Kalteyer hall. The furnishings are subordinated to the architectural details. The fireplace, for example, is not a welcoming hearth; instead, largely unembellished, it stands as an architectural monument. The pair of vases on it have become part of the architecture, extending the columnar motif upward. (Several 1938 photographs of this house show the space largely unchanged. As in other Gordon-designed buildings, subsequent owners were apparently reluctant to alter the plan of the professional designers.)[24]

The Kalteyers' dining room — like that of the Wrights — is inspired by aestheticism (fig. 13.8). Wall, ceiling, and floor surfaces are embellished. A powerfully designed nondirectional ceiling paper with fan lights and trailing vines in Japanese fashion dominates the room. The wide, banded frieze and fill papers, as well as the rich design of Gordon's parquet floor in the entry hall and dining room, appear subdued beneath the patterned ceiling.

Along with the strong aesthetic elements, the dining room mixes colonial revival furniture with that of French inspiration, as in the entry hall. Rich ceramics, silver, and glassware contribute other shapes, patterns, and textures to the room, but personalizing wall decorations are absent.

13.7 (facing page). Entry hall, George H. Kalteyer house, 425 King William Street, San Antonio, ca. 1893 (Architectural Drawings Collection, Architecture and Planning Library, General Libraries, University of Texas at Austin).

13.8 (above). Dining room into music room and entry hall, George H. Kalteyer house, ca. 1893 (Institute of Texan Cultures, San Antonio).

The architect provided windows that reach the floor, giving easy access to the porches. He also incorporated wainscoting, a call button or electric bells, and a fine gas-and-electric lighting fixture over the dining table.

Gordon also built the Corpus Christi home of Henrietta Chamberlain King, widow of Colonel Richard King of King Ranch fame, at approximately the same time that he worked on the Kalteyer house in San Antonio.[25] The two residences show divergent streams in Gordon's interior decoration — the Kalteyer house looks backward to Victorian embellishment, the King house, forward to reform taste. Both houses share a spatial virtuosity that overshadows furnishings, perhaps a characteristic of the architect-designer versus the professional decorator.

The proportions of the King entry hall dwarf the furnishings — the hall chairs, rocking chairs, and child's rocker (figs. 13.9, 13.10). Only the hallstand is proportionate, but it appears built-in and architectural, its beveled mirror matching the one on the stair landing. In this space, lines, not furnishings, demand attention: beams grid the ceiling; dramatic diagonals mark the staircase and in turn are strengthened by the balusters, which are echoed in the grilles and reflected by the mirrors.

Floral garlands texture the ceiling grid and a parquet floor stretches across the space. Strong geometric designs pattern the hall rug and the stair carpet. Interrupting the unadorned plaster walls, a window that reaches to the floor is decorated by a ball-fringe looped valance over the mission panels, an unusual pairing, exemplifying the transition from revival to reform styles.

13.9 (left) and **13.10 (facing page).** Entry hall, Henrietta Chamberlain King house, 517 North Broadway Street, Corpus Christi, ca. 1894 (Architectural Drawings Collection, Architecture and Planning Library, General Libraries, University of Texas at Austin).

13.11. Parlor, Henrietta Chamberlain King house, ca. 1894 (Architectural Drawings Collection, Architecture and Planning Library, General Libraries, University of Texas at Austin).

In fine French parlor form, Gordon fashioned the King town house presentation space (fig. 13.11). Two upholstered armchairs recall Louis XV and Louis XVI styles; the center table, electric lighting fixture, rococo-pattern wall-to-wall carpet, and tasseled raised drapery valance are in the French taste. But there are colonial revival elements as well. The other seating pieces are based upon Queen Anne, Chippendale, and Windsor styles. The lightness of these pieces enhances the feminine atmosphere of the parlor, a quality reinforced by the presence of the draped piano and floral still lifes. A portrait of an unidentified child provides an element of family.

In addition to the style of the room, Gordon displayed his characteristic concern for adequate ventilation. As in other rooms of the house, windows reach to the floor, and interior shutters keep out the sun yet allow coastal breezes to enter.

Across the hall from the parlor, through a pair of identical portières, the Gordon-designed dining room projects a much different air (fig. 13.12). The wainscoting and beamed and patterned ceiling recall the entry hall. A dark scrollwork rug covers the parquet; an extension table, sideboard, and corner china cabinet fill the large space; and sturdy leather-upholstered dining chairs encircle the room. Relief plaques of game hang from the picture molding.

Sunlight streams into the room from the bay windows of the conservatory, which nurtures palms, ferns, and rubber plants. When the conservatory is shut off from the dining room (by lowering the blinds in the three openings), the large electric lighting fixture and drop light illuminates the room.

Two photographs of an unidentified house, probably located in San Antonio, give other evidence of Gordon's early architecture and interior finishes.[26] The sitting room shown in figures 13.13 and 13.14 bespeaks the credo of picturesqueness. The multiple patterning of the surface coverings and the curving shapes of the furniture offer visual animation in a small space. The wall and ceiling papers use a lily pattern, and floral and foliate motifs also adorn the upholstery on several of the occasional chairs.

Scrolls pattern the conventional floral-design, wall-to-wall, borderless strip carpeting. Framing the room's voids, a fanciful rococo-pattern fabric serves as curtains, valances, and portières. The ball-fringe mirror-image textile has been folded, twisted, and dangled through the grilles by the room's designer, either Gordon or a decorating firm he hired.

The variety of seating pieces contributes a stylistic medley — a spindle-back divan, a painted ball-turned stool, a deep-tufted stool, and at least one fan-back chair. A colonial revival corner chair stands in the bright rounded bay, which is illuminated by a kerosene standing floor lamp and a flamboyant electric lighting fixture. Like the Frank W. Ball parlor in Fort Worth (see fig. 9.9), this room projects a variety of fanciful shapes and forms, and as in that house, the distinction between indoors and outdoors is blurred at windows and doors.

The chairs cluster near and in the doorway of the adjacent room into which the carpeting extends (fig. 13.14). The decorator has furnished the parlor with a plush-covered sofa and matching armchairs. The room contains a decorative easel draped with the sitting room's door and window fabric and a brass stand with marble top ready for serving tea.

A comparison of an unidentified parlor of circa 1895 (fig. 13.15) with the rooms shown in previous illustrations reveals differences between earlier and later Gordon designs. Most notable is the shift to plain plaster walls and ceilings. Instead of the elaborated surface decorations and

13.12. Dining room, Henrietta Chamberlain King house, ca. 1894 (Architectural Drawings Collection, Architecture and Planning Library, General Libraries, University of Texas at Austin).

13.13 and **13.14 (following page).** Sitting room, Unidentified house, probably San Antonio, ca. 1890 (Architectural Drawings Collection, Architecture and Planning Library, General Libraries, University of Texas at Austin).

picturesque forms, the room shows the restraint of reform. The narrow valance contrasts with the lavish draping in earlier commissions; even the floor covering is less visually animated.

Some aspects of the aesthetic style remain. Sunflowers, a popular aesthetic motif, embellish the mantel, valance, and table scarf, and their shape is echoed in the outline of the chair backs.

Another circa 1895 house shows a similar restraint (fig. 13.16). About 150 miles north of San Antonio, in Temple, Gordon designed a dwelling for one of Temple's most prominent citizens. Georgia-born W. S. Banks, educated at Baylor University and at Southwestern University, applied his civil engineering training as a member of the surveying corps of the Santa Fe Railroad. He then studied law and in 1883, at the age of twenty-four, was admitted to the bar; eventually he was active in banking, oil, and waterworks interests. His wife, Bennie Walker Banks, was active in civic and public life in Temple.[27]

For the Bankses, Gordon created virtuoso spaces that

13.15. Parlor, Unidentified house, probably San Antonio, ca. 1895 (Architectural Drawings Collection, Architecture and Planning Library, General Libraries, University of Texas at Austin).

blend into one another in an open plan. Wooden columns and paneled wainscoting link adjacent areas, as do the stenciled frieze, outlined ceiling, and carved detailing. The space makes light use of textiles: interior wooden shutters remain uncovered; the mantels feature small scarves; only pillows cushion the built-in bench, the rattan seat, and the hallstand seat; and the hardwood floor is largely exposed, although interrupted by small rugs, including an animal-skin one.

As in his other commissions, Gordon's mantels are significant architectural elements. The mantel in the foreground, with art pottery tiles, in a pattern reminiscent of a textile, faces into the parlor; that in the background, with neither mirror nor columns, adorns the stair hall. Both mantels display an art pottery vase and statuary. Fashionable items decorate the space, but objects relating to Banks' occupations or to his wife's interests — she was active in the Daughters of the American Revolution, Daughters of

13.16. Entry hall, W. S. Banks house, 508 North Ninth Street, Temple, ca. 1895 (Architectural Drawings Collection, Architecture and Planning Library, General Libraries, University of Texas at Austin).

the Republic of Texas, and the United Daughters of the Confederacy — are nowhere to be found.

A rustic stand supports the potted palm beyond the hall tree. Arbiters of taste advocated introducing fashionable rustic elements, and in stylish Texas houses photographed circa 1895, the element was most often a plant stand placed in an entry hall or other public space. A decade later, after its fashionability had peaked, this furniture appears in upstairs bedrooms.

Gordon also designed and built houses for the middle class. In addition to publicizing his commission to build B. F. Yoakum's stone and granite house at an estimated cost of $15,600 and Colonel W. B. Wright's house for $17,000, the architect announced his commission to build a cottage for H. C. Camp in the Alamo Heights area and a one-story shingle cottage for H. Morris on Callaghan Avenue, both in San Antonio. He also built a frame house for John Sherman at a cost of $1,700 and another for C. C. Johnson for $1,850, in the same city. Gordon even ventured into Texas urban housing — apartment buildings — including "Gordon's Madison Square."[28]

Another photo shows Gordon's ability to scale down his designs for more modest homes (fig. 13.17). This small space accommodates multiple functions: entrance, parlor, reception area, and stair hall. The hall portion is narrow, large enough to hold only a hallstand and rattan chair, turned to face the parlor, into which the space blends. The stairs ascend, unceremoniously by comparison with the King house (see figs. 13.9, 13.10), to an upper level. Nevertheless, Gordon has given attention to the room's finishes: paneled pine wainscoting, spindled grilles, art pottery hearth tiles depicting a hunt, an arched window, an electric lighting fixture, and a beamed ceiling, two members of which blend into the stair posts.

The furnishings resemble the chairs in figure 13.15. Despite the portrait photograph on the mantel, the interior looks like a "model" room; its lightweight furnishings, numerous plants, and spare textiles give the only appearance of use. A hooked rug in the center of the room is a nod to colonial revival taste.

About forty miles east of San Antonio, in Seguin, prosperous banker Eugene Nolte and his family moved into a house designed and built by Gordon circa 1896 (figs. 13.18, 13.19). Unembellished plaster walls provide the backdrop for the Noltes' furniture. The upholstered parlor chairs resemble the plush-banded and fringed ones in the Wright-West house (see figs. 13.3, 13.4); the center table is akin to that in the King house (see fig. 13.11); and the rattan rocking chair looks like those in several houses.

Despite furniture similar to that in other professionally designed rooms, the Nolte house has less the look of a decorator's hand than any other Gordon residence. The floral wall-to-wall carpet resembles that in many Texas houses (see figs. 12.2, 12.6). The curtains and portières were widely available to the public via catalogue. The electric lighting fixtures in the parlor and dining room were popular choices for entry halls. Nevertheless, there is little in the room that is obviously personal — only two matted portrait prints, probably of Eugene and Claudia Nolte. Nothing hangs from the gilt picture molding.

Unlike any other dining room pictured in this sample, the Noltes' houses a refrigerator along with a drip pan, on a protective rectangle of linoleum, the rest of which probably covers the kitchen floor (see fig. 13.19). The dining room, like the parlor of the Nolte house, is informal, unimposing, and comfortable. The residence, one of the finest in Seguin, the seat of Guadalupe County, illustrates Gordon's scope as architect of both large urban dwellings and more modest homes in smaller communities.

Photographs of Texas houses designed and built by Gordon during the 1890s contain a variety of useful information. Early views exhibit the continuing preference for

aestheticism and picturesqueness, while later photos illustrate the penchant for less embellished spaces and a growing involvement with architectural reform. The images also document Gordon's range of clients, from the wealthy to those of more limited means, whose relative financial resources affected the scale and finish of their interiors. Gordon's powerful decorative elements and dramatic spatial arrangement reverberate within all these interiors.

13.17 (facing page). Entry Hall, Unidentified house, probably San Antonio, ca. 1895 (Architectural Drawings Collection, Architecture and Planning Library, General Libraries, University of Texas at Austin). **13.18 (above, left).** Parlor into dining room, Eugene Nolte house, 102 East Live Oak Street, Seguin, ca. 1896 (Architectural Drawings Collection, Architecture and Planning Library, General Libraries, University of Texas at Austin). **13.19 (above, right).** Dining room into entry hall, Eugene Nolte house, ca. 1896 (Architectural Drawings Collection, Architecture and Planning Library, General Libraries, University of Texas at Austin).

★ ★ ★ ★

Architect Olle J. Lorehn (1864 – 1939) moved to Houston from St. Louis to supervise the construction of the American Brewing Company complex and stayed to complete the Binz Building, the first tall office building in Houston, in 1895. By the turn of the century, his reputation earned him a variety of commissions for public, religious, and residential structures, including the W. T. Carter, Jr., house (now a property on the National Register of Historic Places) and the Abraham M. Levy house.[29]

In 1906 Lorehn built the Levys' chateauesque residence, and Chicago-based decorators Mitchell & Halbach designed the interiors. Like many other interior decorators in the late nineteenth century, Otto William Mitchell and Frederick A. Halbach had trained as decorative painters. After decorating Chicago's City Hall in 1885, they expanded their business to include interiors of both commercial and residential structures. By 1891, the firm had completed the interiors of Chicago's Hotel Metropole and Spaulding's jewelry store and were remodeling the mansion of Marshall Field, Jr., using "wood work, gas fixtures and electric lighting, furniture, leather, wood floors, carpet . . . decorations, plastic ornamentation and stained glass."[30]

Morris M. Levy had emigrated from Poland to Texas and founded a dry goods business; his children continued the family enterprise. Son Abraham M. Levy occupied his Main Street mansion, as it was called, with an extended family that included sisters Harriet and Fannie and brothers Haskell and Hyman, and later their spouses and children.[31]

Lorehn built the house with an impressive entry hall (fig. 13.20), and Mitchell & Halbach filled it with substantial furniture and statues of Vulcan, Atlas, two lions, and two busts of Roman warriors. In spite of the inviting pillows, leather-upholstered seating pieces, and a fireplace, the entry hall was not designed for lingering. Brightening the dark passage and adding to the embellishment of the space, the electric lighting fixtures include an art nouveau table lamp and wall sconces attached to four fluted columns with composite capitals. Matching the sconces, an impressive fixture is suspended from the tent ceiling, which is supported by the columns; two large torchères mark the uncarpeted stairway and landing.

From the classical entry hall, one could enter a parlor, decorated in the French taste (fig. 13.21). The ceiling and walls are covered in canvas, hand painted with garlands and scrolls that complement the room's textiles. Like the painted walls and upholstery, the window coverings, with elaborate cornices, valances, and draperies, reveal the hand of a professional decorator. Even the wall groupings that personalize the space appear to have been positioned by the designer to enhance the room decoration.

The music room (fig. 13.22) contains colonial revival furniture: the settee was inspired by eighteenth-century sources, and the piano seat is an adaptation of a Windsor chair. The walls appear to be covered with damask, and the canvas or leather frieze above has been painted with musical instruments to underscore the function of the space.

The dining room is marked by strong design and may have been considered "Chippendale" at the time: a wide tapestry landscape frieze and tapestry upholstery give coherence to the room (fig. 13.23).[32] Other textiles include window valances and well-chosen rugs that further mark the room as professionally designed. The furniture resembles pieces produced by the Mitchell Furniture Company of Cincinnati, St. Louis, Memphis, and New Orleans

13.20. Entry hall, Abraham M. Levy house, 2016 Main Street, Houston, ca. 1906 (Houston Metropolitan Research Center).

13.21. Parlor, Abraham M. Levy house, ca. 1906 (Houston Metropolitan Research Center).

(successor to the firm of Mitchell and Rammelsburg), which fashioned furniture shipped to many Texas addresses.

Cut flowers on the table meet the low-hanging art glass fixture. The grape motif of the lighting fixture is repeated in the clusters of purple glass, imitating grapes, that adorn the classically inspired entrance into the well-tended conservatory.[33]

The library (fig. 13.24) expresses the same professional decorating skill as the other rooms. Tabletop portrait photographs of three of the five merchant brothers sit on the library table, facing the camera. These appear to be the only personal accessories in the photographed room. A stenciled frieze embellishes the walls, and appliquéd and fringed valances trim draperies and glass curtains. As in other spaces of the Levy house, the library is illuminated

13.22. Music room, Abraham M. Levy house, ca. 1906 (Houston Metropolitan Research Center).

with art glass lighting fixtures — a table lamp in the art nouveau style and a hanging fixture decorated with shells, urns, candles, and brackets. There is a profusion of statuary: twin statues of Mercury, busts of Shakespeare and others, and freestanding Greek columns.

The handsome "Chippendale" library table stands on an oriental rug that covers the parquet flooring. In addition to the leather-upholstered armchair, matching rocking chair, and cushioned rocker furnishing the space, another chair that resembles the two oriental stands sits in the bay near a desk and a telephone.

The Levy house reveals little personal information about the residents and their household. Only a few portrait photographs document their presence. The cumulative weight of the evidence argues that in pursuit of a stylish and tasteful house, members of the Levy family, like

13.23. Dining room, Abraham M. Levy house, ca. 1906 (Houston Metropolitan Research Center).

13.24. Library, Abraham M. Levy house, ca. 1906 (Houston Metropolitan Research Center).

others in the upper classes, were willing to accept the dictates of the architect and design firm and all but erase their occupational, familial, ethnic, and even regional identities.

★ ★ ★ ★

Architect Henry Trost began a prairie-style house for himself in El Paso the same year Lorehn completed Levy residence in Houston. Although the architecture of the two structures was very different, Mitchell & Halbach provided the interior decoration for both. However, for the Trost commission, the Chicago designers probably functioned as decorative painters rather than as interior designers.

Born in Ohio in 1860, Trost worked for three years as a draftsman following art school graduation. He then moved west and opened a private practice in Pueblo, Colorado, when he was twenty years old. During the next twenty years, he worked in Chicago and in Tucson, among other places, before settling in El Paso and organizing the architectural firm of Trost & Trost, which included his two brothers, G. A. and A. G., and their nephew G. E. Trost.[34]

The Trost house is unusual in this sample because its occupant was also its architect. Clearly influenced by Frank Lloyd Wright, Trost designed his house in 1906 and soon after began building it. Completed in early 1909, the house reportedly cost $15,000. "The art glass, showing a cactus design, was made specially for this home from the design of the architects, and decorations in leather color were also designed by Trost & Trost. . . . Even the furniture in the dining and living room was designed by the architects."[35] Mitchell & Halbach either executed or supervised the stencilwork. The furniture and woodwork designs were consigned to J. P. Paulson, local representative of Brunswick-Balke-Collender Company and, like Mitchell & Halbach, a frequent collaborator with Trost & Trost on commissions.[36]

As in other prairie-style houses, the Trost home was characterized by open, flowing interiors (fig. 13.25). Within one space, sixty feet long and approximately eighteen feet wide, Trost created living room, dining room, breakfast area, entry, stairway, and fireplace-library nook; only buttresses interrupt the eye's progress down its length. Interior details contribute to the unity. A frieze stenciled with southwestern motifs — thistle, palm, and cactus, all executed in shades of tan, brown, burnt orange, light green, and yellow, as the newspaper reported — nearly encircles the long room.

In fashioning his own domestic environment, the architect designed the decorations, lighting fixtures, art glass windows, and freestanding and built-in furniture. The result is a harmonious blend of architectural details and furnishings, much as Wright achieved, that heralds the shift from distinct room settings

The dining area in this long room successfully combines furnishings with interior architecture (fig. 13.26). Rectilinear piers and wall plates are matched by the lines of the dining table, chairs, built-in sideboard, and lighting fixture.

The unified decorating strategy is also evident in the library niche (fig. 13.27). A table holds magazines and books. An oriental carpet covers most of the floor. Leather-upholstered cushions soften the built-in seating pieces. Embellished with art glass door panels, the bookcases are easily accessible. The frieze provides the only wall decoration, and a wall plate serves as a shelf. Typical of the restrained prairie style, Trost's fireplace consists of a simple rectangular firebox opening without a mantel.

The Frederick Henry Farwell house in Orange (figs. 13.28 through 13.32) was designed and furnished by an

13.25. Living room, Henry C. Trost house, 1013 West Yandell Drive, El Paso, 1909 (Southwest Collection, El Paso Public Library).

13.26. Dining room, Henry C. Trost house, 1909 (Southwest Collection, El Paso Public Library).

unknown architect and interior decorator. Its scale, adherence to a new furnishing style, and quality of detailing surpass those in houses lacking professional assistance. A comparison of the Trost and Farwell houses shows that professional designers, becoming more and more active in the state during the early twentieth century, were creating a sameness in fashionable interiors in Texas regardless of region within the state.

These interior spaces share the arts and crafts influence with the Trost house, but unlike the El Paso architect's home, the Farwell home was built in the mission revival style and represents a middlebrow approach to the same arts and crafts aesthetic. Nevertheless, the house was home for the general manager of Lutcher & Moore Lumber Company and a showplace that graced several city promotional brochures over the next fifty years.[37]

13.27. Fireplace/library nook, Henry C. Trost house, 1909 (Southwest Collection, El Paso Public Library).

The tables, chairs, and settles, fashioned of oak and leather, fill the Farwell living room, a space indebted to Wright's designs (figs. 13.28, 13.29). The long room blends into the entry hall, conservatory, and stair hall. Oriental carpets on wooden floors provide pattern, foil to walls covered with a solid paint or paper. Exposed beams divide the high ceiling, creating panels in which clusters of ceiling-mounted electric lighting fixtures are hung. Matching single fixtures hang from the intersecting beams and serve as sconces above the fireplace.

The mantel (fig. 13.29) holds colonial revival and arts and crafts adornments, illustrating how both styles overlapped in reform interiors. And the motto on the fireplace ties the home to the reform ethic: "But every house where love abides, And friendship is a guest, Is surely home and home sweet home, For there the heart can rest." As if to

 13.28 (above) and **13.29 (facing page).** Living room, Frederick Henry Farwell house, 812 Green Avenue, Orange, ca. 1909 (Nelda C. and H. J. Lutcher Stark Foundation, Orange).

13.30. Dining room, Frederick Henry Farwell house, ca. 1909 (Nelda C. and H. J. Lutcher Stark Foundation, Orange).

underline the message, a pierced heart decorates the arms of the rocking chair in the foreground.

The dining room, inspired by arts and crafts design, is filled with mission furniture (fig. 13.30). The rectilinear quality of the beamed ceiling and lighting fixtures carries over to mantel, wainscoting, and furniture. Unlike the Henry Trost house, the Farwell dining room is a discrete space containing fewer built-ins. The bordered carpet is of American manufacture.

The house features an attached conservatory filled with ferns (fig. 13.31). A cast-stone fountain provides humidity for the thriving plants. A cast-iron settee in a grape design peeks out from the overhanging Boston ferns.[38]

The library (fig. 13.32) is more visually animated than

13.31. Conservatory, Frederick Henry Farwell house, ca. 1909 (Nelda C. and H. J. Lutcher Stark Foundation, Orange).

the other photographed spaces of the Farwell house — displaying loving cups, pictures, and an overlapping of boldly patterned rugs. The unmatched furniture in this room — a leather rocker, a colonial revival armchair, and a Morris chair — contrasts with the coordinated furnishings in others rooms. The fireplace motto — "I cannot warm you if your heart be cold" — echoes the sentiment on the living room fireplace.

Farwell sits at his leather-top desk, his reading illuminated by a mission table lamp. His love of dogs is explicitly stated by the oil painting of a fox terrier over the desk. Unlike most of the homeowners in this chapter, the Farwells have, at least in this space, kept tokens of their personal interests prominently visible — in this case, of their avocation. In 1900 Farwell had established Sabine Kennels on Bonnie Street in western Orange where he raised English fox terriers. He entered national competitions, often earning first-place awards, many of which can be seen in the library showcases.[39]

★ ★ ★ ★

Just as the Trost and the Farwell houses offer representative examples of the interiors of professionally designed houses in West and East Texas, the Duff and Shuford houses provide a similar opportunity to discuss houses in Southeast Texas and in North Texas. The architect and the designer of the Duff house are unknown; the architectural firm of Shepard, Farrar & Wiser and the decorating firm of Keith and Company built and furnished the Shuford house.

13.32. Library, Frederick Henry Farwell house, ca. 1909 (Nelda C. and H. J. Lutcher Stark Foundation, Orange).

Railroad magnate Robert C. Duff occupied the house at McGowen Avenue and Milam Street near downtown Houston with his wife, Geraldine, and their two daughters (figs. 13.33 through 13.37). The classical revival residence sat on landscaped grounds that included expansive gardens and statuary: life-size figures of a dancing faun, Psyche, and Venus, all by Viennese sculptor Oswald Lassig, were incorporated into the landscape plan.[40] The prominence of the family, their imposing dwelling, and the gardens made 803 McGowen Avenue a Houston showplace for many years.

The design and furnishing patterns reveal the work of professionals. The large, dramatic reform-style hall leads to a central stairway framed by a wide arch (fig. 13.33). The oak wainscoting, pilasters, newels, and stairway are well detailed; a stenciled border outlines the perimeter of the ceiling. The pale ceiling, rugs, and stair carpet relieve the darker surfaces. The globes of the central lighting fixture match corner fixtures that supply modest illumination. A baroque settee, matching side chairs, and a tall case clock on the landing provide the colonial revival hall furniture. A Chinese stool serves as a fern stand.

The photograph provides a view of the floor plan. To the left of the entry is the living room. The door by the stairs indicates that the dining room is behind it, as can be seen in other photographs (see figs. 13.34, 13.37).

Eighteenth-century design informs the Duff family's living room (fig. 13.34). The armchair, side chair, and settee exhibit the shield-back motif of Sheraton design, while Queen Anne inspiration is clear in the rocking chair. Scrollwork becomes the visual subtheme of the space via the room's textiles — in the rug border and the matching borders on the portières and draperies. On the ceiling, more scrollwork outlines the panels created by the crisscrossing beams.

The room displays few decorative accessories, none of

13.33. Entry hall, Robert C. Duff house, 803 McGowen Avenue (reoriented on same block, 2421 Milam Street), Houston, 1909 (Courtesy Mr. and Mrs. Robert D. Maddox).

13.34. Living room, Robert C. Duff house, 1909 (Courtesy Mr. and Mrs. Robert D. Maddox).

them personal. Instead, it exhibits the skill of the decorator who embellished the surfaces — the mosaic panel above the mantel, the art glass panels on the door to the entry hall, and the trim of the room's textiles and ceiling.

The library also shows similar influence (figs. 13.35, 13.36). Its large bearskin rug, as much a trophy as antlers above the mantel would be, announces the masculine character of the space. The largest and most impressive of the downstairs rooms, the library is almost the size of the living room and the dining room combined. The bookcases, with their volumes carefully positioned according to size and spine, suggest an educated man, an important message to communicate to visitors (see figs. 13.24, 13.27, 13.45). We do not know at this time if Duff's extensive book collection prompted the built-in bookcases or if the architect included this feature and thereby encouraged

13.35 and **13.36 (facing page).** Library, Robert C. Duff house, 1909 (Courtesy Mr. and Mrs. Robert D. Maddox).

Duff to fill them. In either case, "this home boasted one of the finest libraries of the south."[41] But the decorator has placed most of the chairs with little regard for reading light.

The room's impressive woodwork includes ceiling beams the length of the room and strapwork above the mantel. The dark tones of the wood are continued by the somber fabric woven in a stylized tree design covering the side walls above the bookcases. The large bordered rug in a conventional leaf pattern, custom made for the Duff library, exposes little hardwood floor at the room's perimeter. At the windows, a shaped, fringed, and bordered flat valance tops shades, short glass curtains, and draperies. The furniture consists primarily of leather-upholstered armchairs and oak rocking chairs, a classically detailed library table illuminated by a table lamp with an art glass shade, and a Chinese table and matching stand, which, according to family history, the Duffs purchased at the Louisiana Purchase International Exposition in 1904.[42]

The professional architect and the decorator have largely determined the look of this room. Rather than showcasing family photographs, for example, the mantel highlights the strapwork, a design detail unobstructed by personal objects.

The dining room (fig. 13.37) holds an expensive set of American Empire furniture. The pedestal table can be extended to seat at least six, probably more. Matching the table and leather-seat chairs, the china cabinet and sideboard display a collection of cut glass, which is reflected in the mirrors at the back of each.

The dining room in the Duff house has a dramatic quality created by the high color contrasts, especially between the light walls and highly polished woodwork. The fabric wall panels and portières share a border design that is coordinated with that on the curtains. The pale bordered carpet is in turn framed by the dark flooring. The effect is one of restraint, control, and precision.

The decorator who worked on the J. D. Shuford house some five years later used a different approach but nonetheless arrived at a similarly restrained design. Shuford, a general livestock agent for the Fort Worth & Denver City Railway Company, built his family's home in Amarillo in 1913 – 1914. The Kansas City architectural firm of Shepard, Farrar & Wiser designed the house in the Jacobean revival style, and the Kansas City decorating firm of Keith and Company designed the interiors in various revival styles. Keith and Company had already gained a regional reputation, having helped to furnish the McFaddin-Ward house in Beaumont and possibly the Martin Luther Hinchee house, also in Beaumont, some 800 miles from Kansas City.[43]

The colonial revival living room contains a diversity of eighteenth-century furniture styles, freely interpreted by the manufacturer Keith and Company chose (fig. 13.38). The absence of personal elements and the calculated use of light and dark here as in other professionally decorated houses tells nothing of the Shufords' intended or actual use of this room.

In the dining room, the decorator has fashioned a "classical" space through the careful combination of paneling, molding, and furniture style (fig. 13.39). The sideboard and server display a measured arrangement of silver, richness in a room of restraint. In addition to the same wall-to-wall carpeting as in the living room, the two spaces share fabric wall covering, although here the panels appear to be damask. Belying the room's classicism, the sloping arms of the electric lighting fixture evoke medieval candlelight, and Gothic quatrefoils embellish the curtains mounted between window shades and velvet panels. The decorator has coordinated every detail so that the oak

13.37. Dining room, Robert C. Duff house, 1909 (Courtesy Mr. and Mrs. Robert D. Maddox).

twist-turned plant stand and fern disrupt the room's matched precision.

The plant stand accompanies the oak twist-turned gateleg table, side chairs, and server that furnish the small breakfast room (fig. 13.40). The woodwork serves as the room's primary adornment. On an otherwise blank wall, a small framed print is seemingly an afterthought. Inviting the outdoors inside, a bright trellis-pattern chintz decorates two walls of windows.

In the Shuford kitchen, a service area not usually seen by visitors or photographed, stark white surfaces conform to the period's keen awareness of hygiene and the notion of scientific housekeeping (fig. 13.41). Tile floors and ceramic countertops were thought to be easier to keep clean

13.38 (above). Living room, J. D. Shuford house, 1608 South Polk Street, Amarillo, 1914 (Panhandle-Plains Historical Museum, Canyon). **13.39 (facing page).** Dining room, J. D. Shuford house, 1914 (Panhandle-Plains Historical Museum, Canyon).

and thus to ensure health. The table provides a work area; the only wall decorations consist of a match holder for the Great Majestic stove and the call box, which indicated to servants where they were needed.

* * * *

Next door to the Shuford house is the Landergin residence, also designed by Shepard, Farrar & Wiser and decorated by Keith and Company. Interior views show how designers compressed the telling element of the occupants' personal identity into a defined space and then relegated it to a secondary area of the home. Occupational identity, however strong, was overwhelmed by the more powerful voice of the architectural and interior design firms.

A quarter of a century after contractor E. S. Berry had completed his commission to build a house for Pat and John Landergin, he recalled:

> The Landergin house cost at the time of erection, $90,000 and if built two years later would have cost $225,000 [due to] its extreme size — 96 by 113 feet, four floors fully finished.
>
> I remember the rough electric wiring cost $2500, and the pulleys in the windows [cost] $420.00. When the Germans bombarded Brussels in 1914, a $2500 rug being made for the living room was destroyed.
>
> Shepard, Farrar and Wiser of Kansas City were the architects and I worked closely with them. The building was begun September 1913 and required nearly two years to complete. It was my first large contract, together with the Shuford home. I was just 35 years old and was very proud of the finished houses.[44]

13.40. Breakfast room, J. D. Shuford house, 1914 (Panhandle-Plains Historical Museum, Canyon).

Located in the Plemons addition of Amarillo, just south of the central business district, the Shuford and the Landergin houses are two of the few Polk Street mansions that remain on Amarillo's main thoroughfare, once lined with grand homes.

The sons of Irish emigrants, the two Landergin boys decided to come west from New York in 1870. Pat, sixteen, and John, fourteen, hired on as trail drivers. By the turn of the century, the Landergin brothers were prosperous cattlemen in Eureka, Kansas. In 1905 a depressed cattle market drove them to the Texas Panhandle where, in an effort to revitalize their herd and to recoup their losses, they acquired additional pasturelands including about 200,000 acres of two famous Texas ranches: the XIT and the LS. The brothers built their family residence in Amarillo in 1913; with a population of about 10,000, Amarillo

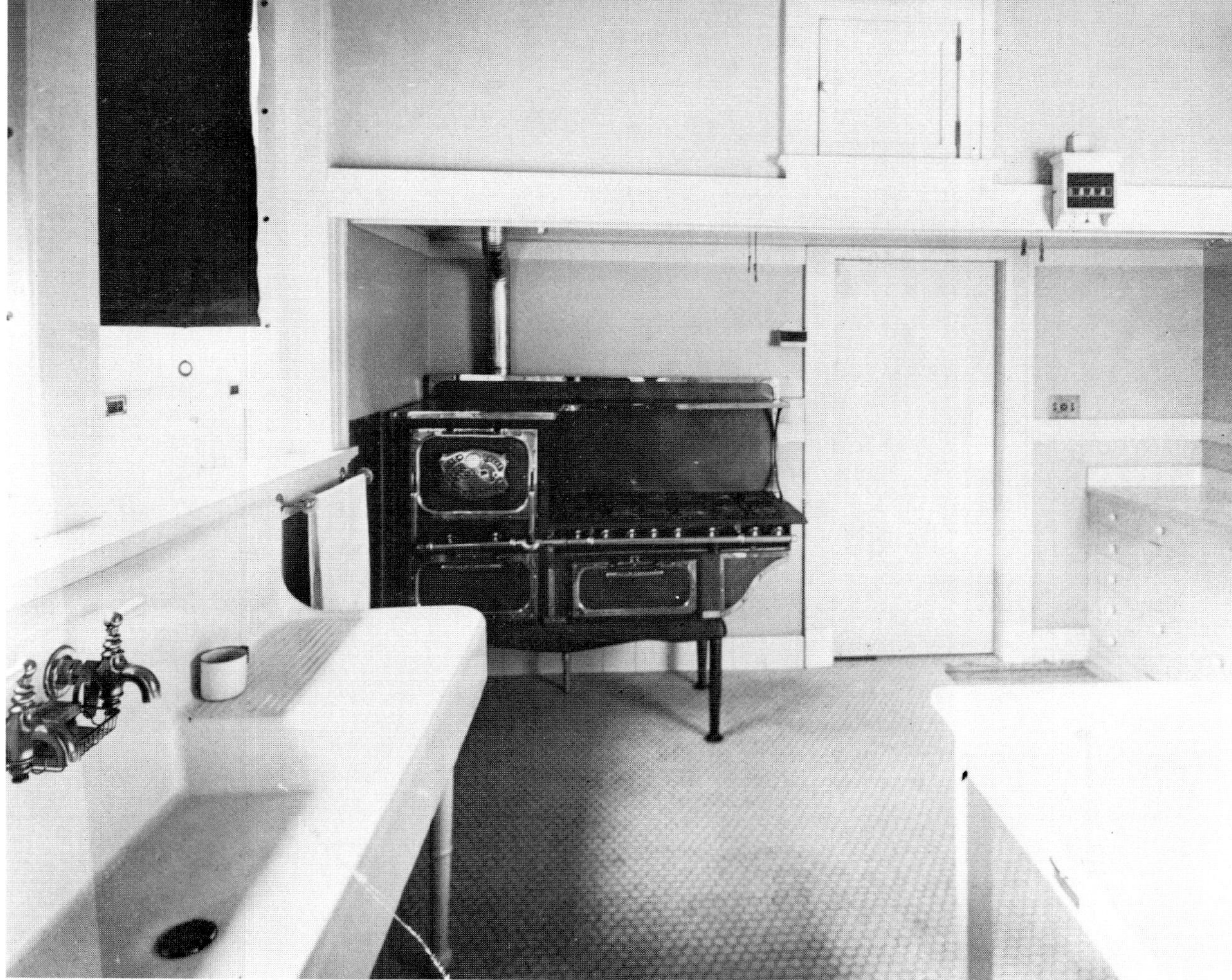

13.41. Kitchen, J. D. Shuford house, 1914 (Panhandle-Plains Historical Museum, Canyon).

was the largest town in the area of their primary ranching activities. Both brothers occupied the home, with Pat's wife and daughter.[45]

Shepard, Farrar & Wiser prepared a set of plans that drew on a variety of architectural antecedents and styles: the combined use of brick and stone and segmental arched openings in the Jacobean style, an Ionic portico with coupled columns, monumental stairs of beaux arts classicism, and selected prairie-style details. Keith and Company probably supplied carpeting, wall and window treatments, and furniture, but since fire destroyed the company's records, the precise extent of their work is difficult to ascertain.

The entry hall contains a wide central stairway leading to a landing with windows containing art glass in shades of greens and browns — "caramels" as one visitor re-

13.42. Entry hall, Patrick H. Landergin house, 1600 South Polk Street, Amarillo, 1915 (Panhandle-Plains Historical Museum, Canyon).

membered — popular colors in prairie-style houses of the period (fig. 13.42).[46] The staircase and the rest of the hall's woodwork are of mahogany; the newels are detailed with bellflowers, a classical motif repeated elsewhere in the house.

For the walls, Keith and Company selected a fabric in shades of ivory, pink, and beige. The ceiling is painted canvas, with a line border in a contrasting color. Oral history recalls that more than one floor covering was delayed by World War I, and the photo confirms this. A temporary carpet has been overlaid with an oriental rug. The George III-style mahogany tall case clock signed Joseph Jennens, Skinner Street, Clerkenwell, London, is the only piece of hall furniture visible in this view. An electric hall lamp, sconce, and complementary globes positioned at strategic points on the ceiling supply artificial illumination for the large entry hall at night. During the day, light flooded into the space from the transom, side lights, and leaded glass panels in the front door. The mirrors flanking the stairway reflect that light, as still more light streams down from the landing.

Blocked by a screen at the left is the stairway to the basement, containing the billiard room, laundry, boiler room, and storage areas, including one section labeled "Fruit Room" on the original plans. To the right of the central stairway, a door leads into the service area of the house — kitchen, pantry, and a back stairway connecting all four floors. Access to all floors was also provided by an Otis elevator. To the left of the clock, a door enters a side hall leading out to the porte cochere. The door immediately to the right of the clock leads to the library. The doors on the left of the hall lead to the living room and dining room.

Dividing the painted canvas ceiling from the walls, wide mahogany molding emphasizes the horizontality of the upstairs hall (fig. 13.43). Mahogany also frames the bay window and forms a window seat cushioned by pillows made from the same fabric that covers the walls of the entry and the stair hall. A shaped, flat, fringed valance and draperies cover glass curtains; strips of carpeting sewn together and bordered stretch wall to wall.

13.43. Landing and upstairs hall, Patrick H. Landergin house, 1915 (Panhandle-Plains Historical Museum, Canyon).

The living room draws its inspiration from a variety of sources (fig. 13.44). Medieval elements, popularized by

13.44. Living room, Patrick H. Landergin house, 1915 (Panhandle-Plains Historical Museum, Canyon).

the arts and crafts movement, have influenced the ceiling fixture and sconces, which are operated by wall switches. Greek motifs embellish the table surfaces, and the pattern of the pale pink silk damask covering the walls contributes a classical element to the space. The living room furniture, possibly marketed as "Hepplewhite," includes a matching cane-back sofa and armchair, detailed with classical paterae and bellflowers, the back and seat cushions of which have been covered with a brown-and-beige cut velvet.

The coordinated upholstery and other textiles bespeak

the hand of a professional decorator. Window treatments match portières that frame the passage between the living room and entry hall where reproductions of colonial and empire furniture mark the entrance to the home.

The "Jacobean" library, too, has been professionally decorated (fig. 13.45). The most notable feature of the room, the pargework ceiling, was made either of plaster from molds decorating companies kept in stock or of wood. A tapestry fabric in browns, black, and greens covers the walls above the oak paneling and upholsters a Jacobean revival armchair and a rocking chair.[47] Built-in bookcases with leaded glass door panels contribute prairie-style elements to the space. As in other rooms of the house, the decorators and furniture manufacturers have liberally borrowed and combined details and designs from early and modern styles — medieval, colonial, and prairie — for the library. The only personalizing object visible in the room is the painting of Landergin's wife, Mary. And even her portrait is not allowed to interrupt the decorative paneling above the fireplace.

The 16-by-20-foot dining room, a small space compared with other downstairs rooms, is filled with oak dining furniture that freely interprets Gothic sources (fig. 13.46). Quatrefoils adorn the sideboard, chair backs, and electric lighting fixture; twist turnings embellish the sideboard pilasters, chair legs, and table pedestals. The decorators have chosen to coordinate the room's oak furnishings and oak interior finishes.

At the windows, the same velvet that frames lightweight curtains also marks the three art glass windows between the dining room and the breakfast room. An oakleaf tapestry of greens, browns, and golds lends pattern to the walls and matches a wall-to-wall carpet that later covered the floor.[48] As in other rooms, an oriental rug is placed on a solid wall-to-wall carpet until the custom carpet arrived.

Identified on the original architectural drawings as the Palm Room, the breakfast room, adjacent to the dining room, functioned as a conservatory and secondary dining area (fig. 13.47). In this "empire" room, references to Greek design abound. Greek key motifs and anthemia adorn the ceiling fixture, the rug border contains the Greek key, while two klismos chairs and the scene in the art glass window continue the theme. The fountain, urns, and bench are of cast stone; gray tiles form the floor surface. The family called this distinctive space the "Pompeian Room" and labeled the window, fashioned of light blue, green, and purple glass, the "Oracle of Delphi."

The room blends with other areas of the house, merging indoor and outdoor spaces. French doors stand open by unnecessary windows to invite viewers into the sun room filled with porch furniture made by the George Hunzinger & Son Furniture Company of New York.[49]

The upstairs bedroom belonging to twenty-six-year-old daughter Alice was furnished in the Louis XVI revival style, popular among the wealthy since the 1890s (fig. 13.48). An aqua-painted canvas with a hand-painted border of pink roses covers the walls.[50] Framed by a valance and side panels in a colorful floral chintz, the windows are covered with shades and sheer curtains. The doorway into the sleeping porch is treated as another window, framed with chintz portières. An aqua pile carpet is dotted with a darker shade of aqua and small pink floral designs. The architecturally ornamented fireplace is an anachronism in a house heated by the radiators. As in the first-floor rooms, wide windowsills cover the tops of the radiators.

In the basement, the Landergins' billiard room contains the single personal feature of their home: a plaster relief mural of ranch scenes forms a frieze on three walls (fig. 13.49). In a residence otherwise designed by architects and decorators, this unique room self-consciously expresses the regional and occupational identities of the home's

 13.45. Library, Patrick H. Landergin house 1915 (Panhandle-Plains Historical Museum, Canyon).

13.46. Dining room, Patrick H. Landergin house, 1915 (Panhandle-Plains Historical Museum, Canyon).

owners. The mural was a planned (by whom is not known), permanent element of the Landergin home. Rather than in the more public first-floor library, the mural is confined to this subterranean room, relegated to the frieze, and permanently installed by the architects, compressed and subordinated to the overall design of the house.

The muralist depicted recognizable landscapes and structures of the Landergin Ranch in the Texas Panhandle, as well as a more standardized chuck wagon scene (appropriately placed over the hearth). As a counterpoint to the flat and vast expanses and native vegetation of the mural, the fire-screen fabric depicts a tree-framed pastoral landscape with hills, lush vegetation, and a stream. Other furnishings consist of a table, used as an informal desk, and a group of unmatched seating pieces, including a rattan

 13.47. Breakfast room, Patrick H. Landergin house, 1915 (Panhandle-Plains Historical Museum, Canyon).

13.48. Bedroom into sleeping porch, Patrick H. Landergin house, 1915 (Panhandle-Plains Historical Museum, Canyon).

chair and a leather-upholstered rocking chair; a settee in the mission style can be seen behind the column, while another in wicker is partially concealed by the billiard table; the other two seating pieces are side chairs possibly from an older dining room set. Unlike the careful, formal compositions in the first-floor spaces, these furnishings emphasize the informality of the room.

The elements of personal identity in the Landergin house are overwhelmed by the program of the architects and designers, especially their agenda of styles. The impact was long-lasting: photographs taken in 1940 show an interior that still reveals little about the family.

★ ★ ★ ★

A Complex of Trails

CONCLUSION

IN 1981 two University of Chicago social scientists, Mihaly Csikszentmihalyi and Eugene Rochberg-Halton, published *The Meaning of Things, Domestic Symbols and the Self.* They had interviewed 315 people in two neighborhoods in the Chicago area in an effort to discover what household possessions the interviewees valued. Their study showed that affection for certain objects is age and gender related. For example, children covet stereos and televisions, whereas grandparents prize photographs, furniture, and books; men favor furniture, televisions, and stereos, while women value furniture, photographs, and visual art.[1]

For this study of late-nineteenth- and early-twentieth-century interiors, interviews with the householders were not possible; photographs and a few family papers had to suffice. Although the photos cannot speak directly, the people who fashioned these rooms tell us what objects were prized by virtue of their *placement* in the interiors. A composite image of what the culture valued is revealed by the *frequency* with which certain objects appear.

Interior views document that convention and personal preference encouraged people to create visual and emotional centers in their houses. Most often the center was a hearth, usually in the parlor. In rooms without hearths, occupants fashioned makeshift mantels on the top of a piano or bookcase and attached small mantel-like shelves to a wall. In some rooms in Texas homes, especially entry halls, householders placed silver-plated pitchers and water glasses — an obvious convenience that offered entrants a cool drink in a warm climate. But the display of a fashionable water pitcher suggests more than quenching a thirst; it became a gesture of hospitality, a greeting of sorts, and a signal to visitors that a home is where needs are met and comforts are found. The frequent placement of plants on stands set as sentinels at doorways was probably also a mixture of convention and preference. Visually, the placement rendered "picturesque" an unportièred passage and perhaps symbolically heralded the transition into a different space. The fanciful adornments hanging from ceiling fixtures show an impulse to render different lighting technologies decorative. The number of spittoons in parlors and other public rooms suggests that some Texans were unaware of or disregarded the advice of etiquette writers.

Other objects appear frequently in these rooms, but we cannot assume that they have the same meaning for all who possessed them. People invest objects with meaning; we are given clues to those meanings by the context in which people place the articles. For example, pianos appear frequently in this group of interior photographs, and yet all do not convey the same message. A piano in a man's dormitory room suggests conviviality; in a family's parlor, it indicates refinement.[2] A popular print of a woman playing the piano for a young child (presumably a mother playing for her daughter) can have different meanings according to its placement in the house: in a bedroom it suggests family identity, while in the parlor of a home belonging to a couple with no children, an identification with refinement.[3]

This group of interior views of Texas houses reminds us that some of our efforts at historic house recreation are speculative and fosters a renewed humility among those who endeavor to fashion in a museum context domestic environments of earlier people. The images call into question many suppositions about houses and furnishings of the late nineteenth century — such as the assumption that late-nineteenth-century Americans lived in sympathy with the design of their houses, within the dictates of floor plans determined by plan-book writers, builders, and architects. A corollary to this notion holds that the individual rooms, strictly designed as places of entertaining, dining, relaxing, and sleeping, were used only for those purposes. The photos reveal exceptions at every turn. Some houses, even those constructed during the late nineteenth century, did not have the elaborated, differentiated spaces. And those that did show that families sometimes ignored the designations the builders applied. People sat, and even posed for pictures, in their bedrooms; they relaxed in halls; and they played in parlors. The frequency with which the combined bedroom and sitting room appears in East Texas houses suggests that there may have been a regional explanation for the phenomenon in addition to issues of class and economics, yet families in West Texas also combined these functions.

Just as the prescribed activity for each room was not followed, so, too, were the recommendations of decorating advisers not always heeded. Many design critics maintained that each room should be decorated in a fashion different from others, reinforcing that different activities took place in them. Yet we have seen exceptions, as in the Walcott house, which differentiates space and blends it at the same time, avoiding dramatic shifts in decoration. And the principle that late-nineteenth- and early-twentieth-century Americans should embrace multiple patterning of walls and floors is undermined by the Little parlor that features a consistent preference for wallpaper and carpet featuring the *C* scroll.

While photographs demonstrating multiple use of space and blending of decoration raise some exceptions to earlier notions about late-nineteenth-century houses and their occupants, other photographs strengthen established beliefs about householders and their furnishings. Even in modest houses, there was often a difference in the quality of furnishings from room to room. Most occupants polished their dining room and wore out their kitchen, adorned the former and made efficient the latter. A dining room unvaryingly expressed abundance — a message demonstrated in opulent statuary and expensive furnishings, in the bounty of the table, or in the sideboard and china cabinet's display of silver and glass. David Potter's observation that Americans were "people of plenty" seems borne out in Texans' dining rooms.[4] In libraries, occupants communicated by displays of books their pursuit of knowledge and their erudition. People most frequently expressed their refinement in parlors, rooms that projected the controlling hand of the woman of the house.

Some assumptions about seasonal changes remain intact, while others have been changed by what these photos reveal. It was not surprising to find netting protecting a hanging parlor lamp in a Comfort house in summer. Conversely, although we expected all heavy portières would be removed from interior doorways in the summer, in the William Jones house in Marlin, they were not. In some homes, matting was a favored summer floor covering — but several interior views in this collection confirm that it remained on hardwood floors during the winter months. The Hill home in Panhandle had matting during February, and the Hanna family home in Galveston was matted in November.

The images also suggest that some householders either did not understand late-nineteenth-century design and its reform or ignored the opposing aesthetics. For example, the highly embellished Simpson sitting room also displayed an elongated pastoral print inspired by the arts and crafts movement, while the Dunlaps shifted to reform curtains but kept their revival style furniture and decorations.

Interior views also document that many families made allusions to ever-changing current styles in fairly predictable manner and measure. To demonstrate one's knowledge of arts and crafts design, for example, one needed only to add a Morris chair, a pastoral print after Jean-François Millet, or a pillow top or print featuring a Native American. Such additions were, after all, less expensive than replacing a renaissance revival parlor suite with mission furniture.

Apart from the addition of a few objects — or even a single object — to indicate fluency in an aesthetic language, families commonly projected an image of "newness" in their home interiors. This does not mean that they were on the cutting edge of design or even that many purchased recently available furnishings. It just means that very little appears to have accumulated over a long period. Little is old in these houses. Part of this newness reflects their recent arrival and the difficulty of carting goods by land and water. But it may also reflect a willingness to embrace new situations unfettered by baggage — real and symbolic — of the past. Texans, unlike New Englanders and others living along the eastern seaboard, did not succumb to "ancestor worship," nor did they retain objects until they were worn beyond use, throwing away virtually nothing. Relatively few pieces of furniture predate mid century; almost nothing reveals an eighteenth-century origin, although householders showed little hesitation about buying revival styles of colonial New England, New York, and Philadelphia. The paucity of old objects might also be a generational or temporal phenomenon whereby people, relishing the opportunity to buy manufactured goods through local stores and catalogues, tossed aside dated or worn furnishings.

William Seale has argued that a geographical "lag" occurs in houses located in the western United States. He estimates that during the nineteenth and early twentieth centuries home interiors beyond the reach of fashionable style centers in the north and east lagged stylistically by "two decades more or less."[5] Some Texas families did have decorations that were twenty years or so old, others forty. But a small group of families incorporated the newest fashion into their homes. The Wulff house photographed in the 1890s looks very much like a home of the 1860s, but the Van Alstyne-Dickson drawing room at the turn of the century is smartly up-to-date with the latest fashion.

The images suggest that at just about any time, there were many possibilities for household decoration. In the 1890s interiors could be as diverse as the Wright house in San Antonio, the McGregor house in Waco, and the Digby-Roberts house in Abilene. Even within one city and within one or two years, as in Houston, there was the wide range represented by the interiors of the Staiti house (1905) and the Levy house (1906).

Identity is one of several issues to consider when interpreting historic interior photographs. By incorporating biography into a reading of the photographs and by examining the images according to the manner in which householders expressed elements of identity in their homes, we can move beyond a simple discussion of style. To state simply that a parlor suite is in the Louis XVI style or to match the suite to one in a manufacturer's trade catalogue tends to stop discussion rather than stimulate it. If being an example of a recognizable and legitimate style were the only criterion for evaluating interior views, we would have to dismiss much of this sample.

Focusing on the varied influences that played on householders as they transformed houses into homes allows us to move toward an understanding of the people who made, bought, or used the goods. And by examining privileged objects within the setting of a room or a house, we put the objects in broader physical and cultural contexts. In this way, Mersfelder's house, which some hasty viewers might dismiss as eccentric, can be more properly viewed as the home of a resourceful, multifaceted man who had cultivated a sense of freedom in his life and who clearly maintained the elements of his talents close at hand in his domestic setting. The Petersen home heightens our appreciation for those Danish settlers who traveled great distances and fashioned a home in a new land while still retaining familial images and loyalties to their homeland. Indeed, the style of Mersfelder's tables and chairs and the Petersens' dresser seems less critical.

A virtual complex of trails, identity is multifaceted, never linear and seldom a hierarchical progression from a smaller sphere to ever larger and eventually less personal ones, as from occupation to family, to ethnic and social group, to region, and finally to refinement, class, and style. At any point, one person may express elements of several identities and in proportions quite different from those of his or her next-door neighbor. Identity is often a reflection of experiences. Thus some Texans identified with the South, incorporating images of the Lost Cause of the Confederacy into their parlors. Others identified with the federal government and Reconstruction. But many, both Southern and Northern in sympathies, also identified with refinement and with style. Still others expressed both familial and social ties in their dwellings or stressed identification with family and with ethnicity. Indeed, the combinations are endless.

While shaping their domestic environments, Texans were influenced by "outside" sources, part of the vast ever-changing landscape of culture. Advice literature, mail-order catalogues, and local authorities at a variety of stores made Texans aware of the increased options for home decoration. And as professional designers became more plentiful and their advice more widely sought, they gained a hand in and then a stronghold on the process.

What effect did decorators and architects have upon how house interiors in Texas looked? They helped to facilitate the change in the ideal middle-class dwelling from "an exuberant, highly personalized display of irregular shapes, picturesque contrasts, and varieties of ornament, supposedly symbolizing the uniqueness of the family, to a restrained and simple dwelling." After the turn of the century, the "model house was more visibly like the others in a planned, homogeneous community," and by 1910 the emphasis was not so much on personalized display and popular participation in home planning as on expertise in home planning.[6] Homogeneity was a byproduct of expertise.

In Texas in the shifting equation of home decoration, professional designers and architects played a major role among the upper-middle and upper classes. Although it is tempting to state that as World War I approached, architects and decorators were making it uniformly impossible for Texans to express their familial or occupational identities, for example, in home interiors, the photographs do not sustain such an argument. But clearly the influence of professional designers tended to standardize house decoration. The Duff house in Houston looks like the Shuford house in Amarillo. Similarly, the Farwell house in Orange on the Louisiana border strongly resembles the Trost house in far West Texas. Farwell, however, managed to express his strong avocational interests in the decoration of his library, a rare occurrence in architect-designed homes. And houses like the Olivers' in Houston, constructed in a popular style, continued to express the occupational identity of the householders at the end of the teens. Likewise, the interior of the Ross house in Pecos shows an identification with family circa 1920.

The issue is more complex than the chronology of events or the weight of authority, and it demands that we look at people and their culture. People did not live in model houses or under model conditions; many were not cowed by professionals or authorities. Although the 1915 King Ranch house was architect designed and professionally decorated, it expresses strong regional identity; indeed it is archetypally Texan. To muddy the waters further, consider those householders who decorated their own domestic environments by embracing and emulating, albeit partially and often imperfectly, the designs of professionals published in books and magazines. The occupants, the prevailing styles, popular notions about taste, and the growing professionalism of architects and designers at once collaborated and contended.

Only by further study of families and interior photographs can we move to a better understanding of the way people expressed themselves in domestic environments that mirrored who they were and the culture in which they lived. Then we can look to other clues in the material culture for help in understanding more fully the identities of the families who occupied the houses. To our increasing knowledge of interior spaces, we can add recent research and scholarship about a building's construction materials and floor plan. We can venture outside to incorporate information about the siting of the house and its relationship to the natural landscape. I hope that these interior views have provided a useful start to this exciting collaborative journey.

Appendix 1

LIST OF STRUCTURES STILL STANDING

Many of the houses whose interiors are included in this book have been destroyed. Listed below are those structures known to be standing. Most are privately owned; those open to the public are noted.

Meredith A. Benton house, *Fort Worth*
James Moreau Brown house, *Galveston* (known as Ashton Villa; owned by the Galveston Historical Foundation; open for scheduled tours)
M. K. Brown's apartment, White Deer Land Company, *Pampa* (currently the White Deer Land Museum; open for scheduled tours)
E. M. Carter house, *Plainview*
Reuben Anderson Cates house, *Palacios*
Cottage Hotel, *Calvert* (currently the Calvert Hotel)
Emil Conitz, Sr., house, *Calvert*
Robert C. Duff house, *Houston*
Benjamin H. Epperson house, *Jefferson* (known as the House of the Seasons; privately owned; open for scheduled tours)
Ira Hobart Evans house, *Austin* (headquarters for the Austin Woman's Club)
August Faltin residence and store building, *Comfort*
W. H. George house, *Beeville*
Fred A. Gildersleeve house, *Waco*
Governor's Mansion, *Austin* (owned by the State of Texas; open for scheduled tours)
John Hanna house, *Galveston*
T. F. Harwood house, *Gonzales*
J. H. Hill house, *Trinity*
Arthur C. Hoover ranch house, *Ozona*
George H. Kalteyer house, *San Antonio*
King Ranch house, *near Kingsville*
Patrick H. Landergin house, *Amarillo* (known as Harrington House and owned by the Panhandle-Plains Historical Society; open for scheduled tours)
Henrietta A. Little house, *Victoria*
LS Ranch, New Headquarters, *four miles south of Tascosa* (standing, but much modified)
Daniel McLean house, *Crockett*
Joseph Magoffin house, *El Paso* (owned by the State of Texas; operated by the Texas Parks and Wildlife Department; open for scheduled tours)
Manton E. Marsh house, *Livingston*
Sam Bell Maxey house, *Paris* (owned by the State of Texas; operated by the Texas Parks and Wildlife Department; open for scheduled tours)
Nick Mersfelder house, *Fort Davis* (operated as the Overland Trail Museum; open for scheduled tours)

Nazareth Academy, *Victoria*
Eugene Nolte house
John T. Price house, *Palacios*
W. L. Ross house, *Pecos*
Josephine Flow Russell house, *Pilot Point*
J. D. Shuford house, *Amarillo*
Thomas Earl Singletary house, *Alto*
Henry Thomas Staiti house, *Houston* (moved to Sam Houston Park in downtown Houston; operated by the Harris County Heritage Society; open for scheduled tours)
Edward Steves house, *San Antonio* (owned by the San Antonio Conservation Society; open for scheduled tours)
Alfred James Taylor house, *Karnes City*
Alexander Thompson house, *Doucette*
Henry C. Trost house, *El Paso*
Paul Gustav Villaret, Sr., house, *Comfort*
Joel B. Wolfe house, *Galveston*
Andrew H. Wootters house, *Crockett*
Anton F. Wulff house, *San Antonio* (headquarters of the San Antonio Conservation Society)

Appendix 2

LISTING BY DATE, STRUCTURE, LOCATION, ROOM, AND FIGURE NUMBER

Historic preservationists and furnishings planners are often interested in particular time periods, areas of the state, and rooms. The following table lists the interior photographs in chronological order and provides the name of the house, the city or town, the room, and the figure number.

Date	Structure	Location	Room	Figure Number
May 1878	Edward Steves house	San Antonio	Sitting room Dining room	4.6 4.7
1879	Edward Steves house	San Antonio	Entry hall	4.5
1885	Francis Newberry and Julia Macy Holbrook house	El Paso	Parlor Parlor into bedroom	9.1 9.2
ca. 1888	Jim Ned Ranch	near Coleman	Sitting room Bedroom	2.1 and 2.2 2.3
ca. 1888	Joseph Magoffin house	El Paso	Parlor Bedroom	11.15 11.16
ca. 1888	Thomas Newton Fleming house	Victoria	Parlor	9.3
1889	Gustav A. Duerler residence	San Antonio	Parlor	4.11
ca. 1890	James Franklin Newman house	Sweetwater	Parlor	3.3
ca. 1890	Andrew Jackson Long house	Sweetwater	Parlor	3.4
ca. 1890	Alexander Rossy house	San Antonio	Parlor into entry hall Parlor	7.15 7.16
ca. 1890	F. A. Taulman house	Hubbard City	Parlor	9.4

Date	Structure	Location	Room	Figure Number
ca. 1890	Albert G. Boyce house	Channing	Parlor	11.8
ca. 1890	Jernigan house	Pecos	Sitting room	11.9
ca. 1890	William B. Wright house	San Antonio	Parlor Dining room	13.3 13.5
ca. 1890	Unidentified house	probably San Antonio	Sitting room	13.13 and 13.14
1890–1895	Benjamin H. Epperson house	Jefferson	Parlor Dining room Bedroom Upstairs hall	9.5 9.6 9.7 9.8
1891	August Faltin residence	Comfort	Parlor	4.8
ca. 1891	Paul Gustav Villaret, Sr., house	Comfort	Parlor	4.14
1892	Frederick Charles Digby-Roberts house	Abilene	Dining room	3.13
1892	Anton F. Wulff house	San Antonio	Parlor	4.9 and 4.10
ca. 1892	Frederick Charles Digby-Roberts house	Abilene	Bedroom Parlor	3.14 3.18
ca. 1892	William A. McVitie house	Galveston	Parlor Dining room	8.21 8.22
1893	Louis Melcher house	La Grange	Parlor	6.6
ca. 1893	George H. Kalteyer house	San Antonio	Entry hall Dining room into music room and entry hall	13.7 13.8
ca. 1894	Paul Gustav Villaret, Sr., house	Comfort	Parlor	4.15 and 4.16
ca. 1894	Henrietta Chamberlain King house	Corpus Christi	Entry hall Parlor Dining room	13.9 and 13.10 13.11 13.12
1895	Frank W. Ball house	Fort Worth	Parlor	9.9
ca. 1895	Sam Bell Maxey house	Paris	Library	2.11
ca. 1895	Unidentified convent	Galveston	Parlor Multipurpose room	2.28 2.29
ca. 1895	Sallie Wade house	Benjamin	Bedroom	3.1

Date	Structure	Location	Room	Figure Number
ca. 1895	Frederick Charles Digby-Roberts house	Abilene	Bedroom	3.15, 3.16, and 3.17
			Parlor	3.19
ca. 1895	Unidentified boardinghouse at Blinn Academy (Blinn College)	Brenham	Dining room	5.6
ca. 1895	Howe house at Blinn Academy (Blinn College)	Brenham	Sitting room	5.7
ca. 1895	Unidentified house (probably the house of Mary Belle Stratton or Lily Moore Field)	Waco	Parlor	7.9
ca. 1895	Unidentified house	Victoria	Parlor into music room	7.14
ca. 1895	William Jones house	Marlin	Sitting room	8.9
ca. 1895	Unidentified house (may be associated with the Howe house, Blinn Academy [Blinn College])	Brenham	Bedroom/office/kitchen	8.19
ca. 1895	J. J. McAdams house	Quanah	Bedroom	11.10
			Parlor	11.11
ca. 1895	Edward and Dolores Welder Dunlap house	Victoria	Parlor	11.14
ca. 1895	Unidentified house	probably San Antonio	Parlor	13.15
ca. 1895	W. S. Banks house	Temple	Entry hall	13.16
ca. 1895	Unidentified house	probably San Antonio	Entry hall	13.17
ca. 1896	Eugene Nolte house	Seguin	Parlor into dining room	13.18
			Dining room into entry hall	13.19
1896	Gregor Carmichael McGregor house	Waco	Parlor	10.1
			Sitting room	10.2
			Dining room	10.3
1897	Unidentified house (possibly the George A. Miller house)	Longview	Parlor	3.2

Date	Structure	Location	Room	Figure Number
ca. 1897	Joel B. Wolfe house	Galveston	Music room	11.17
1897-1898	New Headquarters, LS Ranch	near Tascosa	Office Bedroom Nursery Kitchen Parlor	2.4 2.5 and 2.6 2.7 2.8 2.9 and 2.10
ca. 1898	Paul Gustav Villaret, Sr., house	Comfort	Parlor	4.17
ca. 1898	Henrietta A. Little house	Victoria	Parlor	7.17 and 7.18
ca. 1898	Van Alstyne-Dickson house	Houston	Dining room	8.4
ca. 1898	William H. George house	Beeville	Dining room	11.21
1898-1905	Jack W. and Sydney O. McKee house	Ozona	Parlor or "front room"	8.14
1899	Sheb Williams house	Paris	Sitting room into dining room	2.30
Summer 1900	Josephine Flow Russell house	Pilot Point	Parlor Sitting room Entry hall	3.5 3.6 and 3.7 3.8
August 1900	John Hanna house	Galveston	Parlor	11.19
ca. 1900	Fletcher family's Park Farm	near Beaumont	Art studio	2.20
ca. 1900	P. J. Agerskov Petersen house	Danevang	Bedroom	4.1
ca. 1900	Harry Seele house	San Antonio	Parlor	4.13
ca. 1900	Ella Moore's boardinghouse	Fort Worth	Parlor	5.5
ca. 1900	Unidentified dormitory A&M College (Texas A&M University)	College Station	Dormitory room	5.11
ca. 1900	T. F. Harwood house	Gonzales	Entry hall Dining room	6.15 6.16
ca. 1900	W. A. Fletcher house	Beaumont	Parlor into sitting room Parlor	7.1 7.2
ca. 1900	B. O. Walcott house	Honey Grove	Library	7.7

Date	Structure	Location	Room	Figure Number
ca. 1900	Oscar and Josephine O'Brien Mitchell house	Refugio	Parlor	7.10
ca. 1900	Robert Bruce Barclay house	Wharton	Parlor	7.11
ca. 1900	J. H. Hill house	Trinity	Parlor	7.13
ca. 1900	Van Alstyne-Dickson house	Houston	Entry hall Dining room Drawing room	8.3 8.5 8.6 and 8.7
ca. 1900	Unidentified house	Kaufman County	Dining room into kitchen	8.18
ca. 1900	Peg Bonney store	San Angelo	Paint and paper store	11.2
ca. 1900	Whiteside & Sanford store	Panhandle	Furniture store	11.5
ca. 1900	Captain John H. Williams house, known as Glen Eden	near Sherman	Parlor Bedroom into dining room	11.12 11.13
1901	Unidentified house (Saturday Evening Conversation Club)	Austin	Sitting room	7.3
1901	James Moreau Brown house, known as Ashton Villa	Galveston	Family room	8.15
ca. 1901	B. O. Walcott house	Honey Grove	Parlor into entry hall	7.4
ca. 1901	Benjamin Charles and Rebecca Wheeler Simpson house	Houston	Parlor Sitting room	9.10 and 9.11 9.12
ca. 1901	William H. George house	Beeville	Dining room	11.22
ca. 1901	George Washington West house	San Antonio	Parlor Dining room	13.4 13.6
1901-1902	George Morland Bowie house	Weatherford	Dining room	10.7
September 1902	Charles Otis and Minnie Mae Finley house	near Valentine	Parlor	6.11
December 1, 1902	Hereford House	Hereford	Parlor	5.4
1902	George Morland Bowie house	Weatherford	Entry hall Parlor Library	10.4 10.5 10.6

Date	Structure	Location	Room	Figure Number
November 1903	John Hanna house	Galveston	Sitting room and parlor	11.20
ca. 1903	Joseph M. Maurer Studio	Galveston	Reception room	2.21 and 2.22
1903	Charles Simmang, Jr., house	San Antonio	Parlor	4.12
April 1904	Lavonia Archer house	Mount Calm	Multipurpose room	6.3
October 18, 1904	B. O. Walcott house	Honey Grove	Parlor Entry hall Library	7.5 7.6 7.8
ca. 1904	Mary Hune Waltgenbach house	Brownsville	Sitting room	10.9
1905	Henry Thomas Staiti house	Houston	Entry hall Parlor Dining room Original master bedroom	12.1 12.2 12.3 12.4
ca. 1905	Cottage Hotel (Calvert Hotel)	Calvert	Parlor	5.3
ca. 1905	Unidentified boardinghouse	La Grange	Bedroom/sitting room	5.8
ca. 1905	Unidentified boardinghouse	possibly Fort Worth	Bedroom	5.10
ca. 1905	Manton Edward Marsh house	Livingston	Bedroom/sitting room	6.10
ca. 1905	Unidentified house	possibly Galveston	Sitting room	7.12
ca. 1905	Meredith A. Benton house	Fort Worth	Bedroom	7.19
ca. 1905	William L. Crawford house	Dallas	Art gallery	8.1
ca. 1905	Unidentified house	Houston	Parlor	8.11
ca. 1905	Andrew H. Wootters house	Crockett	Parlor	8.20
ca. 1905	E. E. Thompson store	Waco	Paint and paper store	11.3
ca. 1905	Joel B. Wolfe house	Galveston	Music room	11.18
1905-1910	Henry J. Lutcher Stark's room, Unidentified dormitory building, University of Texas	Austin	Dormitory room	5.14, 5.15, 5.16, and 5.17

Date	Structure	Location	Room	Figure Number
1905-1910	Joe E. Robinson house	Rockhill Community	Bedroom/sitting room	6.9
August/ September 1906	Thomas Earl Singletary house	Alto	Bedroom/sitting room	3.11
1906	Alfred Brown Peticolas house	Victoria	Sitting room/library into dining room	2.12
ca. 1906	Mary Hune Waltgenbach house	Brownsville	Sitting room Parlor	10.10 10.11
ca. 1906	John T. Price house	Palacios	Living room into dining room	11.23
ca. 1906	Abraham M. Levy house	Houston	Entry hall Parlor Music room Dining room Library	13.20 13.21 13.22 13.23 13.24
1907	Llano Furniture Company	Llano	Furniture store	11.7
ca. 1907	Mary Hune Waltgenbach house	Brownsville	Parlor	10.12
1908	Robert Fletcher Avant house	Dilley	Parlor	3.9
1908	Daniel McLean house	Crockett	Entry hall into dining room Entry hall into parlor	6.7 6.8
1908	Taliaferro Furniture Company	Sherman	Furniture store	11.6
ca. 1908	Gillaspie house	Carthage	Sitting room and bedroom	8.10
ca. 1908	Arthur C. Hoover ranch house	Ozona	Dining room	8.17
ca. 1908	Unidentified house	Dallas	Living room into dining room	9.13
ca. 1908	Alexander Thompson house	Doucette	Living room Dining room	9.14 9.15
ca. 1908	Mary Hune Waltgenbach house	Brownsville	Parlor Bedroom	10.13 10.14

Date	Structure	Location	Room	Figure Number
1908-1911	Texas Governor's Mansion	Austin	Parlor Library	6.4 6.5
1909	Emil Conitz, Sr., house	Calvert	Parlor	3.12
1909	Alfred James Taylor house	Karnes City	Parlor	8.8
1909	Henry C. Trost house	El Paso	Living room Dining room Fireplace/library nook	13.25 13.26 13.27
1909	Robert C. Duff house	Houston	Entry hall Living room Library Dining room	13.33 13.34 13.35 and 13.36 13.37
ca. 1909	Mr. and Mrs. James Milton Frame house	Monahans	Sitting room/bedroom	3.10
ca. 1909	Frederick Henry Farwell house	Orange	Living room Dining room Conservatory Library	13.28 and 13.29 13.30 13.31 13.32
1909-1912	Duncan Caldwell Crooks house	Galveston	Entry hall	9.17
1910	Carrie Hofer and May Virginia Warden's room, Nazareth Academy	Victoria	Dormitory room	5.12
1910	Reuben Anderson Cates house	Palacios	Living room Entry hall Dining room	11.24 11.25 11.26
ca. 1910	Unidentified house	Brownsville	Living room	4.2
ca. 1910	Rebecca Sparks Cooperative Home	Waco	Sitting room	5.1
ca. 1910	Unidentified house	Houston	Entry hall	5.2
ca. 1910	Unidentified house, probably the lodgings of photographer Otis A. Aultman	El Paso	Sitting room	6.12, 6.13, and 6.14
ca. 1910	Unidentified house	Houston	Dining room	8.12

Date	Structure	Location	Room	Figure Number
ca. 1910	E. M. Carter house	Plainview	Dining room	8.13
ca. 1910	George Morland Bowie house	Weatherford	Dining room	10.8
ca. 1910	Mary Hune Waltgenbach house	Brownsville	Sitting room	10.15
ca. 1910	Frank H. Hill house	Panhandle	Entry hall	10.16
			Parlor	10.17
			Sitting room	10.18
			Dining room	10.19
			Bedroom	10.20
			Bedroom	10.21
ca. 1910	Ira Hobart Evans house	Austin	Library	10.22
			Entry hall (south)	10.23
			Entry hall (east)	10.24
			Sitting room	10.25
			Dining room	10.26
			Bedroom	10.27
			Bedroom	10.28
January 1912	Henry Thomas Staiti house	Houston	Entry hall	12.5
			Parlor	12.6
			Dining room	12.7
ca. 1912	Fred A. Gildersleeve house	Waco	Dining room	2.23 and 2.24
			Living room into dining room	2.25
			Bedroom	2.26
			Bedroom	2.27
ca. 1912	Harvey Perrin's room, Unidentified dormitory building, A&M College (Texas A&M University)	College Station	Dormitory room	5.13
ca. 1912	George Overton Stoner house	Victoria	Dining room	9.16
April 20, 1913	James Moreau Brown house, known as Ashton Villa	Galveston	Dining room	8.16
April 1914	Lavonia Archer house	Mount Calm	Sitting room	6.3
December 1914	Unidentified boardinghouse	Dallas	Bedroom	5.9

Date	Structure	Location	Room	Figure Number
1914	J. D. Shuford house	Amarillo	Living room	13.38
			Dining room	13.39
			Breakfast room	13.40
			Kitchen	13.41
1915	King Ranch	near Kingsville	Living room	6.1
			Office	6.2
1915	Patrick H. Landergin house	Amarillo	Entry hall	13.42
			Landing and upstairs hall	13.43
			Living room	13.44
			Library	13.45
			Dining room	13.46
			Breakfast room	13.47
			Bedroom into sleeping porch	13.48
			Billiard room	13.49
ca. 1915	Pink L. Parrish, Sr., house	Crosbyton	Entry hall into dining room	8.2
ca. 1915	Sam Bell Maxey house	Paris	Breakfast room	9.18
ca. 1918	M. K. Brown apartment	Pampa	Living room	4.18
1918-1920	Clement Edward Oliver house	Houston	Entry hall into living room	2.13
			Living room into entry hall	2.14
			Living room into library	2.15
			Alcove off living room	2.16
			Library into dining room	2.17
ca. 1920	Nick Mersfelder	Fort Davis	Multipurpose room	2.18 and 2.19
ca. 1920	W. L. Ross house	Pecos	Living room	3.20
ca. 1920	Unidentified house	Big Bend area	Multipurpose room	4.3
			Multipurpose room	4.4

Date	Structure	Location	Room	Figure Number
ca. 1920	Urban S. and Ella Maye Bumpass Russell house	Sherman	Bedroom	9.19
			Dining room	9.20
ca. 1920	Henry F. Hodde house	Brenham	Parlor	10.29, 10.30, 10.31, and 10.32
			Entry hall	10.33 and 10.34
			Dining room	10.35
			Bedroom	10.36 and 10.37
ca. 1920	Henry Thomas Staiti house	Houston	Entry hall and living room	12.8 and 12.9
			Sun room (first story)	12.10 and 12.11
			Dining room	12.12
			Stair landing	12.13
			New master bedroom	12.14
			Sun room (second story)	12.15 and 12.16
			Former master bedroom	12.17
			Bedroom	12.18
			Bedroom	12.19
			Sleeping porch	12.20
			Billiard room	12.21
			Breakfast room	12.22
			Kitchen	12.23 and 12.24
			Bathroom	12.25

Glossary

For more detailed definitions of architectural and design styles, see: John J. G. Blumenson, *Identifying American Architecture: A Pictorial Guide to Styles and Terms, 1600 – 1945* (Nashville: American Association for State and Local History, 1977); A. Allen Dizik, *Concise Encyclopedia of Interior Design* (New York: Van Nostrand Reinhold, 1988, 2d ed.); John Gloag, *A Short Dictionary of Furniture* (New York: Holt, Rinehart and Winston, 1965); Philippa Lewis and Gillian Darley, *Dictionary of Ornament* (New York: Pantheon Books, 1986); Edgar deN. Mayhew and Minor Myers, Jr., *A Documentary History of American Interiors: From the Colonial Era to 1915* (New York: Charles Scribner's Sons, 1980); Milo M. Naeve, *Identifying American Furniture: A Pictorial Guide to Styles and Terms, Colonial to Contemporary* (Nashville: American Association for State and Local History, 1981); Martin Pegler, *The Dictionary of Interior Design* (New York: Crown Publishers, Inc., 1966); Marcus Whiffen *American Architecture since 1780: A Guide to the Styles* (Cambridge: M.I.T. Press, 1969); and Gail Caskey Winkler and Roger W. Moss, *Victorian Interior Decoration: American Interiors, 1830 – 1900* (New York: Henry Holt, 1986).

acanthus: a carved motif, resembling the scalloped leaf of the acanthus tree, used in decoration and architecture.

aesthetic movement (1875 – 1890): a period characterized by the introduction of principles that emphasized art in the production of furniture, metalwork, ceramics, stained glass, textiles, wallpapers, and books, and by great art activity.

American Empire: colonial revival furniture of the 1890s and later, which revived the Grecian style that was especially popular during the 1830s and 1840s.

American renaissance (1876 – 1917): not a rebirth of the best of American design, but a renewed interest by Americans in styles based upon European furnishings of a distant past. In professionally designed homes, the wealthy combined antiques and reproductions to create Renaissance-inspired settings. In this spirit Edith Wharton and Ogden Codman, Jr., authors of *The Decoration of Houses* (1897), looked for design models in Italian interiors of the Renaissance and baroque periods and in French and English styles of the eighteenth century.

anthemion: a motif in classical ornament design that resembles the honeysuckle flower.

art glass: broadly, glass colored by different techniques—enameling, painting, staining — arranged in decorative patterns and used in articles for the home (lampshades, door panels, windows, and bookcase doors).

art nouveau (1900 – 1915): a style of decoration popular at the turn of the twentieth century. It featured sinuous, stylized depictions of organic forms, especially plant and floral forms.

art pottery: a type of ceramics that exhibits a popular manner of decorating forms during the late nineteenth and early twentieth centuries. Ornamentation was applied before the piece was glazed and usually before it was fired. Some of the work was one of a kind, but most came from potteries that produced many copies of the same forms and designs.

arts and crafts (1875 – 1920): a movement to "reform" the decorative arts of the Victorian era. In the place of overornamented, mass-produced furnishings, advocates sought a return to fine craftsmanship and hand fabrication; among the proponents of the arts and crafts movement were Gustav Stickley, manufacturer of Craftsman furniture, and Elbert Hubbard, founder of the Roycroft Shops.

Axminster carpet: a hand-knotted pile carpet originally made in Axminster, England. These carpets, mechanically woven in large, seamless pieces, have a thick, long-cut pile and are like oriental rugs in color and thickness.

banquet lamp: a shaded kerosene lamp, usually with a fanciful metal base.

beaux arts classicism (1890 – 1920): an architectural style generally employed on public buildings; details were incorporated in domestic architecture in Texas and elsewhere. The style called for monumental paired columns, impressive flights of stairs, figure sculpture, and balustrades decorating the projecting facades or pavilions.

bellflower: any one of several plants having bell-shape flowers; the motif was used on classically inspired furniture.

bentwood furniture: chairs tables, and other forms constructed by using a process of bending wood under steam heat. Viennese furniture maker Michael Thonet was a master at using bentwood in furniture design in the late nineteenth century.

Berlin work: embroidery, such as cross-stitch and needlepoint, usually done with Berlin wool on canvas.

bird's-eye maple: a pale brownish-yellow maple patterned with dark brown circles.

Brussels carpet: a floor covering made with three- or four-ply worsted yarns in which uncut loops form a pattern.

Buffalo pottery: one of many products manufactured by the Larkin Company of Buffalo, New York, which began as a soap factory in 1875. John Larkin marketed a variety of articles as gifts with purchase, or premiums, even furniture and lamps. The pottery produced various forms and decorations, including the Blue Willow pattern, Deldware, and historical and commemorative wares.

bungalow style (1895 – 1930): architecture that features broad gables and wide porches on small single-story houses; in larger bungalows the gable is steep, with intersecting cross gables or dormers. Chimneys are often of cobblestone or rough-faced brick; wooden shingles, stucco, or brick usually serve as the exterior finish.

cabinet card: an albumen print popular from 1850 to the turn of the century. A brown image appeared on coated, thin paper that was backed by a mount, usually 4½ by 6½ inches.

captain's chair: a nineteenth-century variation on the Windsor chair having a rounded back formed by a heavy rail resting on vertical spindles and coming forward to form the arms.

caroms — a game played by two or four persons with round wooden counters on a large square board having corner pockets.

carte de visite: a close-trimmed portrait photograph approximately 2½ by 4¼ inches intended as a visiting card.

chair rail: a molding around the interior walls of a room at a height of about thirty inches from the floor. The area below the railing is referred to as a wainscot or dado.

chateau style (1860 – 1890): architecture characterized by massive scale, steeply pitched roof with round towers, wall dormers, and cross windows that are paired and divided by a mullion and a transom bar.

cheval glass: a full-length mirror that pivots from vertical uprights and usually rests on a four-legged frame.

chintz: firm cotton fabric of plain weave, usually glazed, commonly with colorful printed designs.

Chippendale style: named for English cabinetmaker Thomas Chippendale who wrote *The Gentleman and Cabinet Maker's Director* (1754). His furniture designs often blended Chinese, Gothic, baroque, and rococo elements, and featured the claw-and-ball foot, pierced fretwork, and shell motif.

colonial revival style (1870 – 1920): furniture based on designs of seventeenth-, eighteenth-, and early- nineteenth-century styles — William and Mary, Queen Anne, Chippendale, federal, and empire; especially popular after the International Centennial Exhibition in Philadelphia in 1876.

combination case: marketed circa 1890 – 1910, a case piece that had several components — a bookcase, drawers, a writing surface, and a mirror.

composite: a modification of the Corinthian order combining angular Ionic volutes with the acanthus-circled bell of the Corinthian.

conservatory: a greenhouse, sometimes attached to a dwelling, for growing or displaying plants.

cornice: an ornamental horizontal molding used to conceal drapery hardware.

cove molding: a concave molding placed at the juncture of the wall and the ceiling.

cretonne: a strong unglazed cotton or linen fabric similar to chintz but usually printed with large floral designs, woven in plain or fancy weaves, and used especially for curtains and upholstery.

cruciform: forming or arranged in a cross.

cruet: a cut glass bottle used to hold a condiment (such as oil or vinegar) for the table.

curule chair or stool: an *X*-frame upholstered seating piece with two sets of heavy curved legs.

dado: the lower part of an interior wall. It measures approximately thirty inches high and is defined by a wooden molding called a chair rail or a dado molding.

damask: a fabric with reversible, solid color, woven designs on contrasting glossy and dull fabric surfaces; can be woven of any fiber or combination of fibers, most commonly silk or linen.

decalcomania: the art or process of transferring pictures and designs from specially prepared paper to china, glass, and marble.

decoupage: a technique of decorating a surface with paper cutouts, then coating the paper with layers of finish (lacquer or varnish).

de Wolfe, Elsie (1865 – 1950): actress, interior decorator, and bon vivant. Influenced by Wharton and Codman's advocacy of eighteenth-century French and English styles, Elsie de Wolfe wrote *The House in Good Taste* (1915) in which she criticized dark, cluttered interiors. She preached simplicity, suitability, and proportion in house decoration. Responding to her new dicta, rooms in middle-class houses across the country used lighter colored and more delicately proportioned furniture, chintz and other colorful fabrics, and less clutter on tabletops and walls.

diaper work: a regularly repeated surface decoration typically composed of small checkered or geometric designs.

diaphanie: the art or process of imitating stained glass with translucent paper.

drawnwork: decoration on fabric articles, such as clothing and household items, made by drawing out threads according to a pattern and usually grouping and stitching the exposed threads in lacy designs.

Eastlake style: furniture named for Charles Locke Eastlake, an English architect, writer, and designer, whose book *Hints on Household Taste in Furniture, Upholstery and Other Details* was published in England in 1868 and in the United States in 1872. Eastlake emphasized honest construction, simple and functional design, the appropriate use of materials, and conventionalized ornament. To the designer's dismay, American furniture manufacturers misinterpreted his appeal for good design at affordable prices and began machine production of lesser-quality goods. They popularized an "Eastlake" style characterized by rectilinear form, use of oak, walnut, or ebonized wood, turned spindles, balusters, finials, chamfered edges, pierced and cutout decorations, and gilt-incised geometric surface embellishment; also often characterized by its large scale. The so-called style generally shares features with other styles popular during the period, such as renaissance revival.

egg and dart: a carved decorative border ornament common in classical architecture, featuring a running pattern of ovals alternating with arrowheads or darts.

empire style (1810 – 1830): inspired by French design, furniture decorated with ormolu, gilt stenciling, and carved figures of winged caryatids, griffins, and animal forms. Such ornament eventually gave way to furniture featuring plain, mahogany-veneered surfaces. (*See* Grecian style.)

ewer: a large, wide-mouthed pitcher or jug.

fauteuil: an open-sided upholstered armchair.

feather Christmas tree: an artificial Christmas tree usually made of turkey and goose feathers, wire, and wood.

fill paper: the principal wall-covering pattern.

finial: an ornamental knob placed at the top of a piece of furniture or an accessory such as a lamp.

fleur-de-lis: a decorative motif in the form of a lily; a national emblem in France.

fresco: a wall painting in a watercolor-like medium on wet plaster.

fresco paper: plain or patterned wallpaper used during the middle of the nineteenth century to create the illusion of panels.

frieze: the area at the upper portion of the wall above the picture molding.

gargoyle: a grotesque carved human or animal figure.

gasolier: a lighting fixture equipped with gaslights.

gateleg table: a table with folding, hinged leaves supported by legs that swing closed like a gate, allowing the leaves to drop down.

Georgian revival style (1890 – 1925): architecture that features rectangular plans, few projections, symmetrical facades, hipped roofs, and classical details.

Gibson girl: an image of a young American woman regarded as representative of the fashions and manners of the 1890s; named after Charles Dana Gibson, an American illustrator.

Gothic revival style (1840 – 1870): furniture distinguished by pointed arches, tracery, trefoils, quatrefoils, and clustered columns.

Grecian style (1825 – 1855): also referred to as empire, Victorian classical, and pillar and scroll. Characterized by *C* and *S* scrolls and broad, plain surfaces (often of mahogany veneer); suited to mass-production techniques.

Greek key: a pattern formed by a geometrical repetition of intertwined hook-shape square forms.

guilloche: a classical ornamental border consisting of interlaced curves or circles enclosing foliate rosettes.

half-tester: a half canopy on a bed or chair.

heraldic emblems: designs that relate to heraldry and pedigree.

hipped roof: a roof with sloping ends and sides.

horn furniture: chairs, sofas, and hat racks, for example, made from the horns or antlers of elk, deer, and other animals. This furniture, first made in the Middle Ages, experienced a revival in Europe and the United States in the nineteenth century.

horsehair fabric (also **haircloth):** a durable, stiff fabric made from the mane or tail of a horse and used for upholstery.

incised decoration: carved or cut ornament, below the level of a surface.

ingrain paper: beginning in the late 1870s, a wallpaper made from cotton and woolen rags dyed before being made into pulp; a similar process was used to make less expensive "oatmeal" papers popular in the late nineteenth and early twentieth centuries.

ingrain carpeting: an American term for a flatwoven, reversible wool carpet resembling a coverlet in which the colors of the design on one side reverse on the other.

Ionic: a classical Greek order of architecture and decoration, characterized by two opposed volutes in the capital.

Italianate and Italian villa styles (1830 – 1880): architecture that features low-pitched roofs, paired brackets supporting wide eaves, and tall narrow windows and doors. The buildings are usually two or three stories and are sometimes finished with smooth stucco and detailed with quoins.

Jacobean revival style (1890 – 1915): architecture characterized by brick and stone buildings with rectangular windows divided by stone mullions, gables typically rising above the roofs, tall chimneys with a separate shaft for each flue, and round-arched doorways.

jardiniere: a decorative stand or pot designed to hold indoor plants and flowers.

jute: a strong, glossy material made when fibers of two Asian plants are carded and spun into strong, durable yarns; used to add strength, weight, and stiffness to carpets.

klismos chair: a classic Greek type of seating furniture with a concave curved back rail and curved legs that splay out front and back.

lambrequin: usually a stiff horizontal covering for curtain or drapery headings; can also be a decorative fabric used to drape a mantel, tabletop, or shelf.

Louis XV revival style (1865 – 1895): furniture that had earlier inspired the rococo style; painting and gilding were dominant elements in its revival. In rooms inspired by this style, elaborate moldings and panels adorned walls and framed oil paintings, frescoes, and tapestries.

Louis XVI revival style (1865 – 1895): furniture that featured the classic straight line. Carving, inlay, gilding, and ormolu provided decoration. This style was used for less expensive furnishings, which probably lengthened its life span.

McKim, Meade & White: an influential architectural firm during the 1890s in New York, which used Roman and Renaissance forms and constructed such buildings as the Metropolitan Museum of Art, Madison Square Garden, the Henry Villard house, and the Rhode Island state capitol.

Millet, Jean-François (1814 – 1875): a French painter and graphic artist who depicted scenes of rural life.

mission furniture (1895 – 1915): forms of heavy, square shaping and simple, angular construction. Popular examples included the Morris chair with its adjustable back, small portable tables, circular tables often covered with leather, and square chairs with leather seats or leather-upholstered cushions. Among the woods used were chestnut, willow, and oak. (*See* arts and crafts.)

mission revival style (1890 – 1920): architecture characterized by round arches supported by piers, smooth plaster walls, and tile roofs.

mitered: a connection between two pieces of wood or fabric made by beveling an edge of each piece and placing the beveled edges at an angle, usually to form a corner.

modern Gothic furniture (1865 – 1880): also known as art furniture or Eastlake furniture; featured rectilinear forms, compartmentalized spaces or panels, surface decoration, ebonized or dark wood, low-relief carving combined with inlaid, incised, or pierced motifs, elaborate metalwork, and conventional motifs. The publication of Charles Locke Eastlake's *Hints on Household Taste in Furniture, Upholstery and Other Details* (1868) did much to popularize the reform Gothic style. (*See* Eastlake.)

moire paper: wallpaper resembling moire, a fabric with a watered or wavy effect.

Moorish revival style (1876 – 1895): a design incorporating objects with Moorish flavor, such as inlaid furniture, armor, hanging lamps, brass accessories, statuary, and Turkish-style, deeply tufted, upholstered, and fringed furniture. Some Moorish revival rooms simply contained a special niche that became the hallmark of the style: the cozy corner, with a low sofa piled high with pillows and cushions, its walls draped with fabric for a mysterious effect.

Morris chair: a large wooden lounging chair with loose cushions and an adjustable back.

neo-Grec style (1860 – 1890): allied with both the renaissance revival and the Louis XVI styles, neo-Grec used motifs found in both and borrowed elements from ancient Greek architecture like columns, flutes, anthemia, foliate scrolls, and keys.

newel: a heavy upright post or turning at the end of the handrail of a stairway.

oriental revival style (1876 – 1895): featured the use of Japanese- and, to a lesser extent, Chinese-inspired furnishings. In Japanese-style rooms bamboo furniture, fans, parasols, and ceramics abounded. Chinese rooms sported deeply carved teak furniture and Chinese motifs: dragons, fretwork, and pagodas.

parfleche: an article made of a rawhide soaked in lye to remove the hair and dried.

pargework: stucco or plaster applied to a wall or ceiling, forming an ornamental design in relief.

parian: a relatively low-fired white to pale ivory porcelain body made of feldspar and china clay; typically used for bisque statuary and ornamental items.

parquet: an inlaid or mosaic wooden floor; a design is created on the floor by strips of wood laid out in a definite pattern.

patera: a round or oval disk usually decorated with a rosette or other ornament.

pergola: a garden arbor of trelliswork supported on columns or posts over which vines are trained.

picture molding: a grooved wooden strip on a wall, placed close to the ceiling line, or the lowest border of a frieze.

pier mirror: a mirror that is positioned on a section of wall between two windows or doors.

pilaster: a rectangular or half-round column or pillar attached to the face of a wall or an article of furniture as an ornamental motif.

plate rail: a shelflike wooden molding along a wall, intended to hold ornamental plates and other forms.

plateau: a decorative stand, set on low feet, used to raise a centerpiece above the table's surface.

platform rocker: a chair that is so sprung on a stable platform as to be capable of motion like that of a conventional rocking chair.

plissé: a crinkled fabric made from cotton or synthetic fibers.

plush: a long-pile velvet used as an upholstery fabric.

portière: a curtain or drapery used in a doorway to separate areas and provide privacy.

prairie style (1900 – 1920): architecture that features two-story houses, finished with stucco, with low-pitched roofs extending well beyond the exterior walls; exhibiting an overall horizontality, prairie-style houses often have casement windows grouped in horizontal bands and contrasting dark wooden strips against a lighter stucco finish; based on the designs of midwestern architect Frank Lloyd Wright.

putto: a very young boy resembling a wingless cherub or cupid — a popular subject for decoration, painting, and sculpture in the Italian Renaissance.

pyrography: the process of producing designs or pictures on wood or leather by burning or scorching the surface with hot instruments.

Queen Anne style (1880 – 19[illegible]0): architecture that features an encircling porch or veranda, a tower with conical roof, turrets, tall chimneys, and an overall asymmetry expressed by various forms, textures, materials, and colors.

rag carpet: a floor covering using strips of fabric as weft in a woven carpet or, if braided, as the entire carpet.

quatrefoil: an ornament composed of four lobes, leaves, petals, or flowers.

rattan: the slender, tough, vinelike stems of several climbing Asian palm trees, used for caning and weaving furniture.

récamier sofa: a daybed having ends of unequal height; named after the renowned Parisian social and literary figure, Madame Jeanne Récamier.

renaissance revival style (1865 – 1895): massive and solid furniture embellished with deeply carved ornament, cabochon decoration, portrait medallions, classical busts, and architectural motifs such as pediments and pilasters, all combined with varying degrees of historical accuracy.

rococo revival style (1850 – 1870): furniture with curves in *C* or *S* shapes, cabriole legs, and carvings of shells, fruits, flowers, and leaves.

romanesque revival style (1870 – 1890): architecture characterized by rock-faced stone finish detailed with contrasting colored and textured stone or brick trim and semicircular arches typically supported by short polished stone columns.

Roseville pottery: Roseville Pottery Company began in Roseville, Ohio, and in 1898 moved to Zanesville, Ohio. In 1900 the company began production of art pottery; some of the patterns manufactured were Rozane Ware, Dogwood, and Donatello.

rustic style (1870 – 1895): a taste for "primitive" objects led manufacturers to produce rustic picture frames, easels, plant stands, and chairs sporting the wood's bark.

Savonarola chair: a nineteenth-century term for an Italian Renaissance folding chair, featuring six or more serpentine, interlaced *x*-shape frames; the wooden back was ornamented with carving and inlay work named after an Italian monk.

second empire style (1860 – 1890): architecture identified by a projecting central pavilion, mansard roof covered with multicolored slates or tinplates, and dormer windows. Houses in the style also featured classical moldings and details such as quoins and cornices, often of different textures and colored materials, arched and pedimented windows, and arched entrance doors.

settle: a long wooden bench, often with a chest boxed in beneath the seat.

shadow box: a shallow enclosing case, usually with a glass front, which displayed a painting, a relief, or decorative articles and was hung on the wall.

shellwork: work composed of a pattern of shells or adorned with shells.

Sheraton style: named for Thomas Sheraton who wrote *Cabinet-maker and Upholsterer's Drawing Book* (1793 – 1794), which included illustrations of chairs with rectangular backs and crossbars just above the seats. The published patterns inspired American furniture design during the federal period and its revivals.

shingle style (1880 – 1900): architecture that features, as the name suggests, wooden shingles covering exterior walls. Houses built in this style are also recognizable by the horizontal effect that they project, emphasized by small-paned windows that form horizontal bands.

sotol: a plant of the lily family found in the southwestern United States and Mexico; the plant resembles a yucca.

stereoscope: an optical instrument for obtaining a single three-dimensional image from two pictures by means of a separate lens for each eye.

stereograph: a double photographic image designed to be viewed three-dimensionally by means of the stereoscope; mount measures approximately 3 by 7 inches.

stick style (1860 – 1890): architecture that features steep gable roofs, towers, pointed dormers, and large verandas or porches with prominent stick-like details in vertical, horizontal, and diagonal patterns.

strapwork: type of ornamental pattern in architecture and decorative arts consisting of interlacing bands or straps sometimes combined with foliage and resembling fretwork or cut leather.

taboret: an unupholstered stool which can function as a stand or small table.

tidy: a piece of fancywork used to protect the back, arms, or headrest of a chair or sofa from wear or soil.

torchère: originally, a small table designed to hold a candlestick or other illuminating device; in current terminology, a standing floor lamp, sometimes with an inverted bowl shade that casts the light upward.

transom: a hinged window over a door or another window.

trompe l'oeil: French for "fool the eye," a type of painting that appears three dimensional and realistic.

valance: a border of fabric used as a heading over draperies to achieve a finished look and to conceal drapery hardware.

vernacular style: relating to the common building practices of a period or place, displaying a mixture of indigenous and more broadly distributed folk and academic styles, combined in a distinctive local or regional manner.

voile: a plain-weave, sheer, transparent fabric made with highly twisted yarn; can be made in any fiber.

wainscot (also **wainscoting**): a wooden lining of an interior wall, usually paneled; also the lower thirty inches or so of an interior wall when finished differently from the rest of the wall.

western stick style (1895 – 1915): architecture emphasizing wood, with stick-like roof rafters and purlins projecting beyond the ends of the roof and wooden shingles or wooden siding, covered with earth-tone stains.

whatnot: a cabinet with open shelves used for the display of curios or accessories; sometimes called an étagère.

Windsor chair: a wooden chair first popular in England and America in the early eighteenth century. It has a high, spoked back of slender turned spindles, a wooden saddle-like seat, and splayed legs connected by a crossbar. The back is designed in a variety of ways, including fan-back, comb-back, and hoop-back.

Notes

PREFACE

1. Robert Taft, *Photography and the American Scene: A Social History, 1839 – 1889* (New York: Macmillan, 1938; reprint, New York: Dover Publications, 1964), pp. 388 – 89.
2. Donald R. Adams, Jr., "Prices and Wages," in *Encyclopedia of American Economic History,* 3 vols., ed. Glen Porter (New York: Charles Scribner's Sons, 1980), 1: 242.
3. Gail Caskey Winkler, letter to author, March 13, 1991; Bonnie Parks, "Historic Photos as an Aid to Paint Analysis" (Paper delivered at the Association for Preservation Technology Annual Meeting, Boston, Mass., October 1989).
4. Taft, *Photography,* pp. 313 – 14.
5. Clifford Geertz, *The Interpretation of Cultures: Selected Essays* (New York: Basic Books, 1973), p. 448. This is a paraphrase of Geertz' comment, "a story they tell themselves about themselves."

CHAPTER ONE

1. Rupert N. Richardson, Ernest Wallace, and Adrian Anderson, *Texas: The Lone Star State* (5th ed.; Englewood Cliffs, New Jersey: Prentice Hall, 1988), pp. 188 – 90.
2. Charles P. Zlatkovich, *Texas Railroads: A Record of Construction and Abandonment* (Austin: Bureau of Business Research, 1981), p. 5.
3. *Statistics of the Population of the United States at the Tenth Census* (1880) (Washington, D.C.: Government Printing Office, 1883), table 1e, pp. 6 – 7.
4. Stanley A. Arbingast et al., *Atlas of Texas* (5th ed.; Austin: Bureau of Business Research, 1979), p. 31.
5. *Statistics . . . at the Tenth Census* (1880), table 6, p. 424; table 34, p. 847.
6. *Fourteenth Census of the United States, Vol. 1, Population 1920, Bulletin, Population: Texas* (Washington, D. C.: Government Printing Office, 1921), p. 2; Mike Kingston, ed., *Texas Almanac and State Industrial Guide, 1986 – 1987* (Dallas: A. H. Belo Corp., 1985), p. 443.

7. *Fourteenth Census of the United States Taken in the Year 1920: Vol. IV, Population* (Washington, D.C.: Government Printing Office, 1923), table 15, pp. 110 – 27.
8. Zlatkovich, *Texas Railroads*, p. 6.
9. Richardson, *Texas*, pp. 359 – 60.
10. This is due in large part to the ground-breaking study, Lonn Taylor and David B. Warren, *Texas Furniture: The Cabinetmakers and Their Work, 1840 – 1880* (Austin: University of Texas Press, 1975). For a discussion of Sears, Roebuck in Texas, see Patrick H. Butler, III, "Sears in Texas, 1906 – 1913," in *The Consumer Culture and the American Home 1890 – 1930*, ed. Glenda Dyer and Martha Reed (Beaumont: McFaddin-Ward House, 1989), pp. 47 – 55.
11. Eugene C. Barker, ed. *Annual Report of the American Historical Association for the Year 1919*, 2 vols. (Washington, D.C.: Government Printing Office, 1924), 1, Part 1: 785.
12. Ellis A. Davis and Edwin H. Grobe, *The New Encyclopedia of Texas*, 2 vols. (Dallas: Texas Development Bureau [ca. 1930]), 1: 701; *Directory of Greater Dallas Texas 1910* (Dallas: John F. Worley Directory Co., 1910), p. 74.
13. Richardson, *Texas*, p. 180; *Fourteenth Census . . . 1920: Vol. IV, Population*, p. 124.
14. Surveys of American architecture include Marcus Whiffen, *American Architecture since 1780: A Guide to the Styles* (Cambridge: M.I.T. Press, 1969); and John J. G. Blumenson, *Identifying American Architecture: A Pictorial Guide to Styles and Terms, 1600 – 1945* (Nashville: American Association for State and Local History, 1977).
15. Surveys of American interior decoration and furniture include Gail Caskey Winkler and Roger W. Moss, *Victorian Interior Decoration: American Interiors, 1830 – 1900* (New York: Henry Holt, 1986); Edgar deN. Mayhew and Minor Myers, Jr., *A Documentary History of American Interiors: From the Colonial Era to 1915* (New York: Charles Scribner's Sons, 1980); and Milo M. Naeve, *Identifying American Furniture: A Pictorial Guide to Styles and Terms, Colonial to Contemporary* (Nashville: American Association for State and Local History, 1981).
16. For example, the Edward Steves house in San Antonio, figure 4.6, shows one Texas household that did contain a Gothic revival pier mirror and rococo revival chairs and sofa.
17. For a discussion of Victorian culture, see Daniel Walker Howe, "American Victorianism as a Culture," *American Quarterly* 27, no. 5 (December 1975): 507 – 32. The term *Victorian* is commonly used to describe a period of time from 1837 to 1901, the reign of Queen Victoria of the United Kingdom of Great Britain and Ireland.
18. Harvey Green, *The Light of the Home: An Intimate View of the Lives of Women in Victorian America* (New York: Pantheon Books, 1983), p. 93.
19. Carroll Louis Vanderslice Meeks, *The Railroad Station, an Architectural History* (New Haven: Yale University Press, 1956), pp. 1 – 25.
20. Ibid., p. 4.
21. Walter E. Houghton, *The Victorian Frame of Mind, 1830 – 1870* (New Haven: Yale University Press, 1957), p. 33.
22. Clifford Edward Clark, Jr., "Domestic Architecture and the Cult of Domesticity in America, 1840 – 1870," *Journal of Interdisciplinary History* 7, no. 1 (Summer 1976): 33 – 56; Clifford Edward Clark, Jr., *The American Family Home 1800 – 1960* (Chapel Hill: University of North Carolina Press, 1986), pp. 40 – 43.
23. Howard Mumford Jones, *The Age of Energy: Varieties of American Experience, 1865 – 1915* (New York: Viking Press, 1971), p. 216.
24. Ibid., pp. 259 – 300.
25. Cynthia A. Brandimarte, "Somebody's Aunt and Nobody's Mother: The American China Painter and Her Work, 1870 – 1920," *Winterthur Portfolio* 23, no. 4 (Winter 1988): 210 – 11.
26. *Elegant Arts for Ladies* (London: Ward and Lock, n.d.), p. iv; Addie E. Heron, *Dainty Work for Pleasure and Profit* (Chicago: Danks [ca. 1893]), p. 8.
27. Preface to *Ausgefuhrte Bauten and Entwurfe von Frank Lloyd Wright* (Berlin: Wasmuth, 1910), reprinted in David Hanks, *The Decorative Designs of Frank Lloyd Wright* (New York: E. P. Dutton, 1979), p. 8, as quoted in Eileen Boris, *Art and*

Labor: Ruskin, Morris, and the Craftsman Ideal in America (Philadelphia: Temple University Press, 1986), p. 60.

28. Boris, *Art and Labor*, p. 64.
29. Ibid., p. 77.
30. For current interest in Victorian decoration, see Barbara Kantrowitz and Karen Brailsford, "Victoriana Rules Again," *Newsweek* (January 16, 1989): 60 – 61; and "Victorian Style Comes Home in Fashion," *Austin American-Statesman*, December 4, 1988, sec. F, pp. 1, 19.

CHAPTER TWO

1. *Historical and Biographical Record of the Cattle Industry and the Cattlemen of Texas and Adjacent Territory* (St. Louis: Woodward & Tiernan Printing Co., 1895), p. 435.
2. Mrs. Ford M. Boulware, telephone conversation with author, May 18, 1985.
3. Edith Wharton and Ogden Codman, Jr., *The Decoration of Houses* (New York: Charles Scribner's Sons, 1897; reprint, New York: W. W. Norton, 1978), p. 70.
4. Dulcie Sullivan, *The LS Brand: The Story of a Texas Panhandle Ranch* (Austin: University of Texas Press, 1968), p. 157. Construction on the New Headquarters began in 1896 and the Whitmans lived there during 1897 and 1898, but Charles' health required that they move back to Denver.
5. Ibid., n.p., caption to photograph no. 11, says that the ranchhands and cowboys were fascinated by Charles' typewriter, an indication of its rarity in the Panhandle in the 1890s.
6. Ibid., n.p., caption to photograph no. 13.
7. It is not known how many men lived with the Whitman family at the New Headquarters. In December 1985, a year before the New Headquarters was constructed, Whitman had forty men on his payroll.
8. Historic Sites and Restoration Branch, "Preservation Plan and Program for Sam Bell Maxey House, State Historic Structure" (Austin: Texas Parks and Wildlife Department, 1976), pp. a-1 – a-2.
9. Marilda Maxey in Washington, D.C., to Dora Maxey Lightfoot, January 8, [1881], as quoted in "Preservation Plan," p. a-23.
10. Ibid., p. a-22. Marilda Maxey to Dora Maxey, September 12, 1873, in which she states her intention to buy furniture from Willet Babcock (ca. 1826 – 1881); Lonn Taylor and David B. Warren, *Texas Furniture: The Cabinetmakers and Their Work, 1840 – 1880* (Austin: University of Texas Press, 1975), p. 315.
11. Frank W. Johnson, *A History of Texas and Texans*, 5 vols., ed. Eugene C. Barker (Chicago: American Historical Society, 1914), 4: 1669; extant copies of the *Victoria Advocate* for the years 1881 – 1889 at Barker Texas History Center do not list Peticolas as editor; Alfred Brown Peticolas, *Rebels on the Rio Grande: The Civil War Journals of A. B. Peticolas*, ed. Don E. Alberts (Albuquerque: University of New Mexico Press, 1984).
12. Linda Harsdorff, "Pencil Sketches Hailed," *Victoria Advocate*, November 6, 1978, in biographical clipping file, Barker Texas History Center.
13. Photographs of the Peticolas house, not published here, show additional upstairs and downstairs rooms.
14. Harsdorff, "Pencil Sketches."
15. Houston Press Club, comp., *Men of Affairs of Houston: A Newspaper Reference Work* (Houston: W. H. Coyle, 1913), p. 159.
16. Sister M. Agatha, *The History of Houston Heights, 1891 – 1918* (Houston: Premier Printing Co., 1956), pp. 87, 88.
17. Similar wallpaper is found Crockett, Carthage, Doucette, and Houston and may reflect a regional preference (East and Southeast Texas). Marketed as a wall covering in the arts and crafts style, which incorporated pastoral motifs into its ideology, the paper was an especially popular choice for Texans living in this region perhaps because it echoes the nearby Piney Woods.
18. A screened porch is evident in exterior photos of the Oliver house in the collections of the Harris County Heritage Society.
19. Notes made by W. D. Smithers, Photography Collection, Harry Ransom Humanities Research Center.

20. The Mersfelder photo album now housed at the Overland Trail Museum in Fort Davis shows an image of Mersfelder using the corner with the window, shown in figure 2.18, as a photography studio.
21. See illustrations containing similar room details in Edgar deN. Mayhew and Minor Myers, Jr., *A Documentary History of American Interiors from the Colonial Era to 1915* (New York: Charles Scribner's Sons, 1980), pp. 254, 297.
22. "Early Days Here Recalled by Photographer," *Galveston Daily News*, February 28, 1937, clipping, Maurer Collection, Rosenberg Library.
23. *Directory of the City of Galveston 1903 – 1904* (Galveston: Morrison & Fourmy Directory Co., 1903), p. 193, lists studio and residence as the same address, 418 Tremont. *Directory of the City of Galveston 1905* (Galveston: Morrison & Fourmy Directory Co., 1905), pp. 146 – 47, lists Maurer's residence as that of his parents, 3020 Avenue P.
24. "Early Days."
25. *Directory of the City of Galveston 1901 – 1902* (Galveston: Morrison & Fourmy Directory Co., 1901), p. 171, lists Karolina (Mrs. John) Maurer as a florist and dealer in goldfish.
26. Folding beds appeared in the parlors of Texas houses located in small towns in West, Northwest, and South Texas, but typically not in homes of Texans who lived in large cities, at least those whose interior photographs were located for this study. Possibly the dwellings in Quanah, Abilene, Karnes City, Dilley (figs. 11.10, 3.18, 8.6, 3.9) and other sparsely populated areas had fewer accommodations for guests or fewer beds and bedrooms for occupants.
27. Collection of glass plate negatives, Rosenberg Library. Photographer and photographs are unidentified, and the collection has been named Turn of the Century Collection. Because an interior view (not included here) of Ursuline Academy is contained in this collection, these images may be from that institution. See also files pertaining to Ursuline Academy and the Dominican Sisters in Texas (St. Mary's Cathedral School), Rosenberg Library. Architect Nicholas J. Clayton designed both Ursuline Academy and St. Mary's Cathedral School.
28. Johnson, *History of Texas and Texans*, 1: 397; also 1: 395 – 96.

CHAPTER THREE

1. *International Center of Photography Encyclopedia of Photography* (New York: Crown Publishers, 1984), p. 123.
2. *Sears, Roebuck and Co.* (Chicago: Bokker O'Donnell Printing Co., 1895), n.p.
3. Ellis Arthur Davis, ed., *The New Historical Encyclopedia of Texas*, 2 vols. (n.p.: Texas Historical Society [ca. 1940]), 2: 892.
4. *History of the Cattlemen of Texas* (Dallas: Johnston Printing & Advertising Co., 1914), p. 297.
5. Frank W. Johnson, *A History of Texas and Texans*, 5 vols., ed. Eugene C. Barker (Chicago: American Historical Society, 1914), 4: 2136 – 37.
6. Delila M. Baird and Josie M. Baird, comps., *Early Fisher County Families: Biographical History, 1876 – 1919* (Rotan, Texas: D. M. & J. M. Baird, 1976), p. 61; Douglas Barton Willingham, letter to author, October 13, 1983.
7. Captain B. B. Paddock, *History of Texas, Fort Worth and the Texas Northwest Edition*, 3 vols. (Chicago: Lewis Publishing Co., 1922), 3: 273; Elaine Coffman, interview with author, Abilene, January 19, 1985.
8. Elaine Coffman, letters to author, May 24, 1986, August 11, 1987.
9. The collection contains photographs of a Tom Thumb wedding and other activities of the children as they play and pose in other rooms.
10. Kenneth L. Ames, "Meaning in Artifacts: Hall Furnishings in Victorian America," *Journal of Interdisciplinary History* 9, no. 1 (Summer 1978): 19 – 46.
11. Niny A. Massey, letter to author, September 7, 1987.
12. Ibid.
13. Johnson, *History of Texas and Texans*, 3: 1274 – 75; Beverly Singletary Perdue letter to author, June 1, 1985. The elder Singletary was a Confederate veteran and a fourth-generation Scottish immigrant to the United States, his ancestors

living first in North Carolina and then Mississippi before settling in Texas.

14. Reba Alsup, "Old Families of Calvert: The Conitz Family," *New Calvert Tribune*, March 20, 1985, pp. 10 – 11.
15. Justine Digby-Roberts Grisham, interview with author, Abilene, January 10, 1985; Mr. and Mrs. Frederick W. Digby-Roberts, interview with author, Fort Worth, January 13, 1985.
16. Another view of the room, not published here, shows the location of the piano.
17. Genora B. Prewit, telephone conversation with author, November 10, 1984; Callie Bevill, letter to author, March 15, 1985.

CHAPTER FOUR

1. *Compendium of the Eleventh Census 1890, Part 2* (Washington, D.C.: Government Printing Office, 1894), p. 600; Fred Pass, ed., *Texas Almanac and the State Industrial Guide, 1978 – 1979* (Dallas: A. H. Belo Corp., 1977), p. 184.
2. The term *Tejano* refers to Spanish-speaking people who live in Texas.
3. Robert Thomas Teske, "Living Room Furnishings, Ethnic Idenity [*sic*], and Acculturation among Greek-Philadelphians," *New York Folklore Quarterly* 5 (1979): 21 – 32.
4. John L. Davis, *The Danish Texans* (San Antonio: University of Texas Institute of Texan Cultures, 1979), pp. 50 – 51.
5. Ibid., p. 58.
6. Notes made by W. D. Smithers, Photography Collection, Harry Ransom Humanities Research Center.
7. Ellis A. Davis and Edwin H. Grobe, *The New Encyclopedia of Texas*, 2 vols. (Dallas: Texas Development Bureau [ca. 1930]), 2: 1591. See 2: 1588 – 91 for biographies of Edward Steves and Johanna Steves.
8. The name King William Street was used on nineteenth-century maps of San Antonio; "Kaiser Wilhelm Strasse" may have been used informally.
9. Mary Carolyn Hollers Jutson, "An English Architect in Texas: Alfred Giles, 1853 – 1920" (Master's thesis, University of Texas, 1970), pp. 97 – 103. Giles was the architect for Steves' son Alfred's house which stands at 504 King William Street.
10. See Edward Steves Collection of the San Antonio Conservation Society and the Institute of Texan Cultures, San Antonio.
11. Gail Caskey Winkler, letter to author, March 13, 1991. The Steveses attended the International Centennial Exhibition in Philadelphia in 1876 and may have purchased this and other accessories for their home.
12. Davis and Grobe, *New Encyclopedia* [1930], 2: 1591. A conservatory/sun room was built off the dining room in 1910.
13. John Henry Brown, *Indian Wars and Pioneers of Texas* (Austin: L. E. Daniell, 1880; reprint, n.p., 1978), p. 524; *Diamond Jubilee Souvenir Book of Comfort, Texas* (San Antonio: Standard Printing Co., 1928), pp. 27, 30; Guido E. Ransleben, *A Hundred Years of Comfort in Texas: A Centennial History* (rev. ed.; San Antonio: Naylor Co., 1974), pp. 197 – 98.
14. Giles' drawings of the Faltin Store survive in the Architectural Drawings Collection, Architecture and Planning Library, General Libraries, University of Texas at Austin.
15. Frederick Law Olmsted, *Journey through Texas; or, A Saddle-Trip on the Southwestern Frontier, with a Statistical Appendix* (New York: Dix, Edwards, 1857), p. 430, as quoted in Marilyn McAdams Sibley, *Travelers in Texas, 1761 – 1860* (Austin: University of Texas Press, 1967), p. 97.
16. Lonn Taylor and David B. Warren, *Texas Furniture: Cabinetmakers and Their Work, 1840 – 1880* (Austin: University of Texas Press, 1975), p. 8.
17. Albert Mayer, interview with author, Austin, February 12, 1988.
18. Ibid. Henry Wulff also sculpted the image of sister Carolina that decorates the circular bas-relief in the gable.
19. Ibid.
20. Davis and Grobe, *The New Encyclopedia of Texas,* 2 vols. (Dallas: Texas Development Bureau [ca. 1929]), 1: 589.
21. Mrs. Faulkner Herff Heard, interview with Tom Shelton, San Antonio, October 1983.
22. For a discussion of the meanings and uses of the horseshoe,

see Alan Dundes, ed., *The Evil Eye: A Folklore Casebook* (New York: Garland Publishing, 1981), p. 96; and Clarence Maloney, ed., *The Evil Eye* (New York: Columbia University Press, 1976), pp. 35 – 36.

23. Unpublished biographical sketch of Charles Simmang, Jr. File material on the Wends in Texas, Institute of Texan Cultures, San Antonio.
24. For a history of the migration of the Wends to Texas, see George C. Engerrand, *The So-Called Wends of Germany and Their Colonies in Texas and in Australia*, University of Texas Bulletin, no. 3417 (Austin: University of Texas, 1934).
25. Unpublished biographical sketch of Charles Simmang, Jr. File material on the Wends in Texas, Institute of Texan Cultures, San Antonio.
26. Anne Balsig, *The Wends of Texas* (San Antonio: Naylor Co., 1954), as quoted in Sylvia Ann Grider, *The Wendish Texans* (San Antonio: University of Texas Institute of Texan Cultures, 1982), p. 80.
27. L. E. Daniell, *Types of Successful Men* (Austin: By the author, 1890), pp. 536 – 40; Mary Esther Scholl, "A Pageant in Praise of Learning," *Dallas News*, July 19, 1931, in biographical clipping file, Barker Texas History Center.
28. Catherine Villaret Spinks, letter to author, August 3, 1987. For a photograph of an unidentified parlor that shows the same feature, see William Seale, *The Tasteful Interlude: American Interiors Through the Camera's Eye, 1860 – 1917* (2d ed., rev. and enl.; Nashville: American Association for State and Local History, 1981), pp. 196 – 97.
29. Catherine Villaret Spinks, letter to author [May 1986].
30. An interior view of the Villarets' bedroom documents that the desk and bookcase have been moved to that room. The image is not included here.
31. "M. K. Brown" (obituary), *Cattleman* 51, no. 5 (October 1964): 128. See also "Pampa, Tex., Founder Killed," *Dallas Times Herald*, September 11, 1964; and "Pampa Founder Killed in Crash," *Austin Statesman*, September 11, 1964, both in biographical clipping file, Barker Texas History Center.

CHAPTER FIVE

1. *Directory of the City of Waco 1910* (Galveston: Morrison & Fourmy Directory Co., 1910), p. 318.
2. A. Baldwin Sloane, with lyrics by Edgar Smith, "Heaven Will Protect the Working Girl," n.p., 1909.
3. Reba Alsup, "Old Families of Calvert: The Dirr and Shelander Families," *Calvert Tribune*, November 20, 1985, pp. 10 – 11; Reba Alsup to author, series of correspondence, 1986 – 1987.
4. *Directory of the City of Fort Worth 1896 – 97* (Galveston: Morrison & Fourmy Directory Co., 1896), p. 256. This directory, for example, lists Ella Moore as the proprietress of both the Palace Hotel and the Atlanta House; her husband, John M. Moore, was the proprietor of the Standard Theater and the Palace Hotel saloon.
5. Lonn Taylor and David B. Warren, *Texas Furniture: The Cabinetmakers and Their Work, 1840 – 1880* (Austin: University of Texas Press, 1975), p. 386. Taylor lists twenty-eight cabinetmakers working in Washington County alone between 1840 and 1880.
6. *Bulletin of the Agricultural and Mechanical College of Texas*, 3d ser., vol. 3, June 1, 1917, *Forty-First Annual Catalogue*, Agricultural and Mechanical College of Texas (College Station), p. 213, lists Arthur Charles Perrin, a mechanical engineering student from Boerne, and Stanley Ezra Perrin, a student of agriculture also from Boerne. Catalogues circa 1910 – 1918 do not list a Harvey Perrin.
7. Ellis A. Davis and Edwin H. Grobe, *The New Encyclopedia of Texas*, 4 vols. (Dallas: Texas Development Bureau [ca. 1926]), 4: 2567.
8. *Bulletin of the University of Texas No. 73, Official Series No. 14, Catalogue 1905 – 1906* (Austin: State of Texas [1905]), p. 327; *Bulletin of the University of Texas No. 88, Official Series No. 21, Catalogue 1906 – 1907* (Austin: State of Texas, [1906]), p. 330; *Bulletin of the University of Texas No. 103, Official Series No. 25, Catalogue 1907 – 1908* (Austin: State of Texas [1907]), p. 327; *Bulletin of the University of Texas No. 117, Official Series No. 33, Catalogue 1908 – 1909* (Austin: State of Texas [1908]), p. 333; *Bulletin of the University of*

Texas No. 140, Official Series No. 41, Catalogue 1909 – 1910 (Austin: State of Texas [1909]), p. 299; *Bulletin of the University of Texas No. 140, Official Series No. 54, Catalogue 1910 – 1911* (Austin: State of Texas [1910]), p. 323.

9. *Bulletin of the University of Texas No. 103, Official Series No. 25, Catalogue 1907 – 1908* (Austin: State of Texas [1907]), p. 386.
10. Ray E. Lee, "How Texas' Richest Young Man Spends His Money," *Austin American-Statesman*, May 16, 1926, p. 6.
11. Ibid.

CHAPTER SIX

1. "Texas' Largest Ranch Has Finest Ranch House in World," *San Antonio Express*, May 20, 1915, sec. 3, pp. 12 – 13, 15.
2. Charles J. V. Murphy, "The Fortunes of the Klebergs" (condensed from *Fortune Magazine*), *Corpus Christi Caller-Times*, June 15, 1969, n.p. Biographical clipping file, Barker Texas History Center.
3. "King Ranch House Burns," *Kingsville Record*, 1912 [date incomplete]. Biographical clipping file, Barker Texas History Center; "Finest Ranch House in the World." Receipts in the King Ranch Archives confirm the participation of Tiffany Studios.
4. Murphy, "Fortunes of the Klebergs."
5. Ralph Elder, archivist at the Barker Texas History Center, identified this image.
6. Rosa Kleberg, "Early Experiences in Texas," Part 2, *Texas Historical Association Quarterly* 2, no. 2 (October 1898): 170 – 73. See also L. E. Daniel[l], "The Kleberg Family, for Seventy Years It Has Been Helping to Make the History of Texas," *Houston Post*, July 14, 1907, p. 26.
7. *History of the Cattlemen of Texas* (Dallas: Johnston Printing and Advertising Co., 1914), p. 322.
8. Daniel[l], "Kleberg Family."
9. See Joseph E. Taulman Collection and biographical clipping file, Barker Texas History Center.
10. For an example, see Eugene C. Barker, Charles S. Potts, and Charles W. Ramsdell, *A School History of Texas* (Evanston, Ill.: Row, Peterson, 1913), p. 73.
11. Drew Wommack, interview with author, Palestine, March 8, 1985; "The Campbells Have Come," *Dallas Morning News*, August 17, 1906, p. 1.
12. Jean and Price Daniel and Dorothy Blodgett, *The Texas Governor's Mansion: A History of the House and Its Occupants* (Austin: Texas State Library and Archives Commission and the Sam Houston Regional Library and Research Center, 1984), pp. 128 – 33, 136 – 39, 324. See the photograph on p. 132 that shows some of the same furnishings during the Sayers' tenure as during the Campbells' tenure. See a section of William Seale's contribution to the project, Appendix C, pp. 307 – 19.
13. Ibid., p. 316.
14. The treatment resembles those found in *The Curtain-Maker's Handbook* (New York: E. P. Dutton, 1979), originally published as Frank A. Moreland, *Practical Decorative Upholstery* (Boston: Lee and Shepherd, 1889).
15. Pauline Buck Hohes, *A Centennial History of Anderson County, Texas* (San Antonio: Naylor Co., 1936), p. 392.
16. William Seale, *The Tasteful Interlude: American Interiors through the Camera's Eye, 1860 – 1917* (2d ed., rev. and enl.; Nashville: American Association for State and Local History, 1981), pp. 132 – 33. The image reproduced here is a slightly different view than the one presented by Seale who interprets the image as an example of interest in organic furniture that peaked in the 1890s. Seale notes that in inspiration the settee is renaissance revival and the center table Louis XV.
17. Mr. and Mrs. Wilson E. Hail, Jr., letters to author, October 20, 1983, January 10, 1984.
18. For illustrations of landscape papers, especially friezes, see Catherine Lynn, *Wallpaper in America: From the Seventeenth Century to World War I* (New York: W. W. Norton, 1980), pp. 446 – 49.
19. John W. Cordray, interview with author, Carthage, October 25, 1983.
20. Information on the Marsh house was provided by Linda Cheves Nicklas, archivist and librarian, and Holly C. Batson, student assistant, both of the R. W. Steen Library Special Collections, Stephen F. Austin State University,

Nacogdoches, and by Carol Riggs, director of the Texas Forestry Museum, Lufkin.

21. Some members of the Manton Edward Marsh family worked for the Thompson Lumber Company. For related images, see figures 9.14 and 9.15.
22. *Sears, Roebuck and Co. Fall 1900 Catalogue* (1900; reprint, Northfield, Ill.: DBI Books, 1970), p. 164.
23. Landseer's work, like that of one of his "followers," Rosa Bonheur, was very popular in the United States. See Dore Ashton, *Rosa Bonheur: A Life and a Legend* (New York: Viking Press, 1981), pp. 82 – 83, 106.
24. For an account of the hunt, see C. O. Finley, "Stalking the Unknown," *True West* (May – June 1966): 28 – 29, 63 – 64, originally published in 1902 and reprinted from *Pecos News*, July 2, 1965.
25. Mary Sarber, interviews with author, El Paso, January 16, 1985, February 2, 1987.
26. Helen Rugeley, interviews with author, Austin, May 1, 1987, September 8, 1989.

CHAPTER SEVEN

1. Forbes Watson, "'Art in Every Home': An Educational Movement which Does Not Educate," *Arts & Decoration* 14, no. 3 (January 1921): 195.
2. Kenneth L. Ames, "Material Culture as Non-Verbal Communication: A Historical Case Study," *Journal of American Culture* 3, no. 4 (Winter 1980): 619 – 41; Donald R. Adams, Jr., "Prices and Wages," in *Encyclopedia of American Economic History*, 3 vols. ed. Glenn Porter (New York: Charles Scribner's Sons, 1980), 1: 242. These figures represent an estimate based on unskilled urban workers; skilled workers would have earned higher salaries.
3. Amelia E. Barr, *All the Days of My Life: An Autobiography* (New York: D. Appleton, 1913), p. 207, see also p. 215.
4. Thorstein Veblen, *The Theory of the Leisure Class* (3d ed.; New York: Modern Library, 1934), p. 43.
5. William Andrew Fletcher, *Rebel Private, Front and Rear* (Austin: University of Texas Press, 1954); "Johnny Reb in Ranks," *Dallas News*, April 24, 1955, biographical clipping file, Barker Texas History Center; Dermot H. Hardy and Ingham S. Roberts, eds., *Historical Review of South-East Texas*, 2 vols. (Chicago: Lewis Publishing Co., 1910), 2: 520 – 25.
6. Florence Fletcher Dessart, interview with author, August 28, 1983. See figure 2.20 for a picture of Vallie Fletcher's art studio.
7. Charles P. Roos, "Modern Empire Interior," *Decorator and Furnisher* (November 1893): 63, reproduced in Edgar deN. Mayhew and Minor Myers, Jr., *A Documentary History of American Interiors from the Colonial Era to 1915* (New York: Charles Scribner's Sons, 1980), p. 239.
8. Elizabeth Forsythe Hailey, *A Woman of Independent Means* (New York: Viking Press, 1978; Avon Books, 1979), p. 2.
9. Clifford Clark and others have noted the preference for photographing an interior by providing a view through several rooms and giving glimpse of adjoining spaces; see Clifford Edward Clark, Jr., *The American Family Home, 1800 – 1960* (Chapel Hill: University of North Carolina Press, 1986), p. 120.
10. Tom Shelton, interview with author, San Antonio, February 8, 1987.
11. Ibid.
12. Elizabeth Cauthan, letter to author, June 9, 1986.
13. Mabel Tuke Priestman, *Art and Economy in Home Decoration* (New York: John Lane Co., 1908), p. 191.
14. *Directory of the City of San Antonio 1887 – 1888* (Galveston: Morrison & Fourmy Directory Co., 1887), p. 286.
15. Such humorous images were common, constituting a genre of photographs. Perhaps amateur photography liberated people from the formal portraiture of the photographer's studio; with a Kodak, friends and family could take photos in the privacy of their house.

CHAPTER EIGHT

1. *Sears, Roebuck Catalogue* (1897; reprint, New York: Chelsea House Publishers, 1968), p. 664.

2. For photographs of high-style interiors, see *Artistic Houses, Being a Series of Interior Views of a Number of the Most Beautiful and Celebrated Homes in the United States*, 2 vols. in 4 pts. (1883 – 1884; reprint, New York: Benjamin Blom, 1971).
3. Ellis A. Davis and Edwin H. Grobe, *Encyclopedia of Texas*, 2 vols. (Dallas: Texas Development Bureau [ca. 1922]), 2: 604.
4. Texas Federation of Women's Clubs, ed. and comp., *Who's Who of the Womanhood of Texas* (n.p., 1923 – 24), pp. 47, 187.
5. Frances Battaile Fisk, *A History of Texas Artists and Sculptors* (Abilene: By the author, 1928), pp. 73 – 74.
6. Verna Anne Wheeler and Rubye Parrish Stanton, letter to author, November 24, 1987; "Pink Parrish of Lubbock Dies; Former Mayor, State Senator," *Dallas News*, April 11, 1939, in biographical clipping file, Barker Texas History Center. Parrish served as county judge for twelve years, until 1923 when he and his family moved to Lubbock.
7. Architectural Archives Exhibition, "Thirty Residences of Early Christ Church Parishioners: 1984 May Fete Exhibit," May 1984, Houston Metropolitan Research Center, Houston.
8. Richard Guy Wilson, "Presence of the Past," in *The American Renaissance 1876 – 1917* (New York: Brooklyn Museum, 1979), pp. 38 – 55. Although the phrase "American Renaissance" was period, it is misleading. It is not a rebirth of the best of American styles, but instead a renewed interest by Americans in styles based upon European furnishings of a distant past.
9. Ames illustrates a remarkably similar cabinet and identifies it as a "Commode on buffet; rosewood with inlay, gilt and carving. French, 1870 – 1880," at the Brooklyn Museum. He notes that the piece may be by Kimbel and Cabus of New York. See Kenneth L. Ames, "What is Néo-Grec?" *Nineteenth Century* 2 (Summer 1976): 16 – 17.
10. Wilson, "Presence of the Past."
11. Peter Thornton, *Authentic Decor: The Domestic Interior, 1620 – 1920* (New York: Viking Press, 1984), p. 309.
12. Photographs of the drawings of the remodeling of the drawing room survive in the Nicholas J. Clayton Collection at the Rosenberg Library, Galveston.
13. Martha Hartzog, interview with author, Austin, July 23, 1983.
14. *Plainview Homes and Families* (Plainview: Bicentennial Homes and Families Committee, 1976), pp. 40 – 42.
15. Drury Blakeley Alexander and Todd Webb, *Texas Homes of the Nineteenth Century* (Austin: University of Texas Press, 1966), pp. 198, 258 – 59; Paul Goeldner, comp., *Texas Catalog* (San Antonio: Trinity University Press, 1974), pp. 95 – 96.
16. The difference may be practical as well, since presumably the Hoovers have set out all the food, while at the Brown house, servants would bring the various dishes only after the diners were seated.
17. Catherine Lynn, *Wallpaper in America: From the Seventeenth Century to World War I* (New York: W. W. Norton, 1980), p. 471.
18. This is tentatively identified as the Howe House, a boarding house for Blinn Academy students. John Matthias Kuehne was the photographer who documented several student residences at this German academy which educated both men and women.
19. *Sears, Roebuck Catalogue* (1902; reprint, New York: Bounty Books, 1986), p. 768.
20. Assessor's Abstracts, City Out Lots, 1889 – 1893, Galveston, Texas, p. 67, Rosenberg Library, Galveston.
21. June S. Holly, interview with author, Houston, August 12, 1985.
22. Wall plaques in the collections of Ashton Villa, Galveston Historical Foundation, are marked "Interlaken/Beyer & Co." They are also pictured in a photograph of the C. G. Pillot house in Houston, but not included in this sample; the photo appears in *The Standard Blue Book of Texas* (Houston: Who's Who Publishing Co., 1907 – 1908), p. 87.

CHAPTER NINE

1. Francis Newberry and Julia Macy Holbrook Collection, Southwest Room, El Paso Public Library.

2. See page decorations in women's art magazines beginning in the 1880s and continuing into the 1890s. See also, for example, Emma Haywood, "Painting in Boucher Style, Part I," *Art Amateur* 21, no. 5 (October 1889): 100; and Emma Haywood, "China Painting in Boucher Style," *Art Amateur* 21, no. 6 (November 1889): cover, 123 – 24.
3. For a discussion of Anglo-Japanese papers, see Richard C. Nylander, Elizabeth Redmond, and Penny J. Sander, *Wallpaper in New England* (Boston: Society for the Preservation of New England Antiquities, 1986), pp. 227 – 29.
4. Catherine Lynn, "Surface Ornament: Wallpapers, Carpets, Textiles, and Embroidery," in Doreen Bolger Burke, et al., *In Pursuit of Beauty: Americans and the Aesthetic Movement* (New York: Metropolitan Museum of Art and Rizzoli, 1986), p. 82. Decorative arts historian Catherine Lynn has speculated that people "might have appreciated the way borders set off walls and ceilings in much the same way frames did paintings."
5. Tom Shelton, telephone conversation with author, December 14, 1987.
6. Catherine Lynn, *Wallpaper in America: From the Seventeenth Century to World War I* (New York: W. W. Norton, 1980), p. 431.
7. William DeRyee and R. E. Moore, *The Texas Album of the Eighth Legislature 1860* (Austin: Miner, Lambert & Perry, 1860), p. 73. See "Benjamin H. Epperson," biographical clipping file at Barker Texas History Center. I am grateful to Richard and Susan Collins, owners of the House of the Seasons, and Suzanne Benefield, director of the house, for providing information concerning its history.
8. Nylander, *Wallpaper*, pp. 194 – 98.
9. For an illustration of this use of a Japanese parasol, see "The Dining Room: Economical Home Decoration," *Decorator and Furnisher* 3, no. 6 (March 1884): 209.
10. The Frank W. Ball house should not be confused with the George Ball house, now called the Eddleman-McFarland Home, which still stands on Penn Street in Fort Worth.
11. *History of Texas together with a Biographical History of the Cities of Houston and Galveston* (Chicago: Lewis Publishing Co., 1895), pp. 464 – 66.
12. Fannie Simpson Carter, interview with author, Houston, November 11, 1985.
13. *Sears, Roebuck Catalogue* (1902; reprint, New York: Bounty Books, 1986), p. 926.
14. "Lone Star Pine," *American Lumberman*, no. 1740 (September 26, 1908): 67 – 150.
15. Victor M. Rose, *Some Historical Facts in Regard to the Settlement of Victoria, Texas, Its Progress and Present Status* (Laredo: Daily Times Print, n.d.; reprint, Victoria: Book Mart, 1961), p. 191. Margaret Stoner McLean, letters to author, February 10, 21, 1988; Kemper S. Williams, letter to author [February 1988]. I am grateful to Lois E. Myers for sharing her work on the Stoner family.
16. Christopher Monkhouse, "The Spinning Wheel as Artifact, Symbol, and Source of Design," in *Victorian Furniture: Essays from a Victorian Society Autumn Symposium*, ed. Kenneth L. Ames (Philadelphia: Victorian Society in America, 1983), pp. 155 – 72. The spinning wheel incorporated into late-nineteenth- and early-twentieth-century house decoration is one of the more obvious signals of the popularity of the colonial revival but by no means the only index. For studies of the colonial revival, see Alan Axelrod, ed., *The Colonial Revival in America* (New York: W. W. Norton, 1985); and William B. Rhoads, *The Colonial Revival* (New York: Garland Publishing, 1977).
17. Jo Ella Powell Exley, *Texas Tears and Texas Sunshine: Voices of Frontier Women* (College Station: Texas A&M University Press, 1985), p. 11.
18. Jane S. Smith, *Elsie de Wolfe: A Life in the High Style* (New York: Atheneum, 1982), p. 109.
19. Eleanor H. Gustafson, "The Open Gates: The George Sealy House in Galveston," *Antiques* 103, no. 3 (September 1975): 51.
20. Smith, *Elsie de Wolfe*, pp. 39, 143.
21. See Russell Collection, Sherman Historical Museum, Sherman.
22. *Sherman City Directory 1918* (Sioux City, Iowa: R. L. Polk, 1918), p. 259; *Sherman City Directory 1921* (Sioux City, Iowa: R. L. Polk, 1921), p. 278; Sherrie McLeRoy, letter to author, November 27, 1987.

CHAPTER TEN

1. Lonn Taylor, "The McGregor-Grimm House at Winedale, Texas," *Antiques* 103, no. 3 (September 1975): 515 – 16.
2. Ibid.
3. Unidentified clipping in the collection of William M. and Frances P. Harris. The provenance of the clipping is unknown; newspapers publishing in Waco in 1896 include *Waco Examiner* and *Waco Morning Times*. Unless otherwise noted, quotations for figures 10.1, 10.2, and 10.3 are taken from this article.
4. Henry James, as quoted in Richard McLanathan, *The American Tradition in the Arts* (New York: Harcourt, Brace & World, 1968), p. 202.
5. Ibid.
6. *A Memorial and Biographical History of McLennan, Falls, Bell and Coryell Counties* (Chicago: Lewis Publishing Co., 1893), pp. 713 – 15.
7. Figure 10.8 was taken almost a decade after figures 10.4 through 10.7.
8. George Donald Bowie, letter to author, January 21, 1988. G. A. Holland, *History of Parker County and the Double Log Cabin* (Weatherford, Texas: Herald Publishing Co., 1937), pp. 263 – 64; R. J. Tolson, *A History of William Cameron & Co.* (n.p. [ca. 1926]), n.p.; Captain B. B. Paddock, *A History of Central and Western Texas*, 2 vols. (Chicago: Lewis Publishing Co., 1911), 1: 306; Ellen Bowie Holland, *Gay as a Grig: Memories of a North Texas Girlhood* (Austin: University of Texas Press, 1963).
9. Holland, *Gay*, plate 18, p. 65.
10. Ibid., pp. 63, 67.
11. Ibid., p. 66.
12. Ibid., p. 68.
13. Ibid., pp. 66 – 67.
14. Ibid., p. 68.
15. Ibid.
16. Ibid., p. 65.
17. Barbara Bates Mills, interviews with author, San Antonio, March 29, 1986, and October 23, 1987.
18. Neither Mary Hune Waltgenbach nor her husband appear to have been studio photographers. Judging from her surviving work, she used a small, hand-held camera, such as many amateurs used, processed and printed her own film, or sent away for processing and enlarging of portraits. The Waltgenbach images in this chapter are 4-by-5-inch originals that were placed in a family photo album.
19. Barbara Bates Mills, interviews with author.
20. Cynthia A. Brandimarte, "Japanese Novelty Stores," *Winterthur Portfolio* 26, no. 1 (Spring 1991): 1 – 25.
21. Barbara Bates Mills, interviews with author.
22. Ibid.
23. Captain B. B. Paddock, *A Twentieth Century History and Biographical Record of North and West Texas*, 2 vols. (Chicago: Lewis Publishing Co., 1906), 1: 301 – 02.
24. Ibid., p. 302.
25. George Tyng, Pampa, to F. de P. Foster, New York, April 24, 1902, Tyng Collection, Panhandle-Plains Historical Museum.
26. Paddock, *Twentieth Century History*, p. 302.
27. "Armitage," *Panhandle Herald*, May 16, 1912. I am grateful to Betty O. Ellis for sending me a typescript of the article.
28. For a history of the firm, see Violet Altman and Seymour Altman, *The Book of Buffalo Pottery* (New York: Crown Publishers, 1969).
29. George Washington's image related to the turn-of-the-century phenomenon of a search for a national past and past leaders. He and other heroes in American history became favorite icons in home decoration. See Karal Ann Marling, *George Washington Slept Here: Colonial Revivals and American Culture, 1876 – 1986* (Cambridge: Harvard University Press, 1988).
30. H. Leslie Evans, interview with author, San Antonio, January 9, 1988; Frank W. Johnson, *A History of Texas and Texans*, 5 vols., ed. Eugene C. Barker (Chicago: American Historical Society, 1914), 3: 1280 – 82.
31. Mary Carolyn Hollers Jutson, "An English Architect in Texas: Alfred Giles, 1853 – 1920" (Master's thesis, University of Texas, 1970), pp. 120 – 23.
32. Harold Holzer, Gabor S. Boritt, and Mark E. Neely, Jr., *The Lincoln Image: Abraham Lincoln and the Popular Print*

(New York: Charles Scribner's Sons, 1984), pp. 110 – 11, 122 – 25.

33. Richard C. Nylander, Elizabeth Redmond, and Penny J. Sander, *Wallpaper in New England* (Boston: Society for the Preservation of New England Antiquities, 1986), p. 242.
34. For further information on the construction and remodeling of the house, see Mrs. Bascom B. Hayes, "The Evolution of the North-Evans Home" (Austin Woman's Club [1989], typescript).
35. The collecting mania is documented in books like Alice Morse Earle, *China Collecting in America* (New York: Charles Scribner's Sons, 1892).
36. Colors were observed by the author during a site visit to the Evans house, now the headquarters for the Austin Woman's Club.
37. "Death of Mr. H. Hodde," *Brenham Daily Banner*, July 25, 1901, p. 1. Biographical information on the Hodde family was provided by Norman and Loretta Hodde.
38. August Faltin, also a merchant, emigrated in the late 1850s, but he was older than Hodde; the 1891 photograph of his home in Comfort shows a more conservatively furnished interior.
39. Loretta Hodde, interview with author, Brenham, September 11, 1983.
40. Ibid.
41. Ibid.
42. Ibid.
43. Gail Caskey Winkler and Roger W. Moss, *Victorian Interior Decoration: American Interiors, 1830 – 1900* (New York: Henry Holt, 1986), pp. 123 – 26.
44. Clifford Edward Clark, Jr., *The American Family Home, 1800 – 1960* (Chapel Hill: University of North Carolina Press, 1986), p. 114.
45. Zangerle marketed a range of student chairs — from the plain with minimal incising on the seat rail to a more elaborate model with curule legs and sloping arms with carved acanthus and tassel motifs. One of these featured arm supports "playfully carved in the form of beagles' heads with soulful eyes and protective collars." But Zangerle had his imitators in several other Chicago furniture manufacturers, Gannon & McGrath and D. L. Wullweber & Co. One of these companies may have constructed the Hodde family's chair. Sharon Darling, *Chicago Furniture, Art, Craft, & Industry, 1833 – 1983* (New York: W. W. Norton, 1984), pp. 76, 387 n. 37.

CHAPTER ELEVEN

1. "Correspondence," *Ladies' Home Journal* 5, no. 2 (January 1888): 8; "Correspondence," *Ladies' Home Journal* 4, no. 2 (January 1887): 8.
2. George Ware Fulton Papers, Barker Texas History Center, Austin.
3. "Correspondence," *Art Amateur* 21, no. 5 (October 1889): 112.
4. Fred Pass, ed., *Texas Almanac and State Industrial Guide 1978 – 1979* (Dallas: A. H. Belo Corp., 1977), p. 185.
5. "Correspondence," *Art Amateur* 20, no. 6 (May 1889): 143. Texas women not only queried editors, they contributed. The March 1884 issue of the *Decorator and Furnisher* featured several illustrations of Galvestonian Emma Price Willis' wood-carved floral designs; see "Wood Carving," *Decorator and Furnisher* 3, no. 6 (March 1884): 210.
6. See city directories of Waco for the years 1900 to 1920 inclusive.
7. *General Directory of the City of Dallas 1886 – 87* (Galveston: Morrison & Fourmy, 1886), pp. 81, 305, 343; *Directory of the City of Galveston 188[illegible] – 89* (Galveston: Morrison & Fourmy, 1888), p. 16; *Directory of the City of Austin 1887 – 88* (Galveston: Morrison & Fourmy, 1887), p. 259, cover.
8. Gilbert J. Jordan, trans. and ed., "W. Steinert's View of Texas in 1849," Part 5, *Southwestern Historical Quarterly* 81, no. 1 (July 1977): 57.
9. Kathleen M. Catalano, "Cabinetmaking in Philadelphia, 1820 – 1840: Transition from Craft to Industry," in *American Furniture and Its Makers: Winterthur Portfolio 13*, ed. Ian M. G. Quimby (Chicago: University of Chicago Press, 1979), p. 84.

10. Katherine Hart and Elizabeth Kemp, eds., *Lucadia Pease & the Governor, Letters: 1850 – 1857* (Austin: Encino Press, 1974).
11. George F. Barber & Co., *Artistic Homes: How to Plan and How to Build Them* (Knoxville: S. B. Newman, 1893), pp. 78, 86.
12. *History of the Cattlemen of Texas* (Dallas: Johnston Printing & Advertising Co., 1914), pp. 69 – 70; J. Marvin Hunter, *The Trail Drivers of Texas* (2d ed., rev.; Nashville: Cokesbury Press, 1925), pp. 672 – 73; James C. Shaw, *North from Texas: Incidents in the Early Life of a Range Cowman in Texas, Dakota and Wyoming 1852 – 1883* (Evanston, Ill.: Branding Iron Press, 1952), pp. 89 – 90.
13. As quoted in Elizabeth Wilson, *Adorned in Dreams: Fashion and Modernity* (Berkeley: University of California Press, 1987), p. 123.
14. [George A. Martin], *Our Homes; How to Beautify Them* (New York: O. Judd Co., 1888), p. iii.
15. Bettie B. Gafford, letter to author, December 14, 1984.
16. T. C. Richardson, *East Texas: Its History and Its Makers*, ed., Dabney White, 4 vols. (New York: Lewis Historical Publishing Co., 1940), 2: 930.
17. Glen Eden Collection, Sherman Historical Museum, Sherman.
18. Another interior view located, but not published here, repeats the same constellation of artifacts — center table surrounded by potted plants (and a spittoon).
19. L. E. Daniell, *Personnel of the Texas State Government* (Austin: Smith, Hicks & Jones, State Printers, 1889), pp. 265 – 66. Tom Shelton, letter to author, February 27, 1987, San Antonio. As a descendant of the Dunlaps, Shelton provided valuable information about the family and the photograph.
20. Charles L. Eastlake, *Hints on Household Taste in Furniture, Upholstery and Other Details* (1868; reprint, New York: Dover Publications, 1969), p. 99.
21. As quoted in Historic Sites and Restoration Branch, "Preservation Plan and Program for Magoffin Home, State Historic Site, El Paso, Texas" (Austin: Texas Parks and Wildlife Department, 1977), p. a-46.
22. Ibid., p. a-47.
23. Ibid., p. a-48.
24. Dore Ashton, *Rosa Bonheur: A Life and a Legend* (New York: Viking Press, 1981), p. 87.
25. The reverse of the original photograph of figure 11.17 bears the penciled label "Weatherington house." The Weatheringtons owned the house after the Wolfes. That label may refer to the name of the residence at the time the photograph was accessioned into the collections of the Rosenberg Library. Robert Clark, who owned the house during the 1970s and 1980s, did extensive research on the property and acquired prints of figures 11.17 and 11.18 from a Wolfe descendent then living in California.
26. Obituary of William H. George, undated clipping, courtesy of W. O. McCurdy, Beeville. Mr. McCurdy is related to the George family.
27. "Beeville-Bee County Bicentennial Committee Presents Official Historical Medallions and Markers in Bee County, Texas," Bee County Historical Survey Committee [ca. 1976], n.p.
28. Issues of *Homes* (1911 – 1912) are available at the Houston Metropolitan Research Center, Houston Public Library.
29. Helen Cates Neary, letter to author, February 8, 1988.
30. Ibid.
31. Ibid.
32. Ibid. In the 1920s during the Texas National Guard Encampment, the house was used as the Officers' Club.

CHAPTER TWELVE

1. Finn hired Antil & Baring, General Contractors and Builders, to implement his new design. See Alfred C. Finn Collection, Houston Metropolitan Research Center, Houston Public Library.
2. *Directory of the City of Houston 1907* (Houston: Morrison & Fourmy Directory Co., 1906), p. 418; *Directory of the City of Houston 1908 – 09* (Houston: Morrison & Fourmy Directory Co., 1908), p. 448; *Directory of the City of Houston, 1910 – 11* (Houston: Morrison & Fourmy Directory Co., 1910), p. 665. Harris County Heritage Society files, Staiti

Collection. Brenda Jordan, interview with author, Houston, February 11, 1987.

3. Real estate dealer and building contractor Edwin O. Maynard sold the house to the Staitis. He lists several properties in the 1907 Houston city directory, including Westmoreland pl. 2. See *Directory of the City of Houston 1905 – 6* (Houston: Morrison & Fourmy Directory Co., 1905), p. 275; and *Directory of the City of Houston 1907* (Houston: Morrison & Fourmy Directory Co., 1907), p. 262.
4. Harris County Deed Records, vol. 174, pp. 70 – 72.
5. Houston city directories for 1900 through 1930 chronicle the occupancy of the house. Biographical information was generously supplied by Staiti family members, Lee Averill Lawrence, Carol Jackson, and Jeanette Jackson King. Among the published sources consulted about the Staiti family are H. T. Warner et al., eds., *Texans and Their State: A Newspaper Reference Work* (Houston: Texas Biographical Association [ca. 1920]), p. 86; Houston Press Club, comp., *Men of Affairs of Houston and Environs: A Newspaper Reference Work* (Houston: W. H. Coyle, 1913), p. 55; Ellis A. Davis and Edwin H. Grobe, *The New Encyclopedia of Texas*, 2 vols. (Dallas: Texas Development Bureau [ca. 1923]), 1: 374 – 77.
6. Three photographs — the exterior, parlor, and dining room — appeared in a local magazine in 1905, "Houston's Beautiful Homes," *Houstonian* 1, no. 4 (August 5, 1905). Although the one-page article contains misleading information , such as noting that the parlor furniture is hand carved, it is valuable for documenting colors and other room details.
7. Ibid.
8. Ibid.
9. Exhibition announcement, *Antiques* 133, no. 4 (April 1988): 806 – 07. The recently rediscovered original painting and the reproductions have been called "the icon of the Southern experience" as it depicts two great leaders of the South — Robert E. Lee and Stonewall Jackson.
10. Davis and Grobe, *New Encyclopedia* [ca. 1923], 1: 374.
11. "Houston's Beautiful Homes."
12. See Secretary of State Records, State of Texas, Austin, files 009590 – 6A and 021882-CD, for example.
13. Jeanette Jackson King, interview with author, Houston, November 6, 1985.
14. Houston Press Club, *Men of Affairs*, p. 55; Warner, *Texans*, p. 86.
15. Jeanette Jackson King, interview with author.
16. Catherine Lynn, *Wallpaper in America: From the Seventeenth Century to World War I* (New York: W. W. Norton, 1980), pp. 464 – 69.
17. David P. Handlin, *The American Home: Architecture and Society, 1815 – 1915* (Boston: Little, Brown, 1979), p. 350.
18. Siegfried Giedion, *Mechanization Takes Command: A Contribution to Anonymous History* (1948; reprint, New York: W. W. Norton, 1969), pp. 69[illegible] – 701.

CHAPTER THIRTEEN

1. Ellen Bowie Holland, *Gay as a Grig: Memories of a North Texas Girlhood* (Austin: University of Texas Press, 1963), p. 67.
2. *Thirteenth Census of the United States Taken in the Year 1910, Volume 4, Population 1910, Occupation Statistics* (Washington, D.C.: Government Printing Office, 1914), p. 93; *Ninth Census, Volume I, The Statistics of the Population of the United States* (1870) (Washington, D.C.: Government Printing Office, 1872), p. 674.
3. As noted, the interiors of the George Sealy Mansion in Galveston are attributed to Elsie de Wolfe. The participation of Mitchell & Halbach and Robert Keith and Company will be discussed in this chapter.
4. *Men of Texas: A Collection of Portraits of Men Who Deserve to Rank as Typical Representatives of the Best Citizenship, Foremost Activities and Highest Aspirations of the State of Texas* (Houston: Houston Post, 1903), pp. 244, 257.
5. Ellis A. Davis and Edwin H. Grobe, *The New Encyclopedia of Texas*, 2 vols. (Dallas: Texas Development Bureau [ca. 1930]), 1: 701.

6. *Directory of the City of Houston 1910 – 11* (Houston: Morrison & Fourmy Directory Co., 1910), p. 94 (ads).
7. Davis and Grobe, *New Encyclopedia* [ca. 1930], 1: 701; Ellis S. Davis and Edwin H. Grobe, *The New Encyclopedia of Texas* , 2 vols. (Dallas: Texas Development Bureau [ca. 1923]), 1: 630.
8. *Directory of Greater Dallas, Texas, 1910* (Dallas: John F. Worley Printing Co., 1910), p. 74 (ads); *Directory of the City of Houston 1910 – 11* (Houston: Morrison & Fourmy Directory Co., 1910), p. 98 (ads).
9. *Directory of Greater Dallas, Texas, 1911* (Dallas: John F. Worley Directory Co., 1911), p. 1016.
10. 10. Fred Pass, ed., *Texas Almanac and State Industrial Guide 1978 – 1979* (Dallas: A. H. Belo Corp., 1977), p. 184.
11. Rupert N. Richardson, Ernest Wallace, and Adrian Anderson, *Texas: The Lone Star State* (Englewood Cliffs, N.J.: Prentice Hall, 1988), p. 323.
12. See *The Minutes of the Texas State Society of Architects: 1886 – 1896*, p. 106, in the James Riely Gordon Archive, Architectural Drawings Collection, Architecture and Planning Library, General Libraries, University of Texas at Austin. Unless otherwise noted, all references to the Gordon Archive are located at the Architectural Drawings Collection.
13. Ibid.
14. "Address of J. J. Kane to the Texas State Society of Architects," January 17, 1888, in *Minutes* of Texas State Society of Architects, pp. 45, 47.
15. Ibid., p. 43.
16. Henry F. Withey and Elsie Rathbone Withey, *Biographical Dictionary of American Architects (Deceased)* (Los Angeles: New Age Publishing Co., 1956), pp. 241 – 42; "James Riely Gordon, Texas Courthouse Architect," a Centennial Exhibition Presented by the School of Architecture, the University of Texas at Austin, January 21 – March 18, 1983.
17. For a discussion of ventilation in late-nineteenth-century houses, see Gavin Townsend, "Air-Borne Toxins and the American House, 1865 – 1895," *Winterthur Portfolio* 24, no. 1 (Spring 1989): 29 – 42.
18. Undated clipping in Gordon Archive. Gordon maintained a scrapbook filled with "Notice to Contractors" clippings and other newspaper articles and announcements concerning his architectural activities.
19. W. B. Wright to County Judge, Fayette County, March 22, 1890, Gordon Archive.
20. "Some Fine Buildings," undated clipping, Gordon Archive.
21. *American Biography: A New Cyclopedia* (New York: American Historical Society, 1930), 43: 310.
22. Davis and Grobe, *New Encyclopedia* [ca. 1930], 2: 1728 – 33.
23. Mary V. Burkholder, with photographs by Graham B. Knight, *The King William Area: A History and Guide to the Houses* (San Antonio: King William Association, 1973), p. 53.
24. See Gordon Archive.
25. *Sketches from the Portfolio of James Riely Gordon*, n.p., names the house the "Henrietta M. King's home," Gordon Archive. Dan Reid of Reid & Sutherland, Architects and Builders, Corpus Christi, was the builder of the house; Gordon was the architect.
26. A code on the original images suggests the client was an individual whose name begins with "G." Presuming this is not Gordon's own house, it may be the J. N. Groesbeck house on Tobin Hill or the Frank Grice house on Alamo Heights, both of which Gordon designed in the 1890s.
27. *A Memorial and Biographical History of McLennan, Falls, Bell and Coryell Counties* (Chicago: Lewis Publishing Co., 1893), pp. 878 – 79; Texas Federation of Women's Clubs, ed. and comp., *Who's Who of the Womanhood of Texas* (n.p., 1923 – 24), p. 12.
28. Undated clippings, Gordon Archive.
29. "Houston Architectural Survey," vol. 1, Southwest Center for Urban Research and the School of Architecture, p. 266. Besides the American Brewing complex and the Binz Building, Lorehn designed other commercial buildings, like the James Bute Company Warehouse. The architect was also responsible for a religious structure, the Sacred Heart Co-Cathedral, in Houston.
30. In *Trost & Trost, Architects* (El Paso: Trost & Trost, 1907), p.

61, Mitchel[l] & Halbach advertised that Hyman Levy of Houston was one of their clients; Sharon Darling, *Chicago Furniture: Art, Craft, & Industry, 1883 – 1983* (Chicago: Chicago Historical Society; New York: W. W. Norton, 1984), p. 181. Darling notes that the name of the firm is Mitchell & Halbach. The Levy family's experience in building their home by employing professional designers was not their last. In 1911 the Levys secured a second store building on Congress Avenue which joined their primary structure on Main Street. Both new construction and remodeling took place as a "firm of expert interior designers and architects were set to work on plans for the arrangement and equipment of the entire store, and in rapid succession came the institution as Houston finally came to know it — absolutely modern in every particular, and the finest equipped as well as the largest of its kind in the entire South." *American Biography*, p. 354.

31. Marge Crumbaker, "To Leopold Meyers, 2016 Main Revives Memories of Gracious Days Long Past," *Houston Post*, February 5, 1967, sec. 1, pp. 1, 18; *American Biography*, p. 352.
32. The Levy dining room resembles the breakfast room of the McFaddin-Ward house in Beaumont, also built in 1906, and not included in this collection. The McFaddins enlisted the aid of Kansas City interior decorating firm Keith and Company.
33. The McFaddin-Ward House in Beaumont features frosted green glass lighting fixtures in the shape of grape clusters in the breakfast room/conservatory. These fixtures were from Lecoutour Brothers in St. Louis, circa 1907.
34. Frank W. Johnson, *A History of Texas and Texans*, 5 vols., Eugene C. Barker, ed. (Chicago: American Historical Society, 1914), 4: 1764 – 65.
35. "Annual Summary of Southwestern Progress," *El Paso Herald*, January 1, 1909, p. 12, as quoted in Lloyd C. Engelbrecht and June-Marie F. Engelbrecht, *Henry C. Trost, Architect of the Southwest* (El Paso: El Paso Public Library Association, 1981), p. 126, n. 24.
36. Engelbrecht and Engelbrecht, *Trost*, p. 47. See also *Trost & Trost*, p. 61; there Mitchell & Halbach list J. P. Paulson of the National Bank of Commerce in Denver, Colorado, as one of their clients. The decorating firm, established in 1885, advertised in the 1907 promotional brochure of Trost & Trost, Architects, as Decorators and Furnishers who had executed the interiors for a number of domestic and public buildings in Denver, Houston and El Paso.
37. Map of Orange, Texas, April 1909, Sheet 5 (New York: Sanborn Map & Publishing Co.), notes that the house, located at the northeastern corner of the intersection of Green Avenue and Eighth Street, was made of stucco. The house, because of its materials and style, was considered anomalous in Orange, suggesting its professional design. Elizabeth Williams, director of the Heritage House Museum, Orange, telephone conversation with author, June 18, 1987.
38. Patricia M. Tice, *Gardening in America: 1830 – 1910* (Rochester, N.Y.: Strong Museum, 1984), p. 68.
39. Unpublished file notes, Collection of Heritage House Museum.
40. "Stone Lions' Tenure to End," *Houston Chronicle*, February 21, 1937.
41. Ibid.
42. Cindy Crane, interview with author, Houston, November 6, 1984; Mr. and Mrs. Robert D. Maddox, interview with author, Aledo, January 23, 1985.
43. E. S. Berry to Marianne B. Garland, December 8, 1940, Collection of the Panhandle-Plains Historical Society; Charles Hall Page & Associates, Inc., *Amarillo Historic Building Survey & Preservation Program Recommendations* (Amarillo: City of Amarillo, 1981), p. 88. Mrs. Grady Nobles, interview with author, Amarillo, December 14, 1984; Mr. Clarence Williams, interview with author, Amarillo, January 21, 1985; William Seale, *The Tasteful Interlude: American Interiors through the Camera's Eye, 1860 – 1917* (2d ed., rev. and enl.; Nashville: American Association for State and Local History, 1981), pp. 226 – 28.
44. E. S. Berry to Marianne B. Garland.
45. James Oren Palmer, "A History of the Landergin Brothers

Company Ranch" (Master's thesis, West Texas State University, 1967), pp. 73 – 75.

46. Mrs. Grady Nobles, interview with author.
47. Ibid.; Mr. Clarence Williams, interview with author.
48. Mrs. Grady Nobles, interview with author.
49. See Plate 16 in Richard W. Flint, "Prosperity through Patents: The Furniture of George Hunzinger & Sons," in Kenneth L. Ames, ed., *Victorian Furniture: Essays from a Victorian Society Autumn Symposium* (Philadelphia: Victorian Society in America, 1983), pp. 115 – 30.
50. Other painted rooms in the residence (not pictured here) exhibit techniques of freehand, infill, and stencil painting and thus continue the long tradition of painted interiors in Texas.

CONCLUSION

1. Mihaly Csikszentmihalyi and Eugene Rochberg-Halton, *The Meaning of Things: Domestic Symbols and the Self* (Cambridge: Cambridge University Press, 1981), pp. 250 – 53, 95, 107.
2. Compare figures 5.14, 5.15, and 5.16 with figures 7.9 and 7.10.
3. Compare figure 11.10 with figures 3.18 and 3.19.
4. David M. Potter, *People of Plenty: Economic Abundance and the American Character* (Chicago: University of Chicago Press, 1954).
5. William Seale, *The Tasteful Interlude: American Interiors through the Camera's Eye, 1860 – 1917* (2d., rev, and enl.; Nashville: American Association for State and Local History, 1981), p. 13.
6. Gwendolyn Wright, *Moralism and the Model Home: Domestic Architecture and Cultural Conflict in Chicago, 1873 – 1913* (Chicago: University of Chicago Press, 1980), pp. 3, 199 – 227. Geographer Kimberly Dovey makes this observation about professional expertise and the dynamics of making a home: "Strong forces within the architectural profession mitigate against the emergence of a sense of home. Design professions are strongly peer-group oriented, and the designer's reputation is determined more by the visual images of buildings in professional journals than by the experience of the users. . . . Thus, a personal relationship and connectedness between the designer and the image of the place emerges. This highly personal relationship, together with its assumptions of professional superiority, tends to paralyze the emergence of similar yet deeper relationships between dweller and place. Because designers receive their kudos from the image of their products as judged by their peers, they have an interest in keeping these fine-tuned symbols free from contamination by the dwellers. The problems here, even when the dwellers share the values of the designer, is that whereas the designer's concern is with the image, the experience of home is dynamic and action based — it is an experience of 'living in' rather than 'looking at' buildings. . . . A home cannot be someone else's work of art." See Kimberly Dovey, "Home and Homelessness," in *Home Environments,* ed. Irwin Altman and Carol M. Werner (New York: Plenum Press, 1985), p. 58.

Select Bibliography

Books

Agatha, Sister M. *The History of Houston Heights, 1891 – 1918.* Houston: Premier Printing Company, 1956.

Alexander, Drury Blakeley, and Todd Webb. *Texas Homes of the Nineteenth Century.* Austin: University of Texas Press, 1966.

Altman, Violet, and Seymour Altman. *The Book of Buffalo Pottery.* New York: Crown Publishers, 1969.

American Biography: A New Cyclopedia. Vol. 43. New York: American Historical Society, 1930.

Kenneth L. Ames, ed. *Victorian Furniture: Essays from a Victorian Society Autumn Symposium.* Philadelphia: Victorian Society in America, 1983.

Arbingast, Stanley, et al. *Atlas of Texas.* 5th ed. Austin: Bureau of Business Research, 1979.

Artistic Houses; Being a Series of Interior Views of a Number of the Most Beautiful and Celebrated Homes in the United States. 2 vols. 1883 – 1884. Reprint. New York: Benjamin Blom, 1971.

Ashton, Dore. *Rosa Bonheur: A Life and a Legend.* New York: Viking Press, 1981.

Axelrod, Alan, ed. *The Colonial Revival in America.* New York: W. W. Norton, 1985.

Baird, Delila M., and Josie M. Baird, comps. *Early Fisher County Families: Biographical History, 1876 – 1919.* Rotan, Texas: By the authors, 1976.

Barber, George F., & Co. *Artistic Homes: How to Plan and How to Build Them.* Knoxville: S. B. Newman, 1893.

Barker, Eugene C., Charles S. Potts, and Charles W. Ramsdell. *A School History of Texas.* Evanston, Ill.: Row, Peterson, 1913.

_____. *Annual Report of the American Historical Association for the Year 1919.* 2 vols. Washington, D.C.: Government Printing Office, 1924.

_____. *The Austin Papers: October 1834 – January 1837.* Austin: University of Texas, 1927.

_____. *Annual Report of the American Historical Association for the Year 1922.* 2 vols. Washington, D.C.: Government Printing Office, 1928.

Barr, Amelia E. *All the Days of My Life: An Autobiography.* New York: D. Appleton, 1913.

Blumenson, John J.-G. *Identifying American Architecture: A Pictorial Guide to Styles and Terms, 1600 – 1945.* Nashville: American Association for State and Local History, 1977.

Boris, Eileen. *Art and Labor: Ruskin, Morris, and the Craftsman Ideal in America.* Philadelphia: Temple University Press, 1986.

Branda, Eldon Stephen, ed. *The Handbook of Texas, a Supplement.* Austin: Texas State Historical Association, 1976.

Brown, John Henry. *Indian Wars and Pioneers of Texas.* Austin: L. E. Daniell, 1880.

Bulletin of the Agricultural and Mechanical College of Texas. Catalogues 1910 – 1918.

Bulletin of the University of Texas. Catalogues 1900 – 1920.

Burke, Doreen Bolger, et al. *In Pursuit of Beauty: Americans and the Aesthetic Movement.* New York: Metropolitan Museum of Art and Rizzoli, 1986.

Burkholder, Mary V., with photographs by Graham B. Knight. *The King William Area: A History and Guide to the Houses.* San Antonio: King William Association, 1973.

Census Reports Volume 3, Twelfth Census of the United States, Taken in the Year 1900, Population, Part 2. Washington, D.C.: United States Census Office, 1902.

Clark, Clifford Edward, Jr. *The American Family Home, 1800 – 1960.* Chapel Hill: University of North Carolina Press, 1986.

Compendium of the Eleventh Census 1890, Part 2. Washington, D.C.: Government Printing Office, 1894.

Csikszentmihalyi, Mihaly, and Eugene Rochberg-Halton. *The Meaning of Things: Domestic Symbols and the Self.* Cambridge: Cambridge University Press, 1981.

The Curtain-Maker's Handbook. New York: E. P. Dutton, 1979. Reprint. Frank A. Moreland. *Practical Decorative Upholstery.* Boston: Lee and Shepherd, 1889.

Daniel, Jean and Price, and Dorothy Blodgett. *The Texas Governor's Mansion: A History of the House and Its Occupants.* Austin: Texas State Library and Archives Commission and the Sam Houston Regional Library and Research Center, 1984.

Daniell, L. E. *Personnel of the Texas State Government.* Austin: Smith, Hicks & Jones, State Printers, 1889.

Daniell, L. E. *Types of Successful Men.* Austin: By the author, 1890.

Darling, Sharon. *Chicago Furniture: Art, Craft, & Industry, 1833 – 1983.* New York: W. W. Norton, 1984.

Davis, Ellis A., and Edwin H. Grobe. *The Encyclopedia of Texas.* 2 vols. Dallas: Texas Development Bureau, [ca. 1922].

_____. *The New Encyclopedia of Texas.* 2 vols. Dallas: Texas Development Bureau, [ca. 192[illegible]].

_____. *The New Encyclopedia of Texas.* 4 vols. Dallas: Texas Development Bureau, [ca 1926[illegible].

_____. *The New Encyclopedia of Texas.* 2 vols. Dallas: Texas Development Bureau, [ca. 193[illegible]].

Davis, Ellis Arthur, ed. *The Historical Encyclopedia of Texas.* rev. ed., 2 vols. Texas Historical Society, [ca. 1940].

Davis, John L. *The Danish Texans.* San Antonio: University of Texas Institute of Texan Cultures, 1979.

DeRyee, William, and R. E. Moore. *The Texas Album of the Eighth Legislature 1860.* Austin: Miner, Lambert & Perry, 1860.

Diamond Jubilee Souvenir Book of Comfort, Texas. San Antonio: Standard Printing Co., 192[illegible]

Dizik, A. Allen. *Concise Encyclopedia of Interior Design.* 2d ed. New York: Van Nostrand Reinhold, 1988.

Dundes, Alan, ed. *The Evil Eye: A Folklore Casebook.* New York: Garland Publishing, 1[illegible]81.

Earle, Alice Morse. *China Collecting in America.* New York: Charles Scribner's Sons, 18[illegible].

Eastlake, Charles L. *Hints on Household Taste in Furniture, Upholstery and Other Details.* 1[illegible]68. Reprint. New York: Dover Publications, 1969.

Elegant Arts for Ladies. London: Ward and Lock, n.d.

Engelbrecht, Lloyd C., and June-Marie F. Engelbrecht. *Henry C. Trost, Architect of the Southwest.* El Paso: El Paso Public Library Association, 1981.

Engerrand, George C. *The So-called Wends of Germany and Their Colonies in Texas and in Australia.* University of Texas Bulletin, no. 3417. Austin: University of Texas, 1934.

Exley, Jo Ella Powell. *Texas Tears and Texas Sunshine: Voices of Frontier Women.* College Station: Texas A&M University Press, 1985.

Fisk, Frances Battaile. *A History of Texas Artists and Sculptors.* Abilene: By the author, 192[illegible].

Fletcher, William Andrew. *Rebel Private, Front and Rear.* Austin: University of Texas Press, 1[illegible]54.

Fourteenth Census of the United States, Vol. 1, Population, 1920, Bulletin, Population: Texas. Washington, D.C.: Government Printing Office, 1921.

Fourteenth Census of the United States Taken in the Year 1920: Volume IV, Population. Washington, D.C.: Government Printing Office, 1923.

Geertz, Clifford. *The Interpretation of Cultures: Selected Essays*. New York: Basic Books, 1973.

Giedion, Siegfried. *Mechanization Takes Command: A Contribution to Anonymous History*. 1948. Reprint. New York: W. W. Norton, 1969.

Gloag, John. *A Short Dictionary of Furniture*. New York: Holt, Rinehart and Winston, 1965.

Gove, Philip Babcock, ed. *Webster's Third New International Dictionary of the English Language Unabridged*. Springfield, Mass.: G. & C. Merriam Co., 1976.

Graham, Don. *Cowboys and Cadillacs: How Hollywood Looks at Texas*. Austin: Texas Monthly Press, 1983.

Grider, Sylvia Ann. *The Wendish Texans*. San Antonio: University of Texas Institute of Texan Cultures, 1982.

Haigh, Jane G. *Alaska Pioneer Interiors: An Annotated Photographic File*. Fairbanks, Alaska: Tanana-Yukon Historical Society, 1986.

Hailey, Elizabeth Forsythe. *A Woman of Independent Means*. New York: Viking Press, 1978; Avon Books, 1979.

Handlin, David P. *The American Home: Architecture and Society, 1815 – 1915*. Boston: Little, Brown, 1979.

Hardy, Dermot H., and Ingham S. Roberts, eds. *Historical Review of South-East Texas*. 2 vols. Chicago: Lewis Publishing Co., 1910.

Harrison, Constance Cary. *Woman's Handiwork in Modern Homes*. New York: Charles Scribner's Sons, 1881.

Hart, Katherine, and Elizabeth Kemp, eds. *Lucadia Pease & the Governor, Letters: 1850 – 1857*. Austin: Encino Press, 1974.

Heron, Addie E. *Dainty Work for Pleasure and Profit*. Chicago: Danks [ca. 1893].

Historical and Biographical Record of the Cattle Industry and the Cattlemen of Texas and Adjacent Territory. Saint Louis: Woodward & Tiernan Printing Co., 1895.

History of the Cattlemen of Texas. Dallas: Johnston Printing & Advertising Co., 1914.

History of Texas Together with a Biographical History of the Cities of Houston and Galveston. Chicago: Lewis Publishing Co., 1895.

Hohes, Pauline Buck. *A Centennial History of Anderson County, Texas*. San Antonio: Naylor Co., 1936.

Holland, Ellen Bowie. *Gay as a Grig: Memories of a North Texas Girlhood*. Austin: University of Texas Press, 1963.

Holland, G. A. *History of Parker County and the Double Log Cabin*. Weatherford, Texas: Herald Publishing Co., 1937.

Holzer, Harold, Gabor S. Boritt, and Mark E. Neely, Jr. *The Lincoln Image: Abraham Lincoln and the Popular Print*. New York: Charles Scribner's Sons, 1984.

Houghton, Walter E. *The Victorian Frame of Mind, 1830 – 1870*. New Haven: Yale University Press, 1957.

Houston Press Club, comp. *Men of Affairs of Houston and Environs: A Newspaper Reference Work*. Houston: W. H. Coyle, 1913.

Hunter, J. Marvin. *The Trail Drivers of Texas*. 2d ed., rev., Nashville: Cokesbury Press, 1925.

International Center of Photography Encyclopedia of Photography. New York: Crown Publishers, 1984.

Johnson, Frank W. *A History of Texas and Texans*. 5 vols. Edited by Eugene C. Barker. Chicago: American Historical Society, 1914.

Johnson, Sid S. *Texans Who Wore the Gray*. N.p., n.d.

Jones, Howard Mumford. *The Age of Energy: Varieties of American Experience, 1865 – 1915*. New York: Viking Press, 1971.

Kingston, Mike, ed. *Texas Almanac and State Industrial Guide, 1986 – 1987*. Dallas: A. H. Belo Corp., 1985.

Lewis, Philippa, and Gillian Darley. *Dictionary of Ornament*. New York: Pantheon Books, 1986.

Lynn, Catherine. *Wallpaper in America: From the Seventeenth Century to World War I*. New York: W. W. Norton, 1980.

McLanathan, Richard. *The American Tradition in the Arts*. New York: Harcourt, Brace & World, 1968.

Maloney, Clarence, ed. *The Evil Eye*. New York: Columbia University Press, 1976.

Marling, Karal Ann. *George Washington Slept Here: Colonial Revivals and American Culture*. Cambridge: Harvard University Press, 1988.

[Martin, George A.] *Our Homes; How to Beautify Them*. New York: O. Judd Co., 1888.

Mayhew, Edgar deN., and Minor Myers, Jr. *A Documentary*

History of American Interiors, From the Colonial Era to 1915. New York: Charles Scribner's Sons, 1980.

Meeks, Carroll Louis Vanderslice. *The Railroad Station, an Architectural History.* New Haven: Yale University Press, 1956.

A Memorial and Biographical History of McLennan, Falls, Bell and Coryell Counties. Chicago: Lewis Publishing Co., 1893.

Men of Texas: A Collection of Portraits of Men who Deserve to Rank as Typical Representatives of the Best Citizenship, Foremost Activities and Highest Aspirations of the State of Texas. Houston: Houston Post, 1903.

Moss, Roger W., and Gail Caskey Winkler. *Victorian Exterior Decoration: How to Paint Your Nineteenth-Century American House Historically.* New York: Henry Holt, 1987.

Myers, Denys Peter. *Gaslighting in America: A Guide for Historic Preservation.* Washington, D.C.: Heritage Conservation and Recreation Service, 1978.

Naeve, Milo M. *Identifying American Furniture: A Pictorial Guide to Styles and Terms, Colonial to Contemporary.* Nashville: American Association for State and Local History, 1981.

Neely, Mark E., Jr., Harold Holzer, and Gabor S. Boritt. *The Confederate Image: Prints of the Lost Cause.* Chapel Hill: University of North Carolina Press, 1987.

Nielson, Karla J. *Window Treatments.* New York: Van Nostrand Reinhold, 1990.

Ninth Census, Volume 1, The Statistics of the Population of the United States. Washington, D.C.: Government Printing Office, 1872.

Olmsted, Frederick Law. *Journey through Texas; or, A Saddle-Trip on the Southwestern Frontier, with a Statistical Appendix.* New York: Dix, Edwards, 1857.

Paddock, Captain B. B. *A Twentieth Century History and Biographical Record of North and West Texas.* 2 vols. Chicago: Lewis Publishing Co., 1906.

_____. *A History of Central and Western Texas.* 2 vols. Chicago: Lewis Publishing Co., 1911.

_____. *History of Texas, Fort Worth and the Texas Northwest Edition.* 4 vols. Chicago: Lewis Publishing Co., 1922.

Page, Charles Hall, & Associates, Inc. *Amarillo Historic Building Survey & Preservation Program Recommendations.* Amarillo, Texas: City of Amarillo, 1981.

Pass, Fred, ed. *Texas Almanac and the State Industrial Guide 1978 – 1979.* Dallas: A. H. Belo Corporation, 1977.

Pegler, Martin. *The Dictionary of Interior Design.* New York: Crown Publishers, 1966.

Plainview Homes and Families. Plainview, Texas: Bicentennial Homes and Families Committee, 1976.

Priestman, Mabel Tuke. *Art and Economy in Home Decoration.* New York: John Lane Co., 1908.

Ransleben, Guido E. *A Hundred Years of Comfort in Texas: A Centennial History.* Rev. ed. San Antonio: Naylor Co., 1974.

Rhoads, William B. *The Colonial Revival.* New York: Garland Publishing, 1977.

Richardson, Rupert N., Ernest Wallace, and Adrian Anderson. *Texas: The Lone Star State.* 5th ed. Englewood Cliffs, N.J.: Prentice Hall, 1988.

Richardson, T. C. *East Texas: Its History and Its Makers.* 4 vols. Edited by Dabney White. New York: Lewis Historical Publishing Co., 1940.

Rose, Victor M. *Some Historical Facts in Regard to the Settlement of Victoria, Texas, Its Progress and Present Status.* N.p., n.d. Reprint. Victoria: Book Mart, 1961.

Seale, William. *The Tasteful Interlude: American Interiors through the Camera's Eye, 1860 – 19[illegible].* 2d ed., rev. and enl. Nashville: American Association for State and Local History, 1981.

Sears, Roebuck and Co. Chicago: Bokker O'Donnell Printing Co., 1895.

Sears, Roebuck Catalogue. 189[illegible]. Reprint. New York: Chelsea House Publishers, 1968.

Sears, Roebuck and Co. Fall 1900 Catalogue. 1900. Reprint. Northfield, Ill.: DBI Books 1970.

Sears, Roebuck Catalogue. 190[illegible]. Reprint. New York: Bounty Books, 1986.

Shaw, James C. *North from Texas: Incidents in the Early Life of a Range Cowman in Texas, Dakota and Wyoming, 1852 – 1883.* Evanston, Ill.: Branding Iron Press, 1952.

Sibley, Marilyn McAdams. *Travelers in Texas, 1761 – 1860.* Austin: University of Texas Press, 1967.

Smith, Jane S. *Elsie de Wolfe: A Life in the High Style.* New York: Atheneum, 1982.

The Standard Blue Book of Texas. Houston: Who's Who Publishing Co., 1907 – 1908.

Statistics of the Population of the United States at the Tenth Census (1880). Washington, D.C.: Government Printing Office, 1883.

Sullivan, Dulcie. *The LS Brand: The Story of a Texas Panhandle Ranch.* Austin: University of Texas Press, 1968.

Taft, Robert. *Photography and the American Scene: A Social History, 1839 – 1889.* New York Macmillan, 1938. Reprint. New York: Dover Publications 1964.

Taylor, Lonn, and David B. Warren. *Texas Furniture: The Cabinetmakers and Their Work, 1840 – 1880.* Austin: University of Texas Press, 1975

Texas Federation of Women's Clubs, ed. and comp. *Who's Who of the Womanhood of Texas.* N.p. 1923 – 1924.

Thirteenth Census of the United States Taken in the Year 1910, Volume 4, Population 1910, Occupation Statistics. Washington, D.C.: Government Printing Office, 1914.

Thornton, Peter. *Authentic Decor: The Domestic Interior, 1620 – 1920.* New York: Viking Press, 1984.

Tolson, R. J. *A History of William Cameron & Co.* N.p., [1926].

Trost & Trost, Architects. El Paso: Trost & Trost, 1907.

Veblen, Thorstein. *The Theory of the Leisure Class.* 3d ed. New York: Modern Library, 1934.

Warner, H. T., et al., eds. *Texans and Their State: A Newspaper Reference Work.* Houston: Texas Biographical Association, [1920].

Webb, Walter Prescott, and H. Bailey Carroll. *The Handbook of Texas.* 2 vols. Austin: Texas State Historical Association, 1952.

Wharton, Edith, and Ogden Codman, Jr. *The Decoration of Houses.* New York: Charles Scribner's Sons, 1897. Reprint. New York: W. W. Norton, 1978.

Whiffen, Marcus. *American Architecture since 1780: A Guide to the Styles.* Cambridge: M.I.T. Press, 1969.

Wilson, Elizabeth. *Adorned in Dreams: Fashion and Modernity.* Berkeley: University of California Press, 1987.

Winkler, Gail Caskey, and Roger W. Moss. *Victorian Interior Decoration: American Interiors, 1830 – 1900.* New York: Henry Holt, 1986.

Withey, Henry F., and Elsie Rathbone Withey. *Biographical Dictionary of American Architects (Deceased).* Los Angeles: New Age Publishing Co., 1956.

Wright, Gwendolyn. *Moralism and the Model Home: Domestic Architecture and Cultural Conflict in Chicago, 1873 – 1913.* Chicago: University of Chicago Press, 1980.

Zlatkovich, Charles P. *Texas Railroads: A Record of Construction and Abandonment.* Austin: Bureau of Business Research, 1981.

Museum Exhibitions and Catalogues

The American Renaissance, 1876 – 1917. New York: Brooklyn Museum, 1979.

Green, Harvey. *The Light of the Home: An Intimate View of the Lives of Women in Victorian America.* New York: Pantheon Books, 1983.

Grier, Katherine C. *Culture and Comfort: People, Parlors, and Upholstery.* Rochester, N.Y.: Strong Museum, 1988.

Hudson River Museum. *Eastlake-Influenced American Furniture 1870 – 1890.* Exhibition catalogue. Yonkers, N.Y.: By the museum, 1973.

Kaplan, Wendy. *"The Art That Is Life": The Arts & Crafts Movement in America, 1875 – 1920.* Boston: Little, Brown, 1987.

Nylander, Richard C., Elizabeth Redmond, and Penny J. Sander. *Wallpaper in New England.* Boston: Society for the Preservation of New England Antiquities, 1986.

Reichlin, Ellie, Jean Caslin, and Dan Younger. *A Photographic Intimacy: The Portraiture of Rooms, 1865 – 1900.* Boston: Society for the Preservation of New England Antiquities, 1984.

Talbot, George. *At Home: Domestic Life in the Post-Centennial Era.* Madison: State Historical Society of Wisconsin, 1976.

"Thirty Residences of Early Christ Church Parishioners: 1984 May Fete Exhibit." Library exhibition. Houston Metropolitan Research Center, Houston, Texas, 1984.

Tice, Patricia M. *Gardening in America: 1830 – 1910.* Rochester, N.Y.: Strong Museum, 1984.

University of Texas. School of Architecture exhibition brochure. "James Riely Gordon, Texas Courthouse Architect." January 21 – March 18, 1983.

Williams, Susan. *Savory Suppers and Fashionable Feasts: Dining in Victorian America.* New York: Pantheon Books, 1985.

Articles

Adams, Donald R., Jr. "Prices and Wages." In *Encyclopedia of American Economic History,* 3 vols., edited by Glenn Porter, vol. 1, pp. 229 – 46. New York: Charles Scribner's Sons, 1980.

Alsup, Reba. "Old Families of Calvert: The Conitz Family." *New Calvert Tribune,* March 20, 1985, pp. 10 – 11.

_____. "Old Families of Calvert: The Dirr and Shelander Families." *Calvert Tribune,* November 20, 1985, pp. 10 – 11.

Ames, Kenneth L. "What is the Néo-Grec?" *Nineteenth Century* 2 (Summer 1976): 13 – 21.

_____. "Sitting in (Néo-Grec) Style." *Nineteenth Century* 2 (Autumn 1976): 51 – 58.

_____."Meaning in Artifacts: Hall Furnishings in Victorian America." *Journal of Interdisciplinary History* 9, no. 1 (Summer 1978): 19 – 46.

_____. "Material Culture as Non-Verbal Communication: A Historical Case Study." *Journal of American Culture,* 3, no. 4 (Winter 1980): 619 – 41.

"Armitage." *Panhandle Herald,* May 16, 1912.

Cynthia A. Brandimarte. "Somebody's Aunt and Nobody's Mother: The American China Painter and Her Work, 1870 – 1920." *Winterthur Portfolio* 23, no. 4 (Winter 1988): 203 – 24.

_____. "Japanese Novelty Stores." *Winterthur Portfolio* 26, no. 1 (Spring 1991): 1 – 25.

Breisch, Kenneth A. "The Richardsonian Interlude in Texas: A Quest for Meaning and Order at the End of the Nineteenth Century." In *The Spirit of H. H. Richardson on the Midland Prairies: Regional Transformations of an Architectural Style,* edited by Paul Clifford Larson with Susan M. Brown, pp. 86 – 105. Ames: Iowa State University Press, 1988.

Butler, Patrick H., III. "Sears in Texas, 1906 – 1913." In *The Consumer Culture and the American Home, 1890 – 1930,* edited by Glenda Dyer and Martha Reed, pp. 47 – 55. Beaumont: McFaddin-Ward House, 1989.

"The Campbells Have Come," *Dallas Morning News*, August 17, 1906, p.1.

Catalano, Kathleen M. "Cabinetmaking in Philadelphia, 1820 – 1840: Transition from Craft to Industry." In *American Furniture and Its Makers: Winterthur Portfolio 13*, edited by Ian M. G. Quimby, pp. 81 – 138. Chicago: University of Chicago Press, 1979.

Clark, Clifford Edward, Jr. "Domestic Architecture and the Cult of Domesticity in America, 1840 – 1870." *Journal of Interdisciplinary History* 7, no. 1 (Summer 1976): 33 – 56.

"Correspondence." *Art Amateur* 20, no. 6 (May 1889): 143.

"Correspondence." *Art Amateur* 21, no. 5 (October 1889): 112.

"Correspondence." *Ladies' Home Journal* 4, no. 2 (January 1887): 8.

"Correspondence." *Ladies' Home Journal* 5, no. 2 (January 1888): 8.

"Correspondence." *Ladies' Home Journal* 5, no. 5 (April 1888): 8.

Crumbaker, Marge. "To Leopold Meyers, 2016 Main Revives Memories of Gracious Days Long Past." *Houston Post*, February 5, 1967, pp. 1, 18.

Daniel[l], L. E. "The Kleberg Family, for Seventy Years It Has Been Helping to Make the History of Texas." *Houston Post*, July 14, 1907, p. 26.

"Death of Mr. H. Hodde," *Brenham Daily Banner*, July 25, 1901.

"The Dining Room: Economical Home Decoration." *Decorator and Furnisher* 3, no. 6 (March 1884): 209.

Dovey, Kimberly. "Home and Homelessness." In *Home Environments,* edited by Irwin Altman and Carol M. Werner, pp. 33 – 64. New York: Plenum Press, 1985.

"Early Days Here Recalled by Photographer." *Galveston Daily News*, February 28, 1937.

Exhibition announcement. *Antiques* 133, no. 4 (April 1988): 806 –07.

Harsdorff, Linda. "Pencil Sketches Hailed." *Victoria Advocate,* November 6, 1978.

Haywood, Emma. "China Painting in Boucher Style." *Art Amateur* 21, no. 6 (November 1889): 123 – 24.

———. "Painting in Boucher Style." Part I. *Art Amateur* 21, no. 5 (October 1889): 100.

Homes. Houston Metropolitan Research Center, Houston Public Library, Houston, Texas.

"Johnny Reb in Ranks." *Dallas News,* April 24, 1955.

Jordan, Gilbert J., trans. and ed. "W. Steinert's View of Texas in 1849." Part 5. *Southwestern Historical Quarterly* 81, no. 1 (July 1977): 45 – 72.

Kleberg, Rosa. "Early Experiences in Texas." Part 2. *Texas Historical Association Quarterly* 2, no. 2 (October 1898): 170 – 73.

Lee, Ray E. "How Texas' Richest Young Man Spends His Money." *Austin American-Statesman,* May 16, 1926, p. 6.

"Lone Star Pine." *American Lumberman,* no. 1740 (September 26, 1908): 67 – 150.

"Mothers Corner." *Ladies' Home Journal* 4, no. 3 (February 1887): 5.

"M. K. Brown." *Cattleman* 51, no. 5 (October 1964): 128.

Murphy, Charles J. V. "The Fortunes of the Klebergs." *Corpus Christi Caller-Times,* June 15, 1969.

"Pampa Founder Killed in Crash." *Austin Statesman,* September 11, 1964.

"Pampa, Tex., Founder Killed." *Dallas Times Herald,* September 11, 1964.

"Pink Parrish of Lubbock; Former Mayor, State Senator." *Dallas News,* April 11, 1939.

Pratt, Gerry. "The House as an Expression of Social Worlds." In *Housing and Identity: Cross-cultural Perspectives,* edited by James S. Duncan, pp. 135 – 80. New York: Holmes & Meier Publishers, 1982.

Scholl, Mary Esther. "A Pageant in Praise of Learning." *Dallas News,* July 19, 1931.

"Stone Lions' Tenure to End." *Houston Chronicle,* February 21, 1937.

Taylor, Lonn. "The McGregor-Grimm House at Winedale, Texas." *Antiques* 103, no. 3 (September 1975): 515 – 16.

Teske, Robert Thomas, "Living Room Furnishings, Ethnic Idenity, [*sic*], and Acculturation among Greek-Philadelphians." *New York Folklore Quarterly* 5 (1979): 21 – 32.

Watson, Forbes. "'Art in Every Home': An Educational Movement which Does Not Educate," *Arts & Decoration* 14, no. 3 (January 1921): 195.

"Wood Carving." *Decorator and Furnisher* 3, no. 6 (March 1884): 210.

Personal Communications

Alsup, Reba. Series of correspondence with author, 1986.

Bevill, Callie. Letter to author, March 3, 1985.

Boulware, Mrs. Ford M. Series of correspondence and telephone conversations with author, 1985 – 1991.

Bowie, George Donald. Letter to author, January 21, 1988.

Carter, Fannie Simpson. Series of interviews, correspondence, and telephone conversations with author, 1984 – 1991.

Cauthan, Elizabeth. Series of correspondence with author, 1985 – 1986.

Coffman, Elaine. Series of interviews, correspondence, and telephone conversations with author, 1984 – 1989.

Cordray, John W. Series of interviews, correspondence, and telephone conversations with author, 1983 – 1989.

Crane, Cindy. Series of interviews, correspondence, and telephone conversations with author, 1985 – 1989.

Cunningham, Craig Maddox. Series of interviews, correspondence, and telephone conversations with author, 1984 – 1989.

Dessart, Florence Fletcher. Series of interviews and correspondence with author, 1983 – 1985.

Digby-Roberts, Mr. and Mrs. Frederick W. Series of interviews and telephone conversations with author, 1984 – 1985.

Ellis, Betty O. Series of interviews, correspondence, and telephone conversations with author, 1985 – 1989.

Evans, H. Leslie. Series of interviews, correspondence, and telephone conversations with author, 1988.

Gafford, Bettie B. Series of correspondence and telephone conversations with author, 1984 – 1988.

Grisham, Justine Digby-Roberts. Series of interviews, correspondence, and telephone conversations with author, 1985 – 1990.

Hail, Mr. and Mrs. Wilson E., Jr. Series of correspondence and telephone conversations with author, 1983 – 1987.

Jackson, Carol. Interview with author. Houston, Texas, September 19, 1985.

Jordan, Brenda. Series of interviews, correspondence, and telephone conversations, 1986 – 1988.

King, Jeanette Jackson. Series of interviews and telephone conversations with author, 1985.

Lawrence, Lee Averill. Series of interviews, correspondence, and telephone conversations with author, 1983 – 1991.

McLean, Margaret Stoner. Series of interviews and correspondence with author, 1988.

Maddox, Mr. and Mrs. Robert D. Series of interviews, correspondence, and telephone conversations with author, 1984 – 1986.

Massey, Niny A. Letter to author, September 7, 1987.

Mills, Barbara Bates. Series of interviews, correspondence, and telephone conversations with author, 1983 – 1991.

Neary, Helen Cates. Series of correspondence and telephone conversations with author, 1983 – 1987.

Nobles, Mrs. Grady. Interview with author. Amarillo, Texas, December 14, 1983.

Perdue, Beverly Singletary. Series of correspondence and telephone conversations with author, 1983 – 1988.

Prewit, Genora B. Series of correspondence and telephone conversations with author, 1985 – 1987.

Rugeley, Helen. Series of interviews and telephone conversations with author, 1986 – 1989.

Sarber, Mary. Series of interviews, correspondence, and telephone conversations with author, 1984 – 1988.

Shelton, Tom. Series of interviews, correspondence, and telephone conversations with author, 1983 – 1991.

Spinks, Catherine Villaret. Series of correspondence and telephone conversations with author, 1985 – 1991.

Wheeler, Verna Anne. Series of correspondence with author, 1983 – 1987.

Williams, Clarence. Interview with author. Amarillo, Texas, January 21, 1984.

Williams, Elizabeth. Series of interviews, correspondence, and telephone conversations with author, 1984 – 1990.

Williams, Kemper S. Letter to author, [February 1988].

Willingham, Douglas Barton. Series of letters and telephone conversations with author, 1983 – 1989.

Winkler, Gail Caskey. Letter to author, March 13, 1991.

Wommack, Drew. Series of interviews, correspondence, and telephone conversations with author, 1985 – 1988.

Manuscript Collections and Unpublished Sources

Assessor's Abstracts, City Out Lots, 1889 – 1893, Galveston, Texas.

"Beeville-Bee County Bicentennial Committee Presents Official Historical Medallions and Markers in Bee County, Texas." Bee County Historical Survey Committee, [ca. 1976].

Clayton, Nicholas J. Papers. Rosenberg Library. Galveston, Texas.

Finn, Alfred C. Papers. Houston Metropolitan Research Center, Houston Public Library, Houston, Texas.

Fulton, George Ware. Papers. Barker Texas History Center, Austin.

Glen Eden. Papers. Sherman Historical Museum, Sherman, Texas.

Gordon, James Riely. Papers. Architectural Drawings Collection, Architecture and Planning Library, General Libraries, University of Texas, Austin.

Hayes, Mrs. Bascom B. "The Evolution of the North-Evans Home." Austin Woman's Club, [1989]. Typescript.

Harris County, [Houston, Texas]. Deed Records.

Historic Sites and Restoration Branch. "Preservation Plan and Program for Sam Bell Maxey House, State Historic Structure." Austin: Texas Parks and Wildlife Department, 1976.

Historic Sites and Restoration Branch. "Preservation Plan and Program for Magoffin Home State Historic Site, El Paso, Texas." Austin: Texas Parks and Wildlife Department, 1977.

Holbrook, Francis Newberry, and Julia Macy. Papers. Southwest Room, El Paso Public Library, El Paso, Texas.

Jutson, Mary Carolyn Hollers. "An English Architect in Texas: Alfred Giles 1853 – 1920." Master's thesis, University of Texas, 1970.

Landergin-Harrington House Collection. Panhandle-Plains Historical Museum, Canyon, Texas.

Palmer, James Oren. "A History of the Landergin Brothers Company Ranch." Master's thesis, West Texas State University, 1967.

Patton, Glenn. Papers. Architectural Drawings Collection, Architecture and Planning Library, General Libraries, University of Texas at Austin.

Russell, Urban S., and Ella Maye Bumpass. Papers. Sherman Historical Museum, Sherman, Texas.

Sanborn Map Collection. Barker Texas History Center, Austin.

Sloane, A. Baldwin, with lyrics by Edgar Smith. "Heaven Will Protect the Working Girl." N.p. 1909.

Smithers, W. D. Papers. Harry Ransom Humanities Research Center, Austin, Texas.

Staiti, Henry T. Papers. Harris County Heritage Society, Houston, Texas.

Stanton, Rubye Parrish. "The Pink L. Parrish, Sr., Family." Files of the Crosby County Pioneer Memorial, Crosbyton, Texas.

Taulman, Joseph E. Papers. Barker Texas History Center, Austin.

Texas. Secretary of State. Incorporation Papers. Austin.

Turn of the Century Collection. Rosenberg Library. Galveston, Texas.

Tyng, George. Papers. Panhandle-Plains Historical Museum, Canyon, Texas.

City directories

Austin. City directories. [Various titles.] 1882 – 1882 through 1920.

Dallas. City directories. [Various titles.] 1886 – 1887 through 1920.

El Paso. City directories. [Various titles.] 1898 – 1899 through 1920.

Fort Worth. City directories. [Various titles.] 1885 – 1886 through 1920.

Galveston. City directories. [Various titles.] 1878 – 1879 through 1919.

Houston. City directories. [Various titles.] 1879 – 1880 through 1929.

San Antonio. City directories. [Various titles.] 1879 – 1880 through 1918.

Waco. City directories. [Various titles.] 1878 through 1919 – 1920.

Index

Page numbers in **bold face type** refer to illustrations.